A SCIENTIFIC
THEOLOGY

VOLUME 3

THEORY

A SCIENTIFIC
THEOLOGY

VOLUME 3
THEORY

Alister E. McGrath

William B. Eerdmans Publishing Company
Grand Rapids, Michigan

Published in Great Britain by T&T Clark Ltd,
The Tower Building, 11 York Road London SE1 7NX, UK
www.continuumbooks.com

This edition published 2003 in the USA
under license from T&T Clarke Ltd by
Wm. B. Eerdmans Publishing Co.
255 Jefferson Ave. S.E., Grand Rapids, Michigan 49503
www.eerdmans.com

First published 2003

ISBN 0-8028-3927-4

Manufactured in Great Britain

FOR

WYCLIFFE HALL, OXFORD

Contents

Preface

This third volume in the *Scientific Theology* trilogy deals with the critical question of the place of theory in the natural sciences and Christian theology. The first volume in the series addressed the problematic question of the theological status of nature; the second considered the epistemological and ontological status of the real world; the final volume turns to the immensely complex question of how such a reality may be represented theoretically, developing the theologically productive idea that theory is to be regarded as a communal beholding of reality.

A 'scientific theology' represents a principled negotiation between classic Christian theology and the working assumptions and methods of the natural sciences, based on a unitary vision of reality which is grounded and sustained by the specifics of the Christian tradition. This final volume of the trilogy deals with the question of the genesis, development and reception of theory in the natural sciences and in Christian theology. The present volume thus brings this prolegomenon to a future systematic theology to a conclusion by addressing the question of how an existing reality is to be represented and interpreted, taking into account the active nature of the human process of perception. A scientific theology holds that theories, whether scientific or theological, are not free creations of the human mind, but are constructed in response to an encounter with an existing reality. Theory is responsible, in that it is *accountable* to the community of faith for the manner in which it depicts its corporate vision of reality – a vision which it did not create in the first place, and to which it represents a considered and faithful *response.*

In the previous volume of this extended essay on theological method, I attempted to sketch the contours of an authentically Christian meta-narrative realism which is mediated by the Christian community of faith. Such a realism, though specific to the Christian tradition, possesses a tradition-transcending ability to engage with – and, perhaps more importantly, to account for – the existence of other traditions and the rationalities which they mediate. It is essential that a tradition possesses the moral imperative and intellectual resources to account both for its own existence as well as that of others. The central place which a natural theology plays in this process of engagement can be seen as a constructive restatement of the traditional Reformed notion of 'common grace',[1] entailing the rejection of those construals of Christian theology which absolutely deny any common ground between Christian faith and the secular realm.

The theological realism advocated in the previous volume, though ultimately grounded on a Christian account of the natural world, has been partly shaped through a conscious dialogue with the form of 'critical realism' associated with Roy Bhaskar. For Bhaskar, the world of reality possesses an ordering which is independent of the human recognition of its existence. Human agents thus find themselves existing, acting and reflecting within a world that is already structured, and find that they are 'always acting in a world of structural constraints and possibility that they did not produce'.[2] We are born into pre-existing structures, some of which can be transformed by our activity and others not. The physical, biological and social worlds are always pre-structured; the question is how that structuring is to be investigated, and subsequently how it is to be represented.

As Bhaskar stresses, the recognition that all sciences seek to investigate the nature of an independently existing reality leads to the conclusion that 'the social sciences can be "sciences" in exactly the same sense as natural ones, but in ways that are as different (and specific) as their objects'. We see here a concise statement of a fundamental theme of a scientific theology – namely, that each object or aspect of reality is investigated and represented according to its distinctive nature. But how, it must be asked, may this variegated reality be *represented* in a manner that is accommodated to its nature, yet tempered by the limitations of the human language which must be the vehicle of its transmission?

---

[1] For a feisty restatement of this notion, see the excellent study of Richard J. Mouw, *He Shines in All That's Fair: Culture and Common Grace*. Grand Rapids, MI: Eerdmans, 2001.

[2] Roy Bhaskar, 'General Introduction', in Margaret Archer et al. (eds), *Critical Realism*. London: Routledge, 1998, ix–xxiv, especially xvi–xvii.

The approach developed within this volume builds on the insights of writers such as Martin Heidegger and Jürgen Habermas, and argues that theory is to be conceived in terms of the *communal beholding of reality*. On such accounts, seeing gives way to telling; beholding to witnessing; experiencing to representing. J. Hillis Miller acknowledges theory's 'focus on referentiality' – that is, that it 'reliably and unambiguously relates a reader to the "real world" of history, of society, and of people acting within society on the stage of history'[3] – yet sees this as calling its legitimacy into question in a cultural situation suspicious of any such notion. Yet it may reasonably be pointed out both that Miller's focus on issues of *social* reality subtly avoids the major theoretical issues raised by the successes of the natural sciences, and that it is open to challenge in the light of the growing acceptance that 'social reality' is open to a much greater degree of referential analysis than Hiller concedes.[4]

This fundamental tenet of a scientific theology engenders an '*eros* of the mind' (Augustine) – an attitude of expectation and anticipation concerning an engagement with the world, affirming that what is encountered and experienced can be at least partly comprehended; and that when such an understanding is less than complete, it is because we are wrestling with a mystery, rather than with an incoherency.[5] Theory does not detract from mystery; rather it serves the pivotal role of allowing a mystery to be *recognized as such*, rather than being relegated to the lesser categories of irrationality and confusion, and thus marginalized in the quest for knowledge and understanding. An appeal to the mystery of faith is of major importance to the Christian quest to capture the imagination of our culture, to excite the strongest energies of our thinking and feeling and direct them to the exploration and representation of the 'vision of God', while simultaneously affirming the inner coherence of this foundational mystery. Where Jacques Derrida speaks of theory's 'feigning coherence' through an absolute exclusion of what it cannot assimilate, Christian theology sees itself as *discerning* such a coherence, which it grounds in the dual divine creation of world and interpreter. On a Christian reading of the world, the coherence of reality is thus not something that is optimistically and improperly *imposed* upon a formless

[3] J. Hillis Miller, 'The Triumph of Theory, the Resistance to Reading, and the Question of the Material Base', *Publications of the Modern Language Association* 102 (1987), 281–91, especially 283.

[4] See, for example, the lines of argument in John R. Searle, *The Construction of Social Reality*. New York: Free Press, 1995.

[5] A point developed in a Christological context by Robert Sokolowski, *The God of Faith and Reason: Foundations of Christian Theology*. Notre Dame, IN: University of Notre Dame Press, 1982, 34–9.

or inchoate actuality, but is something that can be *discerned*, within the limits of our capacities as created beings.

Given the ontology which is entailed by a Christian doctrine of creation, it is legitimate to suggest that a study of the origins, reception and development of scientific theories illuminates some significant issues which arise in relation to theological theories. Theories are determined and controlled by the external reality to which they are a response. Yet theories are not passive responses to reality; they are constructed by human minds, and therefore bear at least something of a socially located imprint. We must therefore give thought to the process by which theories are generated, developed and received within the scientific and theological communities from a critical realist perspective.

In engaging with reality in this way, it is appropriate to recognize a spectrum of theoretical possibilities, located between positions which might reasonably be styled 'objectivity' and 'social construction'. These modes of interplay are governed by the nature of the strata of reality under investigation, each of which demands its own distinctive mode of engagement. Ontology here determines epistemology. The recognition of some degree of social construction in some of the natural sciences, such as psychology, does not entail the notion that we are free to invent ideas as the individual thinker or community of discourse believes. As Austin Farrer once remarked, 'reality is a nuisance to those who want to make it up as they go along'.[6]

The development of such social constructs as are appropriate to an intellectual discipline is to be seen as nothing other than a principled exercise in attempting to understand the world as best as possible, and to develop for this purpose whatever tools or conceptualities are demanded by any given natural science and the strata of reality it engages.[7] This underlying assumption allows writers such as Roy Bhaskar to propose a common coherent scientific methodology across the natural and social sciences, such differences as exist being the direct outcome of the different levels of reality appropriate to the science in question.

Yet one of the most fundamental objections to theoretical reflection is its intrinsically reductionist agenda. How can the mystery of God be

---

[6] For a full discussion, see Charles C. Conti, *Metaphysical Personalism: An Analysis of Austin Farrer's Metaphysics of Theism.* Oxford: Clarendon Press, 1995.

[7] See in particular Steven Weinberg, *Facing Up: Science and Its Cultural Adversaries.* Cambridge, MA: Harvard University Press, 2001. While acknowledging the influence of social and cultural factors on the development of the sciences, Weinberg insists that scientific truth claims cannot be reduced to social conventions.

expressed in words? How can the radiant glory of the Lord be captured in a doctrine? In defending the legitimacy of theory, it is important to safeguard glory, mystery and beauty in the face of a relentless pressure to categorize – and hence evacuate of precisely those qualities which evoked our joy, worship and adoration in the first place. For this reason, this volume gives careful consideration to how theoretical reflection can be set alongside a loving, reverential concern for particularities, ensuring that theory is seen as an additional level of interpretation of reality, rather than its surrogate. When theory becomes a substitute for an engagement with the vision of God or the wonder of nature, the outcome can only be spiritual impoverishment. The present volume seeks to develop an approach to theory which affirms its critical role, while at the same time safeguarding the greater reality which it seeks to represent.

The theological counterpart of scientific theories are, of course, Christian doctrines, which serve the dual function of *explication* and *conservation*. For example, the doctrine of the person of Christ attempts to make sense of the complex and variegated Christian experience and knowledge of Jesus Christ, and ring-fence the hard-won insights accumulated by the community of faith as it wrestles with these questions. For some, an interest in Christian doctrine is a mark of narrow-mindedness comparable to the tunnel vision of a particularly fastidious stamp collector. In the intellectual environment in which I began to study theology in the 1970s, it was regarded as axiomatic that it is more blessed to pursue truth than to achieve it. We are questing for something that cannot be achieved; only fools believe that it is possible to *know* the truth. Like all overstatements, this incorporates genuine insights – most notably, that the belief that one has firmly secured the truth (and may thus cease questing and enquiring) is intellectually stifling, inhibiting its further exploration.

Yet what happens if one encounters something that is real and transformative, an insight which demands to be preserved, affirmed and proclaimed? What happens if the merchant stumbles across a pearl of great price, and wants to ensure that it never departs from his possession, and never diminishes in his appreciation? It is here that one of the most fundamental human instincts comes into play – the deep-rooted yearning to *preserve* precious insights, lest they are lost. It is precisely this instinct which underlies the development of Christian doctrine. The core motivation for doctrinal development is the desire to 'preserve the mystery', to place a fence around the pasture-ground of the New Testament,[8] to

---

[8] Charles Gore, *The Incarnation of the Son of God.* London: John Murray, 1922, 97. For a more general exploration of this theme, see Andrew Louth, *Discerning the Mystery: An Essay on the Nature of Theology.* Oxford: Clarendon Press, 1983.

transmit to future generations the insights which both sustain the Christian tradition and distinguish it from rival visions of divine identity and human destiny.

Yet this desire to preserve and develop insights and discoveries is not the exclusive preserve of Christian theology. The same fundamental animus underlies the natural sciences. The basic concern to 'save the phenomena' is supplemented by a principled determination to identify deeper patterns within the fabric of the world that these phenomena in some way disclose and exemplify. Scientist and theologian alike are concerned to observe, explore and explain, regarding the sphere of observation (including its extended variant, experimentation) as the foundation of all legitimate theorizing. The grand generalizations of theory gain both their credibility and their specific forms from a sustained engagement with the particularities of human experience and observation. Both the natural sciences and a scientific theology explicitly reject the notion that theories may be derived and legitimated *a priori*. It is through *a posteriori* reflection on what has actually happened that true (including non-tautological) knowledge[9] is derived.

This final volume opens by considering the legitimacy of theory in the natural sciences and theology, confronting those who regard any attempt at theoretical formulation within theology as premature and inappropriate. After arguing for the propriety of theory in the Christian life, I move on to deal with the complex question of how reality may be represented in any intellectual engagement with reality, before turning to deal specifically with the explanatory aspects of theory. A short and somewhat speculative final section of this chapter offers new approaches to two highly complex and contentious issues – the concept of 'heresy' and the development of doctrine – which demonstrate the creative potential of a scientific theology. While each of these topics demands a full book-length treatment in itself – books, it may be added, which will appear within the next five years – these brief sketches of significant

---

[9] Ludwig Wittgenstein famously persuaded Bertrand Russell that the propositions of logic and pure mathematics were 'tautologies' – that is, true propositions which nevertheless introduce no new knowledge (see *Tractatus Logico-Philosophicus* 6.1). In the end, the distinction between tautologies and propositions can only be decided by appealing to their correspondence with empirical observation. A proposition may be thought of as a picture or representation of a possible fact or state of affairs in the world. A proposition in this sense may be either true or false. Yet it is impossible to determine whether it is true or false simply by considering its meaning (*Sinn*). The demarcation of proposition from tautology rests upon a comparison with the empirical world. For some of the issues arising from this point, see the intriguing (and only modestly speculative) article of Laurence Goldstein, 'Wittgenstein's Ph.D. Viva – A Re-Creation', *Philosophy* 74 (1997), 499–514.

developments point to the viability and intellectual potential of the style of theology advocated in these volumes. The final chapter argues for a place for a warranted metaphysics within a scientific theology, against those who reject its *a posteriori* possibility on *a priori* grounds. A scientific theology is shown to be open to various metaphysical developments, and is not in any way reduced to a 'naturalist' account of reality. And finally, the conclusion of the work points ahead to a work that is yet to come, which builds on the foundations laid in these three volumes – a scientific dogmatics.

In bringing this project to a close, I take great pleasure in thanking those who have made it possible. I particularly wish to thank the John Templeton Foundation for funding the research that underlies these three volumes. Dr Darren C. Marks, my research assistant, patiently tracked down and copied even the most obscure references. My colleagues at Oxford University have offered me the double benefit of intellectual stimulus and personal support, and I gratefully acknowledge this. No theologian is an island, and I could not even begin to express my gratitude to the Oxford intellectual environment, which is perhaps unrivalled as a stimulus to creative, responsible and informed theological reflection. If anyone wants to understand my approach to theology, they will have to attempt to come to terms with the remarkable intellectual phenomenon which is called 'Oxford University', and the opportunities for intellectual cross-fertilization that it affords at every level. In particular, I wish to thank Professors John Barton, John Hedley Brooke and John Webster for especially helpful discussions of points of detail. The faculty and students of Wycliffe Hall, Oxford, have provided me with an outstanding environment in which to work, think and write over the last twenty years, and I owe this institution more than I can ever express through dedicating this volume to them. They have given me far more than I can ever hope to give in return, and this small token of appreciation does not even begin to do justice to the debt that I owe this community of faith and learning at the heart of one of the world's greatest universities.

PART FOUR

Theory

Chapter 12

The Legitimacy of Theory within a Scientific Theology

Gloria enim Dei vivens homo; vita autem hominis visio Dei.[1] Within the parameters of the Christian tradition, humanity is to be seen as the height of God's creation, whose life is shaped by the overwhelming radiance of the vision of God. The church is called into being through its apprehension of this vision of God, which it is called to pursue in its theology, spirituality and ethics.[2] Theology begins within this community of faith, as it seeks to give an account of its communal beholding of the vision of God. Indeed, it could be argued that the supreme task of theology is to keep this sense of wonder alive, as the process of unfolding the object of wonder and worship proceeds – in other words, as apprehension gives way to reflection, and supremely the formulation of theory. The Christian community regards itself as being under an obligation to tell what it has seen, like the appointed observers at the great festivals of classical Greece. To behold is to report; theory is an attempt to render in words the great wonders and mysteries of faith.

The Christian tradition posits a unitary reality, holding that the entire creation has the potential to bear witness to its creator. To capture the full vision of God involves an appeal to the entire economy of salvation – creation, redemption, and the hope of final consummation. The Christian doctrine of creation provides a fundamental motivation to the investigation and appreciation of nature, in terms of both providing an intellectual framework which allows nature to be seen as a coherent

---

[1] Irenaeus, *adversus haereses*, IV.xx.7.

[2] One of the best accounts of the ethical dimensions of the matter is provided by Kenneth E. Kirk, *The Vision of God: The Christian Doctrine of the Summum Bonum*. London: Longmans, Green & Co., 1931.

witness to God, and enkindling an intellectual curiosity, a love of truth, a desire for knowledge, and a yearning for understanding which impels the baptized mind to explore what it finds around it and within it.[3]

That vision of God destroys any restrictive categorizations which insist that certain domains of knowledge are to be deemed religious, and others secular. A scientific theology, grounded in a unitary conception of reality, insists that the engagement with every aspect of the world offers the potential to deepen an appreciation of its creator, according to its own distinctive nature and the capacity of a fallen human mind to discern it. A scientific theology gladly and joyfully embraces the totality of reality, while never losing sight of the fact that the theological grid which allows it to affirm and engage the world in this manner is grounded in the specifics of the Christian revelation, and mediated through the Christian tradition.

This grand engagement with public reality is made possible and made significant by the particularities of the Christian vision of God. The natural world which is to be interpreted is a publicly observable entity; the process of *observation* entails '*seeing nature as God's creation*', which entails that a publicly accessible entity is to be observed and interpreted on the basis of a tradition-mediated framework of rationality. The theological engagement with nature is thus powered and directed by a specific understanding of the nature of reality, which must be sustained and safeguarded if this process of encounter and appreciation is to continue. Something of its power can be sensed in the great hymns of the Christian tradition. The hymn often known as the 'Deer's cry' or the 'Lorica', traditionally ascribed to Patrick, patron saint of Ireland, is an excellent example of a theological vision embracing the totality of the economy of salvation.[4]

> I arise through a mighty strength, the invocation of the
> Trinity, through belief in the Threeness, through confession
> of the Oneness of the Creator of creation.
>
> I arise today through the strength of Christ with his Baptism,
> through the strength of his Crucifixion with his Burial
> through the strength of his Resurrection with his Ascension,
> through the strength of his descent for the Judgment of Doom.

[3] For an outstanding account of these issues in Augustine's approach to understanding, see Jean Bethke Elshtain, *Augustine and the Limits of Politics*. Notre Dame, IN: University of Notre Dame Press, 1995.

[4] Whitley Stokes and John Strachan, *Thesaurus Palaeohibernicus: A Collection of Old-Irish Glosses, Scholia, Prose, and Verse*, 2 vols. Cambridge: Cambridge University Press, 1901, vol. 2, 354–8.

I arise today through the strength of the love of Cherubim
in obedience of Angels, in the service of the Archangels,
in hope of resurrection to meet with reward,
in prayers of Patriarchs, in predictions of Prophets,
in preachings of Apostles, in faiths of Confessors,
in innocence of Holy Virgins, in deeds of righteous people.

I arise today, through the strength of Heaven:
light of Sun, brilliance of Moon, splendour of Fire,
speed of Lightning, swiftness of Wind, depth of Sea,
stability of Earth, firmness of Rock.

This unitary vision of nature is given intellectual rigour through its theological foundations, and oxygenated through worship, prayer and adoration. The vision of the God who stands behind, and is disclosed through, the economy of salvation has empowered Christian worship and inspired Christian architecture. While it might be a little ambitious to speak of a coherent 'theology of the Gothic cathedral',[5] there can be no doubt of the spiritual aspirations of their designers and the importance of their sacred spaces in anticipating their heavenly counterparts and sustaining the vision of God. One of the most distinctive features of this architectural style is its deliberate and programmatic use of height and light to generate and sustain a sense of the presence of God and heaven on earth. The extensive use of buttresses allowed the weight of the building to be borne by outside supports, thus allowing the external walls to have large glass windows, which ensured that the building was saturated with the radiance of the sun. The use of stained glass helped generate an other-worldly brilliance within the cathedral, while simultaneously allowing gospel scenes to be depicted to worshippers. The use of tall, thin internal columns created an immense sense of spaciousness, again intended to evoke the hope of heaven. The cathedral thus became a sacred space, bringing the vast spaciousness and brilliance of heaven within the reach of believers. Its worship was seen as an anticipation of the life of heaven, allowing the worshipper to step into another world, capturing something of a vision of the radiant glory of God, before returning to the dull routines of everyday life.

The theological importance of these tactile values is perhaps best explored by considering the ideas of Abbot Suger (1080–1151), who

---

[5] Christoph Markschies, *Gibt es eine 'Theologie der gotischen Kathedrale?' nochmals: Suger von Saint-Denis und Sankt Dionys vom Areopag.* Heidelberg: Universitätsverlag C. Winter, 1995. On Chartres, see Laurence J. James, 'Pseudo-Dionysius' Metaphysics of Darkness and Chartres Cathedral', *Essays in Medieval Studies* 2 (1985), 182–206.

devoted much of his later life to the restoration of the abbey church of Saint-Denis, near Paris.[6] This early example of the classic Gothic style embodies many of its characteristic emphases. Yet perhaps most importantly, Suger's three books of commentary on the renovation process allow us insights into the physical process of construction, along with the spiritual and aesthetic principles which governed his design. The inscription he placed above the great bronze doors of the church points to his theological interpretation of the sense of radiance and spaciousness he had created within the building:[7]

> Nobile claret opus, sed opus quod nobile claret
> Clarificet mentes, ut eant per lumina vera
> Ad verum lumen, ubi Christus ianua vera.

The human mind is to be drawn upwards through the light of the building to the true light, who is the enthroned Christ in heaven – a clear statement of the importance of architecture in embodying, and subsequently sustaining, the vision of God as creator and redeemer.

Just as Gothic churches embodied a sense of the spaciousness of heaven, the worship which was enacted within their walls further strengthened the corporate sense of beholding the vision of God. The idea of liminality – that is, being on the threshold of the sacred, peering into the forbidden heavenly realms – is represented visually in the structure of Orthodox churches, especially the way in which the sanctuary and the altar are set apart from the people on account of a deep sense of the awesomeness of the mystery of God. In their treatises on worship, Chrysostom and other Greek patristic writers repeatedly draw attention to the liturgical importance of this sense of the sacred in sustaining Christian life and thought.[8] The evocation of a sense of mystery both affirms the vitality of the vision of God, while at the same time suggesting that there are limits to the extent that any theoretical accounts of such a mystery can hope to represent it.

Yet some such theoretical account of this vision of God must be offered. The development of theory is as inevitable as it is legitimate, and must be seen as an exercise of theological responsibility, a call to be answerable for and to the Christian gospel. A church which fails to reflect critically upon its identity and proclamation is ultimately a dead or dying

---

[6] Sumner McKnight Crosby and Pamela Z. Blum, *The Royal Abbey of Saint-Denis from its beginnings to the Death of Suger, 475–1151*. New Haven, CT: Yale University Press, 1987.

[7] Abbot Suger of Saint-Denis, *de administratione*, 27.

[8] On which see Hugh Wybrew, *The Orthodox Liturgy: The Development of the Eucharistic Liturgy in the Byzantine Rite*. London: SPCK, 1989. For related issues in the west, see Marie Bernard de Soos, *Le mystère liturgique d'après Saint Léon le Grand*. Münster: Aschendorff, 1971.

church, which has lost confidence in the regenerative power of its ideas. Yet it must be conceded immediately that, while the living God possesses an ability to *excite* worship and delight, theories *about* God often seem to be rather lustreless, plodding and ponderous.

Martin Heidegger, perhaps aware of the ease with which a spine-tingling excitement about nature could give way to some thoroughly pedestrian accounts of nature, suggested revitalizing the notion of theory through a highly creative etymological association. Could not the very term θεωρέω be regarded as deriving from θέος and ὁράω, implying that 'theory' was essentially a beholding of the divine – an idea perhaps more naturally expressed in the Latin term *contemplatio*? Theory is thus to be seen as the outcome of a 'high and lofty' continual process of contemplating the truth.[9] Some justification for such a view can be found in ancient Greek writers such as Plutarch and Philodemus, who held that 'theorizing . . . means seeing what is divine'.[10]

Heidegger's suggestion that theory has strongly religious connotations – the beholding of the divine, or a vision of the gods – is found at a number of points in his writings. In an important study of the notoriously eccentric German poet Hölderlin, Heidegger suggested that his alleged 'madness' arose from gazing too intently on the 'ground and centre' of reality – that is, from too close an encounter with the gods.[11] Theory could thus be argued to designate something that one does *not* see, but is nevertheless under an obligation to express and explore.[12]

The religious leanings of Heidegger's account of theory have met with resistance, not least from the Frankfurt School.[13] Jürgen Habermas sought to reconceive the notion in a purely social context, relocating an ostensibly theological activity within the public discourse of knowledge concerning the universe. The *theoros* was the representative sent by

[9] Martin Heidegger, *The Question concerning Technology, and Other Essays*. New York: Harper & Row, 1977, 163–4. See further William McNeill, *The Glance of the Eye: Heidegger, Aristotle, and the Ends of Theory*. Albany: State University of New York Press, 1999, 252–79.
[10] Plutarch, *de musica*, 27; Philodemus, *de musica*, 23.
[11] See Martin Heidegger, *Erläuterungen zu Hölderlins Dichtung*. Frankfurt am Main: Klostermann, 1944, especially the important essay 'Hölderlin und das Wesen der Dichtung' (31–45). See further Peter Trawny, *'Voll Verdienst, doch dichterisch wohnet der Mensch auf dieser Erde': Heidegger und Hölderlin*. Frankfurt am Main: Vittorio Klostermann, 2000.
[12] Hans Blumenberg, *Das Lachen der Thrakerin: Eine Urgeschichte der Theorie*. Frankfurt am Main: Suhrkamp, 1987, 9. See also the study of Hannelore Rausch, *Theoria: Von ihrer sakralen zur philosophischen Bedeutung*. Munich: Fink, 1982, 148–52, which similarly locates the origin of the idea in a religious context. Note in particular the contrast she draws between the old-style theology of Hesiod and Aristotle's approach (151).
[13] Rolf Wiggershaus, *The Frankfurt School: Its History, Theories and Political Significance*. Cambridge: Polity Press, 1994, 592–6. For etymological concerns about Heidegger's ideas, see Rausch, *Theoria: Von ihrer sakralen zur philosophischen Bedeutung*, 13–15.

Greek cities to public celebrations whose function was *theoria* – that is, to behold what was taking place. In the modern context, such a process of observation is often understood in terms of a neutral or disinterested observer reporting on events;[14] in the ancient world, however, the spectator was understood to be drawn into the events.[15]

> The meaning of the tragedy remains in essence incomprehensible to any 'mere spectator.' The accomplishment of theatrical presentation was rather to involve the spectator in the 'action', to draw him or her into a knowing (seeing) relationship to a world that now became manifest as exceeding or transcending his or her individual actions. The classical Greek 'theatrical' and tragic view of the world was precisely such that it could not be reduced to a merely pictured or represented totality of meaning. Ancient *theōria* entailed, on the contrary, an involved partici- pation in the disclosure of other beings . . . It was also inextricably asso- ciated with experience of the divine and sacred presence of other beings.

In philosophical language, *theoria* was thus readily transferred to con- templation of the cosmos. Wlad Godzich thus argues that theory repre- sents the public beholding of the world and society, through which private perceptions were transcended and reconfigured into socially nor- mative beliefs 'invested with undeniable authority by the polity'.[16]

> The act of looking at, of surveying, designated by *theorein*, does not des- ignate a private act carried out by a cogitating philosopher but a very public one with important social consequences. The Greeks designated certain individuals . . . to act as legates on certain formal occasions in other city states or in matters of considerable political importance. These indi- viduals bore the title of *theoros*, and collectively constituted a *theoria*. (It may be useful to bear in mind that the word is always a plural collective.)

While discarding the religious associations of the notion, Habermas and others have pointed to another element of critical importance to our reflection – namely, that 'theory' designates the reflective activity of a community. The communal dimension of *theoria* is of immense theo- logical importance, and I will return to explore this more thoroughly in due course.

---

[14] See the analysis of Richard J. Bernstein, 'Judging: The Actor and the Spectator', in *Philosophical Profiles: Essays in a Pragmatic Mode*. Philadelphia: University of Pennsylvania Press, 1986, 221–38. More recent studies have stressed the affinities between the *theoria* and a pilgrim- age: Jean Chelini and Henry Branthomme, *Histoire des pèlerinages non-chrétiens: entre magique et sacré – le chemin des dieux*. Paris: Hachette, 1987; Ian Rutherford, '*Theoria* and *Darsan*: Pilgrimage and Vision in Greece and India', *Classical Quarterly* 50 (2000), 133–46.

[15] McNeill, *The Glance of the Eye: Heidegger, Aristotle, and the Ends of Theory*, 254–5.

[16] Wlad Godzich, 'Foreword: The Tiger on the Paper Mat', in Paul de Man (ed.), *The Resistance to Theory*. Minneapolis: University of Minnesota Press, 1986, ix–xviii.

In its developed sense (and especially in its theological forms), theory may be regarded as the initial apprehension by the reflecting mind of a communal revelation, followed by a deliberate attempt to capture and express the sense of an emerging orderedness, underpinned by a sense of authority, which such a revelation elicits. This process of reflection takes place at the communal level, and comes to be authoritative for the community which 'beholds' reality in this manner. For a scientific theology, the inner logic of the Christian faith inexorably points to its theoretical affirmations being grounded and judged with reference to the entire economy of salvation as disclosed in Jesus Christ, who may thus be seen as functioning as both the foundation and the criterion of an authentic theology.

The inevitability of theory

Theory arises precisely because human beings are rational creatures, and feel impelled, both morally and intellectually, to give an account of things. The natural sciences and Christian theology are both rooted in human experience and culture; yet they also aspire to transcend the particularities of time and place to yield truths that claim a more universal significance. The first critical question concerns precisely how one moves from observation of and reflection upon particularities – such as the movements of the planets, the distribution of fossils, or the history of Jesus Christ – to universal theories, having validity and relevance beyond the specific events which evoked and precipitated them. The second critical question has to do with how we ensure that these particularities are not evaporated by the theory which they generate, so that a universal abstraction comes to be valued more than the concrete particularities which it enumerates.

The essence of the process of theorizing may be identified as an attempt to identify universal *a posteriori* patterns in local situations, and represent those patterns in a language appropriate to its subject matter – often, in the case of the natural sciences, the language of mathematics. The intellectual challenge here is to preserve locality while discerning universality – that is to say, to ensure that the particularities of the observed situation are not displaced or superseded by the universal patterns which they are held to disclose.

Theory tames reality, reducing it to manageable proportions and allowing it to be visualized in terms adapted to human reasoning. Experience is to be reduced to repeatable formulas; phenomena are to be represented formally through mathematics. In this sense, theory can

be seen as embodying a central theme of the Enlightenment – the desire
to reduce everything to 'clear and distinct ideas' (Descartes). This
concern can be seen throughout the development of modern natural
science, from Newton to Einstein: reality is to be reduced and represented in terms conforming to three global categories – accuracy, simplicity and generalizability. The Enlightenment set itself the 'double task
of domination and emancipation';[17] the new emphasis upon theory can
be seen as advancing both agendas, in that it facilitated the intellectual,
and subsequently the physical, domination of nature, and the emancipation of the human mind through its ability to comprehend the natural
process it would subsequently redirect towards its own ends.

The relentless human yearning to see the 'big picture' which provides
a framework for the myriad of particular observations leads inexorably
to the formulation and testing of theories. Both the natural sciences and
Christian theology offer such theories as a means of explaining what
may be observed in the world, and are entirely justified in doing so. I
hold Christian doctrine to be the natural, inevitable and proper
outcome of a sustained engagement with the person of Jesus Christ. The
blunt demand for an 'undogmatic Christianity' is as unrealistic as it is
pointless, as we shall presently argue (53–66). To understand more of the
pressures which lead to the development of theory, we may turn to consider Francis Bacon's critique of those who decline to reflect on the intellectual implications of their accumulated observations.

Francis Bacon on theory

One of the most important early defences of theory comes from the pro-
lific pen of Francis Bacon (1561–1626). His *Novum Organum* (1620) contains a set of aphorisms contrasting those who merely collect facts and
observations and those who generate their ideas without any reference
to the external world. Making the point that the human mind must generate ideas in response to what is observed in the natural world, Bacon
suggests that the humble bee might offer a model for a 'true philosophy'.[18]

> Those who have treated of the sciences have been either empiricists or
> dogmatists. The former, like ants, only heap up and use what they accu-
> mulate; the latter, like spiders, spin webs out of their own resources. There

[17] Bruno Latour, *We Have Never Been Modern*. Cambridge, MA: Harvard University Press,
1993, 10.
[18] Francis Bacon, *Novum organum scientiarum*. London: John Bill, 1620, I.95. See further
John C. Briggs, *Francis Bacon and the Rhetoric of Nature*. Cambridge, MA: Harvard University
Press, 1989.

is a true middle way, in that the bee gathers material from the flowers of the garden and the field, but then works and digests it by its own faculties (*quae materiam ex floribus horti et agri elicit; sed tamen eam propria facultate vertit et digerit.*) The true labour of philosophy resembles this, for it neither relies entirely or principally on the powers of the mind, nor yet lays up in the memory the matter afforded by the experiments of natural history or mechanics in its raw state, but changes and works it in the understanding. We have good reason, therefore, to derive hope from a closer and purer alliance of these faculties, (the experimental and rational) than has yet been attempted.

Reflection on observations of the natural world leads to the generation of theories concerning the world, through the intellectual digestion and assimilation of what is observed. Bacon's three analogies merit close attention, in the light of the context in which a scientific theology is set.

First, Bacon rejects the approach of the ant – the mere accumulation of material. His reasons for doing so rest partly on the immense amount of material that requires to be assembled, and partly on the need to go beyond particulars to identify the general patterns that underlie them. In the first place, then, Bacon observes that there is so much material that calls out to be amassed that the task is impossible:[19]

> Moreover, since there is so great a number and army of particulars (*tantus sit particularium numerus et quasi exercitus*), and that army so scattered and dispersed as to distract and confound the understanding, little is to be hoped for from the skirmishings and slight attacks and desultory movements of the intellect.

Yet the task is also somewhat pointless, unless it is possible to use this accumulation of particularities to generate universalities and commonalities – which, in the end, must be seen as one of the central aims of a true science. Bacon thus holds that the generation of 'axioms' is essential if the scientist is to rise from being a mere observer of nature to being a true natural philosopher.[20]

> We may hope well of the sciences when in a true scale of ascent, when we proceed by successive steps which are not interrupted or broken, by which we rise from particulars to lesser axioms; and then to middle axioms, one above the other; and last of all to the most general axioms of all.

A true natural philosopher is thus not to be identified with one who merely 'enumerates' particularities; 'induction which proceeds by simple

---

[19] Bacon, *Novum Organum*, I.102.
[20] Bacon, *Novum Organum*, I.104.

enumeration is childish'.[21] Rather, the true natural philosophy is one which is firmly grounded in the world of particularities, but rises above it through a process of well-argued and empirically grounded induction, through which a series of higher principles or 'axioms' are inferred. To fail to take this step is to squander the potential of a natural philosopher, and become a mere cataloguer, rather than an interpreter, of the world.

Second, Bacon declares the approach of the spider to be invalid, in that it merely constructs a view of the world from internalized assumptions of the mind. The theoretical web is spun from the existing matrix of assumptions and beliefs, whether unconsciously absorbed from the social context or actively generated in the process of logical analysis. For Bacon, axioms must be based on experience and observation. Rationalism is prone to stratospheric flights of speculative fancy, which are not anchored to the real world of particularities, determined through observation. 'The understanding must not therefore be supplied with wings, but rather hung with lead weights, to restrain it from leaping and flying (*itaque hominum intellectui non plumae addendae, sed plumbum potius et pondera; ut cohibeant omnem saltum et volatum*).'[22]

The relevance of Bacon's point to a scientific theology will be clear. The significant commonalities which exist between the scientific and theological enterprises are to be set in the context of their mutual rejection of the foundational themes of the Enlightenment project. That project, as set out by Jean-Jacques Rousseau and endorsed by writers such as Kant, took its cue from the ability of humanity to deploy universally available and globally accessible rational resources to understand and master reality. For Jean-Jacques Rousseau, humanity possessed internalized resources to grasp and master the world and its true destiny through the autonomous exercise of a universal reason that somehow rose above the specificities of history:[23]

> It is a grand and beautiful sight to see man emerge somehow from nothing by his own efforts; dissipate, by the light of his reason, the shadows in which nature had enveloped him; rise above himself; soar by means of his mind into the heavenly regions; traverse, like the sun, the vast expanse of the universe with giant steps; and, what is even grander and more difficult, return to himself in order to study man and know his nature, his duties, and his end.

[21] Bacon, *Novum Organum*, I.105.
[22] Bacon, *Novum Organum*, I.104.
[23] Jean-Jacques Rousseau, *Basic Political Writings*. Indianapolis: Hackett, 1987, 3. For Kant's indebtedness to Rousseau at this point, see Marie Rischmüller, *Bemerkungen in den 'Beobachtungen über das Gefühl des Schönen und Erhabenen'*. Hamburg: Felix Meiner Verlag, 1991, 38.

Universal principles are thus to be determined *a priori*, on the basis of a human reason which is held to be revelationally and soteriologically self-sufficient. Yet the subsequent relentless critical attack on this approach to reality has seen virtually every aspect of its vision of philosophy and ethics diluted, dismantled or abandoned. The Enlightenment project grandly conceived itself in terms of the triumph of a universal rationality, where it was more accurately a local transient victory of an essentially ethnocentric philosophy which was blind to its own limitations and social location. Its attempt to disengage from the particularities and localizations of history led not to a universal philosophy, relieved of the tedious and awkward exigencies of human existence, but to an intellectual utopianism. Believing itself to stand above history, it could not face the dreadful truth of being located within its flux. Preoccupied with the quest for the universal, it devalued and neglected the particularities of history.

A scientific theology eschews such false *a priori* abstractions and universalizations, and seeks to ground general principles *a posteriori*, through an encounter with the world of particularities. If general truths are to be established, this will not take place through the evasion of the particular, but through a sustained and comprehensive engagement with the multi-levelled reality of the world. If that process of engagement leads to the warranted postulation of metaphysical entities, a scientific theology will gladly affirm their propriety. The essential point is that such reflection must take place *a posteriori*, subsequent to an engagement with reality, rather than allowing the nature and outcome of such an engagement to be predetermined on *a priori* grounds.

Bacon's analogy of the bee emphasizes that it is not enough merely to accumulate facts or observations; the key question concerns what this accumulation of observation is seen to entail, and what deeper levels of reality or higher axioms may be inferred from it. The history of science offers countless examples of the application of this general principle. Johann Kepler had access to a remarkably accurate series of observations of the position of the planet Mars against the fixed stars; the question that concerned him, however, was what understanding of the solar system as a whole was indicated by those observations. Charles Darwin's voyage on the *Beagle* provided him with a series of observations, especially of the fauna of the Galapagos islands. But what greater understanding of the origins of the natural world did these point to? Bacon insists that such grand schemes must not be allowed to be the pure product of the human mind, unconstrained by observation of and engagement with the natural world. Positing an interactive mode of reflection, Bacon points to the need to accumulate data and reflect upon it, thus yielding what is recognizably a 'critical realist' approach to nature.

There is thus a theoretical imperative built into the patterns of human thought. It is as if we are designed and intended to yearn to press beyond the world of appearances, and ask what lies beyond or behind it. The same fundamental impulse lies behind philosophy, theology and the natural sciences – the desire to see the 'big picture' which the natural world somehow reflects. The demand to eliminate or avoid theory ultimately amounts to a demand that humans should cease thinking. Theory arises precisely because human beings are rational, inquisitive and exploratory.

Having noted Darwin's theoretical reflections on his observations on the Galapagos islands, we may turn to consider the place of theory in the biological sciences in a little more detail.

Theory in biology

Biology once saw itself as content to catalogue and categorize the plant life of the planet. Yet as that process of accumulating and sifting data proceeded, it became increasingly clear that the data pointed to deeper issues,[24] raising valid theoretical questions which demanded a deeper level of engagement with the natural world. The eighteenth-century Swedish naturalist Carl von Linné (1707–78) – more generally known by the Latinized form of his name, 'Carolus Linnaeus' – discerned that there existed some form of ordering within the natural world.[25] Linnaeus was not an 'experimentalist', as that term is now understood; for him, an 'experiment' referred primarily to the observation or experience of the natural world, which permitted taxonomies to be generated.[26] Linnaeus brought to this taxonomical task an acute ability for accurate observation and logical analysis, allowing him to categorize and classify what might otherwise not be recognized as possessing any form of regularity.

Having established such a taxonomy of species, the question then arose concerning how this was to be interpreted. What did it point to? What theory of the development of the natural world might account for this observed ordering? While Linnaeus was somewhat unorthodox by

---

[24] For a penetrating and controversial exploration of the issue, see Marc Ereshefsky, *The Poverty of the Linnaean Hierarchy: A Philosophical Study of Biological Taxonomy*. Cambridge: Cambridge University Press, 2001.

[25] Margaret J. Anderson, *Carl Linnaeus: Father of Classification*. Springfield, NJ: Enslow, 1997.

[26] Gunnar Broberg, *Homo Sapiens: Studier i Carl von Linnés naturuppfattning och människolära*. Uppsala: Almqvist & Wiksell, 1975.

the norms of contemporary Swedish Lutheranism,[27] there is no doubt that Linnaeus regarded some form of Christian doctrine of special creation as an adequate explanation of his observations. Although Linnaeus does not make any specific appeal to the Christian doctrine of creation in establishing his arguments, he clearly considers that doctrine to be confirmed and strengthened by his arguments concerning the relation of plants and animals.[28]

Linnaeus's views on the origins of the order he perceived were soon subjected to criticism, most notably by George-Louis Leclerc, Comte de Buffon.[29] Yet it was Darwin's account of how such ordering arose which would eventually win the day, largely on account of its elegance and the relatively few assumptions it required, and its resonance with prevailing social assumptions.[30] The Linnaean taxonomy can be seen as providing a significant conceptual foundation for Darwin's subsequent reflections.

Darwin's theory of natural selection thus stands one step removed from the empirical data upon which it is based, and with reference to which it must be defended. Yet the correctness of taking this theoretical step lies beyond dispute. The biologist is under an intellectual responsibility to reflect on the implications of what is observed, and what its wider implications might be. The transition from observations of the natural world to the development of theories concerning the natural world involves a deeper shift, including contested questions relating to human identity and destiny. While it is arguable whether these questions may be answered on biological grounds alone, it is incontestable that they are rightly raised through precisely the theoretical processes which undergird all sciences worthy of that name.

The history of the biological sciences thus demonstrates the irresistible trend from observation to theory. While Linnaeus may be regarded as representing an approach to biology which emphasized the accumulation of data, it is clear that even the Swedish biologist was aware that this data had theoretical implications. For Darwin, those and additional observations pointed to the existence of processes which had

[27] Tore Frängsmyr, *Geologi och skapelsetro: Föreställningar om jordens historia från Hiärne till Bergman*. Stockholm: Almqvist & Wiksell, 1969, 216–17; Broberg, *Homo Sapiens*, 141–9.

[28] Nils von Hoftsen, 'Skapelsetro och uralstringshypoteser före Darwin', *Uppsala Universiteits Årsskrift* 2 (1928), 31–36, especially 35.

[29] Phillip R. Sloan, 'The Buffon–Linnaeus Controversy', *Isis* 67 (1976), 356–75; idem, 'Buffon, German Biology and the Historical Interpretation of Biological Species', *British Journal for the History of Science*, 12 (1979), 109–53.

[30] Thomas F. Glick, *The Comparative Reception of Darwinism*. Austin: University of Texas Press, 1972; James Moore, 'Deconstructing Darwinism: The Politics of Evolution in the 1860s', *Journal of the History of Biology* 24 (1991), 353–408.

not yet been observed, and might even be unobservable, which could only be described theoretically in terms of 'natural selection'. These theoretical insights could, by a process of extrapolation and integration, become the basis of a worldview – such as individualist economic competition and laissez-faire economics,[31] or an explicit atheism.[32] As Alex Rosenberg points out in his survey of recent philosophical naturalisms, Darwinism is widely regarded as offering the theoretical insight 'that makes almost everything else coherent'.[33] The (contested) transition from the observation of finches in the Galapagos to atheism is thus indirect, proceeding by theoretical intermediates by means of a trajectory which may be represented as follows:

$$observation \Rightarrow theory \Rightarrow worldview$$

This process can be illustrated from every science, whether natural or social, and is equally significant for a scientific theology.

Theory in physics

The transition from observation to theoretical reflection is equally marked in the physical sciences. A significant defence of the legitimacy and necessity of theory is found in the writings of the Danish physicist Niels Bohr in the later 1920s, as he sought to give a theoretical account for a complex and somewhat mystifying series of observations relating to quantum phenomena. Bohr was especially concerned with the arguments set out in two papers published by Louis de Broglie in September 1923. De Broglie, who had been deeply impressed by Einstein's discussion of the wave–particle duality for light, argued that the general principle established by Einstein in 1905 was capable of generalization, and could be extended to all material particles, particularly electrons. In his first paper, he suggested that it was possible to assign a 'fictitious associated wave' to any moving body, whose momentum and wavelength (λ) were related as follows:

$$\lambda = h/p$$

[31] Richard Weikart, 'A Recently Discovered Darwin Letter on Social Darwinism', *Isis* 86 (1995), 609–11. This 1872 letter from Charles Darwin to Heinrich Fick, a law professor at the University of Zurich, strongly suggests that Darwin himself was sympathetic to the economic application of his theory.

[32] For reflection on the implications of Darwin's theory, see works such as Richard Dawkins, *The Blind Watchmaker: Why the Evidence of Evolution Reveals a Universe without Design*. New York: W. W. Norton, 1986; Daniel C. Dennett, *Darwin's Dangerous Idea: Evolution and the Meaning of Life*. New York: Simon & Schuster, 1995.

[33] Alex Rosenberg, 'A Field Guide to Recent Species of Naturalism', *British Journal for the Philosophy of Science* 47 (1996), 1–29.

where *h* is Planck's constant and *p* is the momentum of the moving body. What is truly radical about this proposal is that it abolishes the idea of a total distinction between particles and waves; any moving particle has an associated 'de Broglie wavelength' λ. The de Broglie equation proposes a fusion of what had hitherto been considered to be opposites, in that momentum had been considered to be a property of particles, and wavelength a property of waves. De Broglie proposed a fundamental relationship between these. In his second paper, published two weeks later, de Broglie proposed a means of testing his proposed relationship. Experimental confirmation of his ideas, he wrote, could be obtained by allowing electrons to traverse an aperture whose dimensions were small in relation to the predicted de Broglie wavelength.

De Broglie's predictions were confirmed in 1925 by Clinton Joseph Davisson and Lester Halber Germer at the Bell Laboratories in New York, who observed the diffraction of electrons by atoms in a crystal of nickel. The resulting diffraction pattern was consistent with the de Broglie wavelength predicted by the equation. Further confirmation came shortly afterwards, when G. P. Thomson demonstrated the diffraction of electrons by thin films of celluloid and goal. In both cases, the electron velocity and its associated 'de Broglie wavelength' were measured, and found to be related by the precise formula proposed by de Broglie – namely, $\lambda = h/p$.

Matters developed further in 1926, when Werner Heisenberg and Erwin Schrödinger developed these insights into a consistent theory (independently of each other), using different (yet mathematically equivalent) formalisms.[34] Heisenberg developed his 'matrix mechanics' by beginning from the assumption that matter was particulate, whereas Schrödinger pioneered his 'wave mechanics' on the assumption that matter possessed wave properties.[35] Yet how could both be true? Was the electron a wave, or was it a particle? The two mathematical schemes proposed by Schrödinger and Heisenberg were mathematically equivalent and consistent, but seemed to begin from significantly different starting points, and reflect radically different assumptions. It seemed to Bohr that the two mathematical tools reflected different philosophical interpretations of what was happening.[36]

[34] Max Jammer, *The Conceptual Development of Quantum Mechanics*. New York: McGraw-Hill, 1966.
[35] For a full discussion, see David C. Cassidy, *Uncertainty: The Life and Science of Werner Heisenberg*. New York: W. H. Freeman, 1992, 204–25.
[36] Abraham Pais, *Niels Bohr's Times, in Physics, Philosophy and Polity*. Oxford: Clarendon Press, 1991, 302–16.

For Bohr, the central dilemma was how to make sense of the experimental and mathematical materials. Would classical notions, such as 'waves' and 'particles', have to be abandoned or could they continue to be used? Bohr's colleague Werner Heisenberg was inclined to the view that they should be abandoned; the words simply did not make sense at the level of quantum phenomena. Bohr was quite convinced that this was not so. As he declared in a lecture given on 16 September 1927 in the Italian town of Como to mark the centenary of the death of the Italian physicist Alessandro Volta, 'our interpretation of the experimental material rests essentially upon the classical concepts' – the issue concerned how these were to be related to each other in a 'complementary' manner:[37]

> The very nature of the quantum theory . . . forces us to regard the space–time coordination and the claim of causality, the union of which characterizes the classical theories, as complementary but exclusive features of the description . . . complementary pictures of the phenomena . . . only together offer a natural generalization of the classical mode of description.

The decision to use the term 'complementary' and related terms to refer to the way in which classical terms were to be used to describe quantum phenomena was no easy one, and caused some confusion within his audience.

As developed by Bohr in the Como lecture, the notion of 'complementarity' is a means by which those conflictual aspects of quantum phenomena which cannot be accounted for within the framework of classical theories may be completely described. The term carries with it the dual associations of 'the bringing together of mutually exclusive ideas' and 'a completeness of description', both of which can be argued to be integral to Bohr's understanding of the concept. He argued that the implications of the quantum postulate were 'completely foreign to the classical theories'. For Bohr, 'the quantum theory is characterized by the acknowledgement of a fundamental limitation in the classical physical ideas when applied to atomic phenomena'. After explaining this point in more detail, Bohr argues that 'the quantum postulate presents us with the task of developing a "complementarity" theory'.

The outcome of this is well known. Faced with the experimental data, Bohr argued that the only possible theoretical outcome was an approach which affirmed the complementarity of wave and particle approaches to

---

[37] Niels Bohr, *Niels Bohr: Collected Works*, ed. Leon Rosenfield and Erik Rudiger, 6 vols. Amsterdam: North Holland, 1972–85, vol. 6, 147.

quantum phenomena, despite the contradictions this seemed to entail.[38] The phenomena, he declared, admitted no other interpretation. They demanded an explanation, and it was intellectually irresponsible to evade the question of the theoretical implications of these observations. The theoretical conclusions must be drawn. Once more, we see the same fundamental trajectory from observations to theory – from the particularities to the generalities which may be held to lie behind or beneath them.

Niels Bohr is of particular interest to our analysis, in that the theoretical notion of 'complementarity', derived from the interpretation of observation, was expanded to become a worldview. Bohr himself never saw the need to restrict this mode of thinking to issues solely related to quantum theory, but extended it (often, it has to be said, in a rather tenuous manner) to include such areas as the problem of human consciousness, the description of living organisms, and aspects of human culture.[39] He had occasion to develop some religious aspects of these issues in his unpublished Gifford Lectures, entitled 'Causality and Complementarity: Epistemological Lessons of Studies in Atomic Physics', given at the University of Edinburgh in 1949.[40] Although it is open to question how significant Bohr's religious reflections might be, it is clear that he considered his theoretical reflections to offer him a matrix or framework through which he could view and address other issues.

In the end, however, it is not Bohr's specific views which matter, but the general ideational trajectory which he pursues – moving from observation to theory to a worldview. For Bohr, it is not enough to view reality; it is necessary to develop a theoretical account of its significance. Here, as elsewhere, we find a theoretical imperative built into the very fabric of the natural scientific enterprise. Yet, as we shall see, it is not limited to the natural sciences. On any unitary vision of reality, precisely the same impetus will be present at every level of human engagement with reality, natural or social.

[38] For discussion of the detail of these difficulties, see the rather different accounts presented in Henry J. Folse, *The Philosophy of Niels Bohr: The Framework of Complementarity.* Amsterdam: North Holland, 1985; John Honner, *The Description of Nature: Niels Bohr and the Philosophy of Quantum Physics.* Oxford: Clarendon Press, 1987; Dugald Murdoch, *Niels Bohr's Philosophy of Physics.* Cambridge: Cambridge University Press, 1987.

[39] Pais, *Niels Bohr's Times,* 438–47.

[40] These remain unpublished, and have received scant attention in the literature. See, for example, the very brief reference at Pais, *Niels Bohr's Times,* 450 n. 1. There is also a brief allusion to them in John Baillie, *The Sense of the Presence of God.* London: Oxford University Press, 1962, 217.

Theory in the human sciences

The human sciences, in that they involve a quest for understanding which goes beyond the cataloguing of particularities, manifest the same strong theoretical drive we have already noted with the biological and physical sciences. Thus for the Marxist, history is amenable to theoretical analysis.[41] It is not simply an assembly of happenings, but a process which is going somewhere, and which discloses that direction to its more intelligent and perceptive observers. On a Marxist reading, history is ultimately heading towards the inevitable triumph of socialism – a perception which informs political action in the present, in that this leads to the acceleration of the historical process, and the shortening of the birth-pangs of the perfect socialist state.[42] The scientific investigation of historical events thus leads to a specific theory of history, which in turn leads to a specific worldview, and actions directed towards its achievement. The trajectory which leads to this deeper engagement with the structures of reality may be represented as follows:

$$\text{observation} \Rightarrow \text{theory} \Rightarrow \text{worldview}$$

One of the reasons that some have difficulty with the development of theory is that it is seen to be metaphysically or conceptually inflationary, an issue to which we shall return later (Chapter 15). Yet a Marxist would respond that, if such metaphysical or conceptual adumbrations are required on the basis of a valid analysis of the phenomena, their postulation is as necessary as it is natural.

Perhaps the most contentious area in which theory makes a decisive intervention is the field of literary studies.[43] Once more, the fundamental impulse is a yearning to understand – why certain books are written, what determines their characters and outcomes, and how closure is secured or evaded.[44] The field of American literary studies offers a rich tapestry of scholarship, demonstrating how it is impossible to avoid

---

[41] Melvin Rader, *Marx's Interpretation of History*. New York: Oxford University Press, 1979, especially 86–136.

[42] For some reflections on such issues, see Roger S. Gottlieb, *History and Subjectivity: The Transformation of Marxist Theory*. Philadelphia: Temple University Press, 1987. For a classic critique of Marxist approaches to history, see Karl R. Popper, *The Poverty of Historicism*. London: Routledge & Kegan Paul, 1957.

[43] For useful recent surveys of the field, see the somewhat different perspectives offered by Valentine Cunningham, *Reading after Theory*. Oxford: Blackwell, 2002, 13–53; and Jean-Michel Rabaté, *The Future of Theory*. Oxford: Blackwell, 2002.

[44] Such analysis is usually undertaken on the assumption that cultural presuppositions determine the narrative: 'The story, however pleasurable or absorbing, is shoring up ideological propositions.' Catherine Gallagher and Stephen Greenblatt, *Practicing New Historicism*. Chicago: University of Chicago Press, 2001, 82.

theoretical engagement with the issues it raises, even if this involves the risk of ideological commitment or collusion.[45] (How else can we explain how Chinua Achebe grossly misrepresents Joseph Conrad's anti-imperialist *Heart of Darkness* as a racist work of pro-colonialism – in which he is uncritically followed by Edward Said in pursuit of his post-colonialist agenda in *Culture and Imperialism*?[46]) Even those literary scholars who are most dismissive of 'theory' direct their criticisms against a specific form of theory, rather than against the notion as such. Thus Camille Paglia, while excoriating much contemporary literary theory as little more than 'a mask for fashion and greed' is clear that a theoretical engagement with literature is essential, preferably on the basis of 'mastery of the complete history of philosophy and aesthetics'.[47]

The legitimacy of theory for a scientific theology can thus be seen to rest on a broad foundation, in that any intellectual discipline which is concerned with the exploration of what is encountered and experienced in this unitary yet stratified world will wish to proceed from what is thus known and observed to a greater vision of things, as observation gives way to theory, and theory to a worldview.

Theory and theology: the place of doctrine in Christianity

Given this ineluctable pressure to develop theory, it ought to be the occasion for neither surprise nor undue concern that theology is also confronted by this demand. As Thomas Aquinas insisted, while the revealed truths of the Christian faith may ultimately lie beyond reason, they call out for rational theoretical analysis. Theology might thus be defined as 'taking rational trouble over revealed mystery' (Karl Barth). The inevitability of theory in theology may be understood by reflecting on the central figure of Christian life and thought, Jesus Christ, in that one of the supreme tasks of Christian theology is to offer, to the fullest possible extent, an account of his identity and significance.

The development of Christology during the period 100–451 shows a concern to remain faithful to the complex New Testament witness to

---

[45] See especially Jefferson Humphries, 'On the Inevitability of Theory in Southern Literary Study', *Yale Journal of Criticism* 3 (1989), 175–86. There are also useful insights to be found in Sacvan Bercovitch, 'The Problem of Ideology in American Literary History', *Critical Inquiry* 12 (1986), 631–53; Peter Carafiol, 'The New Orthodoxy: Ideology and the Institution of American Literary History', *American Literature* 59 (1987), 628–38.

[46] See Chinua Achebe, 'An Image of Africa: Racism in Conrad's *Heart of Darkness*', *Massachusetts Review* 18 (1977), 782–94; Edward W. Said, *Culture and Imperialism*. London: Chatto & Windus, 1993, 81–2.

[47] Camille Paglia, *Sex, Art, and American Culture: Essays*. New York: Vintage, 1993, 220. These comments are taken from her brilliant essay 'Junk Bonds and Corporate Raiders: Academe in the Hour of the Wolf'.

the identity of Christ to have been of overwhelming importance.[48] Functional and ontological issues interlocked and interplayed, as the debate over how Christ's person was to be construed focused on the apparent ontological implications of his actions. Patristic writers such as Athanasius thus argued that the total thrust of the biblical witness to and Christian experience of Jesus of Nazareth required him to be conceptualized as both divine and human.[49] The biblical phenomena demanded a specific theoretical response. Thus Athanasius insists that God, and God alone, can break the power of sin and bring humanity to eternal life. An essential feature of being a creature is that one requires to be redeemed. No creature can save another creature; only the creator can redeem the creation.

Having emphasized that it is God alone who can save, Athanasius then makes a decisive theoretical move, which in one sense distances him from the biblical material, and in another brings him closer to it. Given that both the New Testament and the Christian liturgical tradition regard Jesus Christ as Saviour, while at the same time affirming the unique identity of *God* as saviour, yet, as Athanasius emphasized, only God can save. A theoretical syllogism is thus constructed as follows:

1. Only God can save.

2. Jesus Christ saves.

3. Therefore Jesus Christ is God.

A related point stressed by Athanasius is that Christians worship and pray to Jesus Christ. This represents an excellent case study of the importance of Christian practices of worship and prayer for Christian theology. By the fourth century, prayer to and adoration of Christ were standard features of the way in which public worship took place. Athanasius argues that if Jesus Christ is a creature, then Christians are guilty of worshipping a creature instead of God – in other words, they had lapsed into idolatry. Christians, Athanasius stresses, are totally forbidden to worship anyone or anything except God himself. Athanasius thus argued that Arius seemed to be guilty of making nonsense of the way in which Christians prayed and worshipped. Athanasius argued that

---

[48] For the best study, see Aloys Grillmeier, *Christ in Christian Tradition*, 2nd edn. London: Mowbrays, 1975.

[49] Wolfgang A. Bienert, 'Zur Logos-Christologie des Athanasius von Alexandrien in *contra gentes* und *de incarnatione*', in E. A. Livingstone (ed.), *Papers presented to the Tenth International Conference on Patristic Studies*. Louvain: Peeters, 1989, 402–19. For a good general account, see T. F. Torrance, 'Athanasius: A Study in the Foundations of Classical Theology', in *Theology in Reconciliation*. London: Geoffrey Chapman, 1975, 215–66.

Christians were right to worship and adore Jesus Christ, because by doing so, they were recognizing him for what he was – God incarnate.

One of the most fundamental impulses towards theoretical development in the early church is a desire to allow the phenomena to dictate their own mode and level of interpretation. The development of patristic Christology makes it clear that simplistic, reductionist modes of representing the identity and significance of Jesus of Nazareth were judged inadequate with reference to the phenomena which they were required or intended to represent.[50] In particular, the model of Jesus of Nazareth as a purely human figure (the Ebionite heresy) or as a purely divine figure (the Docetic heresy) was regarded as quite inadequate. Both the representation of Jesus in the New Testament and the manner in which the Christian church incorporated Jesus into its life of prayer and worship required a more complex and nuanced understanding of his identity and significance than either of these simpler models was able to offer.

The suggestion that some third model could be invoked to explain the phenomenon of Jesus of Nazareth was rejected as unsatisfactory. The debate over the teachings of Apollinarius of Laodicea led to agreement that there was no 'intermediate state', no *tertium quid*, interposing between the two natures.[51] The patristic period witnessed a decisive rejection of any attempt to explain Jesus in terms which involved the construction of a mediating or hybrid concept between divinity and humanity.

It was this awareness that Jesus of Nazareth required to be understood in both divine and human terms which eventually led to what is known as the 'Chalcedonian definition of faith' – the famous assertion that Jesus Christ is truly divine and truly human. Maurice Wiles summarizes the reasons for this development as follows:[52]

> On the one hand was the conviction that a saviour must be fully divine; on the other was the conviction that what is not assumed is not healed. Or, to put the matter in other words, the source of salvation must be God; the locus of salvation must be humanity. It is quite clear that these two principles often pulled in opposite directions. The Council of Chalcedon was the church's attempt to resolve, or perhaps rather to agree to live with, that tension. Indeed, to accept both principles as strongly as did the early church is already to accept the Chalcedonian faith.

[50] See Maurice F. Wiles, *The Making of Christian Doctrine*. Cambridge: Cambridge University Press, 1967; I. Howard Marshall, *The Origins of New Testament Christology*, 2nd edn. Downers Grove, IL: InterVarsity Press, 1992.

[51] G. L. Prestige, *Fathers and Heretics*. Oxford: Oxford University Press, 1940, 193–246.

[52] Wiles, *The Making of Christian Doctrine*, 106.

Theories of the identity of Christ going beyond the statements of the New Testament were developed by the early church for two primary purposes:

1. *Positively*, as a means of ensuring that the Christian community fully appreciated the significance of Christ, by 'unpacking' or 'unfolding' the complex biblical witness to his person and work, and identifying its intellectual implications. It was deemed essential for the Christian church to be made fully aware of the 'unsearchable riches of Christ' (Ephesians 3:8), in order to fully understand its identity and mission in the cultural world of late antiquity.

2. *Negatively*, as a means of safeguarding the church against false understandings of the identity of its central figure, which might impoverish its witness, fragment its unity, or lead to radical incoherence within its proclamation and self-understanding.

This recognition of the communal dimensions of Christian theory leads us on to consider the relation between 'theory' and 'doctrine' within a scientific theology.

Christian doctrine as theory

Those who hold that Christianity merely replicates the common ideational and moral heritage of the human race will fail to see any point in Christian doctrine. Unless Christianity is in the first place distinct, and in the second place regards that distinctiveness as a matter to be preserved and celebrated, there is no point in developing or defending the notion of 'Christian doctrine'. To affirm the importance of doctrine would be to promote social divisiveness, in that it places a line of demarcation between the church and culture as a whole.

This was certainly the view of the Enlightenment, which regarded Christianity as at best a 'republication of the religion of nature'. John Toland's *Christianity not Mysterious* (1696) was more sympathetic to the truth of the Christian revelation than many Deist writings of the period;[53] nevertheless, it is still clear that Toland and others increasingly came to see Christianity as an essentially rational creed, echoing the best that human reason could deliver. Matthew Tindal's *Christianity as Old as the Creation* (1730) hinted darkly that many of Christianity's more opaque and distinctive ideas were to be regarded as 'superstition',

---

[53] Robert E. Sullivan, *John Toland and the Deist Controversy: A Study in Adaptations.* Cambridge, MA: Harvard University Press, 1982; Robert Rees Evans, *Pantheisticon: The Career of John Toland.* New York: Peter Lang, 1991.

representing the influence of a baleful and self-serving 'priestcraft'.[54] Doctrine perpetuated the vested interests of the religious elite, and was thus to be critiqued on political, as much as intellectual, grounds.

Yet the proposal to eliminate Christian distinctiveness has lost its former credibility. In part, this reflects the waning of the plausibility and attractiveness of the Enlightenment worldview and a growing awareness of the coercive agenda which is so easily appended to it – if Christianity has nothing distinctive to say, then it must be forced to echo the common themes of its cultural environment. With the slow and lingering death of modernity has come a renewed interest in rediscovering and reasserting the distinctiveness of the Christian tradition, and particularly its ideas. The terms that have traditionally been used to refer to these distinctive ideas are 'doctrines' or 'dogmas'. In the following chapter, we shall give thought to how the distinct identity of the Christian tradition arises, and what it suggests concerning its origins; our concern here is to stress that Christianity does indeed have a distinctive identity.

The maintenance of this identity has been the subject of no small importance, especially at times when the Christian community has felt itself to be under threat from assimilation into a broader cultural movement – the fate that befell the Jewish community at the Egyptian city of Elephantine, whose origins are to be traced to the fifth century BC, which suffered a radical erosion of its distinctiveness, apparently with assent or equanimity, and eventually ceased to exist as a separate entity.[55] In the course of his controversy against Gnosticism, Irenaeus developed credal statements and formularies designed to differentiate Christianity from its intellectual rivals, and offer both a social and an intellectual demarcation of the two movements. (We shall explore this aspect of Christian doctrine in greater detail later: see 66–76.) This trend was developed through the need for personal statements of faith at the great Easter baptismal festivals of the early church, and growing awareness of the need to clarify Christian positions against other belief systems of the late classical period, and against heretical positions within the church.[56]

[54] For the importance of this theme to the English Enlightenment, see John Redwood, *Reason, Ridicule and Religion: The Age of Enlightenment in England, 1660–1750*. London: Thames & Hudson, 1996.

[55] Bezalel Porten, *Archives from Elephantine: The Life of an Ancient Jewish Military Colony*. Berkeley, CA: University of California Press, 1968.

[56] The best individual study of this trend remains J. N. D. Kelly, *Early Christian Creeds*, 3rd edn. New York: Longman, 1981. There are also important discussions in R. P. C. Hanson, *Tradition in the Early Church*. London: SCM Press, 1962, 52–74, and especially in the older study of Damien van den Eynde, *Les normes de l'enseignement chrétien dans la littérature patristique des trois premiers siècles*. Gembloux: Duculot, 1933.

The term 'dogma' requires comment, not least because it is regarded with suspicion by many within the theological community. Although the term unquestionably possesses unhelpful associations, evoking painful memories of the coercive theological methods of earlier periods in the history of Christianity, it nevertheless articulates a theological notion which remains important and valid – namely, communally authoritative and authorized theories, which are held to be essential to the identity and mission of the Christian community.[57] The modern Roman Catholic use of the term 'dogma' dates from the late eighteenth century, apparently being used in this sense for the first time in the polemical writing *Regula fidei catholicae* (1792) of the Franciscan controversialist P. N. Chrisman (1751–1810) to designate formal ecclesiastical doctrine, and distinguish this from individual theological opinions.[58] The need for the distinction was evident, particularly on account of the seriously detrimental effect of confusion between catholic doctrine and theological opinion in the later Middle Ages.[59] Many, on both sides of the Reformation debates of the first three decades of the sixteenth century, found themselves unable to ascertain what doctrines were officially acknowledged and recognized by the church, and which were merely the private, if publicly expressed, views of theologians.

It is thus possible that Luther may have initiated his reforming programme at Wittenberg in the late 1510s on the basis of the mistaken belief that the opinions of one theological school (the *via moderna*) were to be identified with the views of the catholic church itself. Luther's assertion that virtually the whole church of his day had lapsed into some form of Pelagianism may rest upon the improper extrapolation to the whole western church of what may conceivably have been a valid evaluation of the merits of the soteriology of the *via moderna*.[60]

By introducing the term 'dogma' specifically to designate officially sanctioned ecclesiastical teachings, which were accepted within the

---

[57] See, for example, Wolfgang Bienert, 'Die Funktion des Dogmas für den christlichen Glauben', in *Vom Finden und Verkünden der Wahrheit in der Kirche. Beiträge zur theologischen Erkenntnislehre*. Freiburg and Basel: Herder, 1993, 92–115. Bienert's essays in this same volume on 'Ewiges und Geschichtliches in der Botschaft der Kirche' (56–77) and 'Geschichtlichkeit und Glauben – Dogma heute' (78–91) also repay study.

[58] Johannes Beumer, 'Die Regula Fidei Catholicae des Ph. N. Chrisman, O.F.M. und ihre Kritik durch J. Kleutgen, S.J.', *Franziskanische Studien* 46 (1964), 321–34. Beumer's own views on this issue can be studied from his excellent work *Theologie als Glaubensverständnis*. Würzburg: Echter-Verlag, 1953.

[59] For documentation and analysis, see Alister E. McGrath, *The Intellectual Origins of the European Reformation*. Oxford: Blackwell, 1987, 12–28.

[60] See Alister E. McGrath, *Luther's Theology of the Cross: Martin Luther's Theological Breakthrough*. Oxford: Blackwell, 1985.

community of faith, Chrisman hoped to bring an element of clarity to interdenominational dialogues. 'Dogma' thus specifically designates that which is declared by the church to be revealed truth as part of its universal teaching.[61] Included in the concept of dogma are two quite distinct elements: the notion of divine revelation, or revealed truth; and the church's acceptance or reception of such revelation or truth. All dogma may be theological theories; not all theological theories, however, are dogma. The Jesuit scholar August Deneffe offered the following succinct definition of dogma, which explicitly includes both these elements: *dogma est veritas a Deo formaliter revelata at ab ecclesia sive solemniter sive ordinarie definita.*[62]

The term 'dogma' is not restricted to Roman Catholic usage, but also finds application in both Lutheran and Reformed writings, again tending to bear the general sense of 'an accepted teaching of the church'.[63] The term 'dogmatics', designating an organized body of Christian (or, more accurately, Protestant) theology, first came into use in the seventeenth century, and is now widely used within Christian theology to designate the basic teachings of the Christian church (which can be at least notionally distinguished from what individual theologians have taught, with varying degrees of concern and respect for the church).[64]

It is clear that the term 'dogma' has now come to have strongly negative associations within western culture, which has correspondingly limited its appeal within the Christian community as a whole. I therefore propose to use the term 'doctrine' to designate more or less what Deneffe and others mean by dogma – namely, a theological opinion which has been accepted and received by the church, so that it is now characteristic of the Christian community as a whole, rather than

---

[61] For the implications of this shift for an understanding of the notion of 'heresy', see Albert Lang, 'Der Bedeutungswandel der Begriffe "fides" und "haeresis" von Vienne und Trient', *Münchener Theologische Zeitschrift* 4 (1953), 133–46.

[62] August Deneffe, 'Dogma: Wort und Begriff', *Scholastik* 6 (1931), 381–400. For Deneffe's own working out of this notion, particularly in relation to the theological importance of tradition, see August Deneffe, *Der Traditionsbegriff: Studie zur Theologie.* Münster in Westfalie: Aschendorff, 1931.

[63] The basic notion of an 'authoritative ecclesial statement' was known to and accepted by the ancient church. See Martin Elze, 'Der Begriff des Dogmas in der Alten Kirche', *Zeitschrift für Theologie und Kirche* 61 (1964), 421–38. For some concerns over the notion within Protestant theological circles, see the insightful study of Traugott Koch, 'Dogmatik ohne Frömmigkeit? Zum Konstitutionsproblem protestantischer Theologie', *Neue Zeitschrift für systematische Theologie und Religionsphilosophie* 43 (2001), 300–29.

[64] Gerhard Ebeling, *Wort Gottes und Tradition: Studien zu einer Hermeneutik der Konfessionen.* Göttingen: Vandenhoeck & Ruprecht, 1964, 128–9; 168; Gerhard Sauter, *Zugänge zur Dogmatik.* Göttingen: Vandenhoeck & Ruprecht, 1998, 19–53.

individual theologians. Examples of such 'doctrines' would include the two natures of Christ, and the doctrine of the Trinity.

Doctrine is thus one aspect of the process in which the Christian community beholds reality, and offers a communal account of that reality in a manner which it regards as best adapted to convey its distinct nature. It marks the transition from a communal 'act of *seeing*' to an 'act of *telling*'.[65] The use of the word 'doctrine' in this sense thus implies reference to a tradition and a community,[66] where 'theology' more properly designates the views of individuals, not necessarily within this community or tradition, who seek to explore ideas without any necessary commitment to them. To revert to the distinction drawn earlier by Wlad Godzich, theology entails a *theoros*, whereas doctrine entails *theoria* (recalling that *theoria* is here to be construed as the plural collective of *theoros*: 8).

Doctrine thus defines communities of discourse, possessing a *representative* and *authoritative* character. As Clifford Geertz has emphasized, there are significant inter-relations between doctrine, schemes of symbolization and representation, and communities.[67] We have already stressed the importance of communities and their traditions in relation in this respect (vol. 2, 57–120). Doctrine thus entails a sense of commitment to a community of faith, and a sense of obligation to speak on its behalf, where the corporate mind of the community exercises a restraint over the individual's perception of truth. Doctrine is an *activity*, a process of transmission of the collective wisdom of a community, rather than a passive set of deliverances. The views of theologians are doctrinally significant, in so far as they have won acceptance within the community. As we shall note later, the concept of 'reception' is thus of central importance to the concept of doctrine, in that a community is involved in the assessment of whether a decision, judgement or theological opinion is consonant with their corporate understanding of the Christian faith, as perceived within that community.

Doctrine may thus be provisionally defined as communally authoritative teachings regarded as essential to the identity of the Christian community, in which the community *tells* itself and outsiders what it has *seen*, and what it has become in response to this vision. Christian

[65] I here draw on the excellent analysis of Martin Jay, *Downcast Eyes: The Denigration of Vision in Twentieth-Century French Thought*. Berkeley, CA: University of California Press, 1993, 30–2.

[66] A point stressed by Stephen W. Sykes, *The Identity of Christianity: Theologians and the Essence of Christianity from Schleiermacher to Barth*. Philadelphia: Fortress Press, 1984, 262–86.

[67] Clifford Geertz, 'Religion as a Cultural System', in D. R. Cutler (ed.), *The Religious Situation*. Boston: Beacon Press, 1968, 639–88.

doctrine may be regarded as the present outcome of that long growth of tradition in which the Christian community has struggled to arrive at an interpretation of its foundational traditions, embodied in the New Testament, which both does justice to its own present place in tradition, and attempts to eliminate those doctrinal pre-judgements which are to be judged as inadequate.

Reductionist foreclosures: some hesitations over theory

Theory, from the arguments set out above, would thus seem to be something inevitable, like death and taxes. Yet this does not necessarily mean that it is something that is to be welcomed. The suspicion that theory robs reality of its wonder has been a constant refrain of the last three centuries. Does not theological reflection on the person of Christ evacuate him of his mystery and personal dignity? How can the immense complexity of the person who drew people to him by uttering the simple words 'follow me' ever be captured in metaphysical formulae or dogmatic slogans? How can the mystery of God ever be expressed in human language? C. S. Lewis notes precisely this concern in recalling a talk he once gave to the Royal Air Force:[68]

> In a way I quite understand why some people are put off by Theology. I remember once when I had been giving a talk to the R.A.F., an old, hard-bitten officer got up and said, 'I've no use for all that stuff. But mind you, I'm a religious man too. I know there's a God. I've felt Him: And that's just why I don't believe all your neat little dogmas and formulas about Him. To anyone who's met the real thing they all seem so petty and pedantic and unreal!'

The same concerns have often been expressed concerning the theories of the natural sciences. How can mathematical equations ever convey the spine-tingling excitement at seeing the arc of a rainbow,[69] or the brilliance of the star-studded heavens?

These are familiar concerns, which must be taken with the utmost seriousness. If theology is concerned with evoking the praise and adoration of God, is not the pursuit of doctrine contrary to this goal? Surely wrestling with lexical technicalities is subversive of the entire doxological enterprise? How can anyone immerse themselves in a textbook of systematic theology, and rise up to behold the glory of the living God? Yet there is much that can be added to this critique of theory.

---

[68] C. S. Lewis, *Mere Christianity*. London: Collins, 1952, 130.
[69] Philip Fisher, *Wonder, the Rainbow, and the Aesthetics of Rare Experiences*. Cambridge, MA: Harvard University Press, 1998.

One of the criticisms which is frequently directed against theory is that it is inherently reductionist, and hence prone to the seminal error of distortion by limitation. Consider the following theoretical representation, which graces the pages of Vladimir Propp's classification of Russian folktales.[70]

$$\gamma^1\beta^1\delta^1A^1C\uparrow\left\{\begin{array}{c}[DE^1 \text{ neg. } F \text{ neg.}]\\ d^7E^7F^9\end{array}\right\}G^4K^1\downarrow[Pr^1D^1E^1F^9 = Rs^4]^3$$

To make sense of this remarkable theoretical statement, it is necessary to know that Propp developed a codification system which allowed every folktale to be categorized according to 31 functions that Propp had earlier identified. Propp argues that all folktales are of a single type in regard to their structure, by which he means that they all contain the same functions – namely, the basic structural building blocks – in the same order. The story may thus be reduced to an abstract theoretical representation.

The 'story of the swan-geese' is a rather touching Russian folktale which relates how a young girl attempts to recover her brother from the clutches of the evil witch Baba Yaga before her parents notice he is missing. Her ultimately successful efforts to find him and bring him safely home are assisted in various ways by an oven, an apple tree, a river of milk and a little mouse. The reader will not be surprised to learn that Propp's rather barren morphological formula represents the plot of 'The Swan-Geese'. The contrast between the charming innocence of the story, masking at least some of its distinctly sinister violent undertones, and the abstract formula will be evident, and represents one of the most widely held criticisms of literary theory – that it reduces complex narratives to seductively concise theoretical formulae.

The criticisms directed by Claude Lévi-Strauss against Propp's formalism may be seen as indicating the dangers attending any theoretical account of reality.[71] Formalism destroys its object precisely because its level of analysis is incapable of doing justice to the totality of what it purports to represent. In the case of Propp's rather austere account of Russian folktales, Lévi-Strauss argues that it offers a purely syntactical account of something which demands to be treated at the lexical level.

---

[70] Vladimir I. A. Propp, *Morphology of the Folktale*, 2nd edn. Austin, TX: University of Texas Press, 1968, 99. For further details, see Wulfhild Ziel, *Bibliographien zu 'Slawisch-folkloristisches Schrifigut' aus dem Vorlesungsrepertoire von Vladimir Propp und zu 'Slawische Folklore und Folklore vom Balkan' von Nikita I. Tolstoi*. Frankfurt am Main: Peter Lang, 1995. For an unpersuasive attempt to provide a biblical application, see Pamela J. Milne, *Vladimir Propp and the Study of Structure in Hebrew Biblical Narrative*. Sheffield: Almond Press, 1988.

[71] Claude Lévi-Strauss, 'Structure and Form: Reflections on a Work by Vladimir Propp', in *Structural Anthropology*. Harmondsworth: Penguin, 1977, vol. 2, 115–45.

'No language exists in which the vocabulary can be deduced from the syntax.' Propp's formalism rests on the mistaken belief that 'the grammar can be tackled at once and the dictionary postponed' – a penetrating criticism which can also be applied to George Lindbeck's disappointingly superficial account of the place of doctrine within the Christian community (vol. 2, 38–53).

The cardinal weakness of theorizing is that it discards particularities in favour of generalities, and in doing so weakens, thins, prunes, distorts and limits. And those often austere limits imposed by theoretical analysis, it may be stressed, are often determined by intra-theoretical considerations, rather than by the pressure of external realities. Theory is obliged to leave things out, to deliberately overlook, to systematically truncate. The redeeming of particularities is an essential antidote to the universalization implicit in theoretical approaches. As the 'Swan-Geese' case makes abundantly clear, *theory reduces narratives to formulae.* This is clearly also an issue in the area of Christology, where one of the most persistent criticisms directed against the Chalcedonian definition is that it likewise reduces the richly textured biblical narrative concerning Christ to a neat little formula.

At their most authentic, and hence also at their best, both the natural sciences and Christian theology are characterized by a living empirical curiosity about particulars – particulars which may well lead on to the founding of a universal view of reality, or may equally lead to its foundering through a failure to account for them in sufficient detail or number. As we shall see presently, to abandon reverential attention for particularities – whether these take the form of the gospel accounts of incidents in the life of Christ or painstakingly accurate observations of the planet Neptune against the fixed stars – is to value provisional derived universalities over and above what brought them into being in the first place, and must ultimately determine their credibility and utility. A healthy suspicion of universals is thus the natural epistemological attitude of a scientific theology, which insists upon redeeming particulars, rather than submerging and losing them in an allegedly universal theory. We shall return to this point presently (38–43).

The critique of theorizing in the natural sciences

The late eighteenth century witnessed the clash of two rival schools of thought in England, with very different attitudes towards the role of theory in engaging nature. Enlightenment writers adopted an essentially theoretical approach to the world, aiming to describe it using accurate, simple and generalizable categories so favoured by Descartes and other leading lights of the movement. The Romantic movement, however, held that this theoretical approach to nature despoiled it of its intrinsic wonder, and eliminated any transcendent dimensions to the natural world. We have already seen how the Romantic poet John Keats viewed the scientific objectification of nature as robbing it of its wonder (vol. 2, 88–92), as expressed in his 1820 poem 'Lamia':

> Do not all charms fly
> At the mere touch of cold philosophy?
> There was an awful rainbow once in heaven:
> We know her woof, her texture; she is given
> In the dull catalogue of common things.
> Philosophy will clip an Angel's wings.

Yet the tensions between the Enlightenment and Romantic approaches to nature extend beyond their sharply contrasting attitudes to the place of theory in any account of the natural world. In their important work *Contested Natures* (1998), Phil Macnaghten and John Urry explored these two very different ways of experiencing, perceiving, representing and valuing nature, noting how their differences are laden with significance in terms of the quality and significance of the human encounter with the natural order.[72]

For Macnaghten and Urry, the Enlightenment saw nature in terms of a struggle for power and survival, 'red in tooth and claw' (Tennyson), which regarded life as 'solitary, nasty, brutish and short' (Hobbes). Nature is thus a primeval state which must be mastered and transformed in order to be converted into something more civilized and useful to humanity. This necessitated the development of technology through the natural sciences, which allowed the crudities of nature to be transmuted into commodities and possibilities more acceptable to humanity.

In contrast, the Romantic view took as its starting point the belief that humanity and nature were once in harmony, and that this innocent relationship was disrupted and ultimately all but destroyed through scientific progress and the mechanization of the world. What the Enlightenment termed 'civilization' is actually a process of alienation of humanity from its proper habitat, and the physical destruction of the environment in which humanity ought to exist. Many of these – and other – anxieties surface in the poetry of Friedrich Hölderlin (1770–1843), especially the poem 'Wie wenn am Feiertage':[73]

---

[72] Phil Macnaghten and John Urry, *Contested Natures*. London: Sage, 1998.

[73] For reflection, especially in relation to the Kantian context, see Richard Eldridge, 'Kant, Hölderlin, and the Experience of Longing', in *The Persistence of Romanticism: Essays in Philosophy and Literature*. Cambridge: Cambridge University Press, 2001, 31–51.

Und sag ich gleich,
Ich sei genaht, die Himmlischen zu schauen,
Sie selbst, sie werfen mich tief unter die Lebenden,
Den falschen Priester, ins Dunkel, daß ich
Das warnende Lied den Gelehrigen singe,
Dort.

The English Romantic tradition valued a direct engagement with nature, and saw scientific theorizing concerning that nature as tantamount to its disenchantment.[74] Where scientific theories about nature are reductionist, disconnecting the human observer from involvement with its beauty and wonder, the Romantics argued that a direct, intuitive engagement with nature leads to personal fulfilment and integrity. Shelley expressed this idea in his 'Hymn to Intellectual Beauty', which posits the idea of an intuited higher power, which saturates nature with its presence and beauty:

The awful shadow of some unseen Power
Floats though unseen among us, – visiting
This various world with as inconstant wing
As summer winds that creep from flower to flower.

The human experience of this beauty may be sporadic, rather than continual; it is, nevertheless, an integral aspect of the phenomenon of nature. Nature is not simply to be investigated and understood as 'the other' by detached observers, especially as it is expressed in scientific theorizing; rather, it is to be encountered and it is to evoke wonder at its sheer beauty by a humanity which is aware that it is an active participant of the whole great scheme of things. Nature is thus a 'Thou', rather than an 'It', to anticipate the helpful distinction developed by Martin Buber.[75] As Paul de Man argued, such forms of Romantic poetry appear to 'originate in the desire to grow closer and closer to the ontological status of the subject'[76] – something which abstract theories about nature fail to encourage, let alone permit.

Much the same misgivings were the subject of frequent expression within American transcendentalism, such as the poems of Walt

---

[74] For a detailed engagement with this issue, see Alister McGrath, *The Reenchantment of Nature: The Denial of Religion and the Ecological Crisis.* New York: Doubleday, 2002, 129–38.

[75] See Bernhard Casper, *Das dialogische Denken: Eine Untersuchung der religionsphilosophischen Bedeutung Franz Rosenzweigs, Ferdinand Ebners und Martin Bubers.* Freiburg: Herder, 1967; Joachim Israel, *Martin Buber: Dialogphilosophie in Theorie und Praxis.* Berlin: Duncker & Humblot, 1995.

[76] Paul de Man, 'Structure intentionnelle de l'image romantique', *Revue internationale de philosophie* 51 (1960), 68–84.

Whitman (1819–92), especially those published in the slim volume *Leaves of Grass*. One of these contrasts the explanations and theories of the professional astronomer with the direct experience of the night sky:

> When I heard the learn'd astronomer;
> When the proofs, the figures, were ranged in columns before me;
> When I was shown the charts and the diagrams, to add, divide, and
>   measure them;
> When I, sitting, heard the astronomer, where he lectured with much
>   applause in the lecture-room,
> How soon, unaccountable, I became tired and sick;
> Till rising and gliding out, I wander'd off by myself,
> In the mystical moist night-air, and from time to time,
> Look'd up in perfect silence at the stars.

Whitman's point is simple: a direct encounter with nature is always going to be more moving and evocative than abstract theorizing about it.

In responding to such criticisms of theory, it is important not to deny the clear truth that they articulate – namely, that theory is reductionist. To criticize theory for being 'reductionist' is like criticizing water because it is wet; that is simply the way of things. The problem lies in how we use theory, not in the nature of theory itself. The entire purpose of scientific theories may be said to be the uncovering of universal principles which lie behind specific patterns of behaviour, which may be empirically observed – as, for example, Darwin's theory of natural selection offers an explanation of the observable features of the natural world of plants and animals by reducing those complex observations to a common pattern, capable of theoretical formulation. The quest to find basic explanations for observed patterns of behaviour is inevitably formulated in terms of reducing phenomena to theories.

This process of reduction can also be seen in action in the process of theory development. The classical approach to genetics, pioneered by T. H. Morgan in the opening decades of the twentieth century through a series of studies on the fruit-fly *Drosophila*, was seen in an entirely new light following the discovery of the structure of DNA by James Watson and Francis Crick in 1953. In one sense, classical genetics may be said to have been reduced to molecular genetics.[77] In a major discussion of issues in the logic of reductive explanation, Ernest Nagel argues that the history of the natural sciences can be schematized as an increasingly suc-

---

[77] For a careful study of whether this is, in fact, the case, see Philip Kitcher, '1953 and All That: A Tale of Two Sciences', *Philosophical Review* 93 (1984), 335–73.

cessful series of reductions, sustained by the 'hope of completely reducing the totality of laws in a given area of inquiry to some allegedly
"basic" theory'.[78] Nagel here develops Carl Hempel's deductive-nomo-
logical model of scientific explanation in such a way that reduction can
be viewed as a specific form of scientific explanation. Nagel's attempt to
distinguish between homogenous and inhomogenous intertheoretical
reductions has met with some resistance; for example, Thomas Nickles
has argued forcefully that not all reduction can be regarded as constituting an explanation.[79] Nevertheless, there is sufficient truth in Nagel's
approach to merit attention.

Granted that there is at least some substance to the Romantic agenda,
it is entirely proper to make two points in refutation of their concerns.
First, the scientific quest for theories is not undertaken by discarding the
phenomena once a theoretical explanation has been derived. Those same
phenomena may be of central importance in the ultimate displacement
of that theory, as another is advanced which offers a more successful
account of what is already known. Identifying what lies beneath the
observed structures and patterns of the world does not negate what is
observed; indeed, it may bring a new clarity and precision to the process
of observation, and a deepened appreciation of the natural world itself.

Second, the Romantic refusal to reflect *theoretically* on what they
observed in nature must ultimately be regarded as intellectually indefensible. The early twentieth-century political theorist Carl Schmitt levelled
the charge of *subjective occasionalism* against the Romantic movement,
arguing that it evaded the intellectual responsibility of responding to
nature as it actually existed, preferring to construct its own highly subjective account of nature, in which 'everything becomes an occasion for
anything'.[80] As Charles Larmore summarizes these concerns:[81]

> Refusing to acknowledge the demands that reality places upon thought,
> [the Romantics] see the world as but the occasion for the artistic mind to
> assert its sovereignty. Reality counts only as the pretext for the imagina-
> tion to express itself, to make up how it would like things to be, to 'aes-
> theticize'.

Precisely the same criticism must be brought to bear against those who
hold that theological theorizing is at best inappropriate, and at worst

[78] Ernest Nagel, *Teleology Revisited and Other Essays in the Philosophy and History of Science*.
New York: Columbia University Press, 1974, 95–113.

[79] Thomas Nickles, 'Two Concepts of Intertheoretic Reduction', *Journal of Philosophy* 70
(1975), 181–201.

[80] Carl Schmitt, *Politische Romantik*. Berlin: Duncker & Humblot, 1919, 24.

[81] Charles E. Larmore, *The Romantic Legacy*. New York: Columbia University Press, 1996, 4.

eliminates the mysteries of faith – something we may consider in a little more detail in what follows.

Some concerns from formalism: theory and defamiliarization

A scientific theology recognizes and welcomes the intellectual demands that reality places upon us, realizing that the formulation of a theoretical account of things is an essential aspect of any true engagement with reality. This does not mean that theory displaces observation; it is simply to acknowledge the need for an additional layer of reflection, which adds to what is already known. Keats's protest against 'philosophical' (we might say 'theoretical') accounts of such natural wonders as the rainbow is not intended to be a substitute for its beauty, or the sense of aesthetic delight that it occasions. It is an additional layer of reflection, which adds rational integrity to aesthetic emotions. Theory aims to offer a representation of reality, which allows us to engage that reality at a new and deeper level, while in no way obliging us to abandon its impact on our imaginations and emotions.

Yet there is a serious difficulty about theoretical approaches to such natural wonders as rainbows, or theological mysteries such as the death of Christ on the cross. An emphasis on theory encourages the automatic, unthinking assignment of such phenomena to ready-made categories. It causes the observer to pigeon-hole complex phenomena in terms of simplistic categories, bypassing the immensely important and productive process of deep reflection which any meaningful encounter with reality is meant to engender. So how can this impoverishing process of premature theoretical assignation and reduction be forestalled? How can theoretical analysis proceed without robbing reality of its wonder?

The Russian formalist Victor Shklovsky (1893–1984) develops a notion which is of profound importance to this problem of theoretical representation in a scientific theology – the idea of 'defamiliarization'.[82] The basic idea is widely attributed to the German Romantic poet Novalis (Friedrich von Hardenberg, 1772–1801), who declared that the essence of romanticism was 'to make the familiar strange, and the strange familiar'. This theme is developed in a significant direction by Shklovsky. Any artistic object, according to Shklovsky, runs the risk of becoming routine, habitual or over-familiar, and thus loses its power as an artistic object.[83] 'As perception becomes habitual, it becomes auto-

---

[82] On Formalism, see Boris Eikhenbaum, 'The Theory of the "Formal Method"', in *Russian Formalist Criticism: Four Essays*. Lincoln, NE: University of Nebraska Press, 1965, 99–139.

[83] Terence Hawkes, *Structuralism and Semiotics*. London: Methuen, 1977, 62–7.

matic.'[84] This inevitable process of 'automatization' or 'habitualization' leads to a loss of potency of the form. It is essential to recover the vitality of such modes of representation; this takes place through the process of 'defamiliarization' or 'making strange' (*ostranenie*).[85]

> Art exists that one may recover the sensation of life, it exists to make one feel things, to make the stone *stony*. The purpose of art is to impart the sensation of things as they are perceived and not as they are known. The technique of art is to make objects 'unfamiliar', to make forms difficult, to increase the difficulty and length of perception because the process of perception is an aesthetic end in itself and must be prolonged.

Shklovsky's concern here is that forms may become so familiar that they lack the potential to *stimulate* or *provoke* their intended reaction from their audience. Overfamiliarity leads to the erosion of their aesthetic potential, and consequently an impoverishment of the experience of the reader. Shklovsky's insistence on the need to 'increase the difficulty and length of perception' has important parallels with Christian spirituality, which deplores the brevity and superficiality of the Christian engagement with biblical texts and images, and thus aims to foster an extended and more profound engagement with their form and contents.

From a theoretical point of view, Shklovsky's concerns point to two difficulties for a scientific theology, and also indicate a means by which both might be alleviated. The first difficulty concerns N. R. Hanson's famous assertion that we always *see* things *as* something – for example, the Christian *sees* nature *as* God's creation. Yet this process of perception can become automatic and reflex. We learn to recognize objects 'by their main characteristics' and automatically place them in predetermined categories instead of seeing them 'in their entirety'.[86] The term 'social cognition' designates this automatization of our habitual perception: human beings process information on the basis of preexisting categories such as 'prototypes', 'schemas' and 'heuristics', and in consequence no longer pay attention to the process of perception. To regain our sensation of perception, from the social cognitive aspect, it will be necessary to de-automatize the process of perception, renewing our perception of everyday things and events which are so familiar that our perception of them has become routinized.[87]

---

[84] Victor Shklovsky, 'Art as Technique', in *Russian Formalist Criticism: Four Essays*. Lincoln, NE: University of Nebraska Press, 1965, 3–24, 7.

[85] Shklovsky, 'Art as Technique', 12.

[86] Shklovsky, 'Art as Technique', 8.

[87] See the careful study of Judith A. Howard, 'Social Cognition', in Karen S. Cook, Gary A. Fine and James S. House, *Sociological Perspectives on Social Psychology*. Boston, MA: Allyn & Bacon, 1995, 90–117.

An approach to theology which places an emphasis on theory runs the risk of failing to engage properly with reality precisely because it hastens towards a theory-driven reading of things. Reality is automatically and hastily assimilated to theoretically predetermined theological categories. According to Shklovsky, the essential function of 'defamiliarization' is to counteract the process of habituation encouraged by routine everyday modes of perception – processes which prevent us from fully perceiving the world around us, in that we become anaesthetized to its distinctive features. We are called upon to defamiliarize that with which we are overly familiar.

It is possible to see the world and its events through a rigid theoretical framework, which not merely disinclines us to engage with the particular, but represents a foreclosure of the interpretative process. We are called upon to engage with reality in its entirety, not merely those segments which fit our theories. Martha Nussbaum has stressed the importance of 'seeing a complex, concrete reality in a highly lucid and richly responsive way . . . taking in what is there, with imagination and feeling'.[88] A predisposition to theoretical reduction can hinder the appreciation of *mystery*, not least by impelling us towards premature theological closure.

The reaffirmation of the category of 'mystery' reminds us that our theoretical account of the world will remain partial, rather than total. We cannot hope to reduce the experience of God or the meaning of the cross to neat theoretical statements, and declare that this is all that there is to it. While Shklovsky was not in the least predisposed towards such religious considerations, his notion of 'defamiliarization' can be seen as a principled attempt to safeguard against the reducing of the sublime to the mundane, the transcendent to the theoretical. While theory is a legitimate aspect of the theological enterprise, it cannot be regarded as its ultimate goal.

Such reflections raise the question of how the reductionism of theoretical analysis may in some manner be counterbalanced by a continuing regard for the particularities on which that analysis is ultimately based – a matter which we shall pursue in more detail in what follows.

Theory and the redemption of particulars

In a neglected article 'On Behalf of Theory', Frank Lentricchia points to one of the most fatal vulnerabilities of theory – a pretension to univer-

---

[88] Martha Nussbaum, *Love's Knowledge: Essays on Philosophy and Literature*. New York: Oxford University Press, 1990, 152.

sality, incorrigibility and necessity which refuses to acknowledge its origins in experience and observation. When rightly understood, *theoria* is a process of encounter, rather than any specific outcome of that engagement.[89]

> Theory is primarily a *process* of discovery of the lesson that I am calling historical; any single, formulable theory is a reduced version of the process, a frozen proposition which will tend to cover up the process it grew out of by projecting itself as an uncontingent system of ideas.

Lentricchia's concern was that theory had come to see itself as possessing the character of an *a priori* truth, and had wilfully chosen to ignore its *a posteriori* origins in an engagement with particulars – whether literary texts or empirical observations.[90]

Theory exists in a highly ambivalent relation to particulars. On the one hand, it owes its existence to them; on the other, they perpetually threaten to undermine or overthrow it. The same set of particulars which led to the emergence of one theory may subsequently lead to the emergence and ultimate triumph of another. While Francis Bacon rightly excoriated those natural philosophers who, like ants, merely piled up observational data, the fact remains that such a body of accumulated data is both the foundation and criterion of any resulting theory. The same facts that seem to disconfirm a theory one day may confirm it the next, as a well-known episode in the history of science will make clear.

In 1815, William Prout (1775–1850) put forward an 'atomic' hypothesis, according to which all of the chemical elements – such as carbon, nitrogen, oxygen and so forth – were actually composed of hydrogen. On the basis of this hypothesis, it would be expected that the atomic weights of the elements would be integral multiples of that of hydrogen. Prout provided some preliminary research to suggest that the atomic weights of elements did indeed conform to this pattern: having investigated nitrogen, oxygen and chlorine, he found them to be exactly 14, 16 and 36 times heavier than hydrogen.[91] Some preliminary work by Thomas Thomson of Glasgow University seemed to confirm Prout's

---

[89] Frank Lentricchia, 'On Behalf of Theory', in Gerald Graff and Reginald Gibbons (eds), *Criticism in the University*. Evanston, IL: Northwestern University Press, 1985, 105–10, especially 108.

[90] Hence Lentricchia has recently started to promote the idea of abandoning theory altogether and returning to the 'pure' act of reading a literary text.

[91] William Prout, 'On the Relation between the Specific Gravities of Bodies in their Gaseous State and the Weights of their Atoms', *Annals of Philosophy* 6 (1815), 321–30. Note that the original article was published anonymously.

ideas; it was clear, however, that more detailed work was required to settle the issue.

In order to settle the issue, the atomic weights of many elements were determined with hitherto unparalleled precision, particularly by the Swedish chemist Jöns Jacob Berzelius (1779–1848).[92] Berzelius's results called Prout's hypothesis into question, in that he was able to demonstrate that a number of elements clearly possessed non-integral atomic weights. Where Prout had calculated, on the basis of less than satisfactory experimental data, that chlorine was exactly 36 times heavier than hydrogen, Berzelius demonstrated that the ratio was the non-integral 35.45. This was widely seen as a decisive contradiction of Prout's hypothesis. In 1860, after exhaustive research, the distinguished Belgian chemist Jean S. Stas (1813–91) declared that it was not possible to take this hypothesis seriously: 'As long as we hold to experiment for determining the laws which regulate matter, we must consider Prout's law as a pure illusion, and regard the undecomposable bodies of our globe as distinct entities having no simple relation by weight to one another.'

However, the discovery of isotopes in 1910 reversed this judgement.[93] It was established that a number of elements existed with different atomic weights, while having the same atomic numbers.[94] Thus chlorine existed in two stable isotopes, Cl^{35} and Cl^{37}, distributed in such a manner that the mean apparent atomic weight of the element is 35.4527.[95] The nucleus of Cl^{35} consists of 17 protons and 18 neutrons, whereas Cl^{37} has 17 protons and 20 neutrons. Each of these isotopes thus possesses an atomic weight which is precisely an integral multiple of that of hydrogen. The outcome of this is clear. The experimental results which had once been regarded as disproving Prout now became proof in his favour. As Larry Laudan commented, 'the very phenomena which had earlier constituted anomalies for Prout's hypothesis became positive instances for it'.[96] The particulars were, in one sense, unchanged; they now pointed to a very different conclusion.

Countless other examples could be provided from the history of science to demonstrate how the assembly of meticulously recorded

---

[92] See Ida Freund, *The Study of Chemical Composition: An Account of its Method and Historical Development.* New York: Dover, 1968, 339.

[93] On which see Alfred Romer, *Radiochemistry and the Discovery of Isotopes.* New York: Dover, 1970.

[94] Abraham Pais, *Niels Bohr's Times, in Physics, Philosophy and Polity.* Oxford: Clarendon Press, 1991, 125–7.

[95] There are also two unstable isotopes, which need not concern us here.

[96] Larry Laudan, *Progress and its Problems: Towards a Theory of Scientific Growth.* Berkeley: University of California Press, 1977, 31.

observations – whether of planetary movements, ocean temperatures, or the frequencies of solar or stellar spectral lines – proved to be decisive for the confirmation or disconfirmation of theories. The particulars always take epistemological precedence over the universal, precisely because the validity of the allegedly 'universal' is to be regarded as provisional, rather than final.

This point is of immense theological importance, affirming as it does, for example, that the particularities of Jesus Christ are epistemologically prior to the ensuing Chalcedonian definition. That definition is the outcome of a sustained and loving process of meticulous engagement with the details of the life and impact of Christ, in which each individual particularity – such as the response of others to Christ, the things that Christ did, or what was said about him – is sifted and explored with a lingering tenderness. The ensuing theory about Christ involves a specific reading of the particularities about Christ, which theoretical reflection and debate often stifles or obscures.[97] This loving attention to particularities about Christ is often regarded as the province of Christian spirituality, rather than theology – witness, for example, the comments of Ludolf of Saxony (c. 1300–78) on the importance of fostering a sense of 'lingering delight' over the particulars of the gospel pericopes:[98]

> Be there with the angel, like another witness, at the moment of the holy conception, and rejoice with the Virgin Mother now with child for you. Be present at his birth and circumcision, like a faithful guardian, with St Joseph. Go with the Wise Men to Bethlehem and adore the little king. Help his parents carry the child and present him in the Temple. Alongside the apostles, accompany the Good Shepherd as he performs his miracles. With his blessed mother and St John, be there at his death, to have compassion on him and to grieve with him. Touch his body with a kind of devout curiosity, handling one by one the wounds of your Saviour who has died for you.

One of the central concerns expressed by Christian spiritual writers is that an excessive preoccupation with doctrinal themes can lead to focusing on diffuse and general issues, leading to the marginalization of the particularities of life – both the life of Christ, and the life of the

---

[97] An excellent example being provided by the way in which the early church sought to integrate the particularities of the Fourth Gospel into its Christologies, especially around the time of the Arian controversy: see T. E. Pollard, *Johannine Christology and the Early Church.* Cambridge: Cambridge University Press, 1970.

[98] Ludolf of Saxony, *Vita Jesu Christi Domini ac salvatoris nostri.* Paris: Gering & Rembolt, 1502, praefatio.

individual which is meant to be conformed to its redeeming prototype.

One of the most interesting treatments of this theme of the 'redemption of particularities' is found in the literary works of Iris Murdoch.
Although she deals with the theme in some of her technical writings,[99]
her most impressive treatment of the issue is found in her novels. *Under
the Net* (1954) is arguably the least philosophical of all her novels; nevertheless, it contains an extended reflection on the manner in which a
Wittgensteinian 'net of discourse' is both necessary if particularities are
to be described, yet also shields or conceals those particularities in order
to reinforce itself. As one of her characters writes:[100]

> The movement away from theory and generality is the movement toward
> truth. All theorizing is a fight. We must be ruled by the situation itself,
> and this is unutterably particular. Indeed it is something to which we can
> never get close enough, however hard we may try as it were to crawl under
> the net.

Theory thus possesses simultaneously the ability to illuminate and
conceal the world of particulars. It is as if the two realms are mutually
necessary, yet permanently in tension.

Literary theory, perhaps paradoxically, illustrates Murdoch's point dis-
turbingly clearly. The theory which was perhaps once intended to
heighten the reader's awareness of the distinctiveness of a given text has
become interposed between reader and text, rendering the latter of questionable importance. Theory-led 'readings' of texts subvert their particularities, and lead to their imprisonment within preconceived
theoretical categories. Aware of this, Valentine Cunningham argues for
the need for 'tactful' reading – that is, a reading which is in touch with
the text, valuing its uniqueness and affirming its distinctiveness, rather
than seeking to catalogue it as yet another example of a theory-driven
category.[101]

When rightly understood, theory liberates, rather than imprisons, in
that it allows us to 'see' or 'behold' a particular in a new manner – for

---

[99] Iris Murdoch, 'Nostalgia for the Particular', *Proceedings of the Aristotelian Society* 52 (1952),
243–60. See also the important piece 'A House of Theory', *Partisan Review* 26 (1959), 17–31,
which makes it clear that Murdoch is not opposed to theory as such, but to certain of its possible consequences.

[100] Iris Murdoch, *Under the Net*. London: Vintage, 2002, 91.

[101] See Valentine Cunningham, *Reading after Theory*. Oxford: Blackwell, 2002, passim. See
also Valentine Cunningham, *In the Reading Gaol: Postmodernity, Texts, and History*. Oxford:
Blackwell, 1994, which argues forcefully that much recent theorizing, through its emphasis on
closed texts, solipsistic narratives and the absence of extra-textual reference, has imprisoned
reading in a gaol of its own making.

example, to see a rainbow as a specific instance of a general optical principle, or the orbiting of the satellites of the planet Jupiter as a specific instance of the general theory of gravitation. Theologically, it allows us to gain new and potentially dramatic readings of the particularities of the gospels – for example, reading the birth of Christ in a theoretical manner, so that it speaks of the humility and condescension of God in the incarnation. Some such interpenetration of particularities and theory can, of course, be argued to be implicit within the New Testament itself, in both the gospels and the Pauline letters.

Yet paradoxically, that same theory can lead to us looking *through* rather than looking *at* the particular, asking what universal truth it may illustrate rather than valuing it in its own right, bathed in its inalienable individuality. It is here that Keats's concerns about the demystification of the rainbow come into their own right, in that a wonder-evoking sight of the natural world is seen simply as an example of an optical phenomenon, rather than as a breathtaking thing of beauty in its own right. Rightly understood, theory leads to a deeper engagement with particularities, rather than a retreat from them.

So is that process of engagement and reflection to be infinitely extended, or does there come a point at which theoretical closure can be achieved?

The issue of closure in theory

The above discussion of the continuing role for particularities in theory development raises a critical question. In what way and at what point can the right interpretation of a set of particulars be regarded as being settled?[102] How can a specific theory be regarded as having secured 'closure' of an issue, when the particularities it claims to represent are more open-ended than this closure suggests? The history of Prout's hypothesis vividly illustrates the possibility of premature closure of an issue, when its real solution lies some distance away. Is not the very attempt to secure theoretical closure of questions actually a premature *foreclosure* of a debate which should continue, rather than being regarded as settled?

The term 'closure' has come to be read in various manners. As used by Max Weber and his followers, it refers to the process by which social structures – such as social classes – emerge, often through conflict,

---

[102] An issue explored in some detail in Peter L. Galison, *How Experiments End.* Chicago: University of Chicago Press, 1987.

leading to the exclusion of certain groupings from power.[103] Closure is thus the process of social crystallization, in which certain structures emerge in a manner that is at least in part open to empirical investigation. The term is also used in literary theory, to refer to the manner and extent to which the meaning of a narrative is determined by its ending.[104] The study of closure has played a significant part in contemporary literary criticism and is implicated in many of its concerns, including psychological aspects of the search for an end in narrative (why do we seek closure?) to the order imposed upon a text by its political or cultural environment. This approach can readily be applied to biblical narratives, as has been illustrated from a recent study on the theme of death and closure.[105] Yet the term is also used to refer to the process of theory generation – the means by which we seek to make sense of the world, and especially the process which leads to the identification and commitment to one specific reading of our situation.

The postmodern rejection of closure: Hilary Lawson

One of the most interesting accounts of this process is offered by the postmodern philosopher Hilary Lawson.[106] As Lawson describes 'closure', the concept refers to the crystallization of the world into differentiated entities:[107]

> It is through closure that openness is divided into things. Without closure, we would be lost in a sea of openness: a sea without character and without form. For in openness, there is no colour, no sound, no distinguishing mark, no difference, no thing . . . Closure enables us to realize objects of every type and variety. Closure is responsible for our being able to describe

[103] See, for example, Frank Parkin, *Class Inequality and Political Order: Social Stratification in Capitalist and Communist Societies*. London: Paladin, 1972; Raymond Murphy, *Social Closure: The Theory of Monopolization and Exclusion*. Oxford: Clarendon Press, 1988; Jeff Manza, 'Classes, Status Groups, and Social Closure: A Critique of Neo-Weberian Social Theory', *Current Perspectives in Social Theory* 12 (1992), 275–302.

[104] There is a vast literature. See, for example, D. A. Miller, *Narrative and its Discontents: Problems of Closure in the Traditional Novel*. Princeton: Princeton University Press, 1981; Barbara Hodgdon, *The End Crowns All: Closure and Contradiction in Shakespeare's History*. Princeton and Oxford: Princeton University Press, 1991; Matilda Tomaryn Bruckner, *Shaping Romance: Interpretation, Truth, and Closure in Twelfth-Century French Fictions*. Middle Ages series. Philadelphia: University of Pennsylvania Press, 1993; Deborah H. Roberts, Francis M. Dunn and Don Fowler (eds), *Classical Closure: Reading the End in Greek and Latin Literature*. Princeton, NJ: Princeton University Press, 1997.

[105] Walter B. Crouch, *Death and Closure in Biblical Narrative*. New York: Peter Lang, 2000.

[106] Hilary Lawson, *Closure: A Story of Everything*. London: Routledge, 2001. For the background to this notion, see his earlier work *Reflexivity: The Post-Modern Predicament*. London: Hutchinson, 1985.

[107] Lawson, *Closure: A Story of Everything*, 4.

the atoms of hydrogen and the molecules of water that make up the sea
. . . Closure can be understood as the imposition of fixity on openness.
The closing of that which is open.

The world, then, is by nature open; it is the human observer who secures
closure. For Lawson, the human observer is active in this process. Far from
representing a passive response to observation, closure represents an active
imposition of meaning or pattern upon the world, as someone might
discern the image of a face in a seemingly random pattern of dots.[108]
Closure is not something which the world demands; it is something that
we, as its observers, feel impelled to provide and impose, not least through
narratives which help impose some structure or meaning on events.

In the postmodern context, Lawson argues, there are no universally
agreed criteria by which this process of closure may proceed, nor by means
of which its results may be verified. The collapse of the 'Great Project' of
Enlightenment rationalism – which Lawson regards as inherently self-
referential[109] – eliminates the possibility that there exists one universal means
of securing closure, which would be accepted by all people at all times. Yet
it is clear that the process of closure continues to take place, even without
such consensus. Its theoretical impossibility does not prevent it taking place.
It merely takes place *improperly*. Things are closed which should remain
open. 'No closure can be safe, for there is no closure that can avoid failure.'

Lawson thus offers a vision of the philosophical quest which is fuelled
by a longing to make sense of things, yet perpetually frustrated by its own
inability to secure closure on key issues. We are constantly searching for
theoretical closure, yet have to learn to live with the fact that this cannot
be secured. 'The failure of closure has the consequence that there can be
no final resting place.'[110] The quest for theoretical advance is unending and
permanently in a state of flux. As Lawson argues in closing his work:[111]

> So the story of closure has been told. We have not however arrived at a
> destination, but rather at a temporary resting point. I do not offer here a
> conclusion, for there can be no close to the story of closure. No portrayal
> that would end our attempt to understand where we are. No safe and final
> truth with which to sum up our circumstance . . . We are lost in the play
> of openness and closure.

There are many problems with the scheme that Lawson proposes, as
becomes especially clear in his unsatisfactory account of how closure is

---

[108] Lawson, *Closure: A Story of Everything*, 5.
[109] Lawson, *Closure: A Story of Everything*, xxix.
[110] Lawson, *Closure: A Story of Everything*, 21.
[111] Lawson, *Closure: A Story of Everything*, 327.

secured in the natural sciences.[112] We find here a historically and analyt-
ically deficient account of the development and reception of theory in
the sciences, which generally fails to offer a persuasive account of why
natural scientists believe that they can secure at least a degree of theoretical closure. For Lawson, the best that we can hope for is 'a temporary
form of abode – a means of holding the world that has the appearance
of holding fast that which cannot be held at all'.[113]

The implications of these reflections for Christian doctrine cannot be
understated. If Lawson is correct, Christian doctrine represents an intellectually premature and unwarranted foreclosure of a discussion which
cannot be settled fully, and which ought to be recognized to be permanently 'open'. Doctrines are at the very best 'temporary resting places',
determined by the specifics of history and culture, and cannot be
regarded as a permanent or universal 'safe and final truth'. Reality is
open; it is we who decide to close it. And that process of closure can only
be regarded as partial, provisional and subjective – the outcome, for
example, of a naked assertion of power by a controlling elite, rather than
an intellectually legitimate process.

Lawson's discussion of closure will resonate with those who view the
Christian journey as an endless engagement with questions which must
ultimately remain unanswered, lest by answering them we subvert both
question and answer. The apophatic tradition is strongly resistant to any
notion of reducing mysteries, and insists on a degree of 'reserve' in our
statements concerning matters of faith.[114] The English mystical tradition
emphasized the 'cloud of unknowing' which surrounded God, while
Martin Luther spoke of the 'darkness of faith', intending to caution those
who believed they could make confident and definitive statements about
the 'hidden and crucified God'. Yet there is a defensible and important
distinction between offering reliable yet limited theoretical statements
concerning matters of faith and believing that it is possible to provide a
complete account of the mysteries of faith in propositional form.

Problems and mysteries: the dynamics of theological closure
The fundamental weakness of Hilary Lawson's account of closure is that
the entire project is framed in an essentially rhetorical manner that is
inattentive to the complexities and nuances of reality. Lawson would

---

[112] Lawson, *Closure: A Story of Everything*, 144–64.
[113] Lawson, *Closure: A Story of Everything*, 327.
[114] The theme regularly recurs in the writings of John Henry Newman: see Robin C. Selby,
The Principle of Reserve in the Writings of John Henry Newman. Oxford: Oxford University Press,
1975.

have us believe that the failure of the *grand récit* of the Enlightenment marks the end of any attempt to achieve full closure. The only alternative is that offered by postmodernity, which rejects closure as a matter of principle.

But there is a third approach – an approach that is attentive to the distinct identity of the aspect of reality under consideration. The point at issue can be understood by considering the distinction developed by Gabriel Marcel (1889–1973) between 'problems' and 'mysteries'.[115] Marcel sees reality as existing on two levels which he calls the world of the problematical and the world of the ontological mystery. For Marcel, the world of the problematical is the domain of science, rational enquiry, and technical control. The real is here defined by what the mind can conceptualize as a problem, and hence solve and represent in a mathematical formula. Reality is merely the sum-total of its parts. In the world of the problematical, human beings are therefore viewed essentially as objects, statistics, or cases, and are defined in terms of their vital functions (i.e. biological) and their social functions; the individual is thus considered as merely a biological machine performing various social functions.

Marcel's existentialist concerns lead him to consider how we might enquire about the nature of Being. However, it proves impossible to think of 'Being' as a problem which can be solved through the application of objective modes of reflection. Whereas the realm of the problematic can be thought of as being apart from us, maintaining a convenient existential distance, questions about Being make us realize that in some intimate and perhaps perplexing way we are implicated in it. It proves impossible to separate the question 'What is Being?' from the further and more troubling question 'Who (or what) are we?' In that the question of Being always involves our own existence, Marcel argues that we cannot really speak about the *problem* of Being; we are here dealing not with a *problem* but with a *mystery*. A problem is something which can be viewed objectively, and for which we can find a possible solution. A mystery is something which we cannot view objectively, precisely because we cannot separate ourselves from it. Ontological mystery presupposes and demands engagement and involvement on our part.

---

[115] For what follows, see especially the 1949–50 Gifford Lectures: Gabriel Marcel, *The Mystery of Being*. London: Harvill Press, 1950. The distinction is also developed in his earlier work, Gabriel Marcel, *Être et avoir*. Paris: Aubier Éditions Montaigne, 1935. For studies of Marcel's approach, see Roger Troisfontaines, *De l'existence à l'être: la philosophie de Gabriel Marcel*, 2 vols. Louvain: Nauwelaerts, 1953; Giuseppe Russo, *Gabriel Marcel: esistenza e partecipazione*. Battipaglia: Il Fedone, 1993.

Marcel's ideas were developed in a more explicitly theological manner by Austin Farrer in his 1948 Bampton Lectures, *The Glass of Vision*.[116] Farrer defines the realm of the problematic as 'the field in which there are right answers'. To treat reality as a 'problem' is to 'approach the world with a fixed measuring instrument, whether of the literal and physical, or of the conceptual sort'. The realm of mystery, however, involves engagement with reality at such a level that it cannot be investigated in terms of 'determinate and soluble problems'.

Farrer illustrates this distinction, not entirely successfully, using the illustration of a yardstick – a measuring rod. The realm of the problematic is defined in terms of what may be measured.[117]

> When I approach my environment, yardstick in hand, I do not ask the general question 'What have we here?' or even 'What here is most important?' but always the narrow question 'What will my yardstick tell me about the things that are here?' The true scientist is justly credited with a supreme respect for fact, that is to say, for the real world upon which he makes his experiments. He will stubbornly refuse to record what his yardstick does not bring to light.

We can see here at least something of an anticipation of the more recent concern that scientific knowledge is essentially determined by, and limited to, instrumental measurement.[118] Farrer's point is not unrelated to this more recent concern. His most fundamental agenda, however, is to emphasize that the realm of what may be measured leads on into another, deeper realm – namely, the realm of the metaphysical.[119]

> Where the attitude of almost passive respect combines with a rigorous demand for understanding, metaphysical activity will appear. Since no ready-formulated tests are to be applied, and no yardstick is presupposed, no determinate and soluble problems arise for the metaphysician: to his inquiries there are no 'right answers.' He is not faced with the limited and manageable relation which arises between a conceptual instrument and the object it is applied to: he is faced with the object itself, in all its fullness: and the object meets him not as a cluster of problems but as a single though manifold mystery.

Each of these mysteries is distinct and unique, and must be approached and understood in terms of its own identity, even if some common

---

[116] Austin Farrer, *The Glass of Vision*. London: Dacre Press, 1948, 64–78. Farrer explicitly acknowledges his debt to Marcel at this point: *The Glass of Vision*, x–xi.

[117] Farrer, *The Glass of Vision*, 65–6.

[118] See, for example, Nancy Cartwright, *Nature's Capacities and their Measurement*. Oxford: Clarendon Press, 1989.

[119] Farrer, *The Glass of Vision*, 67.

metaphysical tools – such as the use of analogies – may prove helpful in reaching an understanding of each mystery.[120]

The analysis presented by Marcel and Farrer points to the perennial nature of the theological task, in that each generation is called upon to wrestle with mystery, knowing that it possesses a certain inexhaustibility which cannot be exhausted by any one writer or era. Whereas a problem is seen as an intellectual difficulty that can be resolved through abstract, analytical, and objective reflection, a mystery remains alive and interesting, no matter how successfully one has dealt with it in previous attempts. The problematical is the domain of science and rational enquiry. Once a problem is solved there is no more interest in it. A mystery, however, challenges, refreshes and reinvigorates the theological task, not least through the expectation that fresh light has yet to break forth from mysteries which have been wrestled with by previous generations.

The process of wrestling with a mystery thus remains open, not closed. What one generation inherits from another is not so much definitive answers as a shared commitment to the process of wrestling. This insight has long been recognized within Christian theology. Traditionally, Christian doctrine has been well aware of its limits, and has sought to avoid excessively confident affirmations in the face of mystery. Yet at the same time, Christian theology has never seen itself as totally reduced to silence in the face of divine mysteries. As Charles Gore rightly insisted:[121]

> Human language never can express adequately divine realities. A constant tendency to apologize for human speech, a great element of agnosticism, an awful sense of unfathomed depths beyond the little that is made known, is always present to the mind of theologians who know what they are about, in conceiving or expressing God. 'We see', says St Paul, 'in a mirror, in terms of a riddle;' 'we know in part.' 'We are compelled,' complains St Hilary, 'to attempt what is unattainable, to climb where we cannot reach, to speak what we cannot utter; instead of the mere adoration of faith, we are compelled to entrust the deep things of religion to the perils of human expression'.

Some degree of closure is thus clearly presupposed within the long history of Christian wrestling with revealed mysteries. The desire to develop an ever-enhanced *intellectus fidei* can never exhaust the riches of the *mysterium Christi*.

---

[120] Farrer, *The Glass of Vision*, 72.
[121] Charles Gore, *The Incarnation of the Son of God*. London: John Murray, 1922, 105–6.

Theoretical closure in a scientific theology: three theses

In Austin Farrer's sense of the terms, theology is a response to a single multifaceted mystery, rather than to a multiple series of problems. The category of mystery is on the one hand *resistant* to closure; there is always more to a mystery than we can represent in our theories and formulae; we are always forced to *revisit* mystery, seeking to gain a greater appreciation of its depths than on previous occasions. As Leonardo Boff points out, mystery represents a challenge to theology to expand its vision, allowing itself to accommodate its limited capacities to the greater vision of the glory of God which it is called to communicate:[122]

> Seeing mystery in this perspective enables us to understand how it provokes reverence, the only possible attitude to what is supreme and final in our lives. Instead of strangling reason, it invites expansion of the mind and heart. It is not a mystery that leaves us dumb and terrified, but one that leaves us happy, singing and giving thanks. It is not a wall placed in front of us, but a doorway through which we go to the infinity of God. Mystery is like a cliff: we may not be able to scale it, but we can stand at the foot of it, touch it, praise its beauty.

Problems may be solved, and so lose their interest; curiously, the allure of a mystery increases in direct proportion to our willingness to concede that we cannot fully grasp it.

Yet a degree of closure is possible concerning a mystery, to the extent that its contours may at least be delineated, even if its depths remain less than fully plumbed. Three affirmations may be made concerning the issue of closure.

1. Closure is an activity which takes place, to the extent that it can, within a communal context.

2. Closure is always partial, not total, in matters of Christian doctrine.

3. The extent of closure is determined by the subject matter. The nature of the object determines the extent of closure possible, according to its own distinctive nature.

We shall explore each of these points in greater detail.

1. We have already stressed that doctrine is a *communal* matter (24–9), not to be confused with individual theological opinion; it represents the outcome of an extensive and weighty discussion within the church as to how best to articulate its corporate understanding of the identity of its

---

[122] Leonardo Boff, *Trinity and Society*. London: Burns & Oates, 1988, 159.

God and its saviour. The Chalcedonian definition of the identity of Christ is a good example of this process of clarification and development within the church. The process of closure is inextricably linked with that of communal self-identification, in which a number of issues – including doxological, social and theological elements – converge to yield a closure which is consistent with the community's sense of identity and place in history.

Closure is thus not an arbitrary matter. Given that no universal criteria of closure may be offered, given the failure of the 'Grand Project' of the Enlightenment, the only viable criteria are those which are specific to, and mediated by, a tradition. One of the more obvious weaknesses of Lawson's account of closure is his failure to give due weight to tradition-bound understandings of rationality (thus there is no discussion of Alasdair MacIntyre's theories where one might reasonably expect to find it). As a result, Lawson's fundamental assertion of the impropriety of closure fails to take into account the third alternative to the 'Grand Project' of the Enlightenment, and the endemic ideological pluralism of postmodernity – an alternative which offers a perfectly viable account of how closure might take place, on the basis of a community-mediated understanding of identity and rationality.

2. Closure is not understood to be *total*. The points made so powerfully by the apophatic tradition must be given due weight at this point. Partial closure may be secured on some issues; others may be left open. These may become the subject for closure by individuals, but such closures will not be seen as binding for the community as a whole. The Christian engagement with the identity and significance of Jesus Christ illustrates this point with especial clarity. The Chalcedonian Definition secures closure on one aspect of the Christological question – namely, that Jesus Christ is indeed truly divine and truly human.[123]

> Following the holy Fathers, we all with one voice confess our Lord Jesus Christ to be one and the same Son, perfect in divinity and humanity, truly God and truly human, consisting of a rational soul and a body, being of one substance with the Father in relation to his divinity, and being of one substance with us in relation to his humanity, and is like us in all things apart from sin (Hebrews 4:15).

Yet the precise manner in which the relation of these natures is to be conceived is not stipulated, allowing both an Alexandrian and an Antiochene interpretation of the matter.

Paradoxically, the partial Christological closure determined by

[123] H. Denzinger (ed.), *Enchiridion Symbolorum*, 24–25 edn. Barcelona: Herder, 1948, 70–1.

Chalcedon thus opened up new ways of reflecting on the central figure of Christ within the Christian tradition. Having determined what the tradition regarded as fundamental, new ways of conceptualizing its themes and exploring its implications became possible. The agreeing of a significant degree of closure did not, as at first might be thought, lead to the stifling of creativity; rather, it provided new and remarkably fertile channels through which it could be expressed and developed. F. J. A. Hort made this point in his 1871 Hulsean Lectures at Cambridge University in considering how 'the truth' has been received and transmitted within the Christian tradition:[124]

> It has enabled the Church to be nourished by its inherited store from age to age, while it was engaged in other tasks not less necessary for its active work in the world; and that it has deferred this more difficult task for ascertaining the full value of the inheritance till the maturity procured by that long and varied education . . . Perhaps those who are themselves best exercised in unwearied and courageous search will be the readiest to profess how much they have been helped throughout towards clear and dispassionate vision by the gracious pressure of some legitimate authority, into the limits of which they had seldom occasion to inquire.

As Karl Rahner has argued, Chalcedon thus represents a beginning rather than an end, in that it lays down a 'line of demarcation' on essentials, while leaving open the question how lesser issues are to be addressed and understood.[125] For Rahner, none of the church's dogmatic formulas can claim to be the last word on matters; nevertheless, Chalcedon established a basic framework within which the *mysterium Christi* could be explored further, while remaining within what the community of faith regarded as its authentic limits. Rahner himself deplored the formulaic approaches to Christology that Chalcedon seemed to inspire, and urged a recovery of its deeper meaning (especially in relation to the humanity of Christ) through a process of dynamic engagement with the tradition, and a re-appropriation of its central living themes.

A similar point is made by E. L. Mascall, who argues that while 'the Definition of Chalcedon is the truth and nothing but the truth', it is also necessary to insist that 'it is not the whole truth'.[126] Its basic insights

[124] F. J. A. Hort, *The Way, The Truth, The Life: The Hulsean Lectures for 1871*. Cambridge: Cambridge University Press, 1893, 87.

[125] Karl Rahner, 'Chalkedon – Ende oder Anfang?' in Alois Grillmeier and Heinrich Bacht (eds), *Das Konzil von Chalkedon: Geschichte und Gegenwart*, 3 vols. Würzburg: Echter-Verlag, 1951–4, vol. 3, 3–49.

[126] E. L. Mascall, 'On from Chalcedon', in *Whatever Happened to the Human Mind? Essays in Orthodoxy*. London: SPCK, 1980, 28–53, especially 28–9.

determine a starting point and means of proceeding, rather than conclude a discussion of its full significance.[127]

> [Chalcedon] both needs and is patent of much more exploration and
> extension than it has in fact received. It may well be that the very author-
> ity which it has been accorded in Christendom has led to it being treated
> too often as a static and finished product and to its potentialities for devel-
> opment being ignored.

3. In the third place, it is essential to grasp that the extent of closure is
determined by the identity of the object under investigation, rather than
by a set of *a priori* principles. We have already argued that it is essential
for a scientific theology to seek to know and understand something
strictly in accordance with what it actually is – that is, κατὰ Φυσίν, in
accordance with its distinctive nature as it becomes disclosed in the
course of enquiry, and thus in accordance with what it really is. In the
same way, the extent to which theoretical closure may be secured is
dependent upon the specifics of that reality.

This point has increased importance when viewed from a critical
realist perspective, which stresses the stratification of reality, thus high-
lighting the attending issues concerning how those differing strata may
be identified, investigated and represented theoretically. One degree of
closure may be had in relation to the chemical composition of water;
quite another in relation to the origins of the universe, or to the extinction of dinosaurs. The extent of closure is determined by a number of
factors, including accessibility of the evidence which will be part of any
attempt to interpret or understand a phenomenon, the impact of unique
or stochastic events, and the intrinsic complexity of the object itself.

We shall return to such matters later in this volume. Before going
further, it is necessary to consider the pressures that lead some to reject
the propriety of doctrines in Christianity, and offer a response to those
concerns.

The origins and instability of a non-dogmatic Christianity

One of the greatest challenges to a theoretical approach to the Christian
tradition is the suggestion that only a 'non-dogmatic' Christianity can
hope to remain faithful to the spirit of the New Testament.[128] The

---

[127] Mascall, 'On from Chalcedon', 37.
[128] For a useful overview of the concerns, see Philip Schäfer, '"Dogmenfreies Christentum":
Seine Anliegen in einer Dogmenauslegung', in Eberhard Schockenhoff, Peter Walter and
Walter Kasper (eds), *Dogma und Glaube: Bausteine für eine theologische Erkenntnislehre*. Mainz:
Matthias-Grunewald-Verlag, 1993, 9–27.

demand for a non-dogmatic Christianity is fuelled by a number of factors, some of which trace their historical roots back to the early years of the Enlightenment. One such factor is the perception that religious dogmas entail religious conflict, and that such conflict has a distressing habit of transferring itself from the intellectual to the military arena. While this concern has its origins around the time of the Wars of Religion, it remains a significant issue for many today.[129] We may consider it in more detail in what follows.

The lingering shadow of the Wars of Religion

A growing concern in intellectual and political circles over the potential of religious issues to destabilize the economies and societies of western Europe in the late seventeenth century led to pressure for the various forms of Christianity competing for advancement in that region to set aside their distinctive ideas. These ideas were held to be inimical to peaceful coexistence. The growing aversion to religious dogma at this time was largely a result of the devastating 'Wars of Religion', which so debilitated western Europe during the seventeenth century. With the ending of the last major European War of Religion in 1648, at least a degree of political and social stability settled upon the continent.[130] Although religious controversy continued intermittently, it became generally accepted that certain parts of Europe were Lutheran, Catholic, Orthodox, or Reformed. The sense of weariness which had been created by the seemingly endless and pointless Wars of Religion led to a new interest in fostering religious toleration, and combating anything which might lead to fresh outbreaks of religious violence.[131] John Locke's *Letter Concerning Toleration* (1689) argues for religious toleration on the basis of three general considerations, as follows.[132]

First, it is impossible for the state to adjudicate between competing

[129] See the excellent study of Karen Armstrong, *The Battle for God*. New York: Alfred A. Knopf, 2000.

[130] For the most serious of these wars, see Theodore K. Rabb, *The Thirty Years' War*. Lanham, MD: University Press of America, 1981; Mack P. Holt, *The French Wars of Religion, 1562–1629*. Cambridge: Cambridge University Press, 1995; R. J. Knecht, *The French Wars of Religion, 1559–1598*, 2nd edn. London: Longman, 1996; Ronald G. Asch, *The Thirty Years War: The Holy Roman Empire and Europe, 1618–1648*. New York: St Martin's Press, 1997.

[131] See, for example, Charles H. O'Brien, *Ideas of Religious Toleration at the Time of Joseph II: A Study of the Enlightenment among Catholics in Austria*. Philadelphia: American Philosophical Society, 1969; Andrew R. Murphy, *Conscience and Community: Revisiting Toleration and Religious Dissent in Early Modern England and America*. University Park, PA: Pennsylvania State University Press, 2001.

[132] Herbert McLachlan, *The Religious Opinions of Milton, Locke, and Newton*. Manchester: Manchester University Press, 1941.

religious truth-claims. This does not mean that there is no truth in matters of religion, or that all religions are equal in terms of their insights into reality. Locke points out that no earthly judge can be brought forward to settle the matter. For this reason, religious diversity is to be tolerated. Second, even if it could be established that one religion was superior to all others, the legal enforcement of this religion would not lead to the desired objective of that religion. Locke's argument here is based upon the notion that 'true and saving religion consists in the inward persuasion of the mind, without which nothing is acceptable to God. And such is the nature of the understanding, that it cannot be compelled to the belief of any thing by outward force.' Finally, Locke argues, on essentially pragmatic grounds, that the results of trying to impose religious uniformity are far worse than those brought about by the continuing existence of diversity. Religious coercion leads to internal discord, or even – and here Locke clearly has the recent English experience in mind – to civil war. As Locke concludes: 'These considerations, to omit many others that might have been urged to the same purpose, seem unto me sufficient to conclude that all the power of civil government relates only to men's civil interests, is confined to the care of the things of this world, and hath nothing to do with the world to come.'

While it must be conceded that marks of distinction can easily become transposed into the causes of conflict, this is actually a criticism of what people do with their doctrinal convictions, rather than a fundamental criticism of such convictions themselves. Religious and anti-religious views are equally open to such abuse.[133] Locke's analysis does not lead him to dismiss the importance of religious doctrines, but to the view that religion is a private matter of public indifference. What individuals believe should be regarded as private, with no relevance to the public field. This approach at one and the same time upheld religious toleration, while indicating that religion was a purely private matter. This conclusion resonated with the new emphasis upon religious toleration developed in North America, where Christian communities recognized the risk of religious destabilization, and sought to preserve both the public peace and the distinctive religious identity of communities by developing a polity of tolerance.[134]

---

[133] As the excesses of violence attending Stalin's enforcement of atheism attest: Martin Amis, *Koba the Dread*. London: Cape, 2002.

[134] The best example of this is provided by the Puritan Roger Williams (c. 1604–84), founder of Rhode Island: see Martin E. Marty, *Anticipating Pluralism: The Founders' Vision*. Providence, RI: Associates of the John Carter Brown Library, 1986.

This essentially pragmatic critique of 'dogmatic' Christianity was supplemented by a more radical theoretical line of argument, developed with particular force during the nineteenth century. According to this new critique, the very notion of 'dogma' was alien to Christianity in its original forms. Dogma was the most melancholy and unwelcome result of the expansion of Christianity into Greek culture, and its uncritical absorption of some of its less benign ideas. This critique is of such importance that we shall consider it in more detail in what follows.

The History of Dogma movement

Perhaps the most serious challenge to the legitimacy of Christian doctrine came about through the 'History of Dogma' movement, which had its origins in the eighteenth century and reached the height of its influence in the opening years of the twentieth century, especially in the writings of Adolf von Harnack (1851–1930). The fundamental claim of the movement was that both the phenomenon of 'dogma' itself, as well as the substance of certain central dogmas of the Christian faith (such as the incarnation) were a response to certain culture-specific situations, above all to the prevailing assumptions of a Hellenistic culture into which the early church expanded.[135]

The origins of the movement are probably best seen from the writings of Johann Lorentz von Mosheim (1693–1755).[136] Mosheim argued that the primitive biblicism of the early church was corrupted by two schools of thought: 'eclecticism', which emphasized a mystical approach to knowledge and favoured an essentially allegorical form of biblical interpretation, and 'orientalism', a form of dualism which introduced Gnostic elements into Christianity. Mosheim tends to see these movements as exercising their corrupting influence primarily through biblical exegesis, not least through encouraging the emergence of speculative approaches to Christian doctrine. In particular, Mosheim holds that the allegorical exegesis employed by Greek patristic writers inevitably leads to doctrinal corruption.[137]

[135] On the general theme, see Karl H. Neufeld, 'Gebundenheit und Freiheit: Liberal Dogmengeschichtserforschung in der evangelischen Theologie', in W. Löser, K. Lehmann and M. Lutz-Bachmann (eds), *Dogmengeschichte und katholische Theologie.* Würzburg: Echter-Verlag, 1985, 78–96.

[136] The best study is currently Martin Mulsow, *Johann Lorenz Mosheim (1693–1755): Theologie im Spannungsfeld von Philosophie, Philologie und Geschichte.* Wiesbaden: Harrassowitz, 1997.

[137] As Rowan Williams points out, this criticism of allegorical exegesis is addressed by John Henry Newman in his *Arians of the Fourth Century:* see Rowan Williams, 'Newman's *Arians* and the Question of Method in Doctrinal History', in Ian Ker and Alan G. Hill (eds), *Newman after a Hundred Years.* Oxford: Clarendon Press, 1990, 263–85.

The theme of the corruption of the primitive faith of early Christianity also features in Harnack's writings, but is developed in a significantly different direction. Harnack argued that the historical investigation of the origins of dogma revealed that there was no clear historical continuity between the developed doctrinal teachings of the church – such as the Chalcedonian definition – and the witness of the New Testament.[138] The pressure to construct such dogmatic statements arose almost entirely as a result of the expansion of the Christian church from its original Jewish context, so that the intellectual environment of Hellenistic culture exercised a decisive influence over Christian thinking – an influence which, in Harnack's view, was as dysfunctional as it was pervasive:[139]

> The claim of the Church that the dogmas are simply the exposition of the Christian revelation, because deduced from the Holy Scriptures, is not confirmed by historical investigation. On the contrary, it becomes clear that dogmatic Christianity (the dogmas) in its conception and in its construction was *the work of the Hellenic spirit upon the Gospel soil*. The intellectual medium by which in early times men sought to make the Gospel comprehensible and to establish it securely, became inseparably blended with the content of the same. Thus arose the dogma, in whose formation, to be sure, other factors (the words of Sacred Scripture, requirements of the cult, and of the organization, political and social environment, the impulse to push things to their logical consequences, blind custom, etc.) played a part, yet so that the desire and effort to formulate the main principles of the Christian redemption, and to explain and develop them, secured the upper hand, at least in the earlier times.

For Harnack, the origins of dogma were to be sought in the 'activity of the Hellenistic spirit upon the gospel soil', as the early church attempted to make the gospel comprehensible to the Hellenistic world within which its early expansion took place:[140]

> The gospel entered into the world, not as a doctrine, but as a joyful message and as a power of the Spirit of God, originally in the forms of Judaism. It stripped off these forms with amazing rapidity, and united and

---

[138] For an excellent study of this point, see Karl H. Neufeld, *Adolf Harnacks Konflikt mit der Kirche: Weg-Stationen zum 'Wesen des Christentums'*. Innsbruck: Tyrolia-Verlag, 1979. The 1892 conflict over the Apostles' Creed is of especial interest in this respect: Neufeld, *Adolf Harnacks Konflikt mit der Kirche*, 114–32. For details, see Adolf Harnack, *Das Apostolische Glaubensbekenntnis. Ein geschichtlicher Überblick*. Berlin: Haack, 1896.

[139] Adolf von Harnack, *Outlines of the History of Dogma*. Boston, MA: Beacon Hill Press, 1893, 5.

[140] Adolf von Harnack, *History of Dogma*, 7 vols. Edinburgh: Williams & Norgate, 1894–9, vol. 7, 272.

amalgamated itself with Greek science, the Roman Empire and ancient culture, developing, as a counterpoise to this, renunciation of the world and the striving after supernatural life, after deification. All this was summed up in the old dogma and in dogmatic Christianity.

Having refused to accept dogmatic understandings of the significance of Jesus Christ, Harnack argues that this significance is not to be articulated in terms of doctrines about Jesus, but in the person and teachings of Christ himself. 'Jesus does not belong to the gospel as one of its elements, but *was the personal realization and power of the gospel, and we still perceive him as such.*'[141] Although it is clear that Harnack has the highest possible estimation of Christ, he insists that the irreducible element of the gospel concerns our relationship to God the Father. Such a faith in God the Father is linked to Jesus Christ historically, not theologically. The peculiar significance of Christ in relation to Christianity resides in the power of his religious personality:[142]

> Whoever receives the gospel, and tries to recognize the one who brought it to us, will testify that here the divine appeared as purely as it can appear on earth, and that Jesus was himself the power of the gospel for his followers. What they experienced and recognized in him, however, they have proclaimed, and this proclamation is still a living force.

Dogmatic approaches to the identity of Christ – such as the 'Logos'-Christology and the dogma of the incarnation – are thus to be treated as the result of Hellenization, representing a distortion of the original gospel. The historical accuracy of Harnack's account was soon challenged, and it became increasingly clear that the proposed absolute disjunction between Judaic and Hellenistic elements of Christian doctrine could not be sustained.[143] Nevertheless, the ideas developed by Harnack were widely taken up within theological circles hostile to the idea of dogma, especially within British Protestantism.[144]

A related approach located the impetus for dogmatic formulation in the eschatological frustrations of the early Christian community, rather

---

[141] Adolf von Harnack, *What is Christianity?* New York: Harper, 1957, 145.

[142] Harnack, *What is Christianity?*, 146.

[143] See Aloys Grillmeier, 'Hellenisierung-Judaisierung des Christentums als Deuteprinzipien der Geschichte des kirchlichen Dogmas', *Scholastik* 33 (1958), 321–55, 528–55; E. J. Meijering, *Die Hellenisierung des Christentums im Urteil Adolf von Harnack.* Amsterdam: Kampen, 1985. There is also much perceptive material to be found in the older study of A. E. J. Rawlinson, *The New Testament Doctrine of the Christ.* London: Longmans Green, 1926.

[144] The impact on American Protestantism was less pronounced, as can be seen from William R. Hutchinson, *The Modernist Impulse in American Protestantism.* New York: Oxford University Press, 1976.

than in the transference of Christianity from its original Jewish matrix to a Hellenistic context. In his *Entstehung des christlichen Dogmas* (1941), Martin Werner argued that the new(ish) insights into the eschatology of early Christianity set out by Johannes Weiss and Albert Schweitzer[145] set the scene for a correct understanding of the origins of dogma – and hence for its ultimate elimination.[146] The 'consistent eschatology' developed by Schweitzer provides a framework to make sense of the early Christian community's turn to dogma as a means of coping with its eschatological disappointments. The first major section of the work deals with the theme of the 'abandoning of the basic ideas of early Christianity as a result of the non-fulfilment of the *parousia*'. Werner then traces the development of dogma as a substitute for the eschatological ideas of the early church. The eschatological gospel of Galilee was thus distorted into the Hellenized Catholicism of the first four centuries.

Werner's approach involved the repristination of Schweitzer's 'consistent eschatology', an idea originally developed in the 1890s, which had gradually fallen out of favour. The credibility of his approach was severely undermined by the fact that he merely reasserted Schweitzer's ideas at a time when they were regarded as outdated, and made them the central platform of his ambitious explanation of the origins of dogma. It is generally thought that Werner's approach was rebutted by H. E. W. Turner's major study of the development of doctrine,[147] and it has since received little attention.

The inevitability of doctrine

Despite the waning of the 'History of Dogma' movement, there still remains a strong anti-theoretical constituency within Christianity which argues that there is no need for any 'theory of Christ'; commitment to his person is all that is required. Three points may be made in response to this.

1. The demand for an 'undogmatic' Christianity amounts to little more than a crude embargo on critical reflection in matters of faith. It represents a retreat from precisely the kind of intellectual engagement which

---

[145] For the issues raised by these writers, see Rolf Schäfer, 'Das Reich Gottes bei Albrecht Ritschl und Johannes Weiss', *Zeitschrift für Theologie und Kirche* 61 (1964), 68–88; D. L. Holland, 'History, Theology and the Kingdom of God: A Contribution of Johannes Weiss to Twentieth Century Theology', *Biblical Research* 13 (1968), 54–66.

[146] Martin Werner, *Die Entstehung des christlichen Dogmas problemgeschichtlich dargestellt.* Bern and Leipzig: Haupt, 1941.

[147] H. E. W. Turner, *The Pattern of Christian Truth: A Study in the Relations between Orthodoxy and Heresy in the Early Church.* London: Mowbray, 1954, 20–3.

makes Christian theology such a genuinely exciting and challenging discipline, and demands that we place in its stead an amorphous and shadowy account of things. Instead of encouraging Christians to think about their faith, it represents a demand that they suspend use of their intellectual faculties in any matters to do with God, Christ or human destiny. Precisely because human beings think, they will wish to develop theories concerning the nature of God and Jesus Christ – whatever form those theories may take.

2. Some use the term 'undogmatic Christianity' in a highly invidious manner, meaning something like 'an understanding of Jesus Christ which is opposed to the official teachings of the Christian faith'. There has never been any shortage of individuals who have argued for such an 'undogmatic' faith, seeing it as liberating individuals from the tyranny of ecclesiastical authority or outmoded ideas.[148] Yet the ideas which are held to displace these are generally as dogmatic as their predecessors. It is a new set of dogmas that is being proposed, not the elimination of dogma as such.[149] As Martin Kähler pointed out in 1892, it is impossible to avoid proposing doctrinal affirmations, whether one opts for the ontological exaggerations of Byzantine Christology, or the pseudo-historical Jesuology of the 'Life of Jesus' movement.[150] Both rest upon sophisticated implicit theoretical foundations. 'New presbyter is but old priest wrote large,' wrote John Milton, deploring those who declared themselves to have abolished certain things, yet in reality merely substituted their own equivalents. Theoretical statements, whether implicit or explicit, undergird all reflections on the nature of God or Christ; to pretend that they do not is to close one's eyes to the pervasive influence of theories in religion, which must be honestly addressed and acknowledged at every point.

3. To demand an 'undogmatic' Christianity often involves confusion over the *tone* and *substance* of Christian doctrine. 'Dogmatic' can rightly

---

[148] An excellent example is provided by Robert J. Campbell, *The New Theology*. London: Chapman & Hall, 1907. For a useful analysis, see B. G. Worrall, 'R. J. Campbell and his New Theology', *Theology* 81 (1978), 342–8. See particularly the vigorous response by Charles Gore, *The New Theology and the Old Religion*. London: John Murray, 1907.

[149] See the contradictions on this issue which litter the pages of John Shelby Spong, *Why Christianity Must Change or Die: A Bishop Speaks to Believers in Exile*. San Francisco, CA: HarperSanFrancisco, 1998.

[150] Martin Kähler, *The So-Called Historical Jesus and the Historic, Biblical Christ*. Philadelphia: Fortress Press, 1964, 43. For the background to this essay, see Wilhelm Herrmann, 'Der geschichtliche Christus der Grund unseres Glaubens', *Zeitschrift für Theologie und Kirche* 2 (1892), 232–73; Otto Ritschl, 'Der historische Christus, der christliche Glaube und die theologische Wissenschaft', *Zeitschrift für Theologie und Kirche* 3 (1893), 371–426.

be understood as meaning 'enclosed within a framework of theoretical or doctrinal beliefs', and in this sense, I must insist, reflects some integral themes of the Christian faith. Yet the term can also bear the meaning of 'uncritical', 'unreflective' or 'authoritarian' – referring, in other words, to the tone or voice in which Christian theological affirmations are made, rather than to their substance. I have no interest in supporting shrill, strident, imperious and overbearing assertions of Christian doctrine, which demand silent unthinking compliance on the part of their audiences, and lead to conflict and tension. Yet I remain convinced that such statements are necessary and legitimate, while insisting that they can and should be stated in a more reflective tone. After all, the purpose of Christian doctrine is partly to inspire awe and worship, not to silence and threaten its audiences.

The propriety of doctrine: some British contributions

Given the continuing importance of an anti-theoretical trend within modern theology, we may briefly consider four classic British responses to it, dating from the intellectual high water mark of the anti-theoretical movement within the church.

In his 1891 Bampton Lectures, Charles Gore set out an extended comparison of the 'Christ of dogma' and the 'Christ of Scripture'.[151] Responding to those who argue that the simplicity of the biblical witness to Christ is compromised and distorted by theoretical development within the history of the church, especially during the patristic period, Gore insists that these later theoretical formulations are to be seen as 'the apostolic teaching worked out into formulas by the aid of a terminology which was supplied by Greek dialectics'.[152] There was no distortion, no misrepresentation – merely the 'gradual unfolding of teaching' of 'an unbroken stream of tradition'.[153] The pressure to express the church's witness to Christ in increasingly theoretic terms lies partly in the human desire to understand. For Gore, 'Christianity became metaphysical simply and only because man is rational'.[154] Yet the pressure to enunciate theory also lies partly in the church's need to defend its central teachings against misunderstanding and misrepresentation, which necessitated clarification and restatement of core beliefs in the face of their distortion by others.

Similar anti-dogmatic arguments were considered by James Orr in his

---

[151] Charles Gore, *The Incarnation of the Son of God.* London: John Murray, 1922, 80–112.
[152] Gore, *Incarnation of the Son of God*, 96.
[153] Gore, *Incarnation of the Son of God*, 96, 101.
[154] Gore, *Incarnation of the Son of God*, 21.

Christian View of God and the World (also delivered in 1891). These lectures, which were three years in preparation, countered the predominant
Ritschlianism of the era by insisting that Christianity combined both
religious and theoretical elements; indeed, that these could not be separated.[155] For Orr, the dynamics of the Christian faith and the human
intellect was such that theoretical reflection and conviction was an
inevitability. Christianity is not simply concerned with religious affec-
tions; it possesses 'definite, positive teaching; it claims to be the truth; it
bases religion on knowledge'.[156] To lose sight of the cognitive aspects of
faith is to surrender the distinctive shape of the Christian faith. 'A religion based on mere feeling is the vaguest, most unreliable, most unstable
of all things.' What is required for 'a strong, stable, religious life', Orr
insists, is 'intelligent conviction' – a notion which Orr clearly understands to possess both intellectual and volitional aspects.

It might, of course, be argued that Christianity 'has its centre in living
in Christ, and not a dogmatic creed'.[157] Orr concedes the obvious truth
in this concern, distancing himself from any suggestion that
Christianity is concerned with the mere revelation of abstract ideas. Yet
the incarnation affirms the importance both of God's engagement with
history and of its doctrinal importance.[158]

> The gospel is no mere proclamation of 'eternal truths,' but the discovery
> of a saving purpose for God, executed in time. But the doctrines are the
> interpretation of the facts. The facts do not stand blank and dumb before
> us, but have a voice given to them, and a meaning put into them. They
> are accompanied by living speech, which makes their meaning clear.
> When John declares that Jesus Christ is come in the flesh, and is the Son
> of God (1 John 4:2, 15), he is stating a fact, but he is none the less enunci-
> ating a doctrine.

Orr insists that theology must constantly work to ensure that its doctrinal formulations are adequate to the 'infinite truth' they seek to
mediate. One of Orr's most distinctive contributions lies in his recognition of 'progress in dogma' – in other words, doctrinal development.
Noting the concern of some over a static understanding of doctrine, he
argues that the entire theological enterprise must be dedicated to devel-

[155] James Orr, *The Christian View of God and the World, as Centring in the Incarnation*. New
York: Charles Scribner's Sons, 1908, 16–26. For his detailed assessment of Ritschl's views, see
James Orr, *The Ritschlian Theology and the Evangelical Faith*. London: Hodder & Stoughton,
1897.
[156] Orr, *The Christian View of God and the World*, 20.
[157] Orr, *The Christian View of God and the World*, 22.
[158] Orr, *The Christian View of God and the World*, 22.

oping dogmatic formulations which are adequate to the revelation which they seek to express, yet which ultimately transcends them.[159]

> The dogmatic moulds which were found adequate for one age have often proved insufficient for the next, to which a larger horizon of vision has been granted; and have had to be broken up that new ones might be created, more adapted to the content of a Revelation which in some sense transcends them all.

An equally robust defence of theory in Christian reflections concerning Christ is found in P. T. Forsyth's masterpiece *The Person and Place of Jesus Christ* (1909).[160] In this work, Forsyth directed particular attention to the idea that Christianity aimed to replicate the 'religion of Jesus' rather than propagate theories about Christ.[161]

> There is nothing we are more often told by those who discard an evangelical faith than this – that we must now do what scholarship has only just enabled us to do and return to the religion of Jesus. We are bidden to practise Jesus's own personal religion, as distinct from the Gospel of Christ, from a gospel which calls him its faith's object, and not its subject, founder or classic only. We must learn to believe not *in* Christ, but *with* Christ, we are told.

In response to these concerns, Forsyth offers a defence of 'dogma' – by which he means 'the specific theological constructions from the past which have been sealed with ecclesiastical authority as formally final'.[162] Part of Forsyth's defence of theological dogma lies in his observation that other areas of intellectual enquiry are similarly committed to dogmatic statements. While his discussion of the matter suggests at best a very superficial knowledge of the natural sciences, the point he makes is still valid:[163]

> Dogma is the science of faith. Every department of science has its dogma; and in the hierarchy of the sciences, these dogmas qualify and supplement each other. In one region we have the dogma of gravitation; in another that of evolution; in another that of affinity; in another (if it be another) the molecular dogma; and so on. Thus in the region of spiritual science, we have also a science. We have a science of faith.

[159] Orr, *The Christian View of God and the World*, 25.
[160] P. T. Forsyth, *The Person and Place of Jesus Christ*. London: Independent Press, 1909. For detailed studies, see John H. Rodgers, *The Theology of P. T. Forsyth: The Cross of Christ and the Revelation of God*. London: Independent Press, 1965; Archibald Macbride Hunter, *P. T. Forsyth: per crucem ad lucem*. London: SCM Press, 1974.
[161] Forsyth, *The Person and Place of Jesus Christ*, 35.
[162] Forsyth, *The Person and Place of Jesus Christ*, 213.
[163] Forsyth, *The Person and Place of Jesus Christ*, 215.

If theoretical statements undergird other areas of intellectual enquiry, why should they not equally be applied in Christian theology?

Yet Forsyth is careful not to suggest that dogma, in his sense of the term, is a matter for individuals. Mingling sociological analysis with theological affirmations, Forsyth contends that the identity of the church requires definition if it is to continue in existence as a distinct entity within the historical process. Dogma, according to Forsyth, is essential to the life of the church, in that it both *arises from* and *expresses* that life.[164]

> A Church must always have a dogma, implicit or explicit. A cohesive Church must have a coherent creed. But it must be a dogma the Church holds, not one that holds the Church. The life is in the body, not in the system . . . The idea of a dogma, as the organized declaration or confession by any Church of its collective doctrine, is only the intellectual counterpart of the idea of the organized Church itself.

There thus exist two pressures which make dogma inevitable: the human desire to make sense of things, and extend the horizons of understanding; and the social need for the church to offer a definition of its identity and boundaries – a matter to which we shall return presently.

An 'undogmatic' Christianity is only a possibility if individual Christians cease to exercise their intellectual faculties and if the church ceases to regard itself as having anything distinctive to say to the world around it. As Forsyth points out, the faith of the church must be capable of statement – and that process of formulation of a statement inevitably leads to the development of dogma.[165]

> Revelation did not come in a statement, but in a person; yet stated it must be. Faith must go on to specify. It must be capable of statement, else it could not be spread; for it is not an ineffable, incommunicable mysticism. It has its truth, yet it is not a mere truth but a power; its truth, its statement, is part of it.

The proper debate thus concerns which dogmas should be adopted, rather than the propriety of dogma itself.

A final discussion of note is found in a series of lectures delivered at Cambridge University in 1940 by J. S. Whale. While offering an overview of the basic ideas of Christian doctrine as a whole, Whale repeatedly turned to consider why such doctrines were appropriate in

---

[164] Forsyth, *The Person and Place of Jesus Christ*, 213–14. For further exploration of such points, see H. R. Mackintosh, *The Doctrine of the Person of Jesus Christ*. Edinburgh: T&T Clark, 1913, 285–305, 345–62.

[165] Forsyth, *The Person and Place of Jesus Christ*, 15.

the first place. In his discussion of Christology, Whale argues that two considerations point to the inevitability of dogma.[166] First, the New Testament – which is the foundation on which Christian theologizing proceeds – is itself saturated with dogmatic statements concerning the identity of Christ. Theology thus cannot evade such issues without distorting what was there from the beginning of the Christian witness. Second, there exists an intellectual imperative to wrestle with truth, even if that truth cannot be mastered. 'We are meant to serve God with the mind, even where the mind is impotent to compass ultimate and ineffable mysteries.' For Whale, the determining factors are thus rational and sociological, and have nothing to do with the alleged influence of 'Hellenistic' pressures. Doctrine is inevitable, having its origins in the basic facts of individual and communal life – namely, that human beings are inquisitive animals, and the church is a social organism. In this, he finds support from Brooke Foss Westcott, perhaps the greatest of England's nineteenth-century scholar-bishops. When asked why he chose to go beyond the modest statements of Scripture in his theological reflections, he replied[167]

> that we cannot but speculate: that we are so made that we must strive after some view of the relations and end of the system in which we are placed: that the advance of partial knowledge forces upon us more and more the duty of looking for a more comprehensive synthesis.

Westcott's vision of the gospel is firmly anchored to an ecclesiology which insists that we are placed, historically and intellectually, within both a Christian community and a Christian 'system', a way of living within and beholding the world. We cannot help but want to explore its inner recesses and its hidden depths, any more than we can rebel against being human. To be human is to long to know more of God and the things of God in this world – in brief, to aspire to theoretical reflection.

Christian doctrine is thus an inevitability. As we have argued throughout this work, the task of theological reflection takes place within a communal tradition, nourished by its communal beholding of the vision of God, which shapes and transmits a distinctively Christian understanding of reality – or way of viewing it – which is demarcated from other understandings of reality. Christian doctrine both elaborates the nature of that understanding, and aims to maintain the distinctiveness of the tradition. In one sense, Richard Rorty is right when he speaks of the

---

[166] J. S. Whale, *Christian Doctrine*. Cambridge: Cambridge University Press, 1941, 109–12.
[167] B. F. Westcott, 'The Gospel of Creation', in *The Epistles of St John*. London: Macmillan, 1892, 285–328, 325–6.

importance of doctrines in consolidating social consensus and identity; where he falls short is in believing that such consensus is in and of itself adequate as the basis of an understanding of reality.

Theory and social reality: the ecclesial function of doctrine

A critical realist account of the world proposes a spectrum of modes of interplay between 'objectivity' and 'social construction' in relation to theory construction. It is fatally easy to speak of the 'Christian tradition' without appreciating that this term designates a social reality – or, better, a complex aggregate of fundamentally interconnected yet subtly differentiated social realities. Without this recognition of the social grounding of ecclesial reality, doctrine becomes an essentially idealist conception, divorced from its historical location and improperly separated from the matrix of social forces which shape it in manners that idealists prefer to overlook, yet are essential to a fully orbed account of the place of theory in the Christian life.

We have already seen how it is essential to at least attempt to distinguish 'theology' and 'doctrine' (or 'dogma') on account of the latter's social function in defining and defending the identity of a Christian community (24–9). The ensuing related processes of doctrinal development and reception of doctrine both illustrate the communal dimensions of the process of reflection within the church upon the vision of God which grounds and impels it, and which it seeks to represent in its theorizing. It is thus essential to realize that:

1. At least some aspects of the process of doctrinal development and reception are socially constructed;

2. Social constructs are subject to constant reappraisal and revision in the light of advancing knowledge and experimental observation; and

3. A realist approach to God or to the world is not called into question through the recognition of socially constructed aspects of the theories developed by either Christian theology or the natural sciences.[168]

Recognizing that at least certain aspects of the development of Christian theory are socially constructed opens the way to a much more plausible and responsible understanding of why certain doctrines have developed

---

[168] See, for example, John R. Searle, *The Construction of Social Reality*. New York: Free Press, 1995.

in certain manners, played certain functions at certain times and not others, and been valued by certain groups of Christians rather than others. The present section explores the ecclesial functions of Christian theory, with a view both to documenting some of the trends that are empirically observable within Christian history, and to offering an explanation of those trends.

It must be stressed that the recognition that Christian doctrine plays certain social functions, or is otherwise connected with the social reality of the Christian tradition, does not call into question the *truth* of the doctrine in question. The social role played by a doctrine is shaped by a complex network of social factors, none of which can legitimately be said to lead to a non-realist construal of Christian doctrine. The social function of a doctrine is an aspect of its real identity – but an aspect that is dependent on the cultural and historical specifics of a given era, and which cannot be considered to be identical at every place, at every time, or for all peoples.[169]

While the role of Christian doctrine in shaping understandings of spirituality, doxology and ethics within the Christian community has been thoroughly studied,[170] considerably less attention has been paid to the external social function of doctrine in demarcating the Christian tradition from its rivals. Yet the history of the Christian tradition discloses that this is a virtually perennial feature of doctrinal development. As Niklas Luhmann has pointed out, doctrine comes to play a particularly important role when the identity of a religious tradition is under threat, particularly from other religious communities.[171] Doctrine is thus to be regarded as a means by which the Christian traditions regulate their relationship with the world at large, whether this is perceived in a neutral or hostile sense, and with other Christian traditions.

Doctrine thus defines communities of discourse – the kind of sociolinguistic communities which feature prominently in George

---

[169] On which see Alister E. McGrath, 'Dogma und Gemeinde: Zur soziologische Funktion des christlichen Dogmas', *Kerygma und Dogma* 36 (1990), 24–43; Christoph Danz, 'Dogmatik als Differenzhermeneutik. Überlegungen zur Funktion moderner Systematischer Theologie im Anschluß an Ernst Troeltsch', *Kerygma und Dogma* 47 (2001), 210–26.

[170] For example, see Robin Maas and Gabriel O'Donnell, 'An Introduction to Spiritual Theology: The Theory that Undergirds our Practice', in R. Maas and G. O'Donnell (eds), *Spiritual Traditions for the Contemporary Church*. Nashville, TN: Abingdon, 1990, 11–21; Gerd Theissen, *Social Reality and the Early Christians: Theology, Ethics, and the World of the New Testament*. Edinburgh: T&T Clark, 1993; Terry Tastard, 'Theology and Spirituality in the Nineteenth and Twentieth Centuries', in P. Byrne and L. Houlden (eds), *Companion Encyclopaedia of Theology*. London: Routledge, 1995, 594–619; A. James Reimer, *Mennonites and Classical Theology: Dogmatic Foundations for Christian Ethics*. Kitchener, ON: Pandora Press, 2001.

[171] Niklas Luhmann, *Funktion der Religion*. Frankfurt am Main: Suhrkamp, 1982, 59–61. For critical engagement with such concerns, see Wolfhart Pannenberg, 'Religion in der säkularen Gesellschaft: Niklas Luhmanns Religionssoziologie', *Evangelische Kommentare* 11 (1978), 99–103.

Lindbeck's analysis of the nature of doctrine.[172] It does not merely structure the conceptual frameworks and specific modes of discourse of those communities; it identifies them as social entities, marking them off from other social groupings.[173] It serves as a means of creating a sense of social identity, shaping the outlook of a community and justifying its original and continued existence in the face of rival communities with comparable claims. It assists in defining both the limits of, and the conditions for entering, such a community. Effective social cohesion requires the fixing of boundaries, and the fostering of a sense of community identity.[174] Doctrine thus enhances the sense of identity of a community, and facilitates its distinction from other communities. Other means of social demarcation associated with the Christian communities (such as the sacraments) also have a clear doctrinal component.[175]

The issue, then, is (externally) the demarcation of a Christian tradition from its alternatives, including clarification of their mutual relationship, and (internally) the fostering of a sense of shared identity and purpose within that tradition. To explore this issue further, we shall consider some historical factors which illuminate the points at issue.

Doctrine and demarcation from Judaism

The first major challenge faced by the emerging Christian churches was to clarify their relationship – intellectual and social – with Judaism. Christians declined to adopt the cultic rituals of Judaism (such as food laws, sabbath observance and circumcision) which served to identify Jews within a Gentile community; on the other hand, Marcion's proposal that Christianity should be declared utterly distinct from Judaism failed to gain support.[176] There was an obvious polarity within the relationship of Christianity and Judaism. As a result, Christian self-definition was initially directed towards clarification of the relationship of Christianity and Judaism, centring upon the identity of Jesus, and subsequently upon the

---

[172] Lindbeck is aware of at least something of the social functions of doctrine: see George Lindbeck, *The Nature of Doctrine*. Philadelphia: Westminster, 1984, 74.

[173] N. T. Wright, *The New Testament and the People of God*. Minneapolis, MN: Fortress, 1992, 447–52.

[174] A pattern noted and assessed in Wayne Meeks's excellent study of the social realities of Pauline communities in the New Testament: see Wayne A. Meeks, *The First Urban Christians: The Social World of the Apostle Paul*. New Haven, CT: Yale University Press, 1983, 84–103.

[175] Again, see the social role of the Lord's Supper in early Pauline communities, according to Meeks: Meeks, *The First Urban Christians*, 150–62.

[176] Ulrich Schmid, *Marcion und sein Apostolos: Rekonstruktion und historische Einordnung der marcionitischen Paulusbriefausgabe*. Berlin: de Gruyter, 1995. This corrects the highly influential earlier study of Adolf von Harnack, *Marcion – das Evangelium vom fremden Gott: Eine Monographie zur Geschichte der Grundlegung der katholischen Kirche*. Leipzig: Hinrichs, 1921.

role of the Old Testament Law.[177] (Incidentally, the importance of the person of Jesus of Nazareth in precipitating bifurcation between Christianity and Judaism serves to highlight his function as the fundamental legitimizing resource of Christianity.) It is thus perfectly acceptable to suggest that the Pauline doctrine of justification by faith represents a theoretical justification for the separation of Gentile Christian communities from Judaism, thus identifying the obvious social function of the doctrine.[178] Yet this does not lead to the conclusion that the Pauline doctrine of justification is solely a social epiphenomenon. Its ecclesial function represents a social construction – but on a critical realist approach to matters, this cannot be regarded as implying that the doctrine is an invention or is untrue. It is simply to note that this doctrine came to play a critical role in the demarcation of communities.

Doctrine and demarcation from the world

Even in the New Testament, a sharp distinction can be seen emerging between 'church' and 'world'. The distinction was initially understood, at least in part, in terms of separation from the world. Perhaps encouraged by an expectation of an early end to all things, the first Christians appear to have formed communities based on shared loyalties and specific commitments, rather than explicitly theoretical notions. The early Christian communities do not appear to have regarded precise and elaborate doctrinal formulations as essential to their self-definition, in that they were already distinguished from the world by sharing in their meetings and worship. 'Their doctrinal distinctiveness, however defined, was reinforced, sustained, perhaps even eclipsed, by their sociological distinctness as groups set, literally, apart from the world.'[179] Thus on the basis of one understanding of the Johannine community, this group regarded its circumstances as a group set apart from the world as being explained and legitimated by the accounts of Jesus Christ's words and actions, transmitted within the Fourth Gospel.[180] The very early

[177] See, for example, Francis Watson, *Paul, Judaism and the Gentiles: A Sociological Approach.* Cambridge: Cambridge University Press, 1986, 49–87.

[178] Thus Watson, *Paul, Judaism and the Gentiles,* 178. For a more nuanced approach, see N. T. Wright, *The Climax of the Covenant: Christ and the Law in Pauline Theology.* Edinburgh: T&T Clark, 1991.

[179] R. A. Markus, 'The Problem of Self-Definition: From Sect to Church', in E. P. Sanders (ed.), *Jewish and Christian Self-Definition.* London: SCM Press, 1980–2, vol. 1, 1–15.

[180] Wayne A. Meeks, 'The Stranger from Heaven in Johannine Sectarianism', *Journal of Biblical Literature* 91 (1972), 44–72. See further David L. Balch, *The Social History of the Matthean Community: Cross-Disciplinary Approaches.* Minneapolis: Fortress Press, 1991. For a critique of the notion of such 'communities', see Richard Bauckham (ed.), *The Gospels for all Christians: Rethinking the Gospel Audiences.* Grand Rapids, MI: Eerdmans, 1998.

Christian communities, although clearly bearing a Wittgensteinian 'family resemblance' on account of their beliefs concerning Jesus of Nazareth, did not require doctrinal formulations to distinguish themselves from the world: that distinction was already forced upon them by the world, which isolated them as visible and readily identifiable social groups.[181] To become a Christian was (at least potentially) to be liable to a visible change in social location, which in itself was adequate for the purposes of being demarcated from society without the need for additional discriminants.

Yet there were limits to social and physical approaches to demarcation. The early Christians, unlike the Essenes, did not withdraw into the wilderness; they remained in the world of the cities and their institutions, gradually developing means of existing in the world without being of the world.[182] 'We Christians', Tertullian wrote to his pagan audience, 'live with you, enjoy the same food, have the same manner of life and dress, and the same requirements for life as you.'[183] So how were they distinguished from other communities of the period? Doctrine came increasingly to represent a means by which Christian individuals and communities might be distinguished from the world around them – especially as the beliefs, values and actions of the Christian community came to converge. Controversy with Gnostic and other communities forced the Christian communities to develop their understanding of self-definition, and led to increased pressure for creeds and other authorized statements of faith.[184] Although the contribution of Irenaeus to this process was pivotal, the importance of Tertullian in urging self-definition and the maintenance of self-identity within the Christian communities must not be overlooked. Yardsticks – such as the canon of the New Testament, or adherence to the apostolic rule of faith – were agreed by which the claims of religious communities to be Christian churches could be tested.[185] Doctrine came to be of increasing importance in distinguishing the church from secular culture at large, and increasing a sense of identity and cohesion within its ranks.

[181] Meeks, *The First Urban Christians*, 84–107.

[182] Important exceptions must, of course, be noted, such as the Egyptian monastic movement: Derwas J. Chitty, *The Desert a City: An Introduction to the Study of Egyptian and Palestinian Monasticism under the Christian Empire*. Crestwood, NY: St Vladimir's Seminary Press, 1995.

[183] Tertullian, *Apologia*, 42.

[184] Georg Günter Blum, *Tradition und Sukzession: Studien zum Normbegriff des Apostolischen von Paulus bis Irenaeus*. Berlin: Lutherisches Verlagshaus, 1963. On creeds in general, see J. N. D. Kelly, *Early Christian Creeds*, 3rd edn. New York: Longman, 1981.

[185] S. L. Greenslade, 'Heresy and Schism in the Later Roman Empire', in Derek Baker (ed.), *Schism, Heresy and Religious Protest*. Cambridge: Cambridge University Press, 1972, 1–20.

Yet if doctrine is of importance in distinguishing the church from a pagan culture, what happens if the culture itself becomes Christian, and there is no longer any need to distinguish church and society? This issue became of importance with the emergence of Christendom, to which we now turn.

The redundancy of demarcation: the case of Christendom

The conversion of Constantine marked a major change in the character of western Christianity.[186] With that conversion, Christianity assumed a new status within the Roman Empire, and doctrinal formulations became of increasing political importance. Where the Donatist schism (313–16) had merely obliged Constantine to determine which of two rival *social groupings* could legitimately claim to be the true church, the Arian controversy put him in the rather more difficult position of having to determine which of two rival *doctrines* was the authentic teaching of the catholic church.[187] With the imperial resolution of the Arian crisis, the concept of 'doctrine' rapidly assumed the character of 'legally sanctioned ideology' – a concept perhaps accurately designated 'dogma'. The relative pluralism of an earlier understanding of doctrine (that is, of a central core of ideas, and agreement concerning the texts to be used in teaching, preaching and theological exploration) reflected the unintegrated social structure of the Christian church of the period; with the advent of centralization during the Constantinian period came the idea of the church as a single institutional unit, requiring doctrinal uniformity in order to preserve its new-found social function and status.

By the dawn of the Middle Ages, the distinction between 'church' and 'society' had become so subtle that formal distinctions were often difficult to draw.[188] There were a number of ambiguities within the notion of Christendom, including the question of the secular power of the church. Thus the Bull *Unam Sanctam*, issued by Boniface VII on 18 November 1302, aimed to clarify the relation between the secular and ecclesiastical powers within Christendom.[189] Yet the fundamental notion was that of a Christian region of the world, which was defined socially

---

[186] See the assessments provided in Alan Kreider (ed.), *The Origins of Christendom in the West.* Edinburgh: T&T Clark, 2001.

[187] See the analysis provided in Rowan Williams, *Arius: Heresy and Tradition*, 2nd edn. London: SCM Press, 2001, 48–81.

[188] For some of the issues, see Scott L. Waugh and Peter D. Diehl, *Christendom and its Discontents: Exclusion, Persecution, and Rebellion, 1000–1500.* Cambridge: Cambridge University Press, 1996.

[189] Boniface VII, 'De unitate et potestate Ecclesiae', in H. Denzinger (ed.), *Enchiridion Symbolorum*, 24–25 edn. Barcelona: Herder, 1948, 218–20.

and politically by the authority of the church. With this development, doctrine ceased to play a major social role. Significantly, the heresies to emerge within Christendom were defined primarily as challenges to the authority of the church, rather than as essentially theological movements – and were hence defined in legal, not theological, terms.[190]

The emergence of Christendom can readily be shown to have led to a marked reduction in interest in doctrine. Issues of pastoral care, the legal rights and responsibilities of the church, and the perennial issues of international diplomacy came to be seen as the natural concern of the church. One interesting result of this disengagement with doctrinal issues was that the Roman Catholic church was not well prepared for the doctrinal debates that erupted in the sixteenth century as a result of the Reformation controversies. As Giuseppe Alberigo noted in his magisterial study of the Italian bishops at the Council of Trent, theological competence had clearly not been seen as a priority in the upper echelons of the church for some time.[191]

The emergence of the Reformation may be regarded as marking a transitional point in the history of the social function of Christian doctrine, and we may turn to explore it in a little more detail.

Doctrine and demarcation of the Christian traditions

One of the most dramatic effects of the Reformation was the creation of a series of ecclesial communities throughout western Europe which sought to identify themselves over and against the medieval catholic church. Luther's evangelical faction at Wittenberg, Calvin's reformed city of Geneva, and various Anabaptist communities sought to distinguish themselves from the church from which they had broken away. Certain key doctrines were instrumental in this process, most notably the doctrine of justification by faith alone, which rapidly became the theological hallmark of Protestant communities.[192]

Yet this process did not happen immediately, and it is important to note some individual aspects of the situation. For a period of about a decade (1515–25), the Reformation in eastern Switzerland proceeded on the model bequeathed to it by the Middle Ages. Reformers in this region

[190] Othmar Hageneder, 'Der Häresiebegriff bei den Juristen des 12. und 13. Jahrhunderts', in W. Lourdaux and D. Verhelst (eds), *The Concept of Heresy in the Middle Ages*. Louvain: Louvain University Press, 1978, 42–103.

[191] Giuseppe Alberigo, *I Vescovi Italiani al Concilio di Trento (1545–1547)*. Florence: Sansoni, 1959.

[192] For some aspects of the process leading to this, see Alister E. McGrath, 'Justification and the Reformation. The Significance of the Doctrine of Justification by Faith to Sixteenth Century Urban Communities', *Archiv für Reformationsgeschichte* 90 (1990), 5–19.

– such as Joachim von Watt at St Gallen and Huldrych Zwingli at Zurich – saw themselves as creating a reformed Christendom, through a reformation of life and morality according to the moral and institutional vision of the New Testament.[193] Doctrine was not seen as a major issue; indeed, the vision for a *doctrinal* reformation of the church owes its origins to Luther, rather than to the first generation of Swiss reformers. Similarly, the English Reformation was essentially an act of state, which substituted the authority of the English monarch for that of the Pope.[194] No doctrinal alterations were initially envisaged; their necessity was a later recognition. The reformed English church was under no pressure to define itself in relation to any other ecclesial body in the land, in that none existed. The manner in which the English Reformation initially proceeded demanded no doctrinal self-definition, in that the church in England was defined socially by precisely the same social and institutional parameters before the Reformation as after, whatever political alterations may have been introduced. There was no need for theological demarcation; indeed, such demarcation would arguably have been detrimental to the vision of a national church that Henry wished to sustain.

This is not to say that no theological debates took place in England at the time of the Reformation;[195] it is to note that they were not perceived as possessing decisive significance in relation to the self-definition of the Henrician English church. They were not regarded as identity-giving. The Lutheran church in Germany was obliged to define and defend its social existence and boundaries through explicitly doctrinal criteria precisely because it had broken away from the medieval catholic church; the Henrician church in England, however, was both contiguous and continuous with the medieval church at the institutional and social level, ensuring its adequate self-definition without the need to resort to explicitly doctrinal criteria. The English church was sufficiently well defined as a social entity to require no further definition at the doctrinal level.

[193] See, for example, Norman Birnbaum, 'The Zwinglian Reformation in Zurich', *Past and Present* 15 (1959), 27–47; Conradin Bonorand, *Vadians Weg vom Humanismus zur Reformation und seine Vorträge über die Apostelgeschichte (1523)*. St Gallen: Verlag der Fehr'schen Buchhandlung, 1962; Ernst Ziegler, 'Zur Reformation als Reformation des Lebens und der Sitten', *Rorschacher Neujahrsblatt* (1984), 53–71.

[194] 'The one thing that can be said about the Reformation in England is that it was an act of State . . . the Reformation in England was a parliamentary transaction.' F. M. Powicke, *The Reformation in England*. London: Oxford University Press, 1941, 1, 34.

[195] For some examples, see William A. Clebsch, *England's Earliest Protestants, 1520–1535*. Westport, CT: Greenwood Press, 1980; Patrick Collinson, *The Birthpangs of Protestant England: Religious and Cultural Change in the Sixteenth and Seventeenth Centuries*. Basingstoke: Macmillan, 1988, 1–27.

In mainland Europe, however, religious diversity was in the process of becoming institutionalized, with a corresponding need for ecclesial demarcation. A series of Protestant 'Confessions of Faith' emerged over the period 1530–60, designed to distinguish the emerging Protestant ecclesial communities from the medieval church. The primary demarcators were doctrinal, most notably in relation to the doctrine of justification. While such confessions were seen as subordinate to Scripture and the creeds of Christendom, they were nevertheless regarded as definitive by the communities which developed them. The Council of Trent, convened to deal with the Protestant challenge, now found itself faced with an unfamiliar situation. In the past, such councils had merely to define the views of heretics, and reject them. Now, the church was being called upon to define its own teaching, as well as rebut the alternative construals of Christianity which were emanating from northern Europe.

The situation became increasingly complex through political developments, which led to the gradual erosion of the principle *cuius regio eius religio* set out by the Religious Peace of Augsburg (1555), which laid down that certain forms of Christianity were to be regarded as 'established' in certain regions of Germany. Each prince was to determine whether Lutheranism or Roman Catholicism was to prevail in his lands. Dissenters were allowed to emigrate, and the free cities were obligated to allow both Catholics and Lutherans to practise their religions. No account was taken of the growing influence of Calvinism. By 1560, it was clear that the situation was becoming unstable: both Lutheranism and Calvinism were becoming established in Germany, with the result that two rival Protestant ecclesial communities were in contention for allegiance in the region.

The outcome was inevitable: an increased emphasis was placed upon *doctrinal* issues in ecclesial self-definition. This growing emphasis upon doctrinal criteria of demarcation is an integral aspect of the 'Confessionalism' which is so distinctive a feature of the history of this turbulent period.[196] The pressures to distinguish Lutheran and Reformed ecclesial communities were both internal and external: internal, in that each community found itself needing to enhance its sense of identity and solidarity; and

---

[196] See, for example, Thomas Kaufmann, *Universität und lutherische Konfessionalisierung: Die Rostocker Theologieprofessoren und ihr Beitrag zur theologischen Bildung und kirchlichen Gestaltung im Herzogtum Mecklenburg zwischen 1550 und 1675.* Gütersloh: Gerd Mohn, 1997; Wolfgang Zimmermann, *Rekatholisierung, Konfessionalisierung und Ratsregiment: der Prozess des politischen und religiösen Wandels in der österreichischen Stadt Konstanz, 1548–1637.* Sigmaringen: Thorbecke, 1994; Michael G. Müller, *Zweite Reformation und städtische Autonomie im königlichen Preussen: Danzig, Elbing und Thorn in der Epoche der Konfessionalisierung (1557–1660).* Berlin: Akademie Verlag, 1997.

external, in that clear blue theological water needed to be placed between the two bodies for political and social purposes. In consequence, certain existing doctrinal distinctions – most notably, on the issue of predestination[197] – were given an excessive emphasis, reflecting the need to identify and stress points of difference between the communities. Pressure to demarcate led to real yet unexceptional theological differences being given a profile and status determined by the social situation, not the theological issues involved. The social function of a doctrine is thus *standortsgebunden*, determined by the contingencies of the social situation faced by ecclesial communities at a given moment in history. With a change in historical circumstances, that social function can change, even to the point of being eliminated. It is this insight which underlies the ecumenical reconciliations of recent years, to which we now turn.

Ecumenism: the suspension of demarcation

One of the issues which George Lindbeck found puzzling was how doctrines which had been the source of division in the sixteenth century between, for example, Roman Catholics and Lutherans, might be so no longer at later junctures. Did this not mean abandoning the truth of such doctrines, or at least taking certain questionable liberties with them?[198] How, it may be asked, may agreement be reached between Lutherans and Roman Catholics on the doctrine of justification by faith, when this doctrine has traditionally divided their churches?[199] Have they not altered their beliefs, which is unthinkable?

Recognizing that certain doctrines function as social demarcators between ecclesial traditions, and that this function is historically situated, opens the way to an understanding of how ecumenical rapprochement is possible. It is not the truth of certain doctrines that is being denied or marginalized; a social function of those doctrines, specific to a past age, is declared to be no longer valid. Ecumenical agreement on the doctrine of justification involves the recognition that doctrinal

---

[197] See, for example, Gottfried Adam, *Der Streit die Prädestination im ausgehenden 16. Jahrhundert: Eine Untersuchung zu den Entwürfen von Samuel Huber und Aegidius Hunnius.* Neukirchen: Neukirchener Verlag, 1970.

[198] See Geoffrey Wainwright, 'Ecumenical Dimensions of George Lindbeck's "Nature of Doctrine"', *Modern Theology* 4 (1988), 121–32.

[199] For an excellent overview of these debates, see Anthony N. S. Lane, *Justification by Faith in Catholic–Protestant Dialogue: An Evangelical Assessment.* London: T&T Clark, 2002. For a more critical view, see Eberhard Jüngel, *Das Evangelium von der Rechtfertigung des Gottlosen als Zentrum des christlichen Glaubens: Eine theologische Studie in ökumenischer Absicht.* Tübingen: Mohr, 1998.

matters which were, as a matter of historical contingency, essential to the self-definition of either Lutheranism or Roman Catholicism at the time of the Reformation need no longer be regarded as having this function. The self-identity of Lutheranism is no longer perceived to be shaped by this doctrine. No longer need this doctrine serve as a marker of division between the two ecclesial communities.

The recognition of the social function of doctrines in no way weakens their truth-claims. Certain specific contingent historical circumstances lead to the perception that a given doctrine is of normative importance for the self-definition of a community in that situation. The identification of a given doctrine, with its particular emphases, as a criterion of ecclesial demarcation is to be seen as *standortsgebunden*, linked with a specific set of historical circumstances. With the passing of those circumstances, its social function is eroded, possibly to the point at which it plays no significant role. Central to modern ecumenical discussions is the fact that doctrines which functioned as social demarcators in the Reformation period – or other periods of critical importance to the identity of the ecclesial community in question – have lost that function, partly by a process of historical erosion and partly on account of a recent willingness to set that function aside in the interests of the unity of Christendom. No ecclesial body which defines itself totally or largely in relation to a specific set of historical circumstances can avoid shifts in paradigms of self-identity with the progress of time. The theological category of 'truth' has a contingent relationship to the social category of 'demarcator'. Doctrines which once divided communities need do so no longer, while still remaining 'true'.

As we have seen, Christian doctrine represents a principled response to reality, which shapes the identity and outlook of a community which aligns itself with that view of reality, and seeks to preserve and transmit this view from one generation to another. To view Christian doctrine as a principled communal response to reality is to anticipate an engagement with a number of issues to be explored in greater detail later in this volume. The first of these concerns the manner in which Christian theology can represent the reality to which it bears witness, and which is mediated through the Christian tradition – an issue to which we may turn immediately.

Chapter 13

The Representation of Reality in a Scientific Theology

We have argued that theory is to be conceived in terms of a *communal beholding of reality* – not in the form of passive detached observation, but an active and engaged participation, in which seeing gives way to telling, and experiencing to representing. But how might this process of representation take place? How can human language convey the community's understanding of what it has experienced? How can a vision be stated in words? How can its distinctive contours, its impact and meaning, be articulated? An experience cannot be reduced to words; yet words are required if the experience is to be apprehended and appreciated.[1] T. S. Eliot's lines from *The Dry Salvages* succinctly yet elegantly express the problematic of the situation:

> We had the experience but missed the meaning,
> And approach to the meaning restores the experience.

The philosophical question of how language is adapted to the realities it attempts to describe reflects a much wider debate over the issue of 'representation of reality', which is by no means limited to Christian theology or the natural sciences. The complex development of the theory of art illustrates this well.[2] The twentieth century witnessed a substantial reaction against the classical notion that art could in any way be said to 'represent' reality. In his highly influential *Art*, first published in 1914

---

[1] Dan R. Stiver, *The Philosophy of Religious Language: Sign, Symbol and Story.* Oxford: Blackwell, 1996. See also the discussion of six major modes of divine representation in William P. Alston, 'Functionalism and Theological Language', *American Philosophical Quarterly* 22 (1985), 221–30.

[2] See the outstanding collection of material assembled by Charles Harrison and Paul Wood, *Art in Theory, 1900–1990: An Anthology of Changing Ideas.* Oxford: Blackwell, 1993.

and more or less continually reprinted until the eve of the Second World War, Clive Bell (1881–1964) insisted that the representative value of a work of art was of no significance. A work of art, irrespective of what it might be held to represent, provokes 'the personal experience of a peculiar emotion'. It is, he insists, possible to distinguish the aesthetic response evoked by a work of art from that evoked by a natural object, and ultimately to eliminate the necessity of the latter.[3]

> If a representative form has value, it is as form, not as representation. The representative element in a work of art may or may not be harmful; always it is irrelevant. For, to appreciate a work of art we need bring with us nothing from life, no knowledge of its ideas and affairs, no familiarity with its emotions. Art transports us from the world of man's activity to a world of aesthetic exaltation. . . . The pure mathematician rapt in his studies knows a state of mind which I take to be similar, if not identical. He feels an emotion for his speculations which arises from no perceived relation between them and the lives of men, but springs, inhuman or super-human, from the heart of an abstract science.

There is no need for a 'representative element' in a work of art, which is capable of giving rise to 'the aesthetic emotion' without having to represent anything.

Bell's formalism – that is, an emphasis upon the form rather than anything that is held to be represented through such a form – is clearly unpromising as a dialogue partner for a scientific theology. Russian Formalism, especially in the writings of Roman Jakobson (1896–1982) and Viktor Shklovsky (1893–1984),[4] shows a similar distrust of any notion of the literary 'representation of reality'. Like Bell, Shklovsky and others within the Russian Formalist movement reacted against any notion that content was superior to form, and insisted upon the need to engage with the devices and forms which underlie literature *qua* literature.[5] Shklovsky holds it to be axiomatic that literature is derived from other literary sources, and is hostile to any notion of an extra-textual 'reality' which is somehow 'represented' textually. Yet such a firm stand against any notion of 'representation' in art or literature is seen as the premature closure of an important debate.[6] As will become clear, other

---

[3] Clive Bell, *Art*. London: Chatto and Windus, 1914, 27.

[4] Ann Jefferson, 'Russian Formalism', in Ann Jefferson and David Robey (eds), *Modern Literary Theory: A Comparative Introduction*. London: Batsford, 1986, 24–45.

[5] Boris Eikhenbaum, 'The Theory of the "Formal Method"', in *Russian Formalist Criticism: Four Essays*. Lincoln, NE: University of Nebraska Press, 1965, 99–139.

[6] See, for example, the issues explored in David Papineau, *Reality and Representation*. Oxford: Basil Blackwell, 1987; Krzysztof Stala, *On the Margins of Reality: The Paradoxes of*

voices urge a more careful consideration of how art and literature can be said to 'represent' reality. One such discussion is of especial interest for our discussion.

The fundamental theme to be explored by Erich Auerbach (1892–1957) is the manner in which European literature has sought to represent reality. Auerbach's *Mimesis* (1946), widely acknowledged to be one of the finest works of scholarship to have been written, addresses this question in some detail.[7] As is well known, Auerbach's distinguished academic career in law, art history, comparative literature, Romance languages, and Latin philology came to an abrupt end in 1936, when the Nazis came to power. Exiled from his homeland, he spent the next ten years teaching at Istanbul State University where, without the benefit of his personal library or any basic research materials, he produced a detailed study of western culture and imagination that includes extended discussions of writers as diverse as Homer, Dante, Montaigne, Shakespeare, and Goethe – not to mention biblical material.[8]

Whereas his colleague Leo Spitzer attempted to develop an aesthetic programme by concentrating on the linguistic detail of western literature, and Ernst Robert Curtis by cataloguing the literary *topoi* preferred by classical and medieval writers, Auerbach chose to focus on the specific literary styles adopted within western literature, believing that these offered insights into how reality might be defined and represented.[9] His early research into Dante's style convinced him of the importance of certain stylistic traits,[10] especially the concept of *figura*.[11]

Representation in Bruno Schulz's Fiction. Stockholm: Almquist & Wiskell, 1993; Timothy David Barnes, *Ammianus Marcellinus and the Representation of Historical Reality*. Ithaca, NY: Cornell University Press, 1998.

[7] Erich Auerbach, *Mimesis: dargestellte Wirklichkeit in der abendländischen Literatur*, 10th edn. Tübingen: Francke, 2001. More generally, see Seth Lerer (ed.), *Literary History and the Challenge of Philology: The Legacy of Erich Auerbach*. Stanford, CA: Stanford University Press, 1996. This work has spawned a series of works on similar themes. The most interesting for our purposes are A. D. Nuttall, *A New Mimesis: Shakespeare and the Representation of Reality*. London: Methuen, 1983; Karla L. Schultz, *Mimesis on the Move: Theodor W. Adorno's Concept of Imitation*. Berne: Peter Lang, 1990.

[8] A chapter on Cervantes was added to the Spanish edition of 1950, and to German editions after 1949.

[9] For discussion, see Geoffrey Green, *Literary Criticism and the Structures of History: Erich Auerbach and Leo Spitzer*. Lincoln, NE: University of Nebraska Press, 1982; William Calin, 'Ernst Robert Curtius: The Achievement of a Humanist', *Studies in Medievalism* 9 (1997), 218–27; idem, 'Makers of the Middle Ages: Leo Spitzer', *Journal of Medieval and Early Modern Studies* 27 (1997), 495–506.

[10] Erich Auerbach, *Dante als Dichter der irdischen Welt*. Berlin: de Gruyter, 1929.

[11] Erich Auerbach, 'Figura', in *Gesammelte Aufsätze zur romanischen Philologie*. Bern: Francke, 1998, 55–92. The essay was first published in 1938.

As Auerbach defined this understanding of reality, there is an essential continuity within history so that one historical person or event may be thought to prefigure or signify their later counterparts.[12]

> Figural interpretation (*Die Figuraldeutung*) establishes a connection between two events or persons in such a way that the first signifies not only itself but also the second, while the second involves or fulfils the first. The two poles of a figure are separated in time, but both, being real events or persons, are within temporality. They are both contained in the flowing stream which is historical life, and only the comprehension, the *intellectus spiritualis,* of their interdependence is a spiritual act.

A universal vision of history – such as that identified by C. S. Lewis as unifying the medieval religious, scientific and philosophical perspectives[13] – allows genuine historical events and individuals to serve as types or 'figures' of other aspects of a greater reality, without in any way reducing them to mere allegories or dehistoricized entities. Auerbach illustrates this by considering the way in which Dante treats the Roman Empire as a figure of the Kingdom of God in the *Divine Comedy*.[14]

> It is reminiscent of the figure of the earthly and heavenly Jerusalem, and indeed is presented in a completely figural manner. Just as the Judaeo-Christian method of interpretation, consistently applied to the Old Testament by Paul and the church fathers, conceives of Adam as a figure of Christ, and Eve as a figure of the Church, just as generally speaking every phenomenon (*Erscheinung*) and every event (*Ereignis*) referred to in the Old Testament is conceived as a figure which only the phenomena and events of Christ's Incarnation can completely realize or – to use a conventional expression – 'fulfil', so that the Roman Empire here appears as an earthly figure of heavenly fulfilment in the Kingdom of God.

This vigorous defence of historical realism – the figures really existed in history – is accompanied by an insistence that they are understood to possess a capacity to point to and anticipate other aspects of reality.[15]

> I have emphasized that a figural schema (*die figurale Struktur*) permits both its poles – the figure and its fulfilment – to retain the characteristics of concrete historical reality, unlike what results through symbolic or allegorical forms, so that the figure and fulfilment, while one 'signifies' the other, have a significance which is not excluded by their being real. An

[12] Auerbach, *Mimesis*, 75.
[13] C. S. Lewis, *The Discarded Image: An Introduction to Medieval and Renaissance Literature.* Cambridge: Cambridge University Press, 1964.
[14] Auerbach, *Mimesis*, 187.
[15] Auerbach, *Mimesis*, 187.

event taken as a figure preserves its literal and historical meaning; it does not become a mere sign, but remains an event. The church fathers, especially Tertullian, Jerome, and Augustine, successfully defended figural realism, that is, the maintenance of the basic historical reality of figures, against the prevailing currents of spiritual-allegorical interpretation.

What Auerbach designates as a 'figure' is not therefore to be confused with an analogy; rather, it is to be thought of as a specific historical entity with the capacity to relate to another entity within or beyond – given the Christian vision of history being embraced within eternity – the historical process. As Auerbach observes, within such a scheme as Dante's, 'earthly phenomena are on the whole merely figural, potential, and requiring fulfilment'.[16] Auerbach's account of Dante's approach thus firmly anchors theological speculation in genuine events and figures, avoiding any elimination of their historicity or particularities, while affirming their potential for transcendent signification.[17]

Alongside this insistence upon the importance of figures, Auerbach introduces an understanding of the nature of language as it seeks to speak of this transcendent spirituality. It is not necessary, he insists, to develop an elevated language or form of diction to refer to such exalted spiritual matters; the history of the Christian tradition demonstrates that a *sermo humilis* – a low or 'humble' form of diction – can be adopted and developed for the purposes of representing a transcendent reality. Auerbach thus argues for the origination of a new, Romance sublime style in the *sermo humilis* of late Christian antiquity.[18] Words, events, individuals – all were to be seen as possessed of a capacity, when appropriately interpreted by the *intellectus spiritualis*, to point to other aspects of a greater reality.

Such an understanding of the function of language is certainly retrievable, and has arguably persisted throughout the modern period, despite determined efforts to unseat and displace it. In what follows, we shall consider the issue of how a scientific theology may hope to represent the reality of God and the things of God.

---

[16] Auerbach, *Mimesis*, 188.

[17] The contemporary theological importance of Auerbach's approach is not to be overlooked, and is best appreciated by considering Gillian Rose's criticisms of certain aspects of John Milbank's ambitious theological project as 'utopian', in that it undermines – and perhaps even denies – the realities of actual human historical existence. See the occasionally opaque discussion in Lewis Ayres, 'Representation, Theology and Faith', *Modern Theology* 11 (1995), 23–46, especially 25–9.

[18] See especially the essay Erich Auerbach, 'Sacrae Scripturae sermo humilis', *Neuphilologische Mitteilungen* 42 (1941), 57–67.

On modes of representation: some preliminary reflections

Reality demands to be represented, to be expressed in words or images. The theologian is obliged to give an account of the Christian grasp of reality using the means of representation at our disposal which are best adapted to its unique identity and nature. Such an account makes an appeal to the human imagination as much as to the human reason. The distinct, though related, processes of visualization and understanding are both to be seen as integral aspects of the overall Christian attempt to depict reality.

The representation of a stratified reality

A scientific theology holds that reality is *stratified*. We illustrated this point earlier, by considering the World Health Organization's 'International Classification of Impairments, Disabilities and Handicaps' (ICIDH), which recognizes four distinct 'levels' within the complex notion of 'illness'. The critical realist perspective which informs a scientific theology insists upon the recognition of a plurality of levels within reality, each demanding its own distinct mode of investigation and representation. Ontology determines epistemology. This insight has important implications for any attempt to 'represent' reality. For example, it is necessary to note that each level of reality may demand, not merely its own distinct mode of investigation, but its own correspondingly distinct mode of representation. To revert to the ICIDH: biological *pathology* is investigated and represented in a manner which is significantly different from social *participation*.

The stratification of reality also has important consequences for the type of 'understanding' it may elicit. Certain German schools of thought, doubtless in reaction to the overstatements of Comtean positivism during the nineteenth century, have drawn a polemically sharpened distinction between *Erklären* and *Verstehen* – that is, between a causal explanation on the one hand, and an interpretative understanding on the other.[19] The origins of this distinction may be traced back to F. D. E. Schleiermacher and Wilhelm Dilthey, who shifted the focus of hermeneutical engagement from 'texts' in the strict sense of that term to all human productions or creations, whether textual or nontextual. In part, Dilthey sought to respond to the positivist insistence that all valid

---

[19] For a survey, see Karl-Otto Apel, 'The Erklären–Verstehen Controversy in the Philosophy of the Natural and Human Sciences', in G. Floistad (ed.), *Contemporary Philosophy: A New Survey*. The Hague: Nijhof, 1982, 19–49. Apel's own influential account of the distinction may be found in Karl-Otto Apel, *Die Erklären–Verstehen Kontroverse in transzendentalpragmatischer Sicht*. Frankfurt am Main: Suhrkamp, 1979.

human knowledge must arise through the methods of the physical sciences, whose explanatory successes were increasingly regarded as epistemologically privileged. In countering this trend, Dilthey argued that the fundamental difference between the *Geisteswissenschaften* and the *Naturwissenschaften* lay in their respective objects of study and the methodologies these demanded: '*Naturwissenschaften* explain (*erklären*) nature, *Geisteswissenschaften* understand (*verstehen*) expressions of life.'[20]

Explanation in the natural sciences therefore comprehends its object through causal connections; it may be said to 'know' its object from the outside. Understanding in the human sciences, however, may be said to 'know' its object – which is a human being or a human production – from the inside. To speak of 'understanding' or 'explanation' is thus to become embroiled in a verbal battlefield, ultimately reflecting the belief that there existed an 'absolute contrast between the science of the physical non-human world of nature and the science of the world of mind, of culture and of history'.[21]

A stratified understanding of reality, such as that posited by critical realism, renders this absolute distinction untenable. If the human sciences can be sciences 'in exactly the same sense, though not in exactly the same way' as the natural sciences – I here borrow the celebrated distinction of Roy Bhaskar[22] – then an essential continuity of understanding and explanation must be posited throughout the spectrum of the sciences.[23] While different strata must be handled in different manners, reflecting their individual identity, any notion of an *absolute* distinction of method must be abandoned in terms of a spectrum of methodologies, each adapted to the nature of the level of reality under study.

The affirmation of a stratified creation is entirely in keeping with the Christian understanding of the nature of the world. Brooke Foss Westcott (1825–1901), one of the most creative Anglican theologians of the nineteenth century to give sustained attention to the doctrine of creation,[24] was adamant that the notion of a stratified (or 'hierarchical')

---

[20] Lothar Bredella's distinction between the individual subject as 'sense-producing' (*sinnsetzend*) and 'sense-discovering' (*sinndeutend*) may also be noted here: Lothar Bredella, *Das Verstehen literarischer Texte*. Stuttgart: Kohlhammer, 1980, 38–42. For further reflections, see Lothar Bredella, *Literarisches und interkulturelles Verstehen*. Tübingen: Gunter Narr, 2002.

[21] Roy Bhaskar, *The Possibility of Naturalism: A Philosophical Critique of the Contemporary Human Sciences*, 3rd edn. London: Routledge, 1998, 18.

[22] Bhaskar, *The Possibility of Naturalism*, 159.

[23] For Bhaskar's own account of explanation in a critical realist context, see Roy Bhaskar, *A Realist Theory of Science*, 2nd edn. London: Verso, 1997.

[24] See Brooke Foss Westcott, 'The Gospel of Creation', in *The Epistles of St John*. London: Macmillan, 1892, 285–328.

natural order was entirely consonant with the biblical witness and Christian tradition. There is, he argued, a 'hierarchy of sciences, which are severally subordinated one to another, and each regulated by its peculiar laws'.[25] Theology is the highest such science, and builds upon the insights of lower sciences, such as biology and chemistry. And precisely because it stands at the apex of the hierarchy of sciences, theology is able – and obligated – to 'take account of the "whole"' – that is to say, to offer, as best it can, a total vision of the God who is known in creation and redemption, to which the lesser sciences bear witness.[26] A scientific theology, by affirming a Christian doctrine of creation, set firmly within the context of the economy of salvation as a whole, is thus able to evoke a vision of God in which the entire fabric of nature, human history and culture witnesses to the divine glory and wonder.

But are words capable of even beginning to capture or convey such a vision of God? The theologian is faced with the uncomfortable insight that the words at our disposal are inadequate to the demands that we place upon them. As Wittgenstein once pointed out, human words cannot even describe the aroma of coffee.[27] How can they conceivably depict the Christian vision of God? In what follows, we shall begin to engage with these issues.

Representation through words

The advance of knowledge demands a corresponding advance in human language. As new entities are uncovered, and new patterns of relationships between existing entities established, the pressure to devise a new vocabulary grows correspondingly. There are two quite distinct forces at work here, which must be distinguished with some care. On the one hand, there is the general process of linguistic development, which is catalysed by a variety of factors, including technological advance and growing awareness of other cultures. On the other, there is a much more specific pressure to be able to describe or discuss something *new*, either by coining new terms or adapting existing words in order that they might accommodate such novelties.

The first point is of considerable historical interest and of no small importance to Christian theology. Languages evolve in response to a

[25] Brooke Foss Westcott, *The Gospel of the Resurrection: Thoughts on its Relation to Reason and History*, 8th edn. London: Macmillan, 1891, 259.

[26] Brooke Foss Westcott, *Lessons from Work*. London: Macmillan, 1901, 41.

[27] For comment, see Fergus Kerr, *Theology after Wittgenstein*. Oxford: Blackwell, 1988, 162–7; Simon Blackburn, 'How to Refer to Private Experience', *Proceedings of the Aristotelian Society* 75 (1974), 201–14.

variety of pressures, precisely because they are living and public entities. The development of the English language during the sixteenth century illustrates this point particularly well.[28] During a period of increasing scientific, theological and philosophical advance, medieval English found itself creaking under the pressure to cope with an explosion of new ideas and approaches. Many argued that the solution was to coin new words, based on classic Greek and Latin, to deal with this conceptual crisis of vocabulary. Sir Thomas Elyot (c. 1490–1546) produced an important treatise on what would now be termed 'neologisms' (from the Greek for 'new words') in a deliberate attempt to develop and improve the English language.[29]

This was fiercely resisted by more reactionary writers. Sir John Cheke (1514–57), the first Regius Professor of Greek at the University of Cambridge, was strongly opposed to what his colleague Roger Ascham (1515–68) dismissively referred to as 'inkhorn' terms – that is, words which were coined from Latin or Greek to make the resulting English words sound more sophisticated and dignified.[30] Cheke applied this principle particularly to biblical translation, producing highly idiosyncratic translations of the gospels in which he attempted to avoid as many classical terms as possible, and replace them with Anglo-Saxon equivalents. Examples of Cheke's curious attempts to eliminate 'inkhorn' religious and theological terms include the following: 'frosent' (for 'apostle'); 'hundreder' (for 'centurion'); 'crossed' (for 'crucified'); 'mooned' (for 'lunatic'); 'byword' (for 'parable'); 'uprising' (for 'resurrection'); and 'wizards' (for 'wise men').

In 1587, Arthur Golding set out to develop a new English technical vocabulary, capable of meeting the growing needs of the arts and sciences, which drew on Anglo-Saxon rather than classical roots.[31] Some examples of his recommendations: 'threlike' (for 'equilateral triangle'); 'likejamme' (for 'parallelogram'); 'endsay' (for 'conclusion'); and 'saywhat' (for 'definition'). In every case, the classical alternative would pass into general use, despite Golding's vigorous rearguard action.

Cheke and Golding thus fought a losing battle. English went on to develop its vocabulary in response to a variety of stimuli, losing some

[28] N. F. Blake, *A History of the English Language*. Basingstoke: Macmillan, 1996.

[29] John M. Major, *Sir Thomas Elyot and Renaissance Humanism*. Lincoln, NE: University of Nebraska Press, 1964.

[30] See Hugh Sykes Davies, 'Sir John Cheke and the Translation of the Bible', *Essays and Studies* 5 (1952), 1–12. Cheke's translation was finally published in 1843, tending to be viewed as a quaint intellectual curiosity: John Cheke, *The Gospel according to St. Matthew and Part of the First Chapter of the Gospel according to St. Mark*. London: William Pickering, 1843.

[31] Louis Thorn Golding, *An Elizabethan Puritan: Arthur Golding, the Translator of Ovid's Metamorphoses and also of John Calvin's Sermons*. Freeport, NY: Books for Libraries Press, 1971.

older words, coining new ones, and adapting others to new ends. Thus Robert Cawdry's *A Table Alphabetical* (1604) listed 2,500 unusual or borrowed words, on the assumption that many of his readers would not yet be familiar with them. John Bullokar's *An English Expositor* (1616) listed older native English words which had now become archaic on account of the 'loan words' which had gradually displaced them.

Yet it is the second aspect of the question which particularly concerns us. Discovery demands representation, and hence advances in terminology. An excellent example is provided by the discovery of the electron by J. J. Thomson in 1897. After exhaustive experimentation, Thomson announced his conclusion 'that "negative electrification" is made up of units each having "a charge of electricity of a definite size"' and that 'the magnitude of this negative charge is equal to the positive charge carried by the hydrogen atom (ion) in the electrolysis of solutions'. This hitherto unknown particle demanded a name; standing in the tradition advocated by Thomas Elyot (and excoriated by John Cheke), Thomson coined the term 'electron' to refer to his new discovery.[32] In this instance, a new term was coined to denote a new reality – in much the same manner as the terms 'mitochondria', 'quarks' and 'entropy'.

The situation within Christian theology is somewhat more complex. Certain new, often inelegant, terms have been minted by theological educationalists to denote specific areas or themes in theology – such as 'sacramentology', 'ecclesiology' and 'hamartiology'. These have relatively little importance, in that they are essentially jargon used to designate existing notions referred to in rather more lengthy, if more lucid, manners – for example, 'the doctrine of sin'. Yet it is important to appreciate that the Christian theological community has on occasion found itself under pressure to develop a new theological term to articulate a theological insight which could not be expressed adequately by the mere repetition or rearrangement of existing biblical terms. An excellent example is provided by Athanasius's growing recognition that the clumsy non-biblical term ὁμοούσιος had to be used to do justice to the crystallizing perceptions of the church over the true identity of Christ, and the best manner of conceptualizing this.[33] Athanasius initially pre-

---

[32] Abraham Pais, 'The Early History of the Theory of the Electron: 1897–1947', in A. Salam and E. P. Wigner (eds), *Aspects of Quantum Theory*. Cambridge: Cambridge University Press, 1972, 79–92.

[33] Adolf M. Ritter, *Das Konzil von Konstantinopel und sein Symbol: Studien zur Geschichte und Theologie des II. Ökumenischen Konzils*. Göttingen: Vandenhoeck & Ruprecht, 1965, 270–93. For useful background, see Wolfgang A. Bienert, 'Das vornicaenische ὁμοούσιος als Ausdruck der Rechtgläubigkeit', *Zeitschrift für Kirchengeschichte* 90 (1979), 5–29; U. M. Lang, 'The Christological Controversy at the Synod of Antioch in 268/9', *Journal of Theological Studies* 51 (2000), 54–80.

ferred to use more circumstantial modes of expression – such as ὅμοις κατ᾽ οὐσίαν. Gradually, however, he came to realize the need for the more precise technical term ὁμοούσιος. As the history of the reception of the term makes clear, there was resistance to it, not least on account of a reluctance to accept verbal innovations absent from Scripture.[34] Yet within a generation, the term had become the accepted means of summarizing the Christian community's decisive and distinctive understanding of the person of Christ.[35]

Yet the dominant pattern of theological development has been that of adopting existing terms, and reinterpreting them in a manner which is consonant with the Christian vision of God, as expressed in the economy of salvation. An excellent example of this second pattern of development can be seen in the Christian use of the term 'salvation', a term already widely used within the religious traditions of the Mediterranean world of the classical and late classical periods.[36] Here, an existing word has developed a specific meaning within the Christian tradition on account of the associations imposed by that tradition – a process noted by Karl Barth, who spoke of the manner in which the terms of the 'spoken matter of proclamation' in the Christian faith 'acquire their meaning from the associations and contexts in which they are used'.[37] For Ludwig Wittgenstein, the *Lebensform* ('form of living') within which a word was used was of decisive importance in establishing the meaning of that word. The Christian *Lebensform* is thus of controlling importance in understanding what the Christian concept of salvation implies, presupposes and expresses. As Wittgenstein himself pointed out, the same word can be used in a large number of senses. One way of dealing with this would be to invent a totally new vocabulary, in which the meaning of each word was tightly and unequivocally defined. But this is not realistic, in that languages, like religions, are living entities, and cannot be forced to behave in such an artificial way. A perfectly acceptable approach, according to Wittgenstein, is to take trouble to define the particular sense in which a word should be understood, in order to avoid confusion with its many other senses. This involves a careful study of its associations and its use in the 'form of living

---

[34] Wilhelm Gessel, 'Das "homoousios" als Testfall für die Frage nach der Geltung und dem Verhältnis von Schrift und Tradition auf dem Konzil von Nizäa', *Annuarium Historiae Conciliorum. Internationale Zeitschrift für Konziliengeschichtsforschung* 17 (1985), 1–7.

[35] J. N. D. Kelly, *Early Christian Creeds*, 3rd edn. New York: Longman, 1981, 242–54.

[36] Franz Jung, *Soter: Studien zur Rezeption eines hellenistischen Ehrentitels im Neuen Testament.* Münster: Aschendorff, 2002.

[37] Karl Barth, *Church Dogmatics* I/1, 86.

(*Lebensform*)' to which it relates.[38] 'Salvation' is clearly a case in point. Its use and associations within the Christian tradition, especially in worship, point to a distinctive understanding of what the Christian faith is understood to confer upon believers, its ultimate basis, and the manner in which this comes about.[39]

An examination of the Christian *Lebensform* reveals that, while Christianity may indeed use a common word, it invests it with its own distinctive tradition-specific and tradition-mediated meaning. Thus Christianity has a particular understanding of the nature, grounds and means of obtaining salvation. For example, the Christian understanding of salvation, like the Christian notion of God, is Christologically determined. Equally, the Christian understanding of what form that salvation takes is distinctive, reflecting the belief that Christ is both the basis and the norm of the Christian life.[40] Christian ethics is shaped by the beliefs and *Lebensform* of the Christian community.[41]

Similarly, Christianity uses the simple term 'God' to designate the self-revealing reality which it affirms and discerns to lie behind the economy of salvation. But the associations and connotations of this term are determined by that economy of salvation.[42] The history of the Christian understanding of the word 'God' can be seen in terms of the affirmation and appropriation of the distinctiveness of the God of Israel in relation to the divinities of its pagan neighbours in the Ancient Near East,[43] followed by a period of complex negotiation as the church sought to preserve the unique identity of the 'God and Father of our

---

[38] Ludwig Wittgenstein, *Lectures and Conversations on Aesthetics, Psychology and Religious Belief.* Oxford: Blackwell, 1966, 2: 'If I had to say what is the main mistake made by philosophers . . . I would say that it is that when language is looked at, what is looked at is a form of words and not the use made of the form of words.' For further discussion, see Fergus Kerr, *Theology after Wittgenstein.* Oxford: Blackwell, 1988.

[39] See the important discussion in Joseph-Augustine Di Noia, *The Diversity of Religions: A Christian Perspective.* Washington, DC: Catholic University of America Press, 1992.

[40] See the analysis of Richard B. Hays, *The Moral Vision of the New Testament: Community, Cross, New Creation.* Edinburgh: T&T Clark, 1997.

[41] A point stressed repeatedly by Stanley Hauerwas, especially in *A Community of Character.* Notre Dame, IN: University of Notre Dame Press, 1981; and *In Good Company: The Church as Polis.* Notre Dame, IN: University of Notre Dame Press, 1995. On Hauerwas's communitarian and tradition-specific ethic, see Arne Rasmusson, *The Church as Polis: From Political Theology to Theological Politics as Exemplified by Jürgen Moltmann and Stanley Hauerwas.* Lund: Lund University Press, 1994.

[42] A point stressed by Robert W. Jenson, *The Triune Identity: God According to the Gospel.* Philadelphia: Fortress, 1982.

[43] See the important study of Mark S. Smith, *The Origins of Biblical Monotheism: Israel's Polytheistic Background and the Ugaritic Texts.* Oxford: Oxford University Press, 2001, which clarifies many aspects of the distinctiveness of Israel's religious views.

Lord Jesus Christ' (2 Corinthians 1:3) in the face of assimilationist pressure in relation to the secular concepts of divinity prevalent in Hellenistic culture.[44]

Words, then, play a critical role in the theological enterprise. It is essential to determine what those words mean by considering their contexts and use, rather than assuming that their 'common' usage can be directly transferred to theological concepts. Alan of Lille discussed this issue during the theological renaissance of the twelfth century, pointing out that any terms predicated of God are 'transferred from their proper signification (*transfertur a sua propria significatione*)'; transference of the term (*nomen*) could not be allowed to entail the transference of its meaning (*res*).[45] Theological terms thus possessed 'borrowed meanings' which stood in a complex relationship to their original contexts, making the task of clarifying their relationship of critical theological importance.[46]

As the history of Christian thought makes clear, the community of faith struggled to find a vocabulary adequate to the vision of reality disclosed in the gospel. The old linguistic wineskins proved incapable of containing the new revelatory wine. While generalizations in such a complex field are potentially simplistic, it may nevertheless be suggested that the Christian vocabulary has emerged by a dual process of verbal innovation and renovation, in which new words were coined and older words adopted with new meanings in the face of the conceptual demands of the Christian vision of reality. The meaning of those words was determined and shaped by the Christian understanding of the economy of salvation.

Although Ludwig Wittgenstein and Martin Heidegger had quite different understandings of the nature of language, they were nevertheless united in one important respect: the recognition that issues of representation or communication could not be resolved simply in terms of

---

[44] For some such concepts of divinity, see H. S. Versnel, *Ter Unus: Isis, Dionysos, Hermes. Three Studies in Henotheism*. Leiden: Brill, 1990. For more general considerations, see Wolfhart Pannenberg, 'The Appropriation of the Philosophical Concept of God as a Dogmatic Problem of Early Christian Theology', in *Basic Questions in Theology II*. London: SCM Press, 1971, 119–83; R. B. Edwards, 'The Pagan Dogma of the Absolute Unchangeableness of God', *Religious Studies* 14 (1975), 305–13; Joseph C. McLelland, *God the Anonymous: A Study in Alexandrian Philosophical Theology*. Cambridge, MA: Philadelphia Patristic Foundation, 1976.

[45] Alan of Lille, *Regulae Theologicae* 26. See further Gillian R. Evans, *Alan of Lille: The Frontiers of Theology in the Later Twelfth Century*. Cambridge: Cambridge University Press, 1983, 29–33.

[46] For a discussion of the issues, see G. R. Evans, 'The Borrowed Meaning: Grammar, Logic and the Problem of Theological Language in Twelfth-Century Schools', *Downside Review* 96 (1978), 165–75.

vocabulary – in other words, the identification and analysis of individual words.[47] Words are one thing; the relation of words one to another
represents something quite different, and potentially immensely important. We must therefore move on and consider the place of propositions
in an account of reality offered by a scientific theology.

Representation through propositions

How can reality be reduced to propositions? The critics of dogma in the
1880s declared their hostility to any attempt to 'limit infinite truth
within definite formulae'.[48] For James Orr, unless this 'infinite truth' can
in some way be represented or communicated in words, 'theology
nothing to work on'. Yet Orr was something of a voice crying in the
wilderness. The idea that propositions can be of service to theology continued to be subjected to something approaching utter ridicule in the
closing decades of the twentieth century.[49] The stridently anti-proposi-
tional attitude of George Lindbeck's *Nature of Doctrine* (1980) both
reflects and perpetuates this settled attitude. What Lindbeck designates
as a 'cognitive-propositionalist' understanding of doctrine is a caricature
of how traditional Christian theology has conceived and expressed this
notion; nevertheless, Lindbeck's comments reflect the mood of an anti-
cognitive age, which found appeals to experience or culture more fruitful than what was (prematurely, it must be said) regarded as an
outmoded propositionalism.

In part, the impetus for this critique of propositions in representing
highly complex entities has arisen from the study of classical philosophy,
particularly Plato's theory of Forms. As has often been observed, Plato
attaches an almost religious significance to 'knowing' the Forms.[50] In the
Republic, Plato argues that a proper understanding of the material world
can only result when the essential characteristics of things are separated
and distinguished from their accidental features and superficial appearances. Human sensory perceptions may disclose only something of the
superficial appearance of things, which has no particular value in

---

[47] Anton Grabner-Haider, *Semiotik und Theologie: religiöse Rede zwischen analytischer und hermeneutischer Philosophie*. Munich: Kösel, 1973, 51–143; Anthony C. Thiselton, *The Two Horizons: New Testament Hermeneutics and Philosophical Description with Special Reference to Heidegger, Bultmann, Gadamer, and Wittgenstein*. Exeter: Paternoster, 1980, 24–50, 357–85.

[48] James Orr, *The Christian View of God and the World, as Centring in the Incarnation*. New York: Charles Scribner's Sons, 1908, 26.

[49] See the excellent analysis of Colin E. Gunton, *A Brief Theology of Revelation*. Edinburgh: T&T Clark, 1995, 7–17.

[50] See, for example, Gregory Vlastos, *Platonic Studies*. Princeton, NJ: Princeton University Press, 1981, 43–57.

rationally comprehending the world. Thus Plato is severely critical of artists, whom he regards as being fixated on such outward appearances, and failing to penetrate to the true state of affairs.[51]

To understand a thing properly, we must use our rational natures to know the Forms.[52] Such Forms are required not only to comprehend the material world, but also to understand the manner in which language itself functions, and how it is to be used properly. We come to understand things in the material world by applying to them objective, unambiguous categories; but those categories cannot be identified with anything in the complex amalgam of impulses we perceive through the senses. Plato thus concludes that true knowledge – as opposed to mere opinion or belief – must be predicated upon the Forms.[53] For Plato, such Forms serve two decisively important epistemological functions: in the first place, they are to be regarded as 'universals' – that is, the properties in which things that are properly described as 'good' or 'beautiful' or 'righteous' must participate (at least, to some degree or extent);[54] and in the second, they are to be recognized as the true paradigms of those common names – the perfect instantiations or defining 'paradigms' of goodness, beauty, or righteousness, with which everyone who hopes to understand the concepts must be acquainted.[55] Knowledge of such Forms is thus of critical importance to philosophy, as Plato understands that activity.

But what form does that knowledge take? The prevailing assumption within much twentieth-century philosophy has been that Plato assumes that it takes the form of 'knowledge by acquaintance' – that is to say, a form of personal knowledge which is necessarily non-propositional in character.[56] Yet in an important survey of what he styles 'myths about non-propositional thought' in classical philosophy, Richard Sorabji has pointed out how propositional elements are deeply embedded in Plato's

---

[51] *Republic* 597a–588e; 601c–602b. For Iris Murdoch's fascinating engagement with Plato's views at this point, see Iris Murdoch, *The Fire and the Sun: Why Plato Banished the Artists.* London: Chatto & Windus, 1990.

[52] On which see R. E. Allen, 'Participation and Predication in Plato's Middle Dialogues', in *Studies in Plato's Metaphysics.* London: Routledge & Kegan Paul, 1965, 43–60.

[53] Gail Fine, 'Knowledge and Belief in *Republic* V', *Archiv für Geschichte der Philosophie* 60 (1978), 121–39.

[54] Gerasimos Santas, 'The Form of the Good in Plato's *Republic*', in J. Anton and A. Preuss (eds), *Essays in Ancient Greek Philosophy*, vol. 2. Albany, NY: State University of New York Press, 1983, 232–63.

[55] *Republic* 476c. For comment and criticism, see David Bostock, *Plato's 'Theaetetus'.* Oxford: Clarendon Press, 1991, 17.

[56] For example, see R. S. Bluck, 'Knowledge by Acquaintance in Plato's *Theaetetus*', *Mind* 72 (1963), 259–63.

understanding of the Forms – as they are throughout classical philosophy.[57] Sorabji cites *Republic* 534b–c to make his point:[58]

> Do you not call a man a dialectician, if he gets an account (*logos*) of the being (*ousia*) of each thing? And will you not deny that a man understands something if he does not have such an account, and in so far as he cannot give an account of the thing to himself or others? . . . . And is it not, then, similar with goodness? If someone cannot define (*diorisasthai*) the Form of the Good with an account, separating it from all other things; if he cannot come through all refutations (*elenchoi*) as if in battle; if he does not desire to produce real refutations rather than merely seeming ones; if he does not in all these things journey through with an unfaltering account; will you not deny that such a man knows goodness itself, or anything else that is good?

Sorabji has clearly not demonstrated that Plato's understanding of 'knowledge' of the Platonic Forms is to be envisaged *purely*, or even *predominantly*, as propositional; there are far too many references within the *Republic* and the *Phaedo* which clearly presuppose 'knowledge by acquaintance' to permit any such conclusion. Yet there is no doubt that Sorabji has persuasively shown that Plato's account of the manner in which the Forms are to be known cannot be construed *solely* as 'knowledge by acquaintance'.[59]

On the basis of this analysis of Plato's dialectic, the demand that 'an account be given of the being of each thing' can be seen as a propositionalist component within a complex overall notion of knowledge, involving both 'knowledge by acquaintance' and 'knowledge as statement'. The same has long been recognized in the case of a Christian understanding of revelation, in which the potentially vacuous notion of 'knowing God by acquaintance' is supplemented – but not displaced – by the notion of knowing certain things *about* God. As P. T. Forsyth stressed, the Christian vision of truth is not to be thought of in purely 'propositional or statutory' terms, as if it were solely a 'plexus of doctrine'; rather, it is a revelation of 'spiritual reality, divine life, personal grace' which calls out to be communicated and expressed in words, even though this reality ultimately transcends any such words.[60] Forsyth's

---

[57] Richard Sorabji, *Time, Creation and the Continuum: Theories in Antiquity and the Early Middle Ages*. London: Duckworth, 1983, 137–56.

[58] I must make it clear that the understanding of dialectic set out at 532a5–b5 and 534b3–d1 differs from that found at 510b and 511b3–c2.

[59] Sorabji, *Time, Creation and the Continuum*, 142–4.

[60] P. T. Forsyth, *The Principle of Authority in Relation to Certainty, Sanctity, and Society. An Essay in the Philosophy of Experimental Religion*, 2nd edn. London: Independent Press, 1952, 53.

analysis points to a danger which attends any attempt to theologize, and one that must be taken with the utmost seriousness – namely, the temptation to *replace* the category of personal relationship with propositions in any conceptualization of the gospel. The two belong together; to displace one by the other is to impoverish, and even to distort, the greater reality to which theology bears witness.

Engagement with the natural sciences allows a similar point to be made. It is perfectly possible to summarize a complex set of observations using propositional statements. As an example, we may consider Isaac Newton's reflections on the behaviour of bodies in response to various forces applied to them. Using the three basic concepts of space, time and mass, Newton set out three propositions which he believed to account for all his observations to date, while at the same time predicting the future action of similar objects.[61]

1. Every body continues in its state of rest or of uniform motion in a right line unless it is compelled to change that state by forces impressed upon it.

2. The change of motion is proportional to the motive force impressed and is made in the direction of the right line in which that force is impressed.

3. To every action there is always opposed an equal reaction; or, the mutual actions of two bodies upon each other are always equal and directed to contrary parts.

Each of these statements is capable of being expressed mathematically. Yet Newton chose to set them out as propositional statements, believing – correctly, as events would demonstrate – that they referred to certain quite definite events in the world, while at the same time pointing to some deeper truth which lay behind them. This does not involve *reducing* nature to words, but to using the interrelation of words – to the extent that this is possible – to represent what may be known about nature.

Similar comments must be made concerning theological statements. These are not to be conceived as abstract and disembodied, but as having their origins and validation in the economy of salvation. For example, consider the following propositional statement: 'God is love'

---

[61] For an excellent account, see Peter Guthrie Tait, *Newton's Laws of Motion*. London: A&C Black, 1899. This account is especially interesting from an historical point of view, as it shows no awareness of the modifications that would later require to be introduced to Newtonian kinematics in consequence of either quantum mechanics or general relativity.

(1 John 4:8, 16).[62] This definition is both grounded and embodied in the economy of salvation, in that the love of God is affirmed to be demonstrated in the death of Christ on the cross (1 John 4:9). Far from being a proposition derived from *a priori* theological axioms – to note a distinguishing theological pretension of the Enlightenment – it represents an *a posteriori* account of the significance of the economy of salvation, seen from the unique perspective of the Christian tradition. The love of God is revealed and given ostensive definition through the economy of salvation.

To declare that 'God is love' involves affirming a statement, and subsequently clarifying the relation of its terms.[63] Yet the Christian revelation is by no means constituted solely, or even predominantly, by such prepositional forms. Narratives – such as the story of the prodigal son, or the journey of Israel from Egypt to the promised land – and images form an integral element of the Christian attempt to envision God. So in what way can reality be represented through images?

Representation through images

'A "picture" (*Bild*) held us captive. And we could not get outside it, for it lay in our language and language seemed to repeat it to us inexorably.'[64] Wittgenstein here expresses both the importance of images to the philosophical and theological tasks and their intimate bonding to human language. It has often been observed that humanity possesses the capacity to think. Perhaps it is still better observed that it possesses the unique capacity to *imagine*. Our understanding of the universe, God and ourselves is primarily controlled by images, rather than concepts. Human language finds itself pressed to its limits when trying to depict and describe the divine. Words and images are borrowed from everyday life, and put to new uses in an attempt to capture and preserve precious insights into the nature of God.[65] The Christian understanding of both the divine and human natures is such that – if it is right – we are unable

---

[62] For comment on the Greek text, see Brooke Foss Westcott, *The Epistles of St John*. London: Macmillan, 1892, 148, 156–7.

[63] The theological debate over the theological function of 'sentences' during the later Middle Ages remains instructive, not least because of its anticipation of some Wittgensteinian themes. See Fritz Hoffmann, 'Der Satz als Zeichen der theologischen Aussage bei Holcot, Crathorn und Gregor von Rimini', in Albert Zimmermann (ed.), *Der Begriff der Repräsentatio im Mittelalter: Stellvertretung, Symbol, Zeichen, Bild*. Berlin: de Gruyter, 1971, 296–313. On Gregory of Rimini's views on the matter, see Mario Del Fra, 'La teoria dei "significato totale" delle propositione nel pensiero di Gregorio da Rimini', *Rivista critica di storia della filosofia* 11 (1956), 287–311.

[64] Ludwig Wittgenstein, *Philosophical Investigations*, 3rd edn. Oxford: Blackwell, 1968, §115.

[65] John Bowker, *The Religious Imagination and the Sense of God*. Oxford: Clarendon, 1978.

to grasp the full reality of God. Can the human mind ever hope to comprehend something which must ultimately lie beyond its ability to enfold?

The Christian tradition holds that there are limits placed upon the human ability to grasp the things of God. Our knowledge of God is accommodated to our capacity. As writers from Augustine to Calvin argued, God is perfectly aware of the limitations placed upon human nature – which, after all, is itself a divine creation. Knowing our limits, such writers argued, God both discloses divine truths and enters into our world in forms that are tempered to our limited abilities and competencies.[66] Familiar images from the world around us become windows of perception into the nature and purposes of God. The parables of Jesus Christ are perhaps the most familiar example of this: an everyday event (a sower sowing seed in the fields), or a keenly observed event (a woman's joy on finding a lost coin), or a cultural situation becomes the means by which deeper spiritual truths are disclosed.[67] The woman's joy becomes a powerful symbol of the delight of God when wayward humanity returns home to its tender creator and redeemer. Yet this is not an arbitrary association or connection; it is one which Christians hold to be divinely *authorized.*

This is perhaps best seen in the Old Testament images of God, which are developed and given still greater impact in the New. As the Oxford scholar and theologian Austin Farrer argued, Christianity represents a 'rebirth of images', in terms of both the importance assigned to images in conceiving and sustaining the Christian life and the new impetus given to the religious imagery which the church inherited from Israel.[68] To speak of God as 'king', 'shepherd' or 'mother' is to draw upon a richly textured biblical tradition, which authorizes its users to speak of God in this manner, and whose imagery engages both mind and imagination in a sustained process of reflection and internal appropriation. Such analogies were drawn from the ancient near eastern world of everyday experience; they nevertheless possessed the capacity to point beyond themselves, signifying something of a greater reality lying beyond them and the world which contained them.

Yet why are such images capable of reflecting God's nature? Is this

[66] See, for example, Stephen D. Benin, *The Footprints of God: Divine Accommodation in Jewish and Christian Thought.* Albany: State University of New York, 1993.

[67] For examples, see Mary Ann Tolbert, *Sowing the Gospel: Mark's World in Literary-Historical Perspective.* Minneapolis: Fortress Press, 1989; Warren Carter, 'Resisting and Imitating the Empire: Imperial Paradigms in Two Matthean Parables', *Interpretation* 56 (2002), 260–72.

[68] Austin Farrer, *A Rebirth of Images: The Making of St John's Apocalypse.* London: Dacre Press, 1949.

capacity intrinsic to them? Or is it acquired, perhaps through some external process of authorization or internal process of illumination? In support of the former possibility, it may be noted that both a Christian doctrine of creation and a Platonic doctrine of Forms point to a form of created correspondence between images within the material world and what lies beyond it. Thus one of the most distinctive features of the Italian Renaissance is its pervasive belief that images of reality are in some way determined by that reality, so that there is at least some degree of ontological transference between reality and its images and shadows. Giambattista Vico once commented that it was a distinctive 'property of the human mind, that whenever men can form no idea of distant and unknown things, they judge them by what is familiar and at hand'.[69] This important Vichian analogical principle reflects the pervasive belief of the Italian Renaissance that the relation between symbol and original is ontologically grounded, rather than accidental. Marsilio Ficino's doctrine of the resemblance between a symbol and its original ultimately rests on a Neoplatonic understanding of the relation of the world of senses and ideas.[70] As E. H. Gombrich pointed out in a classic essay, the rich and complex iconography of the Renaissance was ultimately grounded in the belief that the visual image and the reality which it depicted were connected through the Neoplatonic notion of a 'Great Chain of Being', so that the former might somehow intrinsically reflect the latter.[71] Yet the situation is more complex than this, as Karl Barth's formidable criticism of the notion of any 'analogy of being' (*analogia entis*) makes clear. We shall presently move on to a detailed analysis of the place of analogies in a scientific theology.

Yet we must consider a further point before doing so. For some writers, an appeal to religious images is a means of subverting cognitive theistic statements. An excellent example is provided by Paul Tillich's conception of a 'symbol', which he holds to be 'a representation of that which is unconditionally beyond the conceptual sphere'.[72] It is the task of theology 'to interpret symbols':[73]

---

[69] Giovanni Vico, *The New Science*. Ithaca, NY: Cornell University Press, 1968, 60. See further Donald Phillip Verene, *Vico's Science of Imagination*. Ithaca, NY: Cornell University Press, 1981.

[70] Paul Oskar Kristeller, *The Philosophy of Marsilio Ficino*. New York: Columbia University Press, 1943, 96–8.

[71] E. H. Gombrich, '*Icones Symbolicae*: The Visual Image in Neoplatonic Thought', *Journal of the Courtauld and Warburg Institutes* 11 (1948), 163–92.

[72] Paul Tillich, 'The Religious Symbol', in Sidney Hook (ed.), *Religious Experience and Truth: A Symposium*. New York: New York University Press, 1961, 301–23, 303.

[73] Paul Tillich, *Systematic Theology*, 3 vols. Chicago: University of Chicago Press, 1951, vol. 1, 240.

This double meaning of the truth of a symbol must be kept in mind. A symbol has truth adequate to the revelation it expresses. A symbol is true; it is the expression of a true revelation.

In Tillich's view, God's 'otherness' or transcendence is such that God must be revealed symbolically; otherwise, God is reduced to verbal expressions or concepts, and hence robbed of transcendence. An appeal to the symbolic serves, for Tillich, as a critical reminder of the limitations placed upon theological language.

Important though Tillich's affirmations may be, the fundamental limitations placed upon symbols, by their very nature, must not be overlooked. They cannot, for example, serve as adequate substitutes for cognitive discourse. Symbols, at least as Tillich understands them, are divorced from history; they do not relate what happened in the past, or what will happen in the future.[74] Tillich's characteristic disinclination to engage with history entails a fatal loosening of the critical connection between a revelatory symbol and the historical context against which it is to be interpreted. Given our fundamental emphasis upon the economy of salvation, it will be clear that a historically disengaged 'symbol' leads to a philosophy of religion, not a theology – a perennial and timeless study of human existence, rather than a revealed and incarnational faith, called into existence by specific events.

Our discussion thus far has centred on the revelatory and representational possibilities of words and images. Yet a scientific theology is obliged to recognize that there exists a creative dialectic between possibilities and limitations, between authorization and speculation, which opens up a significant debate on the limits imposed upon the representation of reality[75] – a matter to which we may now turn.

Mystery: the limits of representation

In 1966, Ian Ramsey delivered the Zenos Lectures at the McCormick Theological Seminar in Chicago. It was a time of theological turbulence,

---

[74] See, for example, Paul Tillich, *Dynamics of Faith*. New York: Harper & Row, 1957, 42–3, 47.

[75] See the excellent discussion in Denys Turner, *The Darkness of God: Negativity in Christian Mysticism*. Cambridge: Cambridge University Press, 1998, 19–49. Turner's analysis of the tension between apophatic and cataphatic modes of reflection in Denys the Areopagite can profitably be set alongside that of Andrew Louth, *Denys the Areopagite*. London: Chapman, 2001, 101–9. Louth's earlier study of the Christian mystical tradition lends intellectual depth to his discussion: Andrew Louth, *The Origins of the Christian Mystical Tradition from Plato to Denys*. Oxford: Clarendon Press, 1983.

in which any sense of divine transcendence had been jettisoned as a hindrance to the survival of the church.[76] Ramsey spoke of two defining characteristics of the theological mood of the day: 'the loss of the sense of God's presence' and 'a growing inability to see the point of theological discourse'.[77] The two are not unrelated; the loss of any sense of a transcendent dimension to religion inevitably leads to an understanding of theological discourse evacuated of any idea of referring to God; at best, it can bear witness either to what the church has believed (but which it no longer believes),[78] or to the characteristics of an ecclesial community, setting to one side the historical beliefs which once defined and distinguished that community. Christianity would now be discussed in terms of its religious life, or as a socio-linguistic community.

Interesting though that phase in western culture may have been, it has now passed. Cultural obstacles to an appreciation and celebration of the transcendent have been removed, allowing the Christian tradition to recapture a vision which was suppressed by the anti-transcendent exaggerations of the 1960s. The rediscovery of the transcendence of God opens the way to the reappropriation of insights and approaches that should never have been abandoned or suppressed – above all, the recognition of the sheer *mystery* of God, and the intense problems that human language and imagery face when trying to even begin to represent it. The category of mystery provides theological resistance to the natural craving of the human spirit for a clear, transparent and definite system, undermining the Enlightenment demand for unambiguous, incorrigible knowledge that could be stated completely in purely propositional terms. The category of mystery subverts the Enlightenment project, just as the Enlightenment project sought to subvert the category of mystery.

The rediscovery of the category of 'mystery' is of fundamental importance to a scientific theology. The Christian vision of things affirms the ultimate coherence of reality, so that the opacity of existence reflects a mystery, not an incoherence. Perceptions of incoherence are thus to be understood as noetic, rather than ontic. A broken, wounded, chaotic and seemingly purposeless world is affirmed to possess an inner coher-

---

[76] The marked anti-transcendence of the religious mood of the time is well described in Adrian Hastings, *A History of English Christianity 1920–1985*. London: Collins, 1986, 580–6. For the cultural mood, see Arthur Marwick, *The Sixties: Cultural Revolution in Britain, France, Italy, and the United States, c. 1958–c. 1974*. Oxford: Oxford University Press, 1998. For the 'death of God' movement, see William Hamilton, 'The Death of God Theology', *Christian Scholar* 48 (1965), 27–48.

[77] Ian T. Ramsey, *Models for Divine Activity*. London: SCM Press, 1973, 1.

[78] For an excellent example of such an unsatisfactory attempt to reconceive Christianity, see John A. T. Robinson, *Honest to God*. London: SCM Press, 1963.

ence and rationality which human reason can only begin to discern. It is no accident that some recent writers have chosen to follow Luther, and focus on the 'mystery of the cross' as a means of disclosing – and, at least as importantly, of affirming – God's presence and purpose within a seemingly godless, hopeless and pointless situation.[79] *Crucis sapientia nimis hodie est abscondita in mysterio profundo.*[80] Revelation discloses a hidden coherence and divine presence: *contrarium est iudicio homimum,* which sees little more than pointless suffering and purposeless existence.[81]

An excellent example of this process of engagement with a complex and irreducible reality is provided by Hans Urs von Balthasar's appropriation of the concept of *Gestalt* as a means of attempting to represent the inner coherence of the *crucis sapientia.*[82] Christian von Ehrenfels (1859–1932), the Austrian founder of Gestalt theory, introduced the term to designate complex wholes which simply cannot be reduced to their constituent components. The whole is to be seen as *more than,* and *other than,* the sum of its individual parts.[83] Von Balthasar applies such insights to the notion of revelation, which he insists is ultimately irreducible.[84]

> The experience of God in the Bible, in the Old and New Covenants, is completely characterized by the fact that the God who is by nature invisible (John 1:18) and unapproachable (1 Timothy 6:16) becomes, through God's own action, visible to God's creatures. The one who is without *Gestalt* in the world or in history takes on *Gestalt.*

Von Balthasar insists upon the 'totality' of the divine revelation, holding that it necessarily exceeds human comprehension. Conceding the human need and impulse to 'dissect' such a *Gestalt,* he argues that this

---

[79] I here think of writers such as Jürgen Moltmann, *The Crucified God: The Cross of Christ as the Foundation and Criticism of Christian Theology.* London: SCM Press, 1974.

[80] WA 5.84.40.

[81] WA 3.463.15–18.

[82] For an excellent introduction to this concept in von Balthasar's thought, see Hans Urs von Balthasar, 'Die christliche Gestalt', in *Pneuma und Institution.* Einsiedeln: Johannes Verlag, 1974, 38–60.

[83] There is a huge literature, ably summarized in Barry Smith, *Austrian Philosophy: The Legacy of Franz Brentano.* Chicago: Open Court, 1994, 255–311.

[84] Hans Urs von Balthasar, *Herrlichkeit: Eine theologische Ästhetik: 1 – Schau der Gestalt.* Einsiedeln: Johannes Verlag, 1961, 290. Von Balthasar often used the term *Ganzheit* as a synonym for *Gestalt,* bringing out this aspect of 'an irreducible totality': see Manfred Lochbrunner, *Analogia caritatis: Darstellung und Deutung der Theologie Hans Urs von Balthasars.* Freiburg: Herder, 1981, 173. On von Balthasar on the related issue of 'singularity', see Jörg Peter Disse, *Metaphysik der Singularität: Eine Hinführung am Leitfaden der Philosophie Hans Urs von Balthasars.* Vienna: Passagen Verlag, 1996.

represents an attempt to 'master' revelation,[85] and hence subjugate it. Beholding the *Gestalt* as a totality forces us to concede the inadequacy of our fragmented approaches to mystery. We cannot hope to see *behind* that mystery; we must look for that meaning *within* it, accepting the limitations on comprehension and representation that this entails. Liturgically, this could be expressed in terms of the hiddenness of the divine and the transcendent within the publicly accessible liturgy, in which the verbal symbolism – though seen by all – is only grasped by some to lead to the hidden mysteries, wrapped in silence.[86]

The fundamental point we are forced to concede is that there are limits to our understanding and capacity to represent the divine, fixed both by our limitations as fallen, finite human beings and by the nature and extent of divine self-revelation. It has long been recognized that systematic theology encounters serious difficulties of language and imagery in attempting to convey even a hint of the wonder of the vision of God, or the economy of salvation. How can a mystery be explained? Was not Augustine right when he wrote *si comprehendis non est Deus*?[87] To affirm that reality may be *explained* is not to suggest that it may be reduced to the level of our comprehension, but rather that we are enabled to catch a sufficient glimpse of its structures to allow us to grasp its fundamental characteristics, and thus impelled to yearn for the final disclosure of what we now see only in part. To affirm that it may be *represented* is not to suggest that it may be fully and exhaustively disclosed in human words and images, but rather that such words and images are pointers to a greater whole which simply cannot be conveyed in all its totality.[88] This 'constructive interplay of negation and affirmation'[89] is essential if theology is to be responsible, acknowledging the limits under which it is constrained to operate. The essence of a mystery is its epistemological irreducibility – and part of our task as theologians, if we are to wrestle with God and the things of God κατὰ φυσίν, is to acknowledge the reality of this situation, and respond and work within the limits it imposes upon us.

---

[85] von Balthasar, *Herrlichkeit*, 144–5.

[86] Thus Louth, *Denys the Areopagite*, 101–9.

[87] Augustine, *Sermo* 117.

[88] As Turner rightly points out, the theological enterprise cannot be considered to be purely negative in character; negativity refers to the recognition of limits within a positive theology. 'The apophatic . . . is intelligible only as being a moment of negativity within an overall theological strategy which is at once and at every moment both apophatic and cataphatic.' Turner, *The Darkness of God*, 265.

[89] Turner, *The Darkness of God*, 271.

The irreducibility of complex realities is a fundamental theme in the natural sciences, and features prominently in any critical realist account of reality. Complex entities are multilayered, each stratum of which requires exploration in terms of how it is to be investigated and represented, and how it relates to contiguous strata. We have already noted some instances of such irreducibility – for example, the ICIDH-2 model of illness, which posits a multilevelled understanding of this complex entity, each level of which requires its own research methodologies and forms of remediation (vol. 2, 229–31).

The cross offers an example of the theological irreducibility of divine revelation, forcing us to recognize the limits placed on human representation and explanation. Other examples are easily given – for example, the complex pattern of divine presence and activity which we designate the 'economy of salvation'. This can be reduced to theoretical verbal formulae – yet it is thereby robbed of its deep narrative structure, failing to take account of its subtle interplay of action and presence. More seriously, the process of theoretical reduction fails to convey adequately problems posed by the anomalies encountered in any attempt to engage with reality as a whole.

Aware of such problems, C. S. Lewis offers a remarkable means of conceptualizing the mystery of faith in the final chapter of *Perelandra*, the second novel in his science fiction trilogy.[90] Lewis here develops the idea of a final 'seeing' of reality for what it really is. Lewis's hero, Dr Ransom, is depicted as being granted a vision of reality which resolves paradoxes and anomalies, allowing the flux of history to be seen as coherent and purposeful and the apparent inconsistencies of existence to be reconciled with a greater vision of its whole.[91]

> He had never till now seen the reality. For now he saw this living Paradise, this Lord and Lady, as the resolution of discords, the bridge that spans what would else be a chasm in creation, the keystone of the whole arch.

The revelation takes the form of a 'Great Dance'.[92] This image of the economy of salvation allows Lewis to bring together such themes as the interweaving of the complex patterns of existence, and the beginning and end of an extended process, embracing creation, redemption and consummation.[93]

---

[90] C. S. Lewis, *Perelandra*. London: Collins, 1983, 190–206. For the background to this work, see Roger Lancelyn Green and Walter Hooper, *C. S. Lewis: A Biography*. London: Souvenir Press, 1988, 169–73.

[91] Lewis, *Perelandra*, 192.

[92] Lewis, *Perelandra*, 198–9.

[93] Lewis, *Perelandra*, 201–2.

> In the plan of the Great Dance plans without number interlock, and each movement becomes in its season the breaking into flower of the whole design to which all else had been directed. . . all the patterns linked and looped together by the unions of a kneeling with a sceptred love. . . . [The Great Dance] seemed to be woven out of the intertwining undulation of many cords or bands of light, leaping over and under one another and mutually embraced in arabesques and flower-like subtleties.

Lewis develops a number of traditional theological themes in attempting to explain how a 'Wounded World' can be said to be part of this 'Great Dance', most notably that of incarnation.[94]

> All which is not itself the Great Dance was made in order that He might come down into it. In the Fallen World He prepared for Himself a body and was united with the Dust and made it glorious for ever. This is the end and final cause of all creating.

Yet the theme that is of particular importance to our reflections concerns the ability of the fallen human mind to discern the patterns that underlie the seemingly incoherent and discordant events of the real world.[95]

> All that is seems planless to the darkened mind, because there are more plans than it looked for. In these seas there are islands where the hairs of the turf are fine and so closely woven together that unless a man looked at them he would see neither hairs nor weaving at all, but only the same and the flat. So with the Great Dance. Set your eyes on one movement and it will lead you through all patterns and it will seem to you the master movement. But the seeming will be true . . . There seems to be no plan because it is all plan; there seems to be no centre because it is all centre.

Lewis's image of the 'Great Dance' points to the need for the eye of faith to discern the unity of the patterns and activities of the world, and see the single economy of salvation that undergirds and unites them all. A scientific theology, confronted with the many strata of reality, must similarly aim to uncover and express the unity which underlies them all, and to which it is called to bear witness.

Yet perhaps the finest attempt to cast the vision of the mystery of salvation into words is found in Dante's *Divine Comedy*, a vernacular poem in 100 cantos (more than 14,000 lines), telling of the poet's journey through Hell and Purgatory (guided by Virgil) and through Paradise (guided by Beatrice, to whom the poem is a memorial). Although the work belongs to the same genre as the otherworld journeys of the knight

---

[94] Lewis, *Perelandra*, 199.
[95] Lewis, *Perelandra*, 202.

Tondal (1150) and Thurkil of Essex (1206), the sheer imaginative brilliance of Dante's poetic creation completely overshadows them. Written in a complex pentameter form known as *terza rima*, it is a magnificent synthesis of the medieval outlook, picturing a changeless universe ordered by God, studded with the divine presence and glory for those with eyes to see it.[96]

In the third canto of the work – *Paradiso* – we find Dante setting out his vision of the paradise that awaits the saints. His human language fails him as he attempts to put into words the glories and subtleties of what he beholds. 'This passing beyond humanity (*trasumanar*) cannot be set forth in words (*per verba*).' We find Dante deploying a series of verbs used to describe the paradisaical vision of God prefixed with *tras-*, indicating the need to go beyond conventional human limits in describing heaven: we must *trasmodare, trasumanar, transvolare*, if we are to fully grasp the glory of the heavenly paradise. Words fail when faced with such a vision of God – a thought famously expressed by T. S. Eliot in *Burnt Norton*:[97]

> Words strain
> Crack and sometimes break, under the burden
> Under the tension, slip, slide, perish,
> Decay with imprecision, will not stay in place.
> Will not stay still.

The trajectory of Dante's thought in this final canto of the *Comedy* leads through the visible heavens to the invisible Empyrean which lies beyond – a vision which he seeks to set out in words, while knowing that a creative divine transformation of vocabulary, imagery and intelligence is required if it is to be grasped fully. Accommodating himself for the sake of intellectual decency to the intellectual conventions of the time, Dante sets out a complex vision of nine interlocking concentric spheres, which are clearly based on contemporary astronomical wisdom.[98]

Yet Dante's real concern lies with the need to pass beyond the realm of the human and physical, in order to pass into the presence of God, and finally behold the glory of 'the love that moves the sun and the other stars'.[99] Dante's delicate hints of the 'beatific vision' remind us of

---

[96] Alison Morgan, *Dante and the Medieval Other World.* Cambridge: Cambridge University Press, 1990.

[97] T. S. Eliot, *Burnt Norton*, V.13–17.

[98] William Egginton, 'On Dante, Hyperspheres and the Curvature of the Medieval Cosmos', *Journal of the History of Ideas* 60 (1999), 195–216.

[99] On the biblical background to this idea, see Mark S. Smith, '"Seeing God" in the Psalms: The Background to the Beatific Vision in the Hebrew Bible', *Catholic Biblical Quarterly* 50 (1988), 171–83.

the eschatological dimensions of the economy of salvation, and affirm that the vision of God grasped at present through the veiled communal beholding of God's words and works will finally give way to a direct beholding of God's untempered glory – an experience which theology cannot itself mediate, but for which it may prepare, and enkindle the yearning of anticipation.

Analogical reasoning in a scientific theology

Human beings create and deploy images, shaping their understanding of reality through the aid of great images, metaphors and analogies.[100] Early Enlightenment writers such as Descartes and Hobbes dreamed of being able to represent reality through a mental autonomy which need make no reference to extramental realities as analogies; it was, however, a failed dream, which overlooked the iconogenic function of the human mind.[101] Without analogies, we are condemned to silence in many areas of human discourse. The role of analogies in argument has long been recognized, and equally disputed. The prevailing consensus in early modern Europe is summarized in the standard work of reference of the period, the *Encyclopédie ou dictionnaire raisoné des sciences, des arts et des métiers*. This influential work was conceived as 'a general picture of the efforts of the human spirit in all subjects and all centuries', summarizing existing knowledge in many areas, and advocating future changes in others.[102] The article on 'analogy' reflects the consensus of its age and beyond, embodied in much of its scientific writing.[103]

> Les raisonnements par analogie peuvent servir à expliquer et à éclaircir certains choses, mais non pas à les démontrer . . . une analogie tirée de la ressemblance extérieure des objets. Pour en conclure leur ressemblance intérieure, n'est pas une regle infaillible; elle n'est pas universellement vrai.

Analogies thus illuminate things, but do not prove them; an analogy which is drawn on the basis of external appearances cannot be regarded as a demonstration of any corresponding internal similarity.

---

[100] A point stressed by H. Richard Niebuhr, *The Responsible Self: An Essay in Christian Moral Philosophy*. New York: Harper & Row, 1978, 151–2, 160–1.
[101] See the analysis of Keith J. Holyoak and Paul Thagard, *Mental Leaps: Analogy in Creative Thought*. Cambridge, MA: MIT Press, 1995.
[102] John Lough, *Essays on the Encyclopédie of Diderot and d'Alembert*. London: Oxford University Press, 1968.
[103] César Chesnau de Marsais and Claude l'Abbé Yvon, 'Analogie', in Denis Diderot and Jean Le Rond d'Alembert (eds), *Encyclopédie; ou Dictionnaire raisoné des sciences, des arts et des métiers*, 28 vols. Paris: Briasson, David Le Breton, Durand, 1751, vol. 1, 399–400.

The physical sciences would be seriously impoverished unless there was some manner of rendering the quantum world *anschaulich* – that is to say, visualizable.[104] One of Niels Bohr's central concerns throughout the later 1920s, as he wrestled with the implications and inner intelligibility of quantum mechanics, was *Anschaulichkeit* – namely, how quantum phenomena could be visualized. In a postcard sent to Wolfgang Pauli in the late summer of 1927, Heisenberg indicated that one of the main differences between himself and Bohr concerned the issue of how to construct 'visualizable (*anschaulich*)' analogies for quantum phenomena.[105] For Bohr, the answer lay partly in using classical analogies – waves and particles – to represent aspects of the behaviour of quantum phenomena, thus opening up one of the most fascinating and complex areas of philosophical debate to emerge from this field.[106]

In theology, there has been growing awareness of the importance of analogy in theological reflection.[107] Eberhard Jüngel is a particularly important witness to this development, given his position of eminence within the German-language Protestant theological community, and his particular concern to develop the theological agenda of Karl Barth. For Jüngel,[108]

> Without analogy, there can be no responsible talk about God. Every spoken utterance corresponding to God is made within the horizon of what analogy makes possible.

Jüngel pointedly observes that the debate about analogy which has developed within Protestant theological circles has been deeply unsatisfactory. Yet of the necessity of analogy, there is no doubt.

---

[104] See the important essay of A. I. Miller, 'Redefining *Anschaulichkeit*', in A. Shimony and H. Feshbach (eds), *Physics as Natural Philosophy: Essays in Honor of Laszlo Tisza*. Cambridge, MA: MIT Press, 1982, 376–411. I would also point out that William Whewell commented that one of the more appealing aspects of the Cartesian doctrine of 'vortices' was its 'picturability' – the way in which it allowed such things as contact forces to be visualized. See William Whewell, *History of the Inductive Sciences*, 3 vols. London: Parker & Son, 1857, vol. 2, 155.

[105] See the excellent discussion of 'extending visualizability' in Arthur I. Miller, *Imagery in Scientific Thought: Creating 20th-Century Physics*. Boston, Basel and Stuttgart: Birkhäuser, 1984.

[106] Henry J. Folse, *The Philosophy of Niels Bohr: The Framework of Complementarity.* Amsterdam: North Holland, 1985; John Honner, *The Description of Nature: Niels Bohr and the Philosophy of Quantum Physics.* Oxford: Clarendon Press, 1987; Sandro Petruccioli, *Atoms, Metaphors and Paradoxes: Niels Bohr and the Construction of a New Physics.* Cambridge: Cambridge University Press, 1993.

[107] See the comments of J. Wentzel van Huyssteen, *Theology and the Justification of Faith: Constructing Theories in Systematic Theology.* Grand Rapids, MI: Eerdmans, 1989, 137–47.

[108] Eberhard Jüngel, *Gott als Geheimnis der Welt: Zur Begründung der Theologie des Gekreuzigten im Streit zwischen Theismus und Atheismus*, 4th edn. Tübingen: Mohr, 1982, 384.

It might therefore seem that this new interest in the natural sciences and the role of analogy within Christian theology might lead to a re-invigoration of the discussion of the purpose and place of such devices. Yet, as Janet Martin Soskice has suggested, the level of discussion on the part of some theologians has tended to be little more than something along the lines of 'religion need not be ashamed of its reliance on models if science proceeds in the same way'.[109] The underlying assumption is that the explanatory successes of the natural sciences lend credence to a theological use of analogies, and hence justify theology doing the same thing. This approach is as parasitic as it is indefensible, and I do not propose to give it further consideration.

My concern is to develop a responsible use of analogies which is grounded within the parameters of the Christian tradition, and affirms the ontological unity of the natural world, while recognizing its stratification. It may, of course, be argued at this point that the category of the *metaphorical* needs to be placed alongside that of the *analogical*; while conceding this point, I think it fair to point out that divergencies in definition ultimately lead to difficulties in sustaining, let alone clarifying, this distinction. The categories of the 'analogical' and 'metaphorical' are contested, rather than universally accepted.[110] Cajetan, for example, regarded metaphors as instances of the 'analogy of proportionality'.[111] For the limited purposes of this discussion, I propose to follow Bruno de Solages in defining analogy as follows:[112]

> L'analogie consiste dans le rapport entre deux objects, tout en étant différents, ont une certaine ressemblance. Ce rapport présente par suite comme une double face: il y a la face ressemblance, et il y a la face différence.

The issues that concern us have to do primarily with the grounding of such analogies, and the character and status of their use in argumenta-

---

[109] Janet Martin Soskice, 'Theological Realism', in W. J. Abraham and S. Holtzer (eds), *The Rationality of Religious Belief.* Oxford and New York: Clarendon Press, 1987, 105–19, 110.

[110] For useful discussions, see Sallie McFague, *Metaphorical Theology: Models of God in Religious Language.* Philadelphia: Fortress, 1985; Carl G. Vaught, 'Metaphor, Analogy and the Nature of Truth', in Robert C. Neville (ed.), *New Essays in Metaphysics.* Albany, NY: State University of New York Press, 1987, 217–36; Peter Gärdenfors, 'Mental Representation, Conceptual Spaces and Metaphors', *Synthese* 106 (1996), 21–47.

[111] E. J. Ashworth, 'Analogical Concepts: The Fourteenth-Century Background to Cajetan', *Dialogue* 31 (1992), 399–413. For critical comparisons of Cajetan and Aquinas on this point and others, see Paul G. Kuntz, 'The Analogy of Degrees of Being: A Critique of Cajetan's "Analogy of Names"', *New Scholasticism* 56 (1982), 51–79; Ralph McInerny, 'Aquinas and Analogy: Where Cajetan went wrong', *Philosophical Topics* 20 (1992), 103–24.

[112] Bruno de Solages, *Dialogue sur l'analogie.* Paris: Aubier, 1966, 17.

tion, rather than the broader clarification of potential types of analogical representation.

The logical structure of arguments from analogy can be set out in the following manner:[113]

Entities E_1, E_2, E_3 . . . E_n have properties P_2, P_3, P_4 . . . P_n in common.
Entities E_2, E_3 . . . E_n have property P_1 in common.
Therefore it is probable that:
Entity E_1 has property P_1.

Note that the analogy is not confined to a comparison between two entities only, even though this is probably the most common type of analogy to be encountered. Indeed, the larger the number of entities between which the analogy holds, and the greater the number of respects in which the analogy may be said to hold (in other words, the greater the number of analogous properties), the stronger the analogy may be considered to be. Yet, as Shaw and others have pointed out, these considerations are essentially intuitive, and are therefore vulnerable to conflicting intuitions.[114] This aspect of the argument from analogy has led some writers to suggest that they are devoid of real significance.[115] This, however, distinctly seems to be a minority view.

The use of analogies can be traced back to the earliest written texts in western philosophy. Plato deployed three striking analogies in the *Republic*, perhaps most notably the analogy of the sun as an image of the Good.[116] Just as the sun reigns over the entire visible world, so the Good reigns over the entire domain of the intelligible. Plato does not regard it as germane to his argument to explain why his readers should regard this analogy as self-evidently true – given the epistemic weight which he places upon such analogies in the *Republic*, this would seem to be called for – but appears to assume that the analogy will prove compelling on account of its elegance and ease of use.

It is, however, in Aristotle that we find the notion of the analogy receiving its fullest development in the ancient world. While a number of senses of the term may be discerned within his writings, the most important is the 'analogy of proportion'. 'Analogy of proportion is when the second term is to the first as the fourth to the third. We may then

---

[113] William H. Shaw and L. R. Ashley, 'Analogy and Inference', *Dialogue* 22 (1983), 415–32, 420–1.

[114] Shaw and Ashley, 'Analogy and Inference', 422.

[115] Monroe Beardsley, *Practical Logic*. New York: Prentice-Hall, 1950, 105–9.

[116] Robert J. Fogelin, 'Three Platonic Analogies', *Philosophical Review* 80 (1971), 371–82. The two others are the analogy of the 'divided line' and the more extended analogy – often described as an 'allegory' – of the cave.

use the fourth for the second, or the second for the fourth.'[117] The relation posited here is essentially mathematical, and could be represented by the equation $a:b = c:d$. In other words, the relation of a to b corresponds to the relation of c to d. The analogy gains its potency from the similarity of *relationships*, rather than the precise nature of the four entities being posited to exist in such relationships. Yet the question of why there should be some correspondence between these relationships is left frustratingly unresolved. The manner in which Aristotle deploys analogies and metaphors occasionally suggests that his concerns are rhetorical and poetic, rather than more rigorously philosophical; in other words, his primary interest is in effective and interesting communication, rather than rigorous argumentation.

From the perspective of a scientific theology, the grounding of analogies is of central importance. The fundamental point that needs to be made here is that a Christian doctrine of creation entails an analogical mode of argumentation. The created correspondences between humanity, the world and their divine creator entails the use of analogies in both scientific and theological explanation. In each case, four fundamental issues arise.

1. The capacity of an analogy to model or represent another system.

2. The authority of the analogy, which establishes and validates its use as a model.

3. The extent to which an analogy may be deployed before its similarity to the system to be modelled breaks down.

4. The complementary interaction of analogies in representing a system.

In what follows, we shall consider each of these points in more detail.

The capacity of analogies: analogia entis

One of the most fundamental difficulties attending the use of analogies is ambiguity over the status of those analogies in the first place. No general theory of analogical argument has found general acceptance.[118] This is not to say that no such theory has been set out; the point is that none finds general acceptance today. One of the most intriguing

---

[117] On this entire issue, see Enrico Berti, 'L'analogia in Aristotele. Interpretazioni recenti e possibili sviluppi', in Enrico Berti and Giuseppe Casetta (eds), *Origini e sviluppi dell'analogia da Parmenide a S. Tommaso*. Roma: Edizioni Vallombrosa, 1987, 94–115; Virgilio Melchiorre, 'L'analogia in Aristotele', *Rivista di Filosofia Neo-Scolastica* 85 (1998), 230–55, especially 231–2.

[118] A point stressed by Shaw and Ashley, 'Analogy and Inference'.

questions is whether older justifications of argumentation by analogy can be retrieved. For example, there is a clear understanding in classical philosophy that the concept of analogy is somehow grounded in mathematical relations, so that there is some form of proportionality between entities which are held to be analogically related.[119]

As we have seen, the Renaissance witnessed the growing influence of a Neoplatonic ontology, which affirmed a fundamental ontological linkage between an image and its original. This was developed in a number of directions. Erasmus of Rotterdam tended to see analogies more in terms of rhetorically fruitful devices, which aided an appeal to the imagination.[120] Yet for others, there was a far more profound affinity between the image and the reality which it represented. The origins of this trend can be identified in twelfth-century scholasticism, as a growing familiarity with the Arabic Aristotelian tradition led to an increased interest in developing the notion of the analogy between the creator and creation.[121] Although twelfth-century writers preferred to speak of 'ambiguity' rather than 'analogy', a series of influential works by Alexander of Hales and Philip the Chancellor laid the foundation for the extensive use of the latter term, now developed significantly beyond its original Aristotelian sense.

Thomas Aquinas is of critical importance in the development of the medieval notion of analogy, not so much on account of his exploration of the nature of such an analogy, but on account of his concern to develop the ontological foundations of the concept.[122] Although Aquinas made extensive use of the Aristotelian concept of the *analogia proportionalis* in the *Quaestiones disputatae de veritate* (1256–7), he subsequently seems to have abandoned any interest in the notion.[123] The fundamental theme to be developed is that God differs from creatures in that God *is* good, whereas creatures may be said to *possess* goodness – a goodness which originates from, and points back to, God. God differs from creatures in the manner in which God is good, not in the nature

[119] Hampus Lyttkens, *The Analogy between God and the World: An Investigation of Its Background and Interpretation of its Use by Thomas of Aquino*. Uppsala: Almquist & Wiksells, 1952.

[120] Jean-Claude Margolin, 'L'analogie dans la pensée d'Erasme', *Archiv für Reformationsgeschichte* 69 (1978), 24–50.

[121] Alain de Libera, 'Les sources gréco-arabes de la théorie médiévale de l'analogie de l'être', *Etudes philosophiques* 3–4 (1989), 319–45.

[122] E. J. Ashworth, 'Signification and Modes of Signifying in Thirteenth-Century Logic: A Preface to Aquinas on Analogy', *Medieval Philosophy and Theology* 1 (1991), 39–67.

[123] George P. Klubertanz, *St. Thomas Aquinas on Analogy: A Textual Analysis and Systematic Synthesis*. Chicago: Loyola University Press, 1960, 80–100.

of that goodness itself. Consequently, true human goodness has the capacity to serve as an analogy of God.[124]

Does this represent a distortion of Aristotle? For many, the doctrine of the *analogia entis* represents a clear misreading of both Aristotle's intentions and his statements.[125] On the basis of the highly influential Kantian construal of Aristotle, analogies represent little more than inductive tools without any systematic justification, grounded in the structures of the world. However, a powerful challenge to this reading of Aristotle was mounted in 1862 by Franz Brentano, who argued that Aristotle's analysis of analogies could be held to contain the seeds of later medieval development, perhaps even anticipating some of its fundamental themes, if a little opaquely.[126] I find this unpersuasive. Aquinas did not find the doctrine of the *analogia entis* in Aristotle; rather, he found the building blocks for his own position in a Christian doctrine of creation that is not found in Aristotle, and is ultimately inconsistent with his system.

For Aquinas, the capacity of analogies to model God thus rests upon a *created correspondence* between the creation and creator. This idea was developed and intensified by Erich Przywara (1889–1972), perhaps best known in the English-language world through Karl Barth's extended critique of his views.[127] Przywara argued that Greek philosophy could be

---

[124] This does not, however, resolve the many issues involved. For example, consider the difficulties which arise for Nicholas of Cusa, who is able to accept Aquinas's ontology, but not his Aristotelian theory of abstraction: John L. Longeway, 'Nicholas of Cusa and Man's Knowledge of God', *Philosophy Research Archives* 13 (1987–8), 289–313. Or the problems that arise through Duns Scotus's insistence that the concept of 'being' is not analogical but univocal: Olivier Boulnois, 'Duns Scot, théoricien de l'analogie de l'être', in Ludger Honnefelder, Rega Wood and Mechthild Dreye (eds), *John Duns Scotus: Metaphysics and Ethics*. Leiden: Brill, 1996, 293–315.

[125] For what seems to me to be a definitive analysis of this point, see Pierre Aubenque, *Le probléme de l'être chez Aristote: essai sur la problématique aristotélicienne*. Paris: Presses Universitaires de France, 1977, 198–206.

[126] Franz Brentano, *Von der mannigfachen Bedeutung des Seienden nach Aristoteles*. Freiburg im Breisgau: Herder, 1862. For a study, see Enzo Melandri, 'The Analogia Entis according to Franz Brentano: A Speculative-Grammatical Analysis of Aristotle's Metaphysics', *Topoi* 6 (1987), 51–8. I am equally unimpressed by the highly speculative suggestion that Aquinas's idea resulted from a deficient translation from Greek to Arabic, and hence to Latin, made in the otherwise excellent study of Bernard Montagnes, *La doctrine de l'analogie de l'être d'après Saint Thomas d'Aquin*. Louvain: Publications Universitaires, 1963, 178–80.

[127] For biography and assessments, see Bernhard Gertz, *Glaubenswelt als Analogie: Die theologische Analogie-Lehre Erich Przywaras und ihr Ort in der Auseinandersetzung um die analogia fidei*. Düsseldorf: Patmos-Verlag, 1969; Rudolf Stertenbrink, *Ein Weg zum Denken: Die Analogia entis bei Erich Przywara*. Salzburg: Verlag Anton Pustet, 1971; Friedrich Wulf, 'Christliches Denken: Eine Einführung in das theologisch-religiose Werk von Erich Przywara (1889–1972)', in Paul Imhof (ed.), *Gottes Nähe: religiöse Erfahrung in Mystik und Offenbarung: Festschrift zum 65. Geburtstag von Josef Sudbrack*. Würzburg: Echter, 1990, 353–66.

regarded as questing for, rather than achieving, an understanding of 'being' which avoided the *aporia* of purely transcendental or immanentist modes of thought. For Przywara, this *aporia* could be avoided by developing a specifically Christian concept of the *analogia entis*, conceived in a dynamic rather than static manner, which is based upon a Christian doctrine of creation which affirmed the absolute distinction between creator and creation. This theme, which sounds Barthian to inexperienced ears, nevertheless posits a created capacity on the part of the analogy to model God, which seemed to Barth to represent a crude assertion of the revelational autonomy of the creation over its creator.[128] While I wish to take Barth's legitimate concerns with the utmost seriousness, a number of points must be made against him in this matter.

1. Przywara follows the Fourth Lateran Council (1215) in insisting that in every similarity that may be discerned between God and the world, there exists an even greater dissimilarity: *inter creatorem et creaturam non potest tanta similitude notare, quin inter eos maior sit dissimilitude notanda*.[129] At no point can Przywara be thought or held to reduce God to the level of the creation.

2. Przywara does not allow any revelational autonomy on the part of creation, insisting that every human attempt to explore the analogous relation between God and the creation must presuppose, rather than be considered to prove, such a relation. The *analogia entis* is clearly understood to be theologically *derivative*, rather than theologically *autonomous*.

3. It is not clear whether Barth's critique of Przywara can be pressed with equal force against the earlier exponents of the doctrine, such as Thomas Aquinas. For example, in her *Endliches und ewiges Sein* (1934), Edith Stein (1891–42) develops an understanding of the *analogia entis* which distinguishes the logical and ontological aspects of the analogy in a manner quite distinct from Przywara, and closer to the approach of Aquinas.[130]

[128] Here is a characteristically blunt assessment: 'I regard the *analogia entis* as the invention of anti-Christ', *Church Dogmatics* I/1, xiii. More restrained assessments may be found in H. G. Pöhlmann, *Analogia entis oder analogia fidei? Die Frage nach Analogie bei Karl Barth*. Göttingen: Vandenhoeck & Ruprecht, 1965; Martin Bieler, 'Karl Barths Auseinandersetzung mit der *analogia entis* und der Anfang der Theologie', *Catholica* 40 (1986), 229–45.

[129] Cap. 2, 'De errore Abbatis Iochim', in H. Denzinger (ed.), *Enchiridion Symbolorum*, 24–25 edn. Barcelona: Herder, 1948, 202.

[130] Klaus Hedwig, 'Edith Stein und die analogia entis', in R. L. Fetz, M. Rath and P. Schulz (eds), *Studien zur Philosophie Edith Stein*. Munich: Verlag Karl Alber, 1991, 320–52, especially 336–40. Edith Stein died in a gas chamber at Auschwitz on 9 August 1942.

Hans Urs von Balthasar, whose understanding of the place and purpose of the *analogia entis* owes much to Przywara,[131] clearly regards Barth's criticisms as understandable yet misplaced, inevitably leading to a failure on the part of the creator to communicate with the creature. The *analogia entis* is rather to be seen as the necessary presupposition of the *analogia fidei*.

It is not necessary to buy deeply into the assumptions of modern neo-Thomist thought in order to recognize that there are many insights of importance to the capacity of analogies to model the divine. W. Norris Clarke may speak from such a perspective in stressing the importance of analogy as a 'bridge that enables us to pass over the cognitive abyss between ourselves and God';[132] this insight, however, can be argued to be entailed by a Christian doctrine of creation. Clarke is right to insist that 'being, intelligibility and analogy' are inextricably interwoven in Christian theological reflection;[133] yet this relationship is already grounded in a Christian understanding of the creation of the world, and of humanity after the image of God. David Burrell's double concern for an 'ability to recognize' and the 'inner demand for intelligibility' is similarly grounded in such a doctrine, without entailing its specifically neo-Thomist construal.[134]

Furthermore, the concept of an 'analogy of nature', which was itself the consequence of the actualization in creation of certain eternal and archetypal patterns in the mind of God, lies behind much of the scientific philosophizing of the late seventeenth and early eighteenth centuries. This theme was developed further in George Cheyne's *Philosophical Principles of Religion* (1715), which asserted that the observed analogy of nature was to be accounted for theologically, on the basis of a doctrine of creation.[135]

> This analogy of things necessarily infers the existence of the author of these things, and the wisdom of the contriver of this analogy. These things and this analogy could come from nothing else but from their original ideas and archetypal patterns in the divine mind or imagination, and their harmony and proportion can possibly arise from nothing but their being representations of his ideas.

[131] See the excellent exposition in Georges de Schrijver, 'Die analogia entis in der Theologie Hans Urs von Balthasar: Eine genetisch-historische Studie', *Bijdragen* 38 (1977), 249–81.
[132] W. Norris Clarke, *The Philosophical Approach to God: A Neo-Thomist Perspective*. Winston-Salem, NC: Wake Forest University Press, 1979, 54.
[133] Clarke, *The Philosophical Approach to God*, 53.
[134] David Burrell, *Analogy and Philosophical Language*. New Haven, CT: Yale University Press, 1973, 134.
[135] Quoted in J. E. McGuire, 'Atoms and the "Analogy of Nature": Newton's Third Rule of Philosophizing', *Studies in History and Philosophy of Science* 1 (1970), 3–58, 35.

While Cheyne and his contemporaries did not develop this 'analogy of creation' to quite the extent that we find in the writings of Przywara, there are fundamental congruities between their modes of thinking – above all, the belief that the creative mind of God must be recognized in the proportions, ordering and beauty of the creation itself.

Yet although I am disinclined to follow Barth completely in his critique of the *analogia entis*, the general drift of his critique of the notion has merit in relation to another area of critical importance to a scientific theology – namely, the question of how an analogy may be said to have *authority* in theological reflection. We may turn to a consideration of this point immediately.

The authority of analogies: analogia fidei

An analogy may have the capacity to represent God; but who determines that it *shall* represent God in this manner? The potential of an image to represent the vision of God must be complemented by its authorization to do so. In the natural sciences, the concept of 'authorization' of an analogy or model to represent a given complex reality is cast in terms of its explanatory and predictive successes. The acceptance within the scientific community of Darwin's analogy of 'natural selection' is thus grounded in its empirical adequacy. Its 'authorization' derives from its communal acceptance within the scientific community; that 'authorization', however, is a matter of empirical contingency, and is dependent upon continual explanatory success and the absence of a superior analogy or model.[136] There is no question of such an analogy being *imposed* upon the scientific community in an authoritarian manner; the authority of the analogy is derived from that community's perception of its empirical adequacy and theoretical fecundity.

The authorization of a theological analogy resides *proximately* in the judgement of the Christian community, yet *ultimately* in divine revelation. There is an immediate and obvious parallel here with the medieval debate over *ratio meriti*. For what reasons might God regard the action of a Christian believer as meritorious?[137] For Thomas Aquinas, the

---

[136] For related issues in astronomical models, see Imre Lakatos and Elie Zahar, 'Why did Copernicus' Research Program supersede Ptolemy's?' in Robert S. Westman (ed.), *The Copernican Achievement*. London: University of California Press, 1975, 354–83.

[137] For discussion and texts, see Alister E. McGrath, *Iustitia Dei: A History of the Christian Doctrine of Justification*, 2nd edn. Cambridge: Cambridge University Press, 1998, 109–19. A similar issue arises in John Calvin's discussion of merit, in this case focusing on the question of the manner in which Christ's death can be said to 'merit' the salvation of humanity: see Alister E. McGrath, 'John Calvin and Late Medieval Thought: A Study in Late Medieval Influences upon Calvin's Theological Thought', *Archiv für Reformationsgeschichte* 77 (1986), 58–78.

answer lay in the operation of the divine intellect, which recognized the intrinsic value of the human action. The meritorious value of the act was thus held to be directly proportional to its intrinsic moral worth. For William of Ockham, however, the ground of merit lay in the divine will. The correlation between a human action and its meritorious value did not lie in the divine intellect recognizing the intrinsic value of that action, but in the divine decision that such action will possess a given *meritorious* value, which need not be related in any manner to its *moral* value. For Ockham, God cannot be permitted to be bound by the creation, and must be free to determine the merit of an action without being restricted by external considerations.

There are two concerns involved in this debate, which relate directly to the theological use of analogy.

1. Does the ultimate theological justification for the use of a given analogy as a model of God, or of the divine activity, reside in the *intrinsic capacity* of the analogy to represent God, or the *divine authorization* of the analogy to function in this manner?

2. Does not the affirmation of the intrinsic capacity of some aspect of the creation to reveal God represent a compromise of the divine freedom in revelation, in that revelation can occur without the divine will that it *should* occur?

Both these issues emerge in Karl Barth's critique of Erich Przywara's doctrine of the *analogia entis*, and his proposed counter-understanding of the theological basis of analogy in the doctrine of the *analogia fidei*, to which we now turn.

Barth's less than pellucid concept of the *analogia fidei* is best understood as an attempt to maintain the freedom and sovereignty of God in the revelational process. Barth initially maintained this emphasis dialectically (as in the *Romans* commentary), particularly through an appeal to the notion of *Krisis*, and a focus on a distinct *analogia revelationis* determined by the cross.[138] Although there is considerable debate over the chronology of Barth's growing interest in analogy subsequent to this,[139] its basic themes are reasonably well established. The 'dialectical'

---

[138] There are some fascinating parallels here with the revelational aspects of Luther's *theologia crucis* which I cannot pursue here – but see Enrico de Negri, *Offenbarung und Dialektik: Luthers Realtheologie*. Darmstadt: Wissenschaftliche Buchgesellschaft, 1973; Alister E. McGrath, *Luther's Theology of the Cross: Martin Luther's Theological Breakthrough*. Oxford: Blackwell, 1985, 148–75.

[139] The debate is admirably summarized and extended by Bruce L. McCormack, *Karl Barth's Critically Realistic Dialectical Theology: Its Genesis and Development, 1909–1936*. Oxford: Clarendon Press, 1997, 14–23.

element of Barth's early thought was never totally displaced by an appeal to analogy; rather, the fact that there is some correlation between revelation and human language – a notion expressed in the formula *analogia fidei* – is to be seen as a consequence and expression of dialectical concerns. Whereas Hans Urs von Balthasar famously asserted that Barth turned away from dialectic to analogy in the 1920s, the situation is much more nuanced than this simplistic analysis suggests.[140] My concern, however, is not to document the development of this notion, but to explore its final form.

Whereas the *analogia entis*, from Thomas Aquinas to Erich Przywara, grounded the analogical basis of theological language and divine revelation in creation, Barth insists that the proper grounding of any such analogy is in the event of revelation itself. There is thus an *analogia revelationis*, whose foundation and inner rationality is to be discerned within and determined by the act of divine revelation, rather than posited on the basis of a doctrine of creation.[141] For Barth, any analogy between human language and the reality of God is grounded in the divine decision that this shall be so; that such an analogy is called into being by the free revelational act of God, rather than elicited by human enquiry from a consideration of the created order. The *analogia entis* threatens to limit God's freedom to reveal the structures of the created order; whereas in reality, divine revelation is the ultimate ground of any correlation between words and God, or creation and God. The ultimate grounds of any analogical mode of speaking about God are not *creavit Deus* but *dixit quoque Deus*. Analogies rest upon a covenant, not upon nature.

We may begin engaging with these issues by reflecting on Martin Luther's *theologia crucis*, which proposes that the cross of Christ should be recognized as a distinctive locus of divine revelation, subverting human pretensions to autonomy through its contradiction of human preconceptions of what form that revelation should take, and where it should be found.[142] 'True theology and knowledge of God are found in

---

[140] On this, see Michael Beintker, *Die Dialektik in der 'dialektischen Theologie' Karl Barths*. Munich: Kaiser Verlag, 1987. For the older position, see Hans Urs von Balthasar, *Karl Barth: Darstellung und Deutung seiner Theologie*. Cologne: Hegner, 1951.

[141] Bernhard Gertz, 'Was ist Analogia Fidei?' *Catholica* 26 (1972), 309–24.

[142] Willigis Eckermann, 'Christus als Gekreuzigter: Grundzüge einer Kreuzestheologie', in Joachim Kuropka (ed.), *Zur Sache – Das Kreuz! Untersuchungen zur Geschichte des Konflikts um Kreuz und Lutherbild in den Schulen Oldenburgs*. Vechta: Vechtaer Druckerei, 1986, 254–71. Luther's use of the category of the metaphorical is also of importance here: Joachim Ringleben, 'Luther zur Metapher', *Zeitschrift für Theologie und Kirche* 94 (1997), 336–69.

Christ crucified.'[143] Luther argues that one of the central themes of Paul's theology is the deliberate subversion of human preconceptions of divine wisdom through the cross.[144] Luther's conception of the biblical message is essentially antithetical, involving the development of certain fundamental tensions between law and gospel, *crux* and *gloria*, *Gabe* and *Aufgabe*.[145] A *theologia gloriae* seems to correspond to what Barth regards as the inevitable outcome of the theological application of the *analogia entis*, untempered by the *analogia fidei*.[146] Yet it may reasonably be pointed out that a Christian doctrine of creation affirms the capacity of any aspect of nature to serve as a medium of disclosure for the nature and purposes of God. The *analogia entis* affirms the theoretical capacity of any aspects of the created order – including events and entities – to mirror their creator; the *analogia fidei* identifies those aspects that have been authorized to act in this manner – whether or not they correspond to human preconceptions of their suitability for this purpose.

Similarly, Luther develops the idea of *revelation sub contrariis* as an integral aspect of his *theologia crucis*. God chooses to reveal the divine wisdom in the form of what humans deem foolishness, and the divine strength in the form of what humans deem weakness.[147] At first sight, there is clearly a denial of a certain principle of analogy here – namely, that it can be assumed that there is some direct correspondence between divine and human wisdom. Yet on closer examination, the true issue becomes clearer: God chooses to reveal the divine wisdom in a place and manner which challenges human preconceptions of the location and

---

[143] For a discussion of this theme, see McGrath, *Luther's Theology of the Cross*, 149–51. See also Hellmut Bandt, *Luthers Lehre vom verborgenen Gott: Eine Untersuchung zu dem offenbarungsgeschichtlichen Ansatz seiner Theologie*. Berlin: Evangelische Verlagsanstalt, 1958.

[144] It must not be thought that such themes are restricted to Paul. See, for example, Ulrich Luz, '*Theologia crucis* als Mitte der Theologie im Neuen Testament', *Evangelische Theologie* 34 (1974), 141–75; H. W. Kuhn, 'Jesus als Gekreuzigter in der frühchristlichen Verkündigung bis zur Mitte des 2. Jahrhunderts', *Zeitschrift für Theologie und Kirche* 72 (1975), 1–46; Thomas Knöppler, *Die theologia crucis des Johannesevangeliums: Das Verständnis des Todes Jesu im Rahmen der johanneischen Inkarnations- und Erhöhungschristologie*. Neukirchen-Vluyn: Neukirchener Verlag, 1994.

[145] For a remarkable attempt to overcome these antitheses, see Gerhard Ebeling, 'Einfalt des Glaubens und Vielfalt der Liebe: Das Herz von Luthers Theologie', in *Lutherstudien I*. Tübingen: Mohr, 1971, 126–53.

[146] A similar point is made by Gisbert Greschake in his important review of the first two volumes of Hans Urs von Balthasar's *Herrlichkeit*, published in *Una Sancta: Rundbriefe für interkonfessionelle Begegnung* 19 (1964), 370–3. Greschake notes that von Balthasar's emphasis on *splendor* and *gloria* 'often drives him beyond the measure he himself has set, and into possession and vision of a *gloria* which really exists only in hope'.

[147] McGrath, *Luther's Theology of the Cross*, 153–61.

nature of that revelation. The point is to force humanity to meet God on terms of God's choosing, rather than determine in advance what revelation concerns and where it is to be found. In both these matters, the divine freedom is to be affirmed, not least through the overturning of human revelational preconceptions. For Luther, there can be no automatic correlation between divine and human wisdom; the connection needs to be established.

A similar line of thought may be discerned within the western tradition of speaking of revelation as divine accommodation – as, for example, in the writings of Calvin.[148] The words and images of revelation are here understood to derive their signification from the intention of the one who uttered them, with the explicit purpose of 'accommodating' the things of God to the capacities of the fallen and finite human mind. The bases of any analogies posited in divine speech are thus to be grounded primarily in the intentionality of the divine speaker, rather than the mind of the hearer.

Barth's analogical concerns are ably and responsibly developed by Eberhard Jüngel. In his early writings, Jüngel gave careful consideration to the role played by the notion of analogy in the classical period, focusing especially on Parmenides and Heracleitus.[149] Underlying Barth's approach to analogy, according to Jüngel, is a fundamental conviction that all analogical thinking is to be determined *Christologically*.[150] This point is developed in a major discussion of the place of analogy in actualizing the 'speakability (*Sagbarkeit*) of God' in his major work *Gott als Geheimnis der Welt*.[151] The Word of God does not become effective through its *a priori* conformity to the language of humanity, but rather establishes a presence for itself and of itself.[152] To slip into the language of the Barth–Brunner debate over natural theology, Jüngel clearly opposes the notion that a preexisting 'point of contact' (*Verknüpfungspunkt*) is required in order for divine revelation to take place. The incarnation discloses both the possibility and the form of analogical

---

[148] See Ford Lewis Battles, 'God was Accommodating Himself to Human Capacity', *Interpretation* 31 (1977), 19–38; Stephen D. Benin, *The Footprints of God: Divine Accommodation in Jewish and Christian Thought*. Albany: State University of New York Press, 1993.

[149] Eberhard Jüngel, *Zum Ursprung der Analogie bei Parmenides und Heraklit*. Berlin: De Gruyter, 1964.

[150] Eberhard Jüngel, 'Die Möglichkeit theologischer Anthropologie auf den Grunde der Analogie: Eine Untersuchung zum Analogieverständnis Karl Barths', *Evangelische Theologie* 22 (1962), 535–57. This essay anticipates many of the themes developed subsequently in *Gott als Geheimnis der Welt*.

[151] Jüngel, *Gott als Geheimnis der Welt*, 357–83.

[152] Jüngel, *Gott als Geheimnis der Welt*, 391–3.

language concerning God: 'God has become speakable, addressable, visualizable (*anschaulich*), and knowable as God in his Son.'[153]

These considerations are of theological importance, and must not be minimized. Barth and Jüngel are concerned lest the distinctive language of faith should lose its foundation in God, and become rooted in natural events or objects. Such a danger exists, and it is entirely proper to forestall any such development through the formulation of appropriate theological strategies, particularly when these involve gaining an enhanced appreciation of some fundamental themes of the doctrine of revelation.

Nevertheless, when all is said and done, a suspicion must remain. Is this absolute distinction between *analogia entis* and *analogia fidei* tenable? Gottlieb Söhngen had little doubt about this matter: the latter was implicit within the former.[154] Jüngel insists that such a viewpoint can only be maintained by misrepresenting Barth;[155] without disputing this particular assertion concerning Barth's interpretation of matters, it is fair to point out that there are other ways of conceiving and assessing the situation, maintaining a coherent linkage between *analogia fidei* and *analogia entis*, instead of portraying them as diametrically opposed. It may indeed suit Jüngel's polemical purposes to suggest that the two notions stand in 'as unrelenting a contradiction as the opposition of righteousness from the law and righteousness from faith';[156] the positive theological exploration of the notions, however, would seem to point in a rather different direction.

As we have stressed throughout, a scientific theology intentionally *sees nature as creation*, including the critical insight (which distinguishes Christianity from Judaism and Islam at this point) that the agency of creation is Christ.[157] This is a specific and distinguishing insight of the Christian revelation. A responsible *analogia entis* – which I believe to be stated in the writings of Thomas Aquinas and Jonathan Edwards (though neither of these uses this specific phrase) – cannot be conceived as an assertion of human epistemological autonomy, but is rather to be

[153] Jüngel, *Gott als Geheimnis der Welt*, 530.

[154] Gottlieb Söhngen, 'Wesen und Akt in der scholastischen Lehre von der participation und analogia entis', *Studium* 11 (1955), 649–62. For Söhngen's own views on the nature of analogy, see Gottlieb Söhngen, *Analogie und Metapher: Kleine Philosophie und Theologie der Sprache*. Freiburg: Alber, 1962.

[155] Jüngel, 'Die Möglichkeit theologischer Anthropologie auf den Grunde der Analogie', 537.

[156] Jüngel, 'Die Möglichkeit theologischer Anthropologie auf den Grunde der Analogie', 537.

[157] A point which is not sufficiently emphasized in the otherwise excellent study of Johannes Fischer, 'Kann die Theologie der naturwissenschaftlichen Vernunft die Welt als Schöpfung verständlich machen?' *Freiburger Zeitschrift für Philosophie und Theologie* 41 (1994), 491–514.

seen as reflecting a desire to follow through the implications of the revealed notion of the divine creation of the world in and through Christ. The capacity of the created order to model God is thus a revealed, not a natural, insight.

The issue then becomes this: which aspects of the natural order have been authorized to model God or the things of God? The doctrine of creation lays the foundation for the concept of *analogia revelationis*, while neither subverting nor necessitating it. The *analogia entis* lays the foundation for the *analogia fidei*, in that it establishes the possibility of revelation through natural entities without coercing God's self-revelation through any specific aspect of that nature – which, of course, faith recognizes as God's creation. The same Scripture which affirms that only certain analogies are authorized to model God and things of God also affirms that, through the act of creation, the created order possesses a created capacity to witness to its creator. No tension need exist between the two analogies, which are both presupposed by a responsible Christian doctrine of revelation. Rightly understood, they are as two sides of the same revelatory coin.

A rigid statement of the *analogia fidei* raises precisely the difficulties raised by William of Ockham's understanding of the *ratio meriti* – namely, that there appears to be no good reason why a given human action should be correlated with its meritorious reward. A hiatus is introduced between the realms of the moral and the meritorious, where a continuity might be expected. Barth's construal of the *analogia revelationis* can easily lead to the suggestion that there is an arbitrary connection between the sign and the thing signified. Yet the manner in which analogies for God are deployed within Scripture suggests a natural, yet partial, transference of associations from the analogy to God – for example, with God as shepherd, king or rock. Similarly, there is a natural transference of associations between bread, water and wine in sacramental theology. The *analogia fidei* deployed within Scripture can thus be held to presuppose an *analogia entis*, without entailing that it is to be reduced to it. Both forms of analogy have a distinct and necessary role to play in a constructive scientific theology.

The limits of analogies

One of the most distinctive features of the natural sciences is the tendency to use simple or extended analogies (often referred to as 'models') to depict at least certain aspects of complex systems, for *explanatory* and *exploratory* purposes. Such an analogy is to be understood to be a simplified way of representing a complex system, devised partly to help visualize often abstract or microscopic entities, which allows its users to gain an increased understanding on at least some of its many aspects, and encourage further exploration of both the reality being depicted, and the adequacy of the model to that task. Once a model has been constructed and tested, it can be developed in such a way that it includes some more complicated features of the system which were initially ignored in constructing the model. To illustrate some aspects of the use of such models, we may consider one of the most familiar of such models – the kinetic theory of gases.

The behaviour of gases was studied in some detail from the seventeenth century onwards, particularly by Robert Boyle and Jacques Charles. A series of experiments examined the way in which gases behaved when their pressure, volume and temperature were changed. It was found that the behaviour of gases could be described in terms of a series of laws, which applied to all gases at low pressures, irrespective of their chemical identity. The two most famous such laws – 'Boyle's Law' and 'Charles' Law' – can be formulated as follows:

$$\text{Boyle's Law: } pV = \text{constant}$$
$$\text{Charles' Law: } V = \text{constant} \times T$$

where p is the pressure of the gas, V its volume, and T its temperature, expressed in terms of the temperature scale devised by Lord Kelvin according to which 0 degrees centigrade is 273.15 degrees Kelvin. (This scale thus identifies the temperature of 'absolute zero' as being -273.15 degrees centigrade.) The 'perfect gas equation', which combines these two laws and other observations, can be summarized as $pV = nRT$, where R is the gas constant ($8.31451 \text{ JK}^{-1}\text{mole}^{-1}$) and n the number of moles of gas present. This equation holds universally, irrespective of the identity of the gas in question. This formula assumes that the gas molecules are of negligible size. A small adjustment to the formula allows it to take account of the finite size of the molecules. If b is the volume occupied by a mole of gas molecules, then the behaviour of that gas is given by the formula $P(V - nb) = nRT$, where b represents the volume occupied by gas molecules.

So how is this behaviour to be explained? The 'kinetic theory' of gas offers a simple means of visualizing the nature and behaviour of gases, and allowing certain theoretical predictions to be made.[158] The theory of gases is based on three fundamental assumptions:

---

[158] For details, see Kerson Huang, *Statistical Mechanics*. New York: Wiley, 1963, 143–53. See further Charles E. Hecht, *Statistical Thermodynamics and Kinetic Theory*. New York: Freeman, 1990. On its history, see Peter Achinstein, 'Scientific Discovery and Maxwell's Kinetic Theory', *Philosophy of Science* 54 (1987), 409–34.

1. A gas consists of molecules in ceaseless random motion, which do not interact in any manner.

2. The size of the molecules is negligible, in that their diameter is assumed to be insignificant in comparison with the mean distance travelled by the molecule between collisions.

3. On striking the walls of their container, gas molecules make perfectly elastic collisions, in which the translational kinetic energy of the molecule remains unchanged.

In effect, the model suggests that we think of gas molecules as billiard balls, in constant collision with the walls of the container, allowing the theoretician to predict how pressure, volume and temperature are related.

The field of theoretical physics is a particularly rich resource for those looking for examples of the positive use of analogies in scientific thinking. Indeed, in his study of elementary particles, Jeremy Bernstein comments that 'it is probably no exaggeration to say that all of theoretical physics proceeds by analogy'.[159] Yet, as Mario Bunge points out, a study of the history of science discloses that analogies have a marked propensity to mislead.[160] They must be tested against experience, in order to determine their limits.

A good example of the positive contribution of analogical thinking can be seen in Enrico Fermi's 1933 paper, offering a model for the beta decay of radioactive nuclei.[161] The rival model proposed by Niels Bohr for the phenomenon involved the non-conservation of energy, and was widely regarded as unsatisfactory for this reason.[162] Fermi insisted on the conservation of energy and momentum in the process of beta emission, and offered a different approach for understanding what was happening, based on an assumed analogy with a known process. Fermi's model, as he himself noted, was explicitly constructed 'by way of analogy' with an aspect of electromagnetic theory.

Fermi treated the creation and annihilation of electrons in beta emission as being analogous to the creation and annihilation of photons in quantum transitions between electron orbits. The interaction of particles and fields in beta emission was assumed to be analogous to that of

[159] Jeremy Bernstein, *Elementary Particles and their Currents.* San Francisco: Freeman, 1968, vii.

[160] Mario Bunge, *Method, Model, and Matter.* Dordrecht: Reidel, 1973, 125–6.

[161] Enrico Fermi, 'Tentativo di una teoria dell'emissione dei raggi "beta"', *Ricerca Scientifica* 4 (1933), 491–5.

[162] Abraham Pais, *Niels Bohr's Times, in Physics, Philosophy and Polity.* Oxford: Clarendon Press, 1991, 369.

charged particles and fields in electromagnetic theory, with a corresponding Hamiltonian. The overall result was a model which offered a coherent account of various aspects of beta decay which had hitherto proved puzzling, and allowed further investigation of the phenomenon.

Yet analogies are as capable of misleading as they are of informing. The positing of an analogical relationship between two entities can generate false assumptions, create misleading expectations, and occasionally cause the significance of certain pieces of evidence to be overlooked. Perhaps the most celebrated such occasion of a misleading scientific analogy was the perception that light and sound existed in an analogous relationship, so that the latter was somewhat uncritically accepted as an analogy for the former. In that sound required a medium, it was assumed that the same applied to light, by an analogy. The Michelson-Morley experiment called this fundamental assumption of a 'luminiferous ether' into question, eventually leading to it being rejected.[163] A less often cited example is the use of magnetic, mechanical or electrical analogues during the development of genetic theory over the period 1900–26. This research eventually led to the recognition of the existence and specific function of the gene in a seminal paper published by Thomas Hunt Morgan in 1926.[164] Yet it can be argued that this development was hindered at the time by the use of inappropriate analogies as a means of understanding the genetic mechanisms implicated.

Following the rediscovery of the work of Gregor Mendel in 1900, considerable effort was expended in attempting to clarify the principles governing inherited characteristics or traits. By 1905, it was clear that certain traits were linked in some manner, although the pattern of coupling (later to be interpreted as 'complete' and 'incomplete' coupling) was far from clear. Neither the pattern nor its explanation was clear at this early stage. William Bateson, one of the more significant workers in the field, used a series of vague physical or mechanical analogies – in particular, the analogies of 'coupling' and 'repulsion' – in an attempt to explain the puzzling observations.[165] Bateson appears to have thought that there were certain physical forces in operation, capable of attracting or repulsing factors of genetic significance. Although Bateson does not appear to have developed a definite hypothesis along these lines, it is clear that

---

[163] A. A. Michelson and E. W. Morley, 'On the Relative Motion of the Earth and Luminiferous Ether', *American Journal of Science* 34 (1887), 333–45.

[164] Thomas H. Morgan, *The Theory of the Gene*. New Haven: Yale University Press, 1926.

[165] Lindley Darden, 'William Bateson and the Promise of Mendelism', *Journal of the History of Biology* 10 (1977), 87–106; A. G. Cock, 'William Bateson's Rejection and Eventual Acceptance of Chromosome Theory', *Annals of Science* 40 (1983), 19–60.

such analogies were of significance in shaping his thought, and (in this case) hindering him from finding a solution to the observed patterns.

Perhaps the most celebrated use of an analogy in the biological sciences is Charles Darwin's term 'natural selection', which he coined as a metaphorical or non-literal means of referring to a process which he believed to be the most convincing means of explaining the patterns of diversity he observed within the biosphere.[166] Darwin himself claimed that the concept and the term were suggested by the methods of livestock breeders and pigeon-fanciers, who used artificial selection as a means of generating and preserving desirable characteristics within the animal world. The concept of 'natural selection' was thus based on the perception of an analogy between this and the existing and familiar notion of 'artificial selection'.[167] The analogy implies that the active selection of the animal or plant breeder is somehow paralleled within nature itself. This is certainly suggested by his frequent references to 'nature' as an agent who actively 'selects' variants which she approves as good.

There can be no doubt that this analogy was anthropomorphic in character. While Darwin deployed many such images and analogies throughout *The Origin of Species*,[168] 'natural selection' proved to be especially significant and influential. The analogy was regarded as seriously misleading by Darwin's colleague Alfred Russell Wallace, who was alarmed at its implication of active choice and purposefulness on the part of nature. He wrote to Darwin to express his misgivings. 'I am led to conclude that the term itself, and your mode of illustrating it, however clear and beautiful to many of us, are not yet the best to impress it on the general naturalist public.' For Wallace, many had been led to assume that the term 'natural selection' implied an active process of selection on the part of a personified nature, which was thus conceived anthropomorphically as implying rational analysis and an intended goal.[169] The 'analogy' of natural selection deployed by Darwin thus carries over the notions of intention, active selection and ultimate purpose from the explanatory analogy (established procedures of artificial selection) to the *explicandum* (the natural order). At both the verbal

---

[166] Robert M. Young, 'Darwin's Metaphor and the Philosophy of Science', *Science as Culture* 16 (1993), 375–403.

[167] L. T. Evans, 'Darwin's Use of the Analogy between Artificial and Natural Selection', *Journal of the History of Biology* 17 (1984), 113–40.

[168] See the important analysis of such images in Gillian Beer, '"The Face of Nature": Anthropomorphic Elements in the Language of *The Origin of Species*', in L. J. Jordanoca (ed.), *Languages of Nature*. New Brunswick, NJ: Rutgers University Press, 1986, 207–43.

[169] F. Darwin and A. C. Seward, *More Letters of Charles Darwin*, 2 vols. London: John Murray, 1903, vol. 1, 267–8.

and the conceptual level, the anthropomorphic concept of 'purpose' is retained, despite Darwin's apparent intention to eliminate this (and Wallace's more explicit views on this matter).

Two points must be stressed in relation to the use of analogical argumentation in the natural sciences. A failure to appreciate their significance can lead to misleading conclusions and expectations.

1. It cannot be assumed that analogies are *identical* to the systems with which they are associated. Gas molecules are not minute inelastic spheres; the point is that they behave, in some respects, *as if* they are. An analogy offers a visualizable representation of a system, which assists explanation and interpretation, and stimulates exploration. Yet analogy is not the same as identity.

2. The degree of ontological transference from analogy to the reality being depicted must be established *a posteriori*. It cannot be assumed *a priori* that every aspect, or any given individual aspect, of the analogy is necessarily to be transferred to its subject. Darwin's analogy of 'natural selection' can easily be interpreted to mean that an active process of selection is taking place, whereas Darwin intended something less specific to be understood. Recognizing sound as an analogy of light led to the implicit assumption that, since sound required a medium for its propagation, the same was true of light. Analogies are to be seen as *partial*, not *total*, representations of a system, in which it remains to be determined which aspects of the analogy are to be accepted as authentic representations of the reality being depicted, and which are specific to the analogy.

Similar, but not identical, issues arise in the theological development of analogies. There are, for example, hints of a notion of a fundamental analogy within the natural world, which permits one of its aspects to model another. Scientific analogies are often developed on the basis of a perceived congruence between a reality and its proposed analogue. Thus light was deemed to be related to sound, so that modes of sonic propagation were assumed to be cognate to those of light. Equally, Darwin perceived points of similarity between the outcomes of the methods of cattle breeders and the patterns he discerned within the natural world, and thus assumed that an analogy existed between 'artificial' and 'natural' modes of selection. While the *identification* of analogies thus rests with the natural scientist, there is a sense in which this process of identification rests upon the assumption that the best analogies are ultimately those which mirror aspects of the reality thus requiring to be represented.

For the scientific theologian, however, the analogies are *given*, not selected. They are part of the Christian revelation, and have become deeply embedded in the thought, worship and iconology of the Christian tradition.[170] To revert to Barth's language, the *analogia fidei* demands that we limit our theological exploration of those images which are authorized for this purpose, even though the related *analogia entis* hints that a much wider range of images might be of service in this matter. The issue for the theologian is how to interpret, explore and correlate the nexus of biblical images for God and the things of God. It must also be stressed – against Tillich, for example – that such images are not to be divorced from history in general, nor their specific cultural location in particular. If we might revert to Erich Auerbach's notion of *figura* (79–8), this approach to the *analogia revelationis* maintains 'the characteristics of concrete historical reality', yet insists that these possess a derived, authorized revelational capacity, which the Christian community is invited to explore and express.

Theological analogies, it must be stressed, may mislead just as much as their scientific counterparts through misconstrual of their ontological implications, or a failure to respect their proper limits. A classic example of this process can be seen in the patristic discussion of the redemption of the world through Christ, especially focusing on the notion that Christ's death can be said to represent a 'ransom' for humanity. This analogy was developed by a number of patristic writers, such as Rufinus of Aquileia, to imply that Christ's death was a ransom paid to Satan.[171] Four elements to the analogy were identified: human bondage to Satan; a price paid to achieve liberation; the achievement of liberation; and Satan as the one to whom the ransom was paid. The first three such elements were common elements of the patristic doctrine of redemption;[172] the fourth was widely regarded as unorthodox.[173] Unorthodox it may have been; it was, nevertheless, hugely attractive to the popular religious

---

[170] While the importance of imagery in relation to icons must be noted, it extends far beyond this: see, for example, José E. Espinosa, *Saints in the Valleys: Christian sacred images in the history, life, and folk art of Spanish New Mexico*. Albuquerque, NM: University of New Mexico Press, 1960. On icons, see especially the excellent analysis of Ambrosios Giakalis, *Images of the Divine in the Eastern Orthodox Church: The Theology of Icons at the Seventh Ecumenical Council*. Leiden: Brill, 1994.

[171] Rufinus of Aquileia, *Expositio Symboli*, 14.

[172] H. E. W. Turner, *The Patristic Doctrine of Redemption: A Study of the Development of Doctrine during the First Five Centuries*. London: Mowbray, 1952.

[173] It was subjected to a sustained theological critique by Anselm of Canterbury: see *Cur Deus homo* I.vii. See further Felix Hammer, *Genugtuung und Heil: Absicht, Sinn und Grenzen der Erlösungslehre Anselms von Canterbury*. Vienna: Herder, 1967. On the notion of 'Satan's rights' in the period, see C. William Marx, *The Devil's Rights and the Redemption in the Literature of Medieval England*. Cambridge: Brewer, 1995.

imagination, and went on to play a decisive role in Middle English lit-erature, often developed in terms of the imagery of Christ jousting with Satan, or outwitting Satan to gain control of humanity.[174]

This is widely regarded as theologically illegitimate, pressing an analogy beyond its clearly intended limits. That this is so is indicated by two considerations.

1. The analogy is to be interpreted with a matrix of doctrinal affir-mations, which establish the context within which an analogy is to be interpreted, and provide an important check against the improper overinterpretation of any single given analogy.

2. The Christian representation of reality does not take the form of a single, isolated analogy, but of a network of interlocking images, whose interpretation is determined to a substantial extent by their mutual relationship.[175]

In view of the importance of this second point to a scientific theology, we shall explore it in greater detail.

The interlocking of analogies

A complete view of a complex reality requires a series of analogies or models, especially if the reality in question is stratified. Humanity seems to have an innate ability to hold together insights which might be regarded as inconsistent or incoherent, believing that the outcome is an enriched understanding of a complexity, rather than an unstable rep-resentation of an incoherency.[176] Perhaps the most famous illustration of this point is to be found in the Copenhagen account of quantum theory, which postulates the 'complementarity' of the classical wave and particle models in the representation of light.[177] The origins of Bohr's ideas can be traced to a paper published by Prince Louis de Broglie in

---

[174] Kathleen M. Ashley, 'The Guiler Beguiled: Christ and Satan as Theological Tricksters in Medieval Religious Literature', *Criticism* 24 (1982), 126–37; John A. Alford, 'Jesus the Jouster: The Christ-Knight and Medieval Theories of Atonement in Piers Plowman and the "Round Table" Sermons', *Yearbook of Langland Studies* 10 (1996), 129–43.

[175] This point was developed throughout the writings of Ian T. Ramsey. For the general issue, see *Models and Mystery*. London: Oxford University Press, 1964. For an important study of how models of divine activity – some immanent, others transcendant – interact, see his *Models for Divine Activity*. London: SCM Press, 1973, especially 40–55.

[176] Fritz K. Oser and K. Helmut Reich, 'The Challenge of Competing Explanations: The Development of Thinking in Terms of Complementarity of Theories', *Human Development* 30 (1987), 178–86.

[177] James T. Cushing, *Quantum Mechanics: Historical Contingency and the Copenhagen Hegemony*. Chicago: University of Chicago Press, 1994, 32–4.

September 1923.[178] De Broglie had been deeply impressed by Einstein's discussion of the wave–particle duality for light. The essence of de Broglie's approach was to argue that the principle established by Einstein in 1905 was capable of generalization, and could be extended to all material particles, particularly electrons. In his paper, he suggested that it was possible to assign a 'fictitious associated wave' (*onde fictive associée*) to any moving body, whose momentum and wavelength (λ) were related as $\lambda = h/p$, where h is Planck's constant and p is the momentum of the moving body. This radical proposal abolished any idea of a total distinction between particles and waves through its theoretical assertion that any moving particle has an associated 'de Broglie wavelength' λ. The de Broglie equation proposes a fusion of what had hitherto been considered to be opposites, in that momentum had been considered to be a property of particles, and wavelength a property of waves.

In 1927 – three years after de Broglie asserted that particles of matter could possess wavelike properties – the diffraction of electrons from the surface of a solid crystal was experimentally observed by C. J. Davisson and L. H. Germer of the Bell Telephone Laboratory. An investigation of the angular distribution of electrons scattered from nickel showed that the electron beam was scattered by the surface atoms on the nickel at the exact angles predicted for the diffraction of X-rays, with a wavelength given by the de Broglie equation. Further confirmation came shortly afterwards, when G. P. Thomson demonstrated the diffraction of electrons by thin films of celluloid and gold. In both cases, the electron velocity and its associated 'de Broglie wavelength' were measured, and found to be related by the formula $\lambda = h/p$.

De Broglie's ideas were taken further in 1926, in advance of their experimental confirmation, when Werner Heisenberg and Erwin Schrödinger developed these insights into a consistent theory (independently of each other), using different (yet mathematically equivalent) formalisms.[179] In effect, Heisenberg developed his 'matrix mechanics' by beginning from the assumption that matter was particulate, whereas Schrödinger pioneered his 'wave mechanics' on the assumption that matter possessed wave properties, initially using Hamilton's celebrated analogy between

[178] Louis de Broglie, 'Radiations – ondes et quanta', *Comptes Rendus* 177 (1923), 507–10.
[179] For the details, see David C. Cassidy, *Uncertainty: The Life and Science of Werner Heisenberg.* New York: Freeman, 1992, 204–46. For further reflection, with a particular focus on the analogical issues, see Edward MacKinnon, 'Heisenberg, Models and the Rise of Matrix Mechanics', *Historical Studies in the Physical Sciences* 8 (1979), 137–85.

mechanics and wave optics.[180] Yet how could both be true? Was the electron a wave, or was it a particle? The two mathematical schemes proposed by Schrödinger and Heisenberg were mathematically equivalent and consistent, but seemed to begin from significantly different starting points, and reflect radically different assumptions. It seemed to Bohr that the two mathematical tools reflected different philosophical interpretations of what was happening.[181]

Bohr and Heisenberg had extended discussions throughout 1926 and the early months of 1927 over how to make sense of the experimental and mathematical materials. The central question was whether classical physical concepts, such as 'waves' and 'particles', would have to be abandoned or whether they could continue to be used. Heisenberg was inclined to the view that they should be abandoned; the words simply did not make sense at the level of quantum phenomena. Bohr was quite convinced that this was not so. As he declared in a lecture given on 16 September 1927 in the Italian town of Como to mark the centenary of the death of the Italian physicist Alessandro Volta, 'our interpretation of the experimental material rests essentially upon the classical concepts' – the issue concerned how these were to be related to each other in a 'complementary' manner.[182]

The use of this term is, of course, highly significant, and it must be noted that Bohr's early attempts to set out the theory are specifically directed towards wave–particle complementarity. The two models of the nature of light can 'be considered as different attempts at an interpretation of experimental evidence in which the limitation of the classical concepts is expressed in complementary ways'. What were originally regarded in classical physics as being quite distinct are now to be seen as existing in a relationship of 'complementarity', even though, according to the classical model, they cannot be unified into a single picture. For Bohr, the 'wave-picture' applies *only* when the 'particle-picture' does not, and *vice versa*. The approach is *complete* (in that only two analogies are needed) and *complementary* (in that only one of these mutually exclusive analogies can apply at any one time).

Bohr's approach posited pairs of classical concepts that could be manifested only in mutually exclusive experimental arrangements with both

---

[180] For careful studies of the origins and development of Schrödinger's ideas, see Linda Wessels, 'Schrödinger's Route to Wave Mechanics', *Studies in History and Philosophy of Science* 10 (1979), 311–40; Helge Kragh, 'Erwin Schrödinger and the Wave Equation: The Crucial Phase', *Centaurus* 26 (1982), 154–97.

[181] Pais, *Niels Bohr's Times*, 302–16.

[182] For accounts of this notion and its historical development, see Honner, *The Description of Nature*, 54–65.

needed to embrace the full range of physical experience. Yet Bohr's notion of wave–particle complementarity has encountered two major obstacles:

1. It has never been formulated in a manner that has commanded a general consensus within the scientific community;

2. There is considerable empirical evidence which flatly contradicts the claim of mutual exclusivity of particle and wave properties of quantum objects in a single experiment.

One possible way of resolving this *aporia* is to limit the notion of complementarity entirely to the *mathematical formalism* of quantum theory.[183] While the exploration of such issues lies beyond this study, it is important to note such difficulties in order to avoid overstating the theological significance of the notion.

So what is the theological significance of this exploration of a critical phase in the development of quantum theory? The answer lies partly in the recognition of the need for multiple models to represent a complex reality, and partly in the continuing role that Bohr allots to classical concepts in representing quantum phenomena. According to Bohr, we must describe quantum systems using the terms which we use for describing the classical world, in that the language we use derives from that world and our long association with it. As Peter Gibbins explains this point, from Bohr's perspective:[184]

> The language of classical physics is ideally suited to describing the macro-physical world, the world of medium-sized objects, in which we learn and constantly test natural language. The species has evolved classical concepts (of position, speed and so on) for so many generations that they are now an intrinsic part of our worldview. However far we travel from the world of everyday reality, we are stuck with classical concepts.

The issue is essentially heuristic, reflecting the need for the 'accommodation' of quantum entities to the imaginative capacities of the human mind if they are to be 'visualized'. In one sense, there is no need to do this; mathematical representation is perfectly adequate for most purposes.

The theological implications of Bohr's approach have not gone unnoticed. The most significant theological parallel to Bohr's understanding of complementarity lies in the field of Christology.[185] However, the relevance

---

[183] See, for example, G. Wendell Holladay, 'The Nature of Particle–Wave Complementarity', *American Journal of Physics* 66 (1998), 27–33.

[184] Peter Gibbins, *Particles and Paradoxes*. Cambridge: Cambridge University Press, 1987, 9.

[185] For reflections, see Christopher B. Kaiser, 'Quantum Complementarity and Christological Dialectic', in W. Mark Richardson and Wesley J. Wildman (eds), *Religion and Science: History, Method, Dialogue*. New York: Routledge, 1996, 291–8.

of the approach extends beyond specific doctrines to matters of theological method. James E. Loder and W. Jim Neidhardt have identified clear parallels between Bohr's 'principle of complementarity' and Karl Barth's 'dialectical method'. Loder and Neidhardt suggest that a number of significant points of convergence can be noted between the two writers. In the case of Bohr, the 'phenomenon' to be explained is the behaviour of quantum events; for Barth, it is the relation between time and eternity on the one hand, and humanity and divinity in the person of Jesus Christ on the other.[186] Thus they point out that, for both Bohr and Barth, classical forms of reason are pushed to their limits to explain the phenomena in question. In both cases, the phenomenon discloses itself as an irreducible bipolar relationship which imposes itself upon the knower, and thus requires representation in terms of either the *complementarity* or the *dialectic* of classical forms. The relationality between these polarities is asymmetrical.

Equally, both writers vigorously maintain the principle that the phenomenon should be allowed to disclose how it can be known, and avoid reducing the phenomenon to known forms.[187] The issue rather concerns how known forms can be used as analogies as a means of visualizing the new concepts that are demanded by the phenomenon itself. The observation of the phenomena requires that the knower should be able to communicate those observations in language – and that language is based on known analogies, which are deployed in new ways to express the implications of observation.

Theologically, Bohr's approach points to the propriety of using multiple models, grounded in the 'classical' world of human life and experience, to depict and describe entities which are at times counter-intuitive and impossible to 'see' using existing methods. Wave and particle models were both required to depict the known behaviour of light.[188] This, it must be stressed, does not imply ontological transference from the classical to the quantum domain; it merely affirms the ability of the former to model or represent the latter. In a similar way, a responsible understanding of the *analogia revelationis* requires that we acknowledge that a multiplicity of analogies are required to represent the infinity of the divine, all of which are embedded in a complex network of propositional statements, historical narratives and

[186] James E. Loder and W. Jim Neidhardt, 'Barth, Bohr and Dialectic', in W. Mark Richardson and Wesley J. Wildman (eds), *Religion and Science: History, Method, Dialogue*. New York: Routledge, 1996, 271–89.

[187] An emphasis which is also associated with T. F. Torrance, who develops Barth's approach at this point. See, for example, Thomas F. Torrance, *Theological Science*. London: Oxford University Press, 1969, 26–7.

[188] For a more detailed discussion and evaluation, see M. O. Scully, B.-G. Englert, and H. Walther, 'Quantum Optical Tests of Complementarity', *Physical Review A* 39 (1991), 5229–36.

ethical exhortations, shot through with allegory, metaphor, simile, motif, convention and idiom.[189] These images, when rightly understood, both individually and in terms of their interrelationships, disclose something of the nature and purposes of God. When taken together, they build up to yield a richly textured depiction of such theological actualities as the identity of God, or the nature of salvation. These theological entities are often multi-levelled, each level possessing its own set of images.

Bohr argued that it was possible to use models which had been tried and tested in known situations to make sense of what was happening in more complex situations, providing the limits of the model were established and respected. In an important discussion of theological language, Arthur Peacocke makes a similar point in relation to both science and theology.[190]

> The scientific and theological enterprises share alike the tools of groping humanity – our stock of words, ideas and images that have been handed down, tools that we refashion in our own way for our own times in the light of experiment and experience to relate to the natural world and that are available, with God's guidance, to steer our own paths from birth to death.

Peacocke, it may be noted, holds that we are at liberty to modify the traditional Christian imagery, including that inherited from Scripture; I do not agree with him at this point, believing that the critical issue is how these traditional images are to be understood and deployed.

An excellent illustration of the general pattern of disclosure suggested by Peacocke is provided by the biblical modelling of the nature of salvation. Analogies of salvation are drawn from many areas of life, including the following.

1. The *spatial extension of territory*,[191] particularly the creation of a secure region of habitation.

2. The *healing* of a person who has been wounded or acquired an illness. The Greek term σωτηρία can be translated in a number of manners; some early biblical translations stressed the connotations of healing associated with the term by translating it as *sanitas*.[192]

[189] See the analysis of George B. Caird, *The Language and Imagery of the Bible*. London: Duckworth, 1980, 131–82.

[190] Arthur Peacocke, *Intimations of Reality*. Notre Dame, IN: University of Notre Dame Press, 1984, 51.

[191] Recognition of the importance of this motif is generally thought to date back to Albert Schultens, *Origines hebraeae sive Hebraeae linguae antiquissima natura et indoles*. Leiden: Luchtmans and Le Mair, 1761. For a critique of this association, see John F. A. Sawyer, *Semantics in Biblical Research: New Methods of Defining Hebrew Words for Salvation*. London: SCM Press, 1972, 4–10.

[192] Giuseppe Scarpat, '*Sanitas* come traduzione latina di σωτηρία (Sap 6,26; 18,7)', in *Treasures of Wisdom*. Louvain: Louvain University Press, 1999, 241–53.

3. The *vindication* of a person in the face of legal accusations.[193] The development and meanings of the term δικαίωσις have been the subject of considerable debate within the Christian tradition.

4. The *restoration to fellowship* of an individual. While the associations of the Pauline term καταλλαγή are highly nuanced, it is clear that an analogy is assumed between the reconciliation of alienated individuals and the reconciliation of humanity to God.[194]

5. The *liberation of individuals from bondage*, which is conveyed through analogues such as 'ransom' or 'redemption'.[195]

When such analogies are taken together, along with others not noted here, a multilayered and multifaceted conception of the transformation of the human situation is disclosed. The analogues are stratified, both chronologically and in terms of the realities they depict. Salvation emerges as a complex, rich category, with past, present and future aspects, capable of being depicted on the basis of an accumulation of medical, legal, military and pastoral analogies.

The present chapter has explored some aspects of the representation of reality, noting the difficulties and challenges that face any intellectual discipline as it attempts to depict or describe what it encounters in the world, and offer frameworks allowing an enhanced appreciation of the relationships and interconnections that are observed. While doubtless made more complex through the recognition of the stratification of reality, the representation of the world may be concluded to be a theoretically valid and constructive enterprise. Theology may face some particular challenges of its own, but there can be no doubt that most of those challenges are the common property of any attempt to represent and describe the world.

Yet the enquiring human mind has never been content to *describe*, it longs to *explain*. Having worked out how to represent the way things are, how may they be accounted for? In the following chapter, we shall therefore move on to consider the explanatory aspects of a scientific theology.

---

[193] Alister E. McGrath, *Iustitia Dei: A History of the Christian Doctrine of Justification*, 2nd edn. Cambridge: Cambridge University Press, 1998, 4–16.

[194] There are some interesting analogies proposed in Bradley H. McLean, *The Cursed Christ: Mediterranean Expulsion Rituals and Pauline Soteriology*. Sheffield: Sheffield Academic Press, 1996.

[195] For the New Testament use of ἀπολύτρωσις and cognates, see works such as John G. Gibbs, *Creation and Redemption: A Study of Pauline Theology*. Leiden: Brill, 1971.

Chapter 14

The Place of Explanation in a Scientific Theology

A scientific theology is motivated by the quest for a unified explanation of reality. Like Augustine of Hippo, it recognizes an *eros* of the mind, an *amor sapientiae*, an intellectual desire, without which there can be no enquiry, no wonder, no satisfaction, and ultimately no joy.[1] Yet the reality that requires to be explained is complex, multilayered and often opaque. We do not experience that reality as neatly divided into separate compartments, some of which may be designated as 'physical', others 'biological', and others as 'religious'. Rather, we experience reality in its wholeness and interconnectedness before we develop particular disciplines and techniques to study different aspects of it.

The quest for explanation is perhaps one of the most fundamental impulses to motivate intellectual enquiry. Why are things the way they are? What reasons may be adduced for the present ordering of the world? The development of the scientific revolution in western culture has often been conceived as forcing nature to give answers to our questions[2] – an image which, in the hands of Roger Bacon, sometimes suggests that nature is subjected to violence in order to yield her secrets. A theory is, in part, an explanation of the way things are, although it must be stressed

---

[1] See the excellent comments concerning *amor sapientiae* of Hugh of St Victor, *Didascalion*, 2. Similar themes can be found in Bernard J. F. Lonergan, *Insight: A Study of Human Understanding*. London: Darton, Longman & Todd, 1983, 73.

[2] Matti Sintonen, 'How to Put Questions to Nature', in Dudley Knowles (ed.), *Explanation and Its Limits*. Cambridge: Cambridge University Press, 1990, 267–84.

that this identification only partially illuminates the peculiar nature of theory.[3]

The very idea of 'explanation' denotes the highly significant notion that the world is possessed of a rationality and coherence which may be grasped and understood, and thus ultimately affirms the intelligibility of reality by its beholders. Explanation, it must be stressed, is not the same as perceiving patterns of regularity within nature. These may be observed, and even used to predict future patterns, yet themselves remain unexplained. The classic instance of such a situation is Newton's recognition that his mechanics only 'explained' patterns of motion in terms of their observed regularities, which his three laws of motion enumerated and summarized – but did not explain.[4] An explanation, in the fuller sense of the term, required the postulation of an agency of attraction or force – which we would now term 'gravity' – which operated in a manner which Newton could not understand (partly on account of intuitive difficulties in comprehending the notion of 'action at a distance').[5] Explanation, in the view of many, entails recognizing an *ontic* aspect to reality, so that 'an explanation of an event involves exhibiting that event as it is embedded in its causal network and/or displaying its internal causal structure'.[6] In other words, explanation is grounded in an understanding of the way things are, not simply in human attempts to represent it, or discern patterns of regularity. To affirm the possibility of explanation is to affirm the ontological finality of reality itself in relation to every aspect of our theorizing.

Explanation as a legitimate aspect of a scientific theology

Earlier, we insisted that there was an explanatory aspect to a scientific theology (vol. 2, 294–6). Both the natural sciences and a scientific theology

[3] Strictly speaking, scientific theories may be argued to operate at three levels – empirical adequacy, formal explanation, and understanding, although the final two levels tend to merge into each other. For these distinctions, see James T. Cushing, 'Quantum Theory and Explanatory Discourse: Endgame for Understanding?' *Philosophy of Science* 58 (1991), 337–58. In an important essay on the nature of scientific explanation, Wesley Salmon distinguishes three fundamental philosophical understandings of explanation – *epistemic*, *modal* and *ontic*. See Wesley C. Salmon, 'Scientific Explanation: Three Basic Conceptions', *Philosophy of Science Association* 2 (1984), 293–305.

[4] For a full account of the issues, see Ernan McMullin, *Newton on Matter and Activity*. Notre Dame, IN: University of Notre Dame Press, 1978.

[5] For further comment on this specific notion, see Ernan McMullin, 'The Explanation of Distant Action: Historical Notes', in J. T. Cushing and E. McMullin (eds), *Philosophical Consequences of Quantum Theory: Reflections on Bell's Theorem*. Notre Dame, IN: University of Notre Dame Press, 1989, 272–302.

[6] Salmon, 'Scientific Explanation: Three Basic Conceptions', 298.

attempt to offer explanations of reality, by disclosing the way things truly are in order that the correlations established by observation may be accounted for, and additional observations and correlations proposed, in order that they may be subjected to the appropriate validatory processes. Basil Mitchell summarizes a widely held consensus within the Christian tradition as follows:[7]

> It would be somewhat perverse to deny that both within a system of religious belief and in the individual's approach to such a system there appear what look like explanations or demands for explanation. The perplexed individual who asks 'What is this all for, what does it mean?' is ostensibly looking for some explanation of the 'changes and chances of this transitory life.' And if he becomes persuaded that all these things have a purpose in the providence of God, then it would seem that he has found an explanation.

But is explanation the *primary* function of a scientific theology? D. Z. Phillips certainly thought not, and argued vigorously against those who proposed any significant explanatory dimension to religion.[8] This is especially evident in his discussion of the problem of evil, in which he appears to suggest that the potential explanatory difficulties which suffering poses to the existence of God are not of particular importance.[9] Again, in dealing with the cosmological argument for the existence of God, Phillips marginalizes the explanatory aspects of God, arguing that it is quite wrong to suggest that God is a hypothetical postulate on the part of believers. 'Arguments to establish that God is the cause of the world often look like hypotheses about the origin of things. But a great many believers would not be content to regard the existence of God as an hypothesis, as something which may or may not be true. For them, their fundamental beliefs are absolutes, not hypotheses.'[10]

A similar point is made by Alvin Plantinga, who stresses that the origins of Christian belief do not lie in the human longing for explanation; rather, they lie in the self-revelation of God, and the human attempt to respond to that revelation.[11]

> Believers in God do not ordinarily postulate that there is such a person, just as believers in other persons or material objects do not ordinarily

[7] Basil Mitchell, *The Justification of Religious Belief.* London: Macmillan, 1973, 100–1.

[8] This is best seen from D. Z. Phillips, *Religion without Explanation.* Oxford: Blackwell, 1976. For a somewhat negative assessment of Phillips, see Gavin Hyman, 'D. Z. Phillips: The Elusive Philosopher', *Theology* 102 (1999), 271–8.

[9] D. Z. Phillips, *Wittgenstein and Religion.* London: Macmillan, 1993, 152–70.

[10] D. Z. Phillips, *Faith and Philosophical Enquiry.* London: Routledge & Kegan Paul, 1970, 47.

[11] Alvin Plantinga, *Warranted Christian Belief.* Oxford: Oxford University Press, 2000, 370.

postulate that there are such things. Postulation is a process that goes with scientific theories; one postulates entities of a certain sort (e.g. quarks or gluons) as part of an explanatory theory. Christians, however, do not ordinarily propose the existence of God as an *explanation* of anything at all.

Plantinga does not, it must be stressed, deny that Christian doctrine possesses an explanatory dimension; he insists, however, that this is neither the cause nor the primary focus of the Christian vision of God. If the Christian understanding of God were to be explanatorily sterile, would that invalidate its truth? Why should explanatory potential be seen as of fundamental importance in this matter?[12]

> Suppose theistic belief is explanatorily idle: why should that compromise it, or suggest that it has low epistemic status? If theistic belief is not proposed as an explanatory hypothesis in the first place, why should its being explanatorily idle, if indeed it is, be held against it?

Plantinga does not deny that, for example, the Christian doctrine of God has explanatory potency or fecundity; he is merely raising the issue of why this factor should be seen as of importance in the first place. Like Phillips, he turns to the problem of evil to raise questions about the significance of explanatory potential, as focused on a set of propositions *B*.[13]

> How could the existence of a triune God, or the incarnation of the Second Person of the Trinity, or the death and resurrection of the Son of God be sensibly thought of as *hypotheses* designed to explain what we find in *B*? What in *B* do these things explain? Could one sensibly claim that they are worthy of belief because of their high probability with respect to *B*, or because they explain some significant portion of *B*? Obviously not.

In turning to criticize Phillips or Plantinga at this point, it is essential to concede that they have made important points. For the community of faith, God is most emphatically *not* conceived simply as an explanatory hypothesis. Within the context of a scientific theology, the Christian network of doctrines is conceived as a response to revelation, in the belief that such doctrines will possess explanatory potential. Yet the primary reason for developing them is to respond to divine self-disclosure – to gain an understanding of God, in the belief that this will indirectly yield explanations of the world. Once more, the importance of the doctrine of creation becomes evident: knowledge of the creator

---

[12] Plantinga, *Warranted Christian Belief*, 370.
[13] Alvin Plantinga, 'The Probabilistic Argument from Evil', *Philosophical Studies* 35 (1979), 1–53, 51.

leads to an enhanced understanding and appreciation of the creation. The coherence of the created order, and the capacity of the human mind to grasp that coherence, is thus grounded on a doctrinal framework – yet a doctrinal framework which is primarily conceived as a response to self-positing revelation, not a response to a need for explanation.

If I have understood Plantinga correctly, there is no fundamental objection to postulating explanatory depth to the Christian faith, *provided* that such explanatory capacity is not made a precondition for postulating the truth or rationality – a term which Plantinga dislikes – of the Christian faith. According to Plantinga, the Christian believer has access to – and, indeed, has possession of – certain intellectual resources and insights which are not available to the non-theist; these should therefore be employed and deployed in explaining the nature of the world, and our experience. The key point is that the rationality or rational justification of belief in God must not be allowed to rest upon such a consideration.

So what should a scientific theology be able to explain? Three specific areas of explanation require consideration.

1. A tradition must be able to offer an account of its own specific form and contents, and explicate their interconnection. While Schleiermacher, Barth and the Yale school understand this task and its implications in somewhat different manners, it could be argued that this aspect of the theological enterprise is common to most approaches.

2. A tradition must be able to offer an account of why alternative traditions exist. Following the collapse of the artificial notion of a 'universal rationality', any given tradition is under an obligation to explain both its own existence, and that of its rivals. The particularity of a tradition does not call into question its universal applicability; it does, however, demand that it demonstrate this wider validity.

3. A tradition must be capable of seeing the world through theoretical spectacles in such a manner that it is able to offer explanations which may reasonably be regarded as appropriate and convincing to those within that tradition.

Explanation thus possesses both intrasystemic and extrasystemic dimensions – matters which we shall explore throughout this chapter. We may first turn to consider the extent of intrasystemic explanation, exploring how the Christian tradition is able to give an account of its own shape, form and contents. We shall do this by focusing on the concept of revelation, widely agreed to be of critical importance to Christian theology.

The concept of revelation in a scientific theology

We have stressed that, following the failure of the Enlightenment project, it is essential to recognize that rationality is not a 'universal' notion, but something that is mediated and constituted by a tradition. The Enlightenment optimistically presupposed an objectivity and universality of knowledge and judgement that failed to take account of the role of history and culture in their shaping and transmission. It is important to appreciate from the outset that any notion of tradition-mediated rationality entails that the theologian cannot be a detached observer of the tradition, in that the tradition concerned plays a constitutive role in shaping mental habits and outlooks. Theologians do not merely observe the Christian tradition; they inhabit it.[14] It is not something that they possess, but something by which they are possessed.

It is perhaps inevitable that recognition of this situatedness often leads to an essentially *ecclesial* conception of theology, focusing on the church as a sociolinguistic community, or prioritizing aspects of its religious life in such a way that leads to theological overinvestment in the habits and virtues of social existence. The church exists; therefore let us offer an account of its ideas, languages, habits and history – an enterprise admirably undertaken by Schleiermacher. It is therefore not surprising that the Yale school of theology made an inhabited ecclesial tradition its centre of gravity, paying rather less attention than was wise to the question of why that tradition took its form, and how it might be corrected, reformed and advanced, as the situation demanded. This severely attenuated conception of theology represents an overreaction to the failure of the Enlightenment project, and fails to give due place to the Christian tradition's self-understanding of why it is there in the first place.

Yet a scientific theology is ecclesial by *derivation*, not by *nature*. A critical realist approach to theology demands engagement with every aspect of the multilevelled reality which theology addresses, including the church as a community. Yet Barth's fundamental insight remains of critical importance: the centre of gravity of any responsible theology must

---

[14] I have in mind here Michael Polanyi's significant reworking of Dilthey's concept of knowledge as 'indwelling': see, for example, Michael Polanyi, *Knowing and Being: Essays*. London: Routledge & Kegan Paul, 1969, 144–5, 148. There is an excellent account of this relationship in Andrew Louth, *Discerning the Mystery: An Essay on the Nature of Theology*. Oxford: Clarendon Press, 1983, 59–66.

be – precisely because it already is – a Trinitarian vision of God, upon which the actuality of revelation ultimately depends. That is to say, the community of faith bears witness to an understanding of foundational events and insights which constitute its core identity, to which it returns for spiritual refreshment and theological reconstitution.

Theory represents an attempt to express in language the corporate beholding of a reality. In the case of the Christian community, theology is to be seen as a response to the vision of God which is mediated at every level of its reality, in which seeing gives way to telling; beholding to witnessing; experiencing to representing its unique vision of God. The Christian tradition mediates and embodies a distinctive understanding of God, which it proclaims in both its preaching and adoration, and represents in its theology. But how is knowledge of this God to be acquired, and what form does it take? The exploration of this point has constituted one of the most fruitful aspects of twentieth-century theology, and is likely to remain theologically fruitful for some time to come. Traditionally, this question has been explored in terms of the category of 'revelation'.

Karl Barth's affirmation of the fundamental dogmatic interrelation of revelation and Trinity marks one of the turning points in recent theological history, and demonstrates the critical importance of being able to affirm the manner in which the church is distinguished by the 'revelation' it claims to honour, and to which its life and proclamation bear witness.[15] For the early Barth, one of the most dangerous threats faced by the church was the subversion of its own identity through the intrusion of 'religion' as a human construction, leading to the dislodging of the gospel itself. If, as Karl Barth suggests, we are right to speak of the 'fundamentally nonfoundational character of the dogmatic method (*das grundsätzlich Ungründsatzliche der dogmatischen Methode*)',[16] then

---

[15] Among many recent important discussions of such issues, see Graham Ward, *Barth, Derrida and the Language of Theology*. Cambridge: Cambridge University Press, 1995; William Stacy Johnson, *The Mystery of God: Karl Barth and the Postmodern Foundations of Theology*. Louisville, KY: Westminster John Knox Press, 1997. For an historical exploration of the issue, see Bruce L. McCormack, *Karl Barth's Critically Realistic Dialectical Theology: Its Genesis and Development, 1909–1936*. Oxford: Clarendon Press, 1997, 129–290. For a different perspective on the question, see Rowan Williams, 'Trinity and Revelation', *Modern Theology* 2 (1986), 197–212.

[16] *Die kirchliche Dogmatik*, I/2, 972. The authorized English translation of this passage (*Church Dogmatics*, I/2, 869), which speaks of the 'fundamental lack of principle in the dogmatic method', leaves me somewhat perplexed, as it completely misses Barth's preoccupation with the issue of the foundations of dogmatics throughout §24 – for example, note the following challenging assertions (again, badly translated in the official English version): 'Gibt es nun für die Dogmatik keine voraussetzende Grundanschauung, sondern als Fundament und Zentrum nur das selbst voraussetzende und in der Kraft seines Inhalts sich selbst bestätigende Wort Gottes, dann kann es offenbar kein dogmatisches System geben. Gerade das richtig verstandene Materialprinzip der Dogmatik zerstört den Begriff eines dogmatischen Systems im Keime', *Die kirchliche Dogmatik*, I/2, 970–1.

theology takes its cues from a revelation which both 'presupposes and proves itself by the power of its contents'. There is an inherent circularity within the dogmatic method, in that it ultimately rests upon a 'self-positing and self-authenticating Word of God', which explains but is not explicable, and which authenticates without being authenticated. The church may be regarded as the community of faith which is called into existence by this 'self-positing and self-authenticating Word of God', and is prepared to recognize and live with the tensions of this epistemological situation, in a certain sense regarding itself as *defined* by this tension.[17]

In the English-language theological world, the most penetrating exploration of the question of revelation as constitutive of ecclesial identity is due to Robert Jenson.[18] For Jenson, the church is both identified and distinguished by its proclamation. That is to say, the identity of the church is maintained, both internally and externally, by its distinctive understanding of its identity and purpose, which are in turn shaped by the Christian gospel. 'The purpose that constitutes and distinguishes the church and in service of which the church needs to think is maintenance of a particular message, called "the gospel." . . . "Church" and "gospel" therefore mutually define each other.'[19] A central task of theology is therefore to 'speak' that gospel.[20]

> Theology is the thinking internal to the task of speaking the gospel, whether to humankind as a message or to God in praise and petition – for of course the church speaks the gospel also to God, pleading it before him and praising him for it. The church's specific enterprise of thought is devoted to the question, How shall we get it across, in language, with signs other than linguistic – in the church called 'sacrament' and 'sacrifice' – or by other behavior of our community, that Jesus is risen and what that means?

The term 'revelation' is often used to affirm that the 'gospel', which Jenson rightly affirms to be of central importance to Christian life and thought, does not derive its plausibility from being a cunning human invention, nor being the product of a specific influential society or powerful social grouping, but derives its authority *ab extra* – that is to say,

---

[17] *Church Dogmatics*, I/2, 868–9.
[18] See especially Robert W. Jenson, *The Triune Identity*. Philadelphia: Fortress, 1982. For an appraisal, see the essays gathered together as Colin E. Gunton, *Trinity, Time, and Church: A Response to the Theology of Robert W. Jenson*. Grand Rapids, MI: Eerdmans, 2000.
[19] Robert W. Jenson, *Systematic Theology*, 2 vols. New York: Oxford University Press, 1997–9, vol. 1, 4–5.
[20] Jenson, *Systematic Theology*, vol. 1, 5.

something whose origins lie in some sense 'outside' the community, yet which comes to be central to its self-perception and self-definition through a process of insight and appropriation. This notion – expressed by Barth in terms of the 'self-positing and self-authenticating Word of God' – represents a critique of human epistemic and soteriological autonomy, as well as a clear statement of the limits under which the Christian tradition must undertake theological reflection.

Traditionally, the term 'revelation' has been used to designate and endorse the notion that the central ideas of the Christian faith owe their origins directly or indirectly to God, rather than to human reason. Human knowledge of God can only be a true knowledge if it somehow corresponds to the divine reality, and this is secured by insisting that such knowledge of God has, in the first place, its *origins* in God, and in the second place, is *authorized* by God. The Pauline contrast of the 'wisdom of God' with human wisdom (1 Corinthians 2:1–4) is one of the most important instances of the pervasive biblical insistence upon the priority of God in the acquisition of true knowledge of divine things.[21] The precise interplay of direct and indirect aspects of our knowledge of God is often explored with reference to the concepts of *theologia revelata* and *theologia naturalis*, a process which has long been recognized as both illuminating and important.

Thomas Aquinas emphasized that Christian theology was based upon a revelation which ultimately lay beyond the discoveries of the natural sciences.[22] It is interesting to note that Thomas does not deduce the necessity of revelation from human fallenness, sinfulness or corruption, but from the fact that this knowledge ultimately transcends the natural capacities of humanity *as a creature*. Had this knowledge not been revealed to humanity through divine intervention, it would have remained beyond human reach. Revelation thus establishes the axiomatic points of departure for theological speculation, in much the same way as self-evident principles *(principia per se nota)* do in the philosophical disciplines.[23]

---

[21] See the fine studies of Ulrich Wilckens, *Weisheit und Torheit: Eine exegetisch-religionsgeschichtliche Untersuchung zu 1 Kor. 1 und 2.* Tübingen: Mohr, 1959; André Feuillet, *Le Christ sagesse de Dieu d'après les épîtres pauliniennes.* Paris: Gabalda, 1966.

[22] *Summa Theologiae* Ia q.1 a.1 'Necessarium igitur fuit, praeter philosophicas doctrinas, quae per rationem investigantur, sacram doctrinam per revelationem haberi.' Cf. J.-F. Bonnefoy, 'La théologie comme science et l'explication de la foi selon saint Thomas d'Aquin', *Ephemerides Theologicae Lovanienses* 14 (1937), 421–46; 15 (1938), 491–516.

[23] *Summa Theologiae* Ia q.1 a.8 'Haec doctrina non argumentatur ad sua principia probanda, quae sunt articuli fidei, sed ex eis procedit ad aliquid aliud ostendendum.' On the developing role of axioms in theological method, see Gillian R. Evans, 'Boethian and Euclidian Axiomatic Method in the Theology of the Later Twelfth Century', *Archives internationales d'histoire des sciences* 103 (1980), 13–29.

Since the means by which this revelation is transmitted is Scripture, Christian theology may be defined as 'Holy Scripture received in a human intellect'.[24]

Both the Old and New Testaments stress that human knowledge of God is dependent upon God's willingness to be known, and can be regarded neither as an automatic human right nor as an epistemological achievement within the grasp of the individual thinker. The Old Testament emphasis on the 'hiddenness of God' can be seen as a protest against any idea that God's self-disclosure can be brought under human control or subject to human command, while at the same time affirming the divine freedom in the act and content of revelation.[25] This theme has subsequently been developed extensively in Christian theology, particularly in Martin Luther's celebrated 'theology of the cross'.[26] The content of this revelation is often described as a μυστήριον – a complex and highly nuanced term which the English word *mystery* does not adequately translate.[27] As we saw earlier (46–9), Gabriel Marcel's distinction between a 'problem' and a 'mystery' points to the fundamental irreducibility of a mystery to a mere problem that can be solved, once and for all, by scientific enquiry.

This point is made with particular force by John Henry Newman in his critique of rationalism, which he held to fail to concede the limits of human language to penetrate or comprehend the deep structures of divine reality, and of human language to encompass that which it attempts to express. Mystery is thus discarded as an embarrassment, and faith held to 'consist rather in the knowledge of a system or scheme, than of an agent'.[28] Doctrine is capable of evoking understanding mingled

[24] Etienne Gilson, *Le Thomisme: Introduction au système de saint Thomas d'Aquin.* Paris: Librairie philosophique J. Vrin, 1922, 21–2. Cf. *Summa Theologiae* Ia q.1 a.2 'Revelatio divina. . . . super quam fundatur sacra scriptura seu doctrina'.

[25] See the classic study of Artur Weiser, 'Zur Frage nach den Beziehungen der Psalmen zum Kult: Die Bedeutung der Theophanie in den Psalmen und im Festkult', in Walter Baumgartner (ed.), *Festschrift Alfred Bertholet zum 80. Geburtstag.* Göttingen: Mohr, 1950, 513–31. The best study is now Samuel E. Balentine, *The Hidden God: The Hiding of the Face of God in the Old Testament.* Oxford: Oxford University Press, 1983.

[26] On Luther, see Hellmut Bandt, *Luthers Lehre vom verborgenen Gott: Eine Untersuchung zu dem offenbarungsgeschichtlichen Ansatz seiner Theologie.* Berlin: Evangelische Verlagsanstalt, 1958; Alister E. McGrath, *Luther's Theology of the Cross: Martin Luther's Theological Breakthrough.* Oxford: Blackwell, 1985, 148–75. More generally, see J. L. Schellenberg, *Divine Hiddenness and Human Reason.* Ithaca: Cornell University Press, 1993.

[27] Raymond E. Brown, *The Semitic Background of the Term 'Mystery' in the New Testament.* Philadelphia: Fortress Press, 1968.

[28] John Henry Newman, 'On the Introduction of Rationalistic Principles into Revealed Religion', in *Essays Critical and Historical.* London: Pickering, 1871, 30–101, especially 34–42.

with 'awe and wonder'[29] precisely because it offers perceptions of a mystery which cannot be reduced to purely verbal formulae, but which invites us instead to unleash the power of a biblically informed imagination in attempting to visualize what ultimately lies beyond its capacities, knowing that the struggle to do so is itself intellectually and spiritually enriching.

The stratification of revelation

In the previous volume, we introduced Roy Bhaskar's concept of 'critical realism', and suggested that it had considerable potential for a scientific theology, not least because it offered a framework for the engagement with a multilayered reality (vol. 2, 195–244). As an example, we considered how the very complex reality of 'illness' could be addressed at a number of distinct levels, following the pattern established by the World Health Organization's 'International Classification of Impairments, Disabilities and Handicaps' (ICIDH) in 1980.[30] Four 'levels' or 'strata' of illness may be discerned:[31]

Pathology, relating to abnormalities in the structure or function of an organ or organ system;

Impairment, relating to abnormalities or changes in the structure or function of the whole body;

Activity, relating to abnormalities, changes or restrictions in the interaction between a person and his or her environment or physical context; and

Participation, relating to changes, limitations or abnormalities in the position of the person in their social context.

Each level of illness demands a different research methodology, in accordance with its distinctive nature. It is impossible to reduce illness to any single level, in that the concept is so complex that it embraces a range of levels of reality, each demanding to be investigated and addressed in significantly different ways.

---

[29] Newman, 'Introduction of Rationalistic Principles', 59.

[30] *International Classification of Impairments, Disabilities and Handicaps: A Manual of Classification Relating to the Consequences of Disease.* Geneva: World Health Organization, 1980. This was later modified: *ICIDH-2: International Classification of Functioning and Disability.* Geneva: World Health Organization, 1997. For comment and analysis, see E. M. Bradley, 'An Introduction to the Concepts and Classifications of the International Classification of Impairments, Disabilities and Handicaps', *Disability and Rehabilitation* 15 (1993), 161–78.

[31] Derick T. Wade, 'Recent Advances in Rehabilitation', *British Medical Journal* 320 (2000), 1385–8.

It is perfectly reasonable to argue that the pathological level has priority, if this is understood to mean that it originates the subsequent levels of the reality which is an 'illness'. Yet illness is not limited to the original pathogenic stimulus. Once that stimulus has occurred, the illness becomes embedded at a number of levels of reality, each differing in its consequences, and necessitating different modes of investigation and remediation. Yet the full significance of the pathogenic stimulus can only be appreciated by identifying its impact on higher levels. To understand what a brain tumour is, and why it is so significant, its ramifications for every level of reality must be identified.

We must begin our analysis by noting the double meaning of the term 'revelation' within Christian dogmatics, embracing the notions of both revelatory *acts* and *knowledge*. Revelation as divine action gives rise to what the New Testament articulates in terms of categories such as 'tradition (παράδωσις)' and 'deposit (παραθήκη)' – concepts which convey the general idea of holding something in trust as a treasured possession. A series of past revelatory acts gives rise to a present revelation, both of which the church is required to affirm and safeguard. To use an image we shall explore further at a later stage (156), a revelational explosion has generated a multilevelled revelational crater. The New Testament clearly presupposes that revelation has taken place, and that what has been entrusted to the community of faith represents a 'deposit (παραθήκη)' which results from this revelation, and which may in itself legitimately be regarded as revelatory (1 Timothy 6:20; cf. 2 Timothy 1:12–14). It is this seminal construal of the two concepts of revelation which underlies Heinrich Bullinger's dramatic declaration *praedicatio verbi Dei est verbum Dei*,[32] as well as Karl Barth's highly significant notion of the 'threefold form of the Word of God'.

The Christian tradition has been highly alert to its responsibilities in both safeguarding and developing this revelational gift which has been entrusted to it. As developed within the Christian tradition, this concept (often expressed as *depositum fidei*) has come to mean the understanding of faith, resulting from revelational events, received within the church, and passed on to subsequent generations. Vincent of Lérins is representative of the patristic concern to 'safeguard' this *depositum fidei*:[33]

---

[32] For comment and analysis of this famous maxim in the writings of Karl Barth, see Hans Stickelberger, 'Bullingers bekanntester Satz und seine Interpretation bei Karl Barth', in Hans Ulrich Bächtold (ed.), *Von Cyprian zur Walzenprägung: Streiflichter auf Zürcher Geist und Kultur der Bullingerzeit*. Zug: Achius, 2001, 105–14.

[33] Vincent of Lérins, *Commonitorium* 22.

'Keep the deposit.' What is 'the deposit'? That which has been entrusted to you, not that which you yourself have devised: a matter not of inventiveness, but of learning; not of private adoption, but of public tradition; a matter brought to you, not put forth by you. You are obliged to be its keeper, not its author; a disciple, not a teacher; a follower, not a leader. 'Keep the deposit.' Preserve the talent of the Catholic Faith without addition or alteration. What has been entrusted to you must continue in your possession, and must be handed on by you. You received gold; give gold in turn.

The notion has undergone development substantially since Vincent of Lérins; nevertheless, its basic themes remain constant. For example, the 1990 *Catechism of the Catholic Church* stresses that 'the apostles entrusted the "Sacred deposit" of the faith (the *depositum fidei*), contained in Sacred Scripture and Tradition, to the whole of the Church'.[34] The term 'revelation' thus bears an extended meaning, which embraces the original revelational acts and the witness to those acts in Scripture and in the proclamation of the church.

Earlier, we noted how 'illness' could be seen as a coherent concept, enfolding within itself a number of interlocking levels of reality. Precisely the same is true of the 'revelational crater' which Christian dogmatics defines in terms of such concepts as *depositum fidei*. The 'deposit of faith' is a multilevelled reality, embracing a number of revelational strata. In order to appreciate its true identity and nature, the impact of revelation upon every level of Christian reality must be identified and evaluated. And precisely because of this stratification of the aftermath of revelation, it is amenable to a critical realist analysis. In what follows, we shall offer a 'critical realist' account of the Christian tradition, exploring its stratification and its implications for Christian theology. It is not appropriate to speak of these as different 'aspects' of the *depositum fidei*, in that this suggests a single-levelled reality which is merely viewed from different angles or perspectives, when what we are dealing with is actually a *stratified reality*, possessing a number of interrelating layers.

On the ICIDH model 'illness' denotes a complex, multilayered reality which simply cannot be reduced to any one level, aspect or perspective.

---

[34] *Catechism of the Catholic Church*. London: Geoffrey Chapman, 1993, sections 83–4. For comment on the notion of the *depositum fidei*, particularly in relation to the need for ongoing reformation and reflection, see Thomas F. Torrance, 'The Deposit of Faith', *Scottish Journal of Theology* 36 (1983), 1–28; Germano Pattaro, 'De oecumenismi exercitio: indicazioni per una verifica post-conciliare', *Studi Ecumenici* 2 (1984), 485–515; Irénée Henri Dalmais, 'The Liturgy and the Deposit of Faith', in Irénée Henri Dalmais, Pierre-Marie Gy and Pierre Jounel (eds), *Principles of the Liturgy*. London: Geoffrey Chapman, 1987, 272–80.

The totality of its aspects constitutes illness; yet illness is actually more than any of them. There are obvious parallels here with the notion of a *Gestalt*, considered as an irreducible entity whose whole transcends its individual aspects. In its developed, dogmatic sense, 'revelation' must also be recognized to be a complex, multilayered reality which simply cannot be reduced to any one level, aspect or perspective.

On a critical realist reading of the development of Christianity, a number of different levels of social construction may be identified within the complex aggregate of texts, ideas, images, values, communities and events, which may be described as 'revelation' in the developed sense of the term, which were brought into existence, or given a new depth of meaning, as a result of the original revelatory events which lie behind them, and which are handed on and transmitted through history. These are all affirmed to be integral yet distinct aspects of the same fundamental notion, whose interconnectedness may be explored and confirmed by historical and theological analysis. Among these strata of revelation, we may note the following.

1. *Texts*, which are understood both to mediate the events which constitute revelation, and to set the context for the events of revelation, providing a means by which certain events are to be interpreted. The canonical Scriptures of the Christian tradition bear witness to the foundational events of the Christian faith, as well as offering narrated interpretations of their significance.[35] Narrative and proclamation, *kerygma* and *dogma*, are thus interspersed within this textual medium.

2. *Patterns of worship*, which are already evident in the New Testament, which are to be regarded both as social realities (in that they involve a quite definite set of actions) and as ideas (in that the words associated with these actions have certain quite specific meanings). The importance of doxology to theology has often been noted;[36] what has not been sufficiently appreciated is that Christian patterns of worship are to be thought of as constituting a distinct stratum of reality.

---

[35] On the difficulties of seeing revelation *purely* as event, see Francis Watson, 'Is Revelation an Event?' *Modern Theology* 10 (1994), 383–99. Further issues of importance may be explored from Wolfhart Pannenberg, 'Redemptive Event and History', in *Basic Questions in Theology*. London: SCM Press, 1970, 15–80; Donald Davidson, *Essays on Actions and Events*. Oxford: Oxford University Press, 1980.

[36] Most notably, Geoffrey Wainwright, *Doxology: The Praise of God in Worship, Doctrine and Life*. New York: Oxford University Press, 1980; Aidan Kavanagh, *On Liturgical Theology*. Collegeville, MN: Liturgical Press, 1984.

3. *Ideas*, which occasionally build on existing notions, and at other times go beyond or negate existing ideas. Such ideas are clearly evident at the textual level, and play an increasingly important role through the growing emphasis placed upon formal 'Creeds' as a means of defining membership of Christian communities, as much as articulating and communicating their ideas.[37]

4. *Communities*, brought together through a shared faith in the revelational events, which found their sense of identity and purpose to be consolidated through the public and private reading of such texts, and the liturgical commemoration of both the foundational events of faith, and their perceived significance. Of particular importance is the manner in which Christian communities came to be differentiated from Jewish communities, which involves perceptions on both sides of this growing divide concerning the distinctive identities of the two communities.[38]

5. *Institutional structures*, such as the episcopacy, as means of securing the faithful transmission and embodiment of the ideas and values of the Christian communities.[39] While critical of aspects of existing ecclesiastical institutions, the Protestant reformers of the sixteenth century were fully aware of the importance of institutions in this process of transmission, and established variants on existing structures which they believed were more consonant with Scripture.[40]

6. *Images*, above all the cross as the distinctive icon of the Christian faith – a complex process of development of transformation involving the re-reception of traditional images and the forging of new images.[41]

[37] On which see J. N. D. Kelly, *Early Christian Creeds*, 3rd edn. New York: Longman, 1981.

[38] N. T. Wright, *The New Testament and the People of God*. Minneapolis, MN: Fortress, 1992, 447–52.

[39] Kenneth E. Kirk (ed.), *The Apostolic Ministry: Essays on the History and the Doctrine of Episcopacy*. London: Hodder & Stoughton, 1946; Gregory Baum and Andrew M. Greeley, *The Church as Institution*. London: Burns & Oates, 1974.

[40] Gillian R. Evans, *Problems of Authority in the Reformation Debates*. Cambridge: Cambridge University Press, 1992. The specific forms of institutions are considered in works such as Pieter Coertzen, 'Presbyterial Church Government: Ius Divinum, Ius Ecclesiasticum, or Ius Humanum?' in W. van't Spijker (ed.), *Calvin, Erbe und Auftrag: Festschrift für Wilhelm Neuser zu seinem 65. Geburtstag*. Kampen: Kok, 1991, 329–42.

[41] For a classic study, see Austin Farrer, *A Rebirth of Images: The Making of St John's Apocalypse*. London: Dacre Press, 1949. On the emergence of the cross as the distinctive Christian image, see the substantial body of work produced by Erich Dinkler, gathered together as Erich Dinkler, *Signum Crucis: Aufsätze zum Neuen Testament und zur christlichen Archäologie*. Tübingen: Mohr, 1967. More generally, see Carl Andersen and Gunter Klein (eds), *Theologia crucis – Signum crucis. Festschrift für Erich Dinkler*. Tübingen: Mohr, 1979.

7. The distinctive *vocabulary* of the Christian tradition, which may take the form of new words minted to meet theological needs – such as *homoousios* – or the investment of new meanings to existing terms (see the discussion at 84–90).

8. *Religious experience*, which may be taken to include – without being restricted to – the specifically religious experience identified by Schleiermacher as the 'feeling of absolute dependence (*das Gefühl schlechthinniger Abhängigkeit*)'.[42] As can readily be shown, this quite distinct stratum of Christian existence cannot be studied in anything quite like the intellectual isolation which Schleiermacher and his successors believed to be possible.[43]

Each of these eight interconnected strata – to which others could easily be added – may be regarded as an *explicandum* as much as an *explicans* – that is, as something encountered within the ambit of contemporary experience, whose existence required to be explained, with each level requiring investigation and exploration using techniques appropriate to its stratification. Institutional aspects of the 'deposit of faith' may be investigated, within limits, by sociological methods, without being restricted by the assumption that only a social explanation of its origins may be offered. Doctrines may be explored at a more intellectual level, without assuming that the 'deposit of faith' is purely ideational.

In seeking to be governed by and faithful to a past revelation, the Christian community faces two tasks, both of which are integral to the scientific theology set out in these volumes.

1. Attempting to clarify the nature of this revelation, within the limits imposed by the historical location of both the present community and the original nexus of events which constitute this revelation.

2. Maintaining continuity with this revelationally constituted and determined tradition.

A scientific theology thus possesses a double aspect, descriptive and prescriptive. As a descriptive historical-empirical discipline, a scientific theology takes its object of enquiry as a *datum*. It does not need to establish

[42] Wayne Proudfoot, *Religious Experience*. Berkeley, CA: University of California Press, 1985; William P. Alston, *Perceiving God: The Epistemology of Religious Experience*. Ithaca, NY: Cornell University Press, 1991; Dirk-Martin Grube, 'Religious Experience after the Demise of Foundationalism', *Religious Studies* 31 (1995), 37–52.
[43] Terrence W. Tilley, 'The Institutional Element in Religious Experience', *Modern Theology* 10 (1994), 185–212.

this, in that this lies beyond its scope; its proper task is primarily to explicate its levels and contents.

We may therefore explore how this complex multilayered reality which can collectively be considered to be revelation and its outworking is to be explained. Given what we observe, how can we account for it? If the various levels of an illness are all to be accounted for by a pathological development, what revelational development accounts for the various levels of revelation within the Christian tradition? The issue here is abduction – that is, arguing backwards from what is accessible and may be observed in the present to what may be argued to lie behind it. In what follows, we shall explore how this process of abduction is developed in both the natural sciences and Christian theology.

Revelation: theological abduction to the past

An important modern debate concerns whether the concept of 'revelation' is the most appropriate term or concept for the theological analysis of the self-disclosure of God within history in word and deed. The dogmatic category of 'revelation' is problematic, involving the use of a biblical term outside its natural context. As used in its original New Testament context, the Greek term ἀποκάλυψις is specifically associated with a future divine self-revelation – that is to say, with an event of revelation, understood as divine unveiling, which marks the end of the historical process itself, rather than an act or series of acts of divine self-disclosure within that historical process.[44]

Although there is ample historical evidence that the Christian tradition gradually came to accept the category of 'revelation', extending the biblical concept to embrace the Bible itself as a means of revelation,[45] there has always been a degree of unease within that tradition over the propriety of the term. In 1904, Martin Kähler argued that the concept of the 'Word of God' was far more coherent as a theological concept than 'revelation', enabling a correlation of God's acts and deeds in history, while retaining the Christological focus so characteristic of specifically Christian notions of divine self-disclosure. This can be seen as an important historical milestone towards Barth's articulation of the 'three-fold form of the Word of God', which aimed to re-establish both

[44] For the development of the term, see Morton Smith, 'On the History of ΑΠΟΚΑΛΥΠΤΩ and ΑΠΟΚΑΛΥΨΙΣ', in D. Hellholm (ed.), *Apocalypticism in the Mediterranean World and the Near East*. Tübingen: Mohr, 1983, 9–20.

[45] See René Latourelle, 'L'idée de révélation chez les pères de l'église', *Sciences Ecclésiastiques* 11 (1959), 297–344. For Latourelle's own reflections, see René Latourelle, *Théologie de la révélation*, 2nd edn. Bruges: Desclée de Brouwer, 1966.

the historical actuality and the theological coherence of divine revelation.[46] While the criticisms directed against this traditional construal of the concept of revelation by James Barr may be overstated at points, there is no doubt that Barr's concern whether 'revelation' as 'a term for man's source of knowledge of God' can be justified at either the linguistic or the theological level is well founded.[47] Some have suggested that the biblical category of the 'knowledge of God' offers a much more satisfactory means of aggregating the biblical concerns which are often formulated in terms of 'revelation', and there is much to be said for developing this manner of speaking.[48] More recently, Robert Jenson has tended to use the phrase 'the gospel' to designate the message which indeed rests upon, and conveys the meaning of, divine revelation.[49]

It will thus be clear that the question of the identity of the Christian notion of revelation preoccupied many writers in the twentieth century, and seems set to continue to be an issue in the present era.[50] The growing interest in the genre of narrative theology in the final two decades of the last century has inevitably led to a new concern with the idea of revelation itself. Narrative accounts of biblical authority demand a doctrine of revelation.[51] It is therefore to be expected that intense theological energy has been devoted to offering answers, with varying degrees of confidence and provisionality, to the question: 'What is revelation?'[52] Yet I come

---

[46] Barth, *Church Dogmatics* I/1, 125–86.

[47] James Barr, 'Revelation through History in the Old Testament and in Modern Theology', in *Old and New in Interpretation: A Study of the Two Testaments*. London: SCM Press, 1966, 65–103; *Interpretation* 17 (1963), 193–205; idem, 'The Concepts of History and Revelation', *passim*.

[48] This category has been widely used in systematic theology and philosophy of religion. See, for example, John Baillie, *Our Knowledge of God*. London: Oxford University Press, 1963; H. P. Owen, *The Christian Knowledge of God*. London: Athlone Press, 1969; T. H. L. Parker, *Calvin's Doctrine of the Knowledge of God*. Edinburgh: Oliver & Boyd, 1969; Brian Haymes, *The Concept of the Knowledge of God*. Basingstoke: Macmillan, 1988.

[49] See especially Jenson, *Systematic Theology*, vol. 1, 23–4, for the term. For Jenson's use of the category of 'revelation', see *Systematic Theology*, vol. 1, 59–60.

[50] See the very different approaches to be found in, for example, Rudolf Bultmann, *Der Begriff der Offenbarung im Neuen Testament*. Tübingen: Mohr, 1929; Hannelis Schulte, *Der Begriff der Offenbarung im Neuen Testament*. Munich: Kaiser, 1949; Peter Hünermann, *Offenbarung Gottes in der Zeit: Prolegomena zur Christologie*. Münster: Aschendorff, 1989; Stefan Orth, *Das verwundete Cogito und die Offenbarung*. Freiburg: Herder, 1999; Folkart Wittekind, *Geschichtliche Offenbarung und die Wahrheit des Glaubens: Der Zusammenhang von Offenbarungstheologie, Geschichtsphilosophie und Ethik bei Albrecht Ritschl, Julius Kaftan und Karl Barth (1909–1916)*. Tübingen: Mohr Siebeck, 2000.

[51] John Sykes, 'Narrative Accounts of Biblical Authority: The Need for a Doctrine of Revelation', *Modern Theology* 5 (1989), 327–42.

[52] The most interesting English-language works to deal with this question include Ray L. Hart, *Unfinished Man and the Imagination: Toward an Ontology and a Rhetoric of Revelation*. New York: Herder & Herder, 1968; George Stroup, *The Promise of Narrative Theology:*

away from such engagements with not so much a sense of dissatisfaction at the answers offered, but a profound feeling that the wrong question has been asked. If the natural sciences can indeed be the dialogue partner of Christian theology, the question that must be asked differs significantly in its tensing. For the real question is to be phrased as follows: 'What *was* revelation?'

At first sight, asking about the past identity of revelation might appear to be a puzzling and ultimately self-defeating question. Does it not foreclose such important discussions as whether one can speak of a continual revelation, for example through the influence of the Holy Spirit? Or at least prematurely (and probably also improperly) deny the term 'revelation' to the process by which the individual or community presently recognizes an event or text as authentically disclosing the nature and will of God?[53] It is not my intention to dismiss these questions, or preclude them from consideration in a more detailed account of Christian dogmatics. My concern here is with a central issue of theological method, which requires us to focus on the distinctive precipitating and governing influences, operating at a number of levels, which have shaped the Christian tradition.

While cosmologists are concerned to trace the universe back to its first few seconds,[54] and evolutionary biologists to trace the complex ancestry of humanity, a scientific theology sets itself the agenda of determining what brought the Christian tradition into being, and how this can and should continue to sculpture its intellectual contours. Following Brunner, we must affirm that revelation is something that has happened, and that the biblical witness concerns both the nature of such events, and their interpretation. On this definition, revelation is not something we currently experience; rather, we now encounter its aftermath, its indentation on the historical process. As Barth rightly stresses, the reality of God cannot be statically and objectively described. Revelation itself must be conceived as 'a revealing and not a state of being revealed (*eine Offenbarung und nicht eine Offenbarheit*)'.[55] That

---

Recovering the Gospel in the Church. Atlanta, GA: John Knox Press, 1981; Ronald E. Thiemann, *Revelation and Theology: The Gospel as Narrated Promise*. Notre Dame, IN: University of Notre Dame Press, 1985; T. F. Torrance, *Reality and Evangelical Theology: The Realism of Christian Revelation*, 2nd edn. Downers Grove, IL: InterVarsity Press, 1999.

[53] Legitimate and important questions, well explored in Gabriel J. Fackre, *The Doctrine of Revelation: A Narrative Interpretation*. Edinburgh: Edinburgh University Press, 1997, 181–201.

[54] An excellent example being Steven Weinberg, *The First Three Minutes: A Modern View of the Origin of the Universe*. New York: Harper, 1993.

[55] Karl Barth, 'Schicksal und Idee in Theologie', in *Theologische Frage und Antworten*. Zurich: Evangelischer Verlag, 1957, 54–92, 80.

revelational imprint is like the explosion of an artillery shell, leaving a crater which may be investigated long after the immense power of the detonation has passed. Yet it is the detonation, rather than the resulting crater, which is to be considered as 'revelation' in the proper sense of the word.

Precisely this image of revelation is used by Karl Barth in his *Romans* commentary. In insisting that the revealing God remains unknown and unknowable, and all that may be seen of the reality of this unknown God in the history of the world are the effects of revelation, rather than revelation itself, Barth (with the shell-pocked battlefields of the recent Great War clearly in mind) refers to such effects as '*Einschlagstrichter und Hohlraüme* (shellholes and craters)'. God cannot be thought of as 'entering into' history, in that revelation is a 'non-historical event (*unhistorisches Ereignis*)', which impinges upon human history only as a tangent touches a circle – at a 'mathematical point'.[56] God's revelation can no more be pinned down in human history than a bird can be pinned down during its flight, having no 'stationary point (*Standpunkt*)' which permits it to be observed and studied under the control of humanity. Revelation comes 'perpendicularly from above (*senkrecht von oben*)', denying humanity the opportunity to investigate it under conditions of its choosing.[57]

A similar point concerning access to the past is made by Richard J. Evans, in his important recent study *In Defence of History*.[58] For Evans, the past lies behind us; it is only 'present reality' which can 'be felt and experienced by our senses'.[59] Yet the aftermath of that past reality lives on, particularly in the form of textual documentation.[60] As a result, 'the past does speak through the sources', imposing its reality upon the present in a distinctive manner.[61] The historian is able to encounter the past, although in a subtly attenuated form, and thus able to make meaningful judgements concerning both what actually happened, and its intrinsic meaning.[62]

The essential point here is that we do not *presently* have access to the totality of whatever 'revelation' might be. We know it primarily by its

---

[56] For this image in Luther – who declares Christ to be 'the mathematical point of Scripture' – see *D. M. Martin Luthers Werke. Kritische Gesamtausgabe: Tischreden*. Weimar: Böhlau, 1883–, vol. 2, 439.

[57] Karl Barth, *Römerbrief*, 8th edn. Zurich: Zollikon, 1947, 5–6, 72–4.

[58] Richard J. Evans, *In Defence of History*. London: Granta, 1997.

[59] Evans, *In Defence of History*, 96.

[60] Evans, *In Defence of History*, 112.

[61] Evans, *In Defence of History*, 115, 126.

[62] Evans, *In Defence of History*, 253.

effects – by the impact it has had upon history – such as Scripture, various ecclesiastical institutions, and the liturgy, which point to something decisive having happened, and mediate its perceived significance to us. Yet we are not in a position to predetermine what can or cannot have happened in history; we are confronted with a complex multi-levelled amalgam of historical, literary, institutional and experiential clues, embedded at various strata of reality, to what once happened, which is traditionally designated as 'revelation'. If theological analysis is to be based upon presently available experience, the conclusion must be drawn that revelatory events, precisely because they are *past* events, are not directly accessible to us; what is directly accessible to us takes the form of its aftermath – the craters on the landscape of human history which bear witness to its *impact*, including the institutional and textual transmission of the perceived significance of those revelatory acts for humanity.

Earlier in this chapter, we gave a brief description of eight revelation levels of the 'deposit of faith', noting particularly how these were located at different strata of reality. To use a Barthian image, revelation is the explosion; the *depositum fidei*, the resulting stratified crater. Yet it is possible to abduct from the present to the past, simultaneously demonstrating the continuity of past and present while clarifying the nature of the past revelatory event that gave rise to the present 'deposit of faith'. In what follows, we shall demonstrate how this process of abduction is common to both the natural sciences and Christian theology, and explore some of its implications for a scientific theology.

Explanation as abduction to the past in the natural sciences

For many philosophers of science, the scientific study of the past raises a number of issues of difficulty for the scientific method. How, for example, can a unique event be studied, when the achievement of controlled replicability of results – widely regarded as an integral aspect of the scientific method – is, by definition, impossible? Can the scientific method actually be applied to the study of the past, whether this takes the form of historical investigation of human events such as the assassination of President John F. Kennedy or the proposed understanding of the evolution of species? Both involve the use of presently accessible evidence to reconstruct what happened in the past – but with what degree of plausibility?

In his autobiography *Unended Quest* (1976), Karl Popper expressed hesitation over whether the Darwinian theory of natural selection could strictly be said to fall within the scope of a scientific method, and hence be deemed 'scientific' in character.[63] By 1978, he had revised this view;[64] by 1980, he was clear that it was possible to treat the exploration of the past as a 'scientific' pursuit:[65]

> Some people think that I have denied scientific character to the historical sciences, such as paleontology, or the history of the evolution of life on Earth; or to say, the history of literature, or of technology, or of science. This is a mistake, and I here wish to affirm that these and other historical sciences have in my opinion scientific character; their hypotheses can in many cases be *tested*.

Popper's belief is widely shared within the scientific community: extrapolation from current observations provides a means of gaining access to insights to the past, even if there must remain a significant degree of uncertainty and provisionality to any conclusions that are drawn on their basis.[66] For the purposes of a scientific theology, the following points are of particular importance.

1. Observation of the present leads to an attempt to explain how it came to arise. This naturally leads to the question of how the best explanation is to be identified, an issue which is often considered under the rubric of 'inference to the best explanation' (Gilbert Harman) or, to use the more accurate Piercean terminology, 'abduction to the best explanation'.[67] This process may be discerned as underlying Kepler's reflections on the broader implications of observed planetary motion and Darwin's on the explanations of the origin of species.[68]

2. This process is assisted by 'snapshots' of past epochs – most notably, the fossil record, which played no small role in Darwin's reflections on the evolution of living organisms.[69] Despite diffi-

---

[63] Karl R. Popper, *Unended Quest: An Intellectual Autobiography*. London: Fontana, 1976. For a survey of the issues, see David N. Stamos, 'Popper, Falsifiability, and Evolutionary Biology', *Biology and Philosophy* 11 (1996): 161–91.

[64] Karl R. Popper, 'Natural Selection and the Emergence of Mind', *Dialectica* 32 (1978), 339–55.

[65] Karl R. Popper, letter to *New Scientist* 87:611, 21 August 1980.

[66] A major section could easily be added at this point on the scientific foundations of archaeology: see here works such as Joseph B. Lambert, *Traces of the Past: Unraveling the Secrets of Archaeology through Chemistry*. Reading, MA: Addison-Wesley, 1997.

[67] Gilbert Harman, 'The Inference to the Best Explanation', *Philosophical Review* 74 (1965), 88–95.

[68] Scott A. Kleiner, 'A New Look at Kepler and Abductive Argument', *Studies in History and Philosophy of Science* 14 (1983), 279–313.

[69] See the important monographs of 1851–4: Charles Darwin, *A Monograph on the Fossil Lepadidae or Pedunculated Cirripedes of Great Britain*. London: Palaeontographical Society, 1851;

culties and uncertainties over the dating and interpretation of this evidence, the fossil record is widely regarded as offering important insights into the historical process of evolution. For example, the record of fossil horses from the very small and generalized herbivore *Eohippus (Hyracotherium)* to the morphologically distant *Equus* allows the nature of this transition to be at least partially understood,[70] and suggests further that the different perissodactyl groups can be traced back to a group of very similar small generalized ungulates.[71] Snapshots of the past help build up an overall picture of the emergence of the present-day situation, helping us understand how it came about, and what the decisive factors and transitions may have been.

3. It is possible to identify processes which are operational in the present, and which are believed to have operated in much the same way in the past. Thus Darwin argued that the same mechanisms which lay behind the artificial selection of preferred plant and animal breeds were to be seen as implicated in the presumed process of 'natural selection'. This extends the existing presumption of the synchronic uniformity of nature diachronically.

Such assumptions and methods allow something of the past to be reconstructed, although the fundamental notion of confirmation through experimentally derived evidence cannot be brought to bear with anything even approaching its customary rigour. Furthermore, the element of prediction – regarded by some as essential to the scientific method – is severely limited by virtue of the subject matter of, for example, evolution.[72] Retrodiction is perhaps the most that can be hoped for in such situations, particularly in the light of Stephen Jay Gould's emphasis upon the unpredictability of evolution. If the tape of life were to be rewound and played again, he insisted, a quite

---

idem, *A Monograph on the Fossil Balanidae and Verrucidae of Great Britain.* London: Palaeontographical Society, 1854. For the appeal to the fossil record in Darwin's overall argument, see Darwin, *Origin of Species*, 114–72.

[70] R. L. Evander, 'Phylogeny of the family *Equidae*', in D. R. Prothero and R. M. Schoch (eds), *The Evolution of the Perissodactyls.* New York: Oxford University Press, 1989, 109–27.

[71] L. B. Radinsky, 'The Early Evolution of the Perissodactyla', *Evolution* 23 (1979), 308–28. More generally, see B. J. McFadden, *Fossil Horses: Systematics, Paleobiology, and Evolution of the Family Equidae.* Cambridge: Cambridge University Press, 1992.

[72] See the points made by Anthony Ferguson, 'Can Evolutionary Theory Predict?' *American Naturalist* 110 (1976), 1101–4. On prediction, see Hans Reichenbach, *The Rise of Scientific Philosophy.* Berkeley: University of California Press, 1951, 89: 'A mere report of relations observed in the past cannot be called knowledge; if knowledge is to reveal objective relations of physical objects, it must include reliable predictions.'

different set of organisms would probably succeed. Yet, as we shall see from case studies drawn from the physical and biological sciences, we are still able to draw significant conclusions concerning the past from the study of accessible present-day realities. We begin by considering modes of extrapolation to the past in the physical sciences, especially geology.

Cosmic explosions and bolides: the physical sciences

The question of the scientific investigation of the past arises with considerable force when considering the possibility that the universe came into existence *de novo*, as a unique event which, at least in one sense, lies beyond current investigation.[73] Yet this putative event, which took place long ago and cannot be repeated, has left an impact on history – in this case, the 2.9 K background radiation discovered by Arno Penzias and Robert Wilson in 1964, while they were working on an experimental microwave antenna at the Bell Laboratories in New Jersey. Penzias and Wilson had been using an ultra-sensitive microwave receiving system to study radio emissions from the Milky Way, when they found an unexpected background of radio noise with no obvious explanation. It appeared to emanate from outside the galaxy. Penzias and Wilson consulted with Princeton physicist Robert H. Dicke, who had theorized that if the universe was created according to the 'Big Bang' theory – which was then very open to doubt – it was to be expected that there would exist a background radiation at approximately 3 degrees Kelvin throughout the universe. Dicke duly visited Bell Labs and confirmed that the mysterious radio signal Penzias and Wilson detected was, indeed, the cosmic radiation that had survived from the very early days of the universe.[74] This was not merely the first serious proof of the Big Bang hypothesis, which earned Penzias and Wilson a Nobel Prize; it was a demonstration that a past event could be reconstructed from observation of its aftermath.

Studying the aftermath of a unique event thus allows at least something of that event to be reconstructed. This can also be seen from one of the more intriguing questions which has puzzled scientists for many

---

[73] For some of the points, both scientific and philosophical, see James S. Trefil, *The Moment of Creation: Big Bang Physics from before the First Millisecond to the Present Universe*. New York: Scribner, 1983; William Lane Craig, 'Theism and Big Bang Cosmology', *Australasian Journal of Philosophy* 69 (1991), 492–503; Quentin Smith, 'Atheism, Theism and Big Bang Cosmology', *Australasian Journal of Philosophy* 69 (1991), 48–66.

[74] A. A. Penzias and R. W. Wilson, 'A Measurement of Excess Antenna Temperature at 4080 mc/s', *Astrophysical Journal* 142 (1965), 419–21.

years: why did dinosaurs die out? What factors caused their extinction? How could this past event be explained?[75] In the late 1970s Luis and Walter Alvarez, along with a team of scientists from the University of California, were making a study of the rocks marking the Cretaceous–Tertiary (K–T) boundary in Gubbio, Italy. They found a distinctive layer of clay at this boundary point which contained an unusually high concentration of the rare element iridium. The levels of iridium contained in the clay were roughly 30 times the normal levels. Now iridium is also known to be found in relatively high concentrations in asteroids and chondritic meteors. To explain their otherwise puzzling observations, Alvarez and his team proposed that an asteroid hit the earth at the end of the Cretaceous period, 65 million years ago, throwing up a dust layer that encircled the earth and led to the extinction of the dinosaurs.[76]

Two particularly strong contenders for the site of such a bolide collision have been identified, both under the ocean; indeed, it is possible that both relate to the same cataclysmic event, representing separate impact craters from a fragmented bolide. The 180 km wide impact crater Chicxulub, located at the tip of the Yucatán Peninsula in the Gulf of Mexico, dates back to 65 million years ago, and is generally regarded as the more probable site of the Cretaceous/Tertiary meteorite impact. Evidence of Cretaceous/Tertiary period tidal waves (or, more accurately, tsunamis) has been found throughout the Gulf of Mexico.[77] A second possibility is the Shiva crater – thus named by the paleontologist Sankar Chatterjee – located under the Arabian Sea off the coast of India near Bombay, carved through Deccan Traps and into underlying Precambrian granite. This crater also dates from the K–T boundary, 65 million years ago. Although this impact crater has been partially dispersed on account of sea floor spreading, its original dimensions are believed to be about 600 km by 450 km across and 12 km deep. It would

[75] For early responses, see M. T. Schwartz, 'Evolving Ecosystems: Role in Dinosaur Extinction', *Nature* 12 (1976), 16–17.

[76] S. I. Morehouse and R. S. Tung, 'Statistical Evidence for Early Extinction of Reptiles due to the K/T Event', *Journal of Paleontology* 17 (1993), 198–209; J. David Archibald, *Dinosaur Extinction and the End of an Era: What the Fossils Say*. New York: Columbia University Press, 1996; David E. Fastovsky and David B. Weishampel, *The Evolution and Extinction of the Dinosaurs*. Cambridge: Cambridge University Press, 1996. Note that 'K/T' is the accepted abbreviation for 'Cretaceous/Tertiary'.

[77] V. L. Sharpton et al., 'New Links between the Chicxulub Impact Structure and the Cretaceous/Tertiary Boundary', *Nature* 359 (1992), 891–21; V. L. Sharpton et al., 'Chicxulub Multiring Impact Basin: Size and Other Characteristics derived from Gravity Analysis', *Science* 261 (1993), 1564–7.

require a bolide (such as an asteroid or meteoroid) some 40 km in diameter to create such a crater.[78]

Evolution: the biological sciences

A similar issue arises in evolutionary biology. The present distribution of plant and animal life is held to be explicable on account of a complex pattern of biological evolution and natural selection. Yet the observer does not have access to the evolutionary process, which is widely regarded as being historically dispersed over an immense period of time. The challenge is to explain present observations through an understanding of what happened in the past. Inevitably, this involves the reconstruction of the past in the light of the present, attempting to offer an account of certain critical events (one of which, incidentally, may be the K–T event just considered) and processes which cannot be presently observed. What remains for our observation is the aftermath or imprint of those events and processes.

Abduction to the past is a distinguishing characteristic of the scientific writings of Charles Darwin, especially his epoch-making *Origin of Species*. For Darwin, the biological observations which required to be explained included the following:[79]

Adaptation. An explanation was required of the manner in which organisms' forms are adapted to their needs. A ready explanation of one type was available from the doctrine of special creation, which posited that the creator caused each organism's form to be related to its environmental needs.

Extinction. It is known that Darwin's discovery of Thomas Malthus's theories on population growth had a significant impact on his thinking on this issue.[80] It was not initially clear how the extinction of seemingly well-adapted and successful species could be explained without recourse to 'catastrophe' theories.

Distribution. The uneven geographical distribution of life forms throughout the world was the source of some puzzlement.[81]

[78] M. R. Rampino and B. M. Haggerty, 'The "Shiva Hypothesis": Impacts, Mass Extinctions, and the Galaxy', *Earth, Moon, and Planets* 72 (1996), 441–60; M. R. Rampino, B. M. Haggerty, T. C. Pagano, 'A Unified Theory of Impact Crises and Mass Extinctions: Quantitative Tests', *New York Academy of Science Annals* 822 (1997), 403–31.

[79] S. A. Kleiner, 'Problem Solving and Discovery in the Growth of Darwin's Theories of Evolution', *Synthese* 62 (1981), 119–62, especially 127–9.

[80] Robert Young, 'Malthus and the Evolutionists: The Common Context of Biological and Social Theory', *Past and Present* 43 (1969), 109–45; S. A. Kleiner, 'The Logic of Discovery and Darwin's Pre-Malthusian Researches', *Biology and Philosophy* 3 (1988), 293–315.

[81] Malcolm J. Kottler, 'Charles Darwin's Biological Species Concept and Theory of Geographic Speciation: The Transmutation Notebooks', *Annals of Science* 35 (1978), 275–97.

Darwin's personal research trips on the *Beagle* convinced him of the importance of developing a theory which could explain the peculiarities of island populations, such as those found on the Galapagos.[82]

Vestigial structures. The apparent biological redundancy of certain animal structures – such as the nipples of male mammals – was difficult to accommodate on the basis of the concept of special creation, in that they appeared to serve no apparent purpose. Darwin hoped to offer a superior explanation of non-functional or rudimentary anatomical features.[83]

All these points were accessible and verifiable to the present-day observer; they did not require access to the past, or any privileged status – other than what, to the Victorians, was the relatively limited possibility of extensive travel to such exotic regions as the Galapagos Islands.

Darwin's task was to develop an explanation which would account for these observations more satisfactorily than the alternatives which were then available. Although the historical account of how Darwin arrived at his theory of evolution has perhaps been the subject of a certain degree of romantic embellishment,[84] it is clear that the driving force behind his reflections was the belief that the morphological and geographical phenomena could be convincingly accounted for by a single theory of natural selection. Darwin himself was quite clear that his explanation of the biological evidence was not the only one which could be adduced. He did, however, believe that it possessed greater explanatory power than its rivals, such as the doctrine of special creation. 'Light has been shown on several facts, which on the theory of special creation are utterly obscure.'[85]

In the end, Darwin's theory had many weaknesses and loose ends. For example, it required that speciation should take place; yet the evidence for this was conspicuously absent. Darwin himself devoted a substantial section of *The Origin of Species* to detailing difficulties with his theory, noting in particular the 'imperfection of the geological record', which gave little indication of the existence of intermediate species, and the 'extreme perfection and complication' of certain individual organs, such as the eye.

---

[82] For an excellent account, see Frank J. Sulloway, 'Darwin's Conversion: The Beagle Voyage and its Aftermath', *Journal of the History of Biology* 15 (1982), 325–96.

[83] Ingo Krumbiegel, *Die Rudimentation: Eine monographische Studie*. Stuttgart: Fischer, 1960.

[84] See, for example, Frank J. Sulloway, 'Darwin and his Finches: The Evolution of a Legend', *Journal of the History of Biology* 15 (1982), 1–53.

[85] Charles Darwin, *The Origin of Species*. Harmondsworth: Penguin, 1968, 230.

Nevertheless, he was convinced that these were difficulties which could be tolerated on account of the clear explanatory superiority of his approach. Yet even though Darwin did not believe that he had adequately dealt with all the problems which required resolution, he was confident that his explanation was the best available.[86] At least some of the 'loose ends' of Darwin's theory were tied up after the discovery of the physical basis of heredity through the cytological work of A. F. L. Weissmann in the 1880s and 1890s, and the rediscovery of Gregor Mendel's work by Carl Correns in 1900.[87]

Darwin developed the notion of 'natural selection' as a means of making sense of the bewildering diversity of plants and animals, both living and extinct, which had generally been a source of mystery to those who had preceded him. The reasoning deployed by Darwin in *The Origin of Species* assumes that processes that are currently observed as operational within nature were active in the past, and that their mode of operation and outcome were comparable to what may presently be observed. The first chapter of *The Origin of Species* takes the form of a substantial analysis of 'variation under domestication' – that is, the way in which domestic plants and animals are bred, the manner in which variations develop in successive generations through this breeding, and how these can be exploited to bring about inherited characteristics which are regarded as being of particular value by the breeder.[88] The second chapter then sets out the remarkable variation and novelty which can be discerned within the natural order,[89] and introduces the key notions of the 'struggle for existence' and 'natural selection' to account for what may be observed in both the fossil records and the present biosphere.[90]

It is then argued that this process of 'domestic selection' or 'artificial selection' is the outcome of a biological process, as yet not understood, which can be used as a framework for understanding that a related – yet ultimately significantly different – process of selection is taking place within nature itself.[91] 'Variation under domestication' is presented as

---

[86] Darwin, *Origin of Species*, 205.

[87] Carl Correns, 'G. Mendels Regel über das Verhalten der Nachkommenschaft der Rassenbastarde', *Berichte der deutschen botanischen Gesellschaft* 18 (1900), 158–68; W. E. Castle, 'Mendel's Law of Heredity', *Science* 18 (1903), 396–406; Lindley Darden, 'William Bateson and the Promise of Mendelism', *Journal of the History of Biology* 10 (1977), 87–106.

[88] Darwin, *Origin of Species*, 71–100.

[89] Darwin, *Origin of Species*, 101–13.

[90] Darwin, *Origin of Species*, 114–72.

[91] Robert M. Young, 'Darwin's Metaphor: Does Nature Select?' *Monist* 55 (1971), 442–503. In later studies, Young develops this point to include wider issues: see Robert M. Young, 'Darwin's Metaphor and the Philosophy of Science', *Science as Culture* 16 (1993), 375–403.

analogous to 'variation under nature'; both represent the outcome of a process within the natural order which is held to operate both in contexts familiar to English stockbreeders and horticulturalists and in the broader and more complex sphere of the evolutionary process itself. 'As man can produce and certainly has produced a great result by his methodical and unconscious means of selection, what may not nature effect?'[92]

Loose ends still remain in our understanding of the Darwinian process of evolution, and some of the available observational evidence is ambiguous. This is particularly evident in the current somewhat heated debate involving 'continuous' or 'punctuated' evolution. The traditional Darwinian model views evolution as a continuous process, involving a struggle for survival between organisms or – to develop an approach particularly associated with Richard Dawkins – gene lineages.[93] Yet certain aspects of this theory have been challenged in recent years.

In 1972, Stephen J. Gould and Niles Eldredge proposed the theory which has come to be known as 'punctuated equilibrium'. This holds that most evolution occurs in short bursts, interspersed with long periods of stasis. Gould and Eldredge attacked the idea that organisms continually change, adapting by small degrees to fit their environment.[94] Where Darwin viewed evolution as a slow, continuous process, without sudden jumps, Gould and Eldredge noted that the fossils of organisms found in subsequent geological layers indicated long intervals in which nothing changed (hence 'equilibrium'), yet 'punctuated' by short, revolutionary transitions, in which species became extinct and were replaced by wholly new forms. The fossil record, they pointed out, shows that most species change little after their first appearance.[95] New species appear in large numbers over short periods, perhaps because of dramatic events such as asteroid impacts. Gould – perhaps the most influential and best known evolutionary biologist since Charles Darwin – was widely criticized by more conventional Darwinists, who styled his theory 'evolution by jerks'. In championing theories that challenge at

---

[92] Darwin, *Origin of Species*, 132.

[93] See the useful analysis presented in Kim Sterelny, *Dawkins vs. Gould: Survival of the Fittest*. Cambridge: Icon Books, 2001.

[94] S. J. Gould and N. Eldredge, 'Punctuated Equilibria: The Tempo and Mode of Evolution Reconsidered', *Paleobiology* 3 (1977), 115–51. For a fuller statement of the theory, see Niles Eldredge, *The Pattern of Evolution*. New York: Freeman, 1999; Stephen Jay Gould, *The Structure of Evolutionary Theory*. Cambridge, MA: Belknap, 2002.

[95] See further Niles Eldredge, *Time Frames: The Rethinking of Darwinian Evolution and the Theory of Punctuated Equilibria*. London: Heinemann, 1986.

least certain aspects of the modern Darwinian framework, Gould in turn styled certain of his opponents – most notably, Richard Dawkins – as 'Darwinian fundamentalists'.

We have been considering how the physical and biological sciences are able to offer an explanation of present aspects of reality in terms of past events which are held to have brought them into being, and determined their shape and structure. So how does this process of abduction apply in the case of a scientific theology?

Abduction to the origins of the Christian tradition

Earlier in this chapter, we gave a brief description of eight revelational levels of the 'deposit of faith', noting particularly how these were located at different strata of reality. The existence and form of each stratum requires investigation and explanation, on the basis of its own distinct identity and characteristics. So how is this to be done? At this point, we may note that there is already a well-established pattern within the Christian theological tradition of arguing from a present effect to a revelational cause. This can be illustrated from F. D. E. Schleiermacher's analysis of present religious experience to its putative historical cause.

For Schleiermacher, the present experience of the individual Christian believer requires to be explained. Why does she have such an experience? How is it to be accounted for?[96] How do individuals come to develop this feeling of absolute dependence upon God? Schleiermacher answers this question in an early programmatic statement in *The Christian Faith*.[97]

> Christianity is a monotheistic faith, belonging to the teleological type of religion, and is essentially distinguished from other such faiths by the fact that in it everything is related to the redemption accomplished by Jesus of Nazareth.

Schleiermacher argues that the origins of this feeling are to be located in the impact of Jesus of Nazareth upon the collective consciousness of the Christian community. (Note, incidentally, that Schleiermacher avoids a purely individualistic approach to such feelings; the feelings in question are the common property and heritage of the Christian church.) Schleiermacher thus holds that a specific Christology is to be inferred from the present impact of Jesus of Nazareth upon believers within the

[96] W. Schulze, 'Schleiermachers Theorie des Gefühls und ihre religiöse Bedeutung', *Zeitschrift für Theologie und Kirche* 53 (1956), 75–103.
[97] F. D. E. Schleiermacher, *The Christian Faith*, 2nd edn. Edinburgh: T&T Clark, 1928, 52.

church, arguing back from the observed effect in the present experience of believers to its sufficient cause in the person of Jesus of Nazareth.

Redemption comes about through the stimulation and elevation of the natural human God-consciousness (*Gottesbewusstsein*) through the 'entrance of the living influence of Christ'. He attributes to Christ 'an absolutely powerful God-consciousness', which is impregnated with an assimilative power of such intensity that it is able to effect the redemption of humanity. Schleiermacher is perhaps less specific about the nature and manner of conception of this assimilative power than his critics might like. However, he seems to have in mind a model along the lines of a charismatic leader, who is able to communicate his socio-political vision with such clarity and power that it is both understood by his audience and captivates them in such a way that they are transformed by it and come to be caught up in it. Yet it remains his idea; he has assumed others into it, without compromising his personal uniqueness:[98]

> Let us now suppose that some person for the first time combines a naturally cohesive group into a civil community (legend tells of such cases in plenty); what happens is that the idea of the state first comes to consciousness in him, and takes possession of his personality as its immediate dwelling-place. Then he assumes the rest into the living fellowship of the idea. He does so by making them clearly conscious of the unsatisfactoriness of their present condition by effective speech. The power remains with the founder of forming in them the idea which is the innermost principle of his own life, and of assuming them into the fellowship of that life.

Schleiermacher then moves on to ask the question of who Jesus of Nazareth must be if he is able to have this effect, in this manner.

But this is to digress into Schleiermacher's Christology – a matter of some considerable interest, of course, but not directly relevant for our present purposes.[99] The important thing is to note the theological trajectory followed by Schleiermacher, which begins with a specific stratum of reality, as currently experienced within the life of the church, and proceeds to trace it back to its cause. Present experience constitutes the *explicandum*; the complex stratified notion of 'revelation' represents the *explicans*. Schleiermacher's strategy has weaknesses and limitations,

---

[98] Schleiermacher, *The Christian Faith*, 429.

[99] For a discussion of some of the issues, see Dietz Lange, *Historischer Jesus oder mythischer Christus: Untersuchungen zu dem Gegensatz zwischen Friedrich Schleiermacher und David Friedrich Strauss*. Gütersloh: Mohn, 1975; Maureen Junker, *Das Urbild des Gottesbewusstseins: Zur Entwicklung der Religionstheorie und Christologie Schleiermachers von der ersten zur zweiten Auflage der Glaubenslehre*. Berlin: De Gruyter, 1990.

particularly when viewed from the perspective of Ludwig Feuerbach's notion of the 'self-objectification' of religious experience, and has been criticized for its strongly attenuated conception of both Christianity itself, and the person and work of Christ. Yet such criticisms arise primarily on account of Schleiermacher's single-level approach to Christian experience, which fails to take into account the multi-levelled character of the Christian faith. Given the multi-levelled nature of the present-day Christian experience, a correspondingly stratified notion of revelation is required to account for it.

The process of abduction exemplified, although in a limited and not entirely satisfactory form, by Schleiermacher may be applied to the eight strata identified above (146–8) as corporately constituting the dogmatic (as opposed to biblical) concept of revelation. In every case, the argument may be made that the fundamental impetus to the development of this stratum is the words and deeds of God in history, culminating in the death and resurrection of Jesus Christ. It is this which has impacted upon history, and resulted in what is now accessible to our investigation. There is a perfectly legitimate debate to be had over the priority of the strata, and the manner of their interlocking and interaction. Both the horizontal and vertical aspects of theological explanation will require further examination (see vol. 2, 226–44) – something that lies beyond the limited scope of this extended essay in theological method.

Especially in the second volume of this trilogy, I have stressed the inadequacy of two influential models of knowledge, and urged the recognition of the merits of a third (vol. 2, 3–120). The first model that cannot be sustained is the Enlightenment vision of a universal mode of rationality, adopted by all right-minded people at all times, which gives rise to an incorrigible and universal knowledge which may act as the foundation of a theological or moral system. The second, whose origins owe much to the perceived arrogance and blatant historical inaccuracy of the first, argues that there is 'nothing deep down inside us except what we have put there ourselves, no criterion that we have not created in the course of creating a practice, no standard of rationality that is not an appeal to such a criterion, no rigorous argumentation that is not obedience to our own conventions'[100] – in other words, that we are free to create and inhabit our own intellectual worlds, rather than being under an obligation to respond to the way things are. A craven obedience to an external authority – I here lapse into the rhetoric of this position – is

---

[100] Richard Rorty, *Consequences of Pragmatism*. Minneapolis, MN: University of Minneapolis Press, 1982, xlii. For a critical assessment of this position, see vol. 2.

thus rejected in favour of the affirmation of human autonomy and creativity.

As we argued earlier, each of these positions is inherently incoherent and unstable. The third option is to recognize the critical role of tradition and communities in developing and transmitting ideas and values – an understanding of the nature of rationality which, as Alasdair MacIntyre has demonstrated – and as I have argued throughout this work – has an intellectual coherence which is absent from its two rivals (vol. 2, 64–72). Yet this is to raise a question which must now be addressed – namely, what brought this community into being, and governs its understanding of its own identity, place and purpose?

Revelation and history

To ask this question is to turn to history, recognizing that the Christian community was called into being by a series of historical events – including both phenomena and reflections on those phenomena – which caused it to nucleate and distinguish itself from other communities. One of the most significant aspects of this process of social and intellectual cohesion was the growing rift which opened up between Christianity and Judaism, which both reflected and accelerated a process of reflection on the distinctive identity of the early Christian community.[101] The development of baptismal creeds was an important part of this ongoing double process of differentiation of the Christian community from its ideational rivals in late classical antiquity, and fostering a sense of identity and belonging within the community of faith.[102]

This process of nucleation is not unique to the early Christian church, but is a common feature throughout human history. While it is entirely proper to insist that the *origins* of the Christian community lie in divine revelation, the subsequent process of development of a distinctive group identity is well understood, and is open to sociological investigation. The intellectual and social history of the Middle Ages and Renaissance is especially rich in examples of communities which sought to identify

---

[101] This process has been the subject of rigorous enquiry in one of the most important works of New Testament scholarship in recent years: N. T. Wright, *The New Testament and the People of God*. Minneapolis, MN: Fortress, 1992.

[102] On the role of creeds, see J. N. D. Kelly, *Early Christian Creeds*, 3rd edn. New York: Longman, 1981.

themselves with reference to certain distinctive ideas, events or values.[103] Such studies have stressed the importance of the consolidation of a sense of group identity in relation to their missions, and noted the manner in which such groups achieved this – for example, in the case of Swiss humanist sodalities of the late fifteenth and early sixteenth centuries, by using a common language (Ciceronian Latin) which distinguished them from the world at large.[104]

A similar process is evident within the early Swiss Reformation, as can be seen from Huldrych Zwingli's emphasis upon the role of sacraments in creating and sustaining a shared communal identity. For Zwingli, sacraments reaffirm the importance of the foundational events of the Christian faith, and encourage a corporate recommitment to those ideas and their ongoing application.[105] For Zwingli, the sacraments recall the memory of the foundational events of the Christian faith in much the same way as the annual pilgrimage to the battlesite of Nähenfels recalled a foundational event of the Helvetic Confederation, in which the Swiss defeated the Austrians in 1388.[106] The corporate identity of the church is to be maintained by the recollection and celebration of this event, along with its application to the life and mission of the community.

It will be clear that these reflections point to the importance of history – to the past events which brought the Christian community into being, and with reference to which it continues to define itself throughout the historical process. Truth is something that has happened, to pick up on one of the most important themes of Emil Brunner's vision of Christian theology.[107] Revelation, for Brunner, is above all an event, and *the* revelational event is Christ. Nevertheless the content of that revelation is never a bare event but is rather 'the intercourse of event and interpretation'. The notions of 'revelation' or 'the knowledge of God' are thus

---

[103] See Richard C. Trexler, *Persons in Groups: Social Behavior as Identity Formation in Medieval and Renaissance Europe*. Binghamton, NY: Center for Medieval and Early Renaissance Studies, 1985; Christine Treml, *Humanistische Gemeinschaftsbildung: Sozio-kulturelle Untersuchung zur Entstehung eines neuen Gelehrtenstandes in der frühen Neuzeit*. Hildesheim: Olms, 1989; Kenneth Goewens, 'Ciceronianism and Collective Identity: Defining the Boundaries of the Roman Academy, 1525', *Journal of Medieval and Renaissance Studies* 23 (1993), 173–95.

[104] Treml, *Humanistische Gemeinschaftsbildung*, 44–77; Goewens, 'Ciceronianism and Collective Identity'.

[105] See Huldrych Zwingli, *Corpus Reformatorum: Huldreich Zwinglis sämtliche Werke*. Leipzig: Heinsius, 1927, vol. 91, 217–18.

[106] Timothy George, 'The Presuppositions of Zwingli's Baptismal Theology', in E. J. Furcha and H. Wayne Pipkin (eds), *Prophet, Pastor, Protestant: The Work of Huldrych Zwingli after Five Hundred Years*. Allison Park, PA: Pickwick, 1984, 71–87. For the general context, see Robert C. Walton, 'The Institutionalization of the Reformation at Zürich', *Zwingliana* 13 (1972), 497–515.

[107] Emil Brunner, *Wahrheit als Begegnung*. Zurich: Zwingli-Verlag, 1963.

firmly linked to history. This thus raises the question of the manner in which revelation is linked with history, to which we may now turn.

The manner in which revelation impacts upon history was discussed in some detail during the 1960s, when a growing concern over the ahistorical theology of the Bultmann school was catalysed by the rising influence of Marxism, which offered a coherent philosophy of history as its intellectual foundation.[108] It was only a matter of time before theology responded by articulating a theology of history. We shall explore this point by turning to consider the concept of 'revelation in history' developed by Wolfhart Pannenberg in the early 1960s, before moving on to deal with the quite different approach developed by Alan Richardson around the same time.

Wolfhart Pannenberg on revelation in history

Pannenberg's early views on the theological role of history emerged within the context of what eventually came to be known as the 'Pannenberg Circle', an interdisciplinary group of graduate students at Heidelberg, who met weekly during the 1950s in an attempt to forge an integrated theological programme which would overcome the radical separation of biblical studies and systematic theology proposed, although in different manners, by Karl Barth and Rudolf Bultmann. Pannenberg and his colleagues offered an approach to the nature of revelation which conceded its future orientation, yet anchored the notion in salvation history, and especially in the history of Jesus Christ. While revelation did indeed refer to a future divine self-revelation, the resurrection of Christ was to be interpreted as a proleptic disclosure of that final revelation. A part event *in* history thus mirrored a future event outside history.

The theological manifesto of this group was published in 1961 under the highly significant title *Revelation and History*. The tone and general approach of this work is set out in Pannenberg's opening essay 'Redemptive Event and History', which argued that revelation may indeed be discerned within the historical process. Pannenberg states that history, in all its totality, can only be understood when it is viewed from its endpoint, which alone provides the perspective from which the historical process can be seen as a whole, and thus be properly understood. The end of history, which has yet to take place, is *disclosed proleptically*

---

[108] For recent reflection on the role of history in the formation and shaping of Marx's dialectic, see Paul Wetherly, *Marx's Theory of History: The Contemporary Debate*. Aldershot: Avebury, 1992.

in the history of Jesus Christ, and specifically through the resurrection. Although the end of history has yet to happen, its outcome has been revealed within history itself.

So how is this idea of a 'proleptic disclosure of the end of history' to be justified? Pannenberg argues that the apocalyptic worldview alone provides the key to understanding the New Testament interpretation of the significance and function of Jesus. He found support for this approach in Dietrich Rössler's study of the history of Jewish apocalyptic, which argued for the centrality of salvation-history within the movement.[109] According to Rössler, the basic theme of Jewish apocalyptic is 'history in its totality': the apocalyptic visionary sees history as a unified process which is directed towards a goal, determined by the will of God. The apocalyptic visionary gained an understanding of the *end* of history from *within* history. History is a process which can be understood only from the standpoint of its final goal; the visionary, granted a 'preview' of that final goal, is able to understand his own situation in its light.

The theological importance of this point can be seen by considering Pannenberg's 'Dogmatic Theses on the Doctrine of Revelation'.[110] The first five of these seven theses are of especial importance.

1. The self-revelation of God in Scripture did not take place directly, after the fashion of a theophany, but indirectly, in the acts of God in history.

2. Revelation is not completely apprehended at the beginning, but at the end of revelatory history (*am Ende der offenbarenden Geschichte*).

3. In contrast to special divine manifestations, the revelation of God in history is publicly and universally accessible, and open to anyone who has eyes to see it.

4. The universal revelation of God is not fully realized in the history of Israel; it was first realized in the destiny of Jesus of Nazareth, in so far as the end of history is anticipated in that destiny.

5. The Christ-event cannot be regarded as revealing God in isolation; it is set in the context of the history of God's dealings with Israel.

---

[109] Dietrich Rössler, *Gesetz und Geschichte: Untersuchungen zur Theologie der jüdischen Apokalyptik und der pharisäischen Orthodoxie*. Neukirchen: Neukirchener Verlag, 1960.
[110] Wolfhart Pannenberg, 'Dogmatic Theses on the Doctrine of Revelation', in W. Pannenberg (ed.), *Revelation as History*. New York: Macmillan, 1968, 123–58.

Pannenberg insists that meaning is inherent to events, so that it is quite impossible to draw an absolute distinction between an event and its interpretation. The meaning of an event is part of that event, given with it through its historical situation; it is only in the subsequent process of reflection that a distinction between 'event' and 'meaning' arises. The idea of 'meaning-free' events is not to be taken seriously.[111]

> It is simply not the case that one can take uninterpreted (*deutungsfrei*) established facts and then subsequently ascribe to them this or that meaning as one wishes, so that one could, for instance, also place a revelatory meaning on the list next to other equally possible meanings. On the contrary, events always bring their original meaning along with them from the context to which they have been assigned by their having happened.

This general point assumes particular significance in relation to the meaning of the resurrection of Christ:[112]

> [The] splitting up of historical consciousness into a detection of facts and an evaluation of them . . . is intolerable to Christian faith, not only because the message of the resurrection of Jesus and of God's revelation in him necessarily becomes merely subjective interpretation, but also because it is the reflection of an outmoded and questionable historical method . . . We must reinstate today the original unity of facts and their meaning.

Events and their interpretations can be considered only in the unitary totality of their original historical context (*Geschehenzusammenhang*).

The interpretative framework which is historically given along with the resurrection of Christ, and which determines the manner in which it is to be interpreted, is that of its apocalyptic context. Developing this point in his later work *Grundzüge der Christologie*, translated into English as *Jesus – God and Man*, Pannenberg insists that the apocalyptic worldview entails that the end of history includes a general resurrection of the dead. When the resurrection of Christ is set against this specific context, the future realm of revelation is, at least to some extent,

---

[111] Wolfhart Pannenberg, 'Einsicht und Glaube: Antwort an Paul Althaus', *Theologische Literaturzeitung* 88 (1963), 81–92, quote at 88. Pannenberg here responds to the criticisms directed against him in Paul Althaus, 'Offenbarung als Geschichte und Glaube', *Theologische Literaturzeitung* 87 (1962), 321–30.

[112] Wolfhart Pannenberg, 'The Revelation of God in Jesus of Nazareth', in *Theology as History*, ed. J. M. Robinson and J. B. Cobb. New York: Harper & Row, 1967, 101–33, quote at 126–7. For further reflection, see Iain G. Nicol, 'Facts and Meanings: Wolfhart Pannenberg's Theology of History and the Role of the Historical-Critical Method', *Religious Studies* 12 (1971), 129–39.

transposed to the present. Pannenberg's argument can be summarized as follows.[113]

1. If Jesus has been raised, then the end of the world has begun.

2. If Jesus has been raised, a Jew could only interpret this event as God directly confirming the pre-Easter activity of Jesus.

3. Through his resurrection, Jesus came to be so closely identified with the apocalyptic figure of the Son of Man that it could only be concluded that this Son of Man is none other than the man Jesus, who will come again.

4. If Jesus, having been raised from the dead, is ascended to God, and if the end of the world has dawned as a result, then God is ultimately revealed in Jesus.

The end of history has thus taken place *proleptically* in the resurrection of Jesus from the dead. The resurrection of Jesus thus anticipates the general resurrection at the end of time, and brings forward into history both that resurrection and the full and final revelation of God. The resurrection of Jesus is thus organically linked with the self-revelation of God in Christ:[114]

> Only at the end of all events can God be revealed in his divinity, that is, as the one who works all things, who has power over everything. Only because in Jesus' resurrection the end of all things, which for us has not yet happened, has already occurred can it be said of Jesus that the ultimate already is present in him, and so also that God himself, his glory, has made its appearance in Jesus in a way that cannot be surpassed. Only because the end of the world is already present in Jesus' resurrection is God himself revealed in him.

Pannenberg thus retains the apocalyptic notion of 'revelation' as a future event, yet establishes a link with the history of Jesus Christ through an appeal to a specific interpretation of the resurrection of Christ. Yet this link has proved incapable of bearing the weight placed upon it, and must now be regarded as resting upon an unreliable account of apocalypticism.[115] Wisely recognizing this point, Pannenberg's more

---

[113] Wolfhart Pannenberg, *Jesus – God and Man*. London: SCM Press, 1968, 66–73.

[114] Pannenberg, *Jesus – God and Man*, 69.

[115] For a general account of the difficulties, see David P. Polk, *On the Way to God: An Exploration into the Theology of Wolfhart Pannenberg*. Lanham, MD: University Press of America, 1989, 154–62. More specifically, see Hans Dieter Betz, 'The Concept of Apocalyptic in the Theology of the Pannenberg Group', *Journal for Theology and Church* 6 (1969), 192–207; William R. Murdock, 'History and Revelation in Jewish Apocalypticism', *Interpretation* 21 (1967), 167–87; Andreas Nissen, 'Tora und Geschichte im Spätjudentum', *Novum Testamentum* 9 (1967), 241–77.

recent discussion of the category of 'revelation' stresses the multiplicity of biblical concepts, which clearly includes certain generalized 'apocalyptic' elements, yet extends more generally beyond these.[116] Yet it is questionable whether this can salvage his approach from its obvious vulnerabilities.

In an important later reflection on the 'Pannenberg Circle', Rolf Rendtorff set out his own misgivings about Pannenberg's programme, which he had earlier accepted a little uncritically.[117] In particular, he pointed out how the group had been led to place a quite inappropriate emphasis upon the 'proleptic' or 'postponed' element in revelation. Pannenberg, he argues, interprets the entire Old Testament apocalyptically, failing to note those sections in which revelation is understood to be a completed process. God's self-revelation is frequently affirmed to be a completed process, with both particularist and universalist dimensions, relating to both Israel and the Gentiles.[118] A similar concern emerges from even the most cursory analysis of the Pauline corpus, which bears witness to a notion of revelation which embraces the past, present and future.[119]

Yet alongside these exegetical concerns, a much more general theological difficulty must be noted with Pannenberg's programme. As James Barr pointed out, Pannenberg's entire approach seemed to rest on the notion of 'plain history' being 'revelatory'.[120] To his critics, Pannenberg's argument hinges on the capacity of unaided human reason to discern the revelatory significance of the historical process, which seemed to reduce faith to insight, and deny any role to the Holy Spirit in the event of revelation.[121] This weakness within Pannenberg's early theology of

---

[116] Wolfhart Pannenberg, *Systematic Theology*, 3 vols. Grand Rapids, MI: Eerdmans, 1991–8, vol. 1, 198–214, 227–9.

[117] Rolf Rendtorff, 'Offenbarung und Geschichte: Partikularismus und Universalismus im Offenbarungsverständnis Israels', in *Kanon und Theologie*. Neukirchen-Vluyn: Neukirchener Verlag, 1991, 113–22.

[118] Texts which Rendtorff regards as especially important in this respect include Exodus 14:31; Psalm 76:1; and Psalm 98:2–3.

[119] Markus N. A. Bockmuehl, *Revelation and Mystery in Ancient Judaism and Pauline Christianity*. Tübingen: Mohr, 1990, 133–47. For the present–future tension in greater detail, see Peter Stuhlmacher, 'Erwägungen zum Problem vom Gegenwart und Zukunft in der paulinischen Eschatologie', *Zeitschrift für Theologie und Kirche* 64 (1967), 423–50.

[120] James Barr, 'The Concepts of History and Revelation', in *Old and New in Interpretation: A Study of the Two Testaments*. London: SCM Press, 1966, 65–103, especially 67–8.

[121] See Paul Althaus, 'Offenbarung als Geschichte und Glaube', *Theologische Literaturzeitung* 87 (1962), 321–80; Lothar Steiger, 'Offenbarungsgeschichte und theologische Vernunft', *Zeitschrift für Theologie und Kirche* 59 (1962), 88–113. For Pannenberg's response to such criticisms, see Wolfhart Pannenberg, 'Einsicht und Glaube: Antwort an Paul Althaus', *Theologische Literaturzeitung* 88 (1963), 81–92.

revelation has never been entirely resolved.[122] Pannenberg has failed to meet the most fundamental criticism which may be directed against this approach – namely, that it is possible for two observers to watch the same event, and attribute quite different interpretations to it, both of which may be regarded as warranted on the basis of their specific circumstances.

A further difficulty concerns Pannenberg's apparent devaluation of the linguistic aspects of the context within which revelation takes place. In the prophetic tradition, even where revelation takes the form of a vision – such as Jeremiah's almond branch or boiling pot (Jeremiah 1:11–14), or Amos's basket of fruit (Amos 8:1–4) – that vision is accompanied by interpretation, whether by the seer himself or by the text in which the vision is embedded.[123] Hans-Joachim Kraus argues that the distinctive feature of the Old Testament conception of revelation is that it goes beyond the mere intimation of a divine presence, and affirms a God who may be said to 'speak' or 'call'.[124] Revelation involves the use of words – words which may indeed interpret events, but which are nonetheless essential as part of the complex interlocking of event and interpretation that the notion of revelation so clearly demands.[125]

While Pannenberg is to be complimented on his concern to maintain proximity to the biblical conception of revelation, it is questionable whether the outcome of his engagement with the issue is either rigorously biblically grounded or theologically viable. A more theologically responsible approach was developed within the English-language theological world, to which we now turn.

Alan Richardson on revelation in history

In his 1962 Bampton Lectures at Oxford University, Alan Richardson set out an approach to revelation which grounded it in universal history, while simultaneously affirming its particularity within the Christian tra-

---

[122] In his later writings, Pannenberg has sought to address this concern: see Wolfhart Pannenberg, *Systematic Theology*, 3 vols. Grand Rapids, MI: Eerdmans, 1991–8, vol. 1, 249–52.

[123] This point has repeatedly been stressed by scholars concerned with the biblical ideas of revelation, such as the classic study of F. Eduard König, *Der Offenbarungsbegriff des Alten Testamentes*. Leipzig: Hinrichs, 1882.

[124] Hans-Joachim Kraus, *Theologie der Psalmen*. Neukirchen-Vluyn: Neukirchener Verlag, 1979, 45. See also Hans-Joachim Kraus, *Psalmen*. Neukirchen-Vluyn: Neukirchener Verlag, 1978, especially his comments on Psalm 50:3.

[125] For an excellent discussion of the Old Testament context, see Albert de Pury, 'Sagesse et révélation dans l'Ancien Testament', *Review of Theology and Philosophy* 27 (1979), 1–50. For the general point, see William J. Abraham, *Divine Revelation and the Limits of Historical Criticism*. Oxford: Oxford University Press, 1982, 8–10.

dition.[126] Noting the tendency of theologians since the First World War to disengage with history,[127] Richardson offers a strategy of recovery which takes the concerns of writers such as Paul Tillich and Karl Barth seriously, while moving beyond their ultimately unsuccessful approaches. Richardson argues that the misgivings of such writers arise in response to a positivistic construal of the historical agenda, according to which historians believe that it is possible to establish '"facts", which may be objectively ascertained by followed recognized scientific procedures'. As a result, 'there cannot be Christian (or Marxist or anything else) historical facts'.[128] Richardson's thinking at this point has clearly been stimulated by Edward Hallett Carr's George Macaulay Trevelyan Lectures delivered in the University of Cambridge, over the period January–March 1961, which mounted a sustained attack on the idea of historical 'facts':[129]

> The nineteenth century was a great age for facts. 'What I want,' said Mr. Gradgrind in *Hard Times*, 'is Facts . . . Facts alone are wanted in life.' Nineteenth-century historians on the whole agreed with him. When Ranke in the 1830s, in legitimate protest against moralizing history, remarked that the task of the historian was 'simply to show how it really was (*wie es eigentlich gewesen*)' this not very profound aphorism had an astonishing success. Three generations of German, British, and even French historians marched into battle intoning the magic words, *Wie es eigentlich gewesen* like an incantation – designed, like most incantations, to save them from the tiresome obligation to think for themselves. The Positivists, anxious to stake out their claim for history as a science, contributed the weight of their influence to the cult of facts. First ascertain the facts, said the Positivists, then draw your conclusions from them.

Carr pointed out how this 'common-sense' approach to the matter fitted in perfectly with the British empiricist tradition, which was the dominant strain in British philosophy from Locke to Bertrand Russell. The empirical theory of knowledge presupposes a complete separation between subject and object. Facts, like sense-impressions, impinge on the observer from outside, and are independent of his consciousness. Unlike critical realism, which assumes an active role for the knower in the cognitive process, this form of empiricism held that the process of

[126] Alan Richardson, *History, Sacred and Profane*. London: SCM Press, 1964. For an early study, which has not yet been surpassed, see John J. Navone, *History and Faith in the Thought of Alan Richardson*. London: SCM Press, 1966.
[127] Richardson, *History, Sacred and Profane*, 125–53.
[128] Richardson, *History, Sacred and Profane*, 154.
[129] E. H. Carr, *What is History?* New York: St Martin's Press, 1961, 34–5.

reception is passive – the observer merely receives facts, and acts upon them. As Carr points out, this has important implications for any discipline which makes an appeal to history:

> History consists of a corpus of ascertained facts. The facts are available to the historian in documents, inscriptions, and so on, like fish on the fishmonger's slab. The historian collects them, takes them home, and cooks and serves them in whatever style appeals to him.

Richardson mistakenly assumes that Carr is an ally of the Enlightenment, when in fact he is one of its more penetrating critics.[130] Carr argued that history is always constructed, and is thus to be seen as discourse about the past rather than a reflection of it. Carr recognized that history as a discipline does not follow the logic of discovery. Rather, it is the result of the interaction between the historian and alleged facts – a perpetual dialogue between the present and the past.[131]

Carr is no supporter of a sceptical approach to history, which he holds to subvert the possibility of any objective approach to the discipline (a weakness which he discerns in the approach offered by R. G. Collingwood). Yet by undermining the notion of intrinsically objective historical facts, Carr in fact opens the way to a specifically Christian construal of history, in which the worldview of the observer is actively brought to bear on the process of observation and interpretation. 'The facts of history never come to us pure, since they do not and cannot exist in a pure form: they are always refracted through the mind of the recorder.' Publicly observable events may be construed in quite different ways, and thus disclose quite different ideas to those observing them.

It is the Christian construal of historical events which plays such a critical role in Richardson's approach to history. Richardson stresses that both Old and New Testaments regard a series of events as 'disclosure situations' – that is to say, historical events which generate 'the discernment of a meaning which provokes a response to what is discerned'.[132] These events are not understood to be self-interpreting, nor is their full significance apparent to all who observe them. Nevertheless, they resonate with the community of faith's discernment of the divine nature

[130] See Richardson, *History, Sacred and Profane*, 51–2.

[131] For an excellent introduction to such questions, see Michael Cox, *E. H. Carr: A Critical Appraisal*. Basingstoke: Palgrave, 2000.

[132] Richardson, *History, Sacred and Profane*, 223–7. Richardson derives his understanding of such 'disclosure situations' from Ian T. Ramsey, *Religious Language: An Empirical Placing of Theological Phrases*. London: SCM Press, 1957. For Pannenberg's use of Ramsey, see his *Systematic Theology*, vol. 1, 65–7, 70–1, 198.

and purposes, which is both based upon those events and offers an inter-pretative framework within which the hermeneutical spiral may be advanced.

In the case of the Old Testament, Richardson identifies events such as the exodus from Egypt as charged with significance for those who could discern it 'through the activity of prophetic minds', which 'became interpretative of Israel's historic destiny'. The distinctive characteristic of the biblical conception of revelation is that God is understood to be dis-closed through historical events. Richardson thus affirms that the exodus from Egypt was understood, and was rightly understood, as[133]

> a disclosure of the divine purpose and an act of divine redemption in the midst of real, 'secular' history, so that Israel could say, as of all the deliv-erances in her history, 'This is Yahweh's doing, and it is marvellous in our eyes' (Ps. 118.23) . . . . [It represents] a personal disclosure of the divine intention in the midst of history, a disclosure, that is to say, to those whose eyes and ears have been opened and who in faith and obedience are willing to make the appropriate response to it.

Richardson here avoids the fatal weakness of Pannenberg's fundamen-tally modernist approach, which held that the 'revelation of God is open to anyone who has eyes to see, and does not need any supplementary inspired interpretation'.[134] The nature of history is such, he argues, that this simplistic approach cannot be sustained. Interpretations of history are not 'empirically deduced from an objective study of "the facts", for at every point, even at the point of deciding what are the facts, the per-sonal judgement of the historian is involved'.[135]

We are thus confronted with the fact that history requires to be inter-preted; yet history itself does not provide an interpretative framework through which the process of interpretation may take place. The revela-tory events do indeed take place in 'real' history; their significance, however, is only rightly perceived from the standpoint of faith – that is to say, they are only revelatory if they are recognized as divine revelation, in that they do not interpret themselves as such. It is therefore entirely correct to conclude that 'Christian dogmatics is, in essence, the Christian interpretation of history'.[136] Here, we find a decisive move away from Pannenberg's unsatisfactory account of 'plain history'

---

[133] Richardson, *History, Sacred and Profane*, 225. Richardson's thinking here has been shaped in part by Edmond Jacob, *Theology of the Old Testament*. London: Hodder & Stoughton, 1958, especially 183–232.
[134] Pannenberg, *Systematic Theology*, vol. 1, 249.
[135] Richardson, *History, Sacred and Profane*, 247.
[136] Richardson, *History, Sacred and Profane*, 294.

towards an understanding of both existence within history and a concomitant engagement with history which takes seriously the *particularity* of the perspective of the observer.

What Richardson proposes for our consideration is an understanding of revelation in history which continues to be fruitful for Christian theology, as it reflects on its identity and tasks.[137] The past cannot be replicated in the present, nor can it be encountered and known *directly*. What is transmitted within the historical nexus to subsequent generations can be summed up under three broad categories:

1. A summary account of the historical events which are held to constitute revelation.

2. A summary of the perceived significance of those events for faith.

3. A community which is brought into being by those revelational events and their perceived significance, which regards its identity as being constituted and safeguarded by them, and which proclaims them in word and action.

In effect (3) is generated by (1) and (2); and (3) subsequently 'hands down' or 'hands over' (1) and (2) within the historical process.

We may proceed immediately to a consideration of how such revelation, here understood in its developed sense of *depositum fidei*, is transmitted through the historico-social reality of the Christian tradition.

The transmission of revelation

From an orthodox perspective, the precipitating cause of Christian faith and Christian doctrine was and remains Jesus Christ. We know of him only through the traditions of his deeds and words preserved in the New Testament. In a collective act of solidarity of recollection, the community of faith chose to align itself with this history, and none other, as its fundamental legitimizing resource. The history of Jesus of Nazareth was and is the crucible of Christian doctrinal possibilities, the controlling paradigm of conceptual potentialities.

To attribute authority, however this may subsequently be articulated or defended, to Jesus of Nazareth is to attribute authority to this past event not *because* it is past, but because what thus happened in the past is perceived to be charged with significance for the transformation of the

---

[137] See, for example, Avery Dulles, 'Faith and Revelation', in Francis Schüssler Fiorenza and John P. Galvin (eds), *Systematic Theology: Roman Catholic Perspectives*. Minneapolis: Augsburg Fortress, 1992, 89–128, especially 98.

present and the construction of the future. The transmission of the past to the present thus assumes a pivotal position in the quest for Christian authenticity, in both thought and action. In addition to memories of the life and death of Jesus, the New Testament transmits traditions of the impact made by him after he was raised from the dead, and a range of attempts to explain his identity and significance in the light of this event.[138] The New Testament is essentially the repository of the formative and identity-giving traditions of the Christian community, focusing specifically on the person of Jesus Christ. It does not encompass the totality of those traditions; rather, it contains those elements of early tradition which the first Christian communities perceived as decisive for their own identities and purposes, and thus preserved.

It will thus be clear that 'tradition' is a thoroughly biblical notion. Paul reminded his readers that he was handing on to them core teachings of the Christian faith which he had received from others (1 Corinthians 15:1–4).[139] The term can refer to both the action of passing teachings on to others – something which Paul insists must be done within the church – and to the body of teachings which are passed on in this manner. Tradition can thus be understood as a process as well as a body of teaching.[140] As we have noted, the Pastoral Epistles in particular stress the importance of 'guarding the good deposit which was entrusted to you' (1 Timothy 6:20; 2 Timothy 1:14).

The concept of 'tradition'

The notion of tradition embraces the process by which the Christian proclamation is transmitted, as much as what is transmitted. *Traditio* thus designates a process of 'handing over' and 'handing on', which can be thought of as the faithful and responsible transference from one generation to another of the central realities of the Christian faith. It will immediately be clear that tradition – considered both as process of transmission and as transmitted reality – is a socially embedded concept. To clarify this point, we may consider both aspects of the matter.

1. Considered as *process of transmission*, the notion of tradition embraces far more than the mere oral transfer of ideas from one

---

[138] For the issues raised here, see James D. G. Dunn, *Unity and Diversity in the New Testament: An Inquiry into the Character of Earliest Christianity*, 2nd edn. London: SCM Press, 1990; Arland J. Hultgren, *The Rise of Normative Christianity*. Minneapolis: Fortress Press, 1994.

[139] For a full discussion of the relevant texts and issues, see James I. H. McDonald, *Kerygma and Didache: The Articulation and Structure of the Earliest Christian Message*. Cambridge: Cambridge University Press, 1980.

[140] Mark Harding, *Tradition and Rhetoric in the Pastoral Epistles*. New York: Peter Lang, 1998.

individual to another. The process of intergenerational transmission of the faith has been institutionalized. This process is already evident in the Pastoral Epistles, where the importance of offices and institutions in preserving the integrity of the 'deposit of faith' is heavily emphasized.[141] This would become increasingly important during the patristic period, when bishops and ecumenical councils played a decisive role in determining and subsequently preserving orthodoxy.[142] It is impossible to overlook the sociological substructure which increasingly upholds and transmits the realities of faith.[143]

2. Considered as *transmitted reality*, tradition designates *praxis* as much as *theoria*, embracing institutions, practices, systems of symbols, values and beliefs. It is unacceptable to limit the notion of tradition merely to ideas; what is passed on from one generation to another are ways of thinking, existing, seeing, living, belonging and behaving. It is a deeply socially embedded concept, which embraces matters of doctrine while at the same time transcending them. Tradition is not fully expressed in external statements or practices, in that it also contains 'the gospel which our Lord did not write, but taught by word of mouth and implanted in people's hearts, and part of which the evangelists later wrote down, while much was simply entrusted to the hearts of the faithful'.[144]

Although decisive differences must be conceded, there are clear and helpful parallels between the theologian's engagement with tradition and the historian's engagement with the past. Both regard their tasks as a process of responsible dialogue with the past. This point is brought out with particular force by Carr, who deserves to be cited in some detail:[145]

---

[141] For polemical aspects of the development of the concept of 'early catholicism', see Hermann-Josef Schmitz, *Frühkatholizismus bei Adolf von Harnack, Rudolph Sohm und Ernst Käsemann*. Düsseldorf: Patmos Verlag, 1977.

[142] For some of the issues, see Rowan Williams, 'Does It Make Sense to Speak of Pre-Nicene Orthodoxy?' in Rowan Williams (ed.), *The Making of Orthodoxy*. Cambridge: Cambridge University Press, 1989, 1–23.

[143] This point was particularly emphasized by Ernst Troeltsch, in tracking the transition from a charismatic to an institutional localization of authority. Ernst Troeltsch, 'Das Wesen der Religion und der Religionsgeschichte', in *Gesammelte Schriften*. Tübingen: Mohr, 1906, vol. 2, 452–99.

[144] Joseph Ratzinger, 'On the Interpretation of the Tridentine Decree on Tradition', in Karl Rahner and Joseph Ratzinger (eds), *Revelation and Tradition*. New York: Herder & Herder, 1966, 50–68.

[145] Carr, *What is History?*, 35.

The historian starts with a provisional selection of facts and a provisional interpretation in the light of which that selection has been made – by others as well as by himself. As he works, both the interpretation and the selection and ordering of facts undergo subtle and perhaps partly unconscious changes through the reciprocal action of one or the other. And this reciprocal action also involves reciprocity between present and past, since the historian is part of the present and the facts belong to the past. The historian and the facts of history are necessary to one another. The historian without his facts is rootless and futile; the facts without their historian are dead and meaningless. My first answer therefore to the question, What is history?, is that it is a continuous process of interaction between the historian and his facts, an unending dialogue between the present and the past.

The 'unending dialogue' between present and past is an integral aspect of a scientific theology, and highlights the importance of tradition, both as process and as substance.

Yet to speak of 'tradition' is inevitably to engage with a series of controversies over the identity and authority of the theological past, especially during the Middle Ages. In an important discussion of the relation between Scripture and tradition in late medieval theological method, Heiko A. Oberman identifies two main understandings of this relation prevalent during the period. The first approach, which Oberman designates 'Tradition I', treats Scripture and tradition as fundamentally coterminous, so that the *kerygma,* Scripture and tradition essentially coinhere. The second view, which Oberman designates 'Tradition II', recognizes an extra-scriptural oral tradition as a theological source, in addition to Scripture itself, and not necessarily coinherent or coterminous with it.[146] Several influential studies have located the seeds of the disintegration of the medieval synthesis in this second view of the relation of Scripture and tradition.[147]

The rise of Gnosticism, particularly during the second century, led to a growing appreciation of the importance of tradition as a means of identifying and safeguarding the Christian faith against its rivals. The anti-Gnostic polemic of the early church led to the development of a *regula fidei,* by which Scripture, as received by the church, was regarded as embodying the Christian *kerygma* in a materially sufficient manner.[148]

[146] Heiko A. Oberman, *The Harvest of Medieval Theology: Gabriel Biel and Late Medieval Nominalism.* Cambridge, MA: Harvard University Press, 1963, 361–412; idem, *Forerunners of the Reformation: The Shape of Late Medieval Thought.* Philadelphia: Fortress Press, 1981, 53–66.

[147] Most notably, George H. Tavard, *Holy Writ or Holy Church: The Crisis of the Protestant Reformation.* London: Burns & Oates, 1959.

[148] J. N. Bakhuizen van den Brink, 'Tradition und Heilige Schrift am Anfang des dritten Jahrhunderts', *Catholica* 9 (1953), 105–14; Bengt Hägglund, 'Die Bedeutung der "regula fidei" als Grundlage theologischer Aussagen', *Studia Theologica* 12 (1958), 1–44; R. P. C. Hanson, *Tradition in the Early Church.* London: SCM Press, 1962.

In other words, all truths which were in any sense necessary to salvation were those given directly in, or which could be directly inferred from, Scripture. Christian theology was thus essentially to be conceived as the exegesis of Scripture within the context of the living faith of the church, which transmitted this to subsequent generations.[149] Thus Gerald of Bologna, writing in the early fourteenth century, draws attention to the organic relation of Scripture and the living entity of the church, indicating their mutual dependency and coinherence.[150] Oberman, however, argues that this early medieval consensus disintegrated through the adoption of the 'two source' theory of the canonists.

In the twelfth and thirteenth centuries, when theologians generally adopted a 'single source' theory, the canonists (such as Ivo of Chartres and Gratian of Bologna) began to develop a 'two source' theory, based upon Scripture and tradition. According to Oberman, when the influence of the canonists was at its greatest in the fourteenth century, 'the canon-law tradition started to feed into the theological tradition'.[151] In other words, at a time when the theories of the canon lawyers were held in high esteem, theologians began to adopt their methods, thus developing an approach to theological method which differentiated between Scripture and the process of transmission. This approach leads to the conclusion that some fundamental Christian doctrines or practices are not contained within Scripture, but are transmitted solely by an extra-biblical oral tradition – an approach which appears to be adopted by the Council of Trent:[152]

> This truth and discipline are contained in the written books, and the unwritten traditions which, received by the apostles from the mouth of Christ himself, or from the apostles themselves, the Holy Spirit dictating, have come down to us, transmitted as it were from hand to hand; following the examples of the orthodox Fathers, [the church] receives and venerates with an equal affection of piety, and reverence, all the books both of the Old and of the New Testament – seeing that the one God is the author of both – as also the said traditions, whether these relate to faith or to morals, as having been dictated, either by Christ's own word of

---

[149] See the important early study of Gerhard Ebeling, *Kirchengeschichte als Geschichte der Auslegung der Heiligen Schrift*. Tübingen: Mohr, 1947, where this theme is fruitfully developed.

[150] See Paul de Vooght, *Les sources de la doctrine chrétienne d'après les théologiens du XIVe siècle et du début du XVe*. Bruges: De Brouwer, 1954, 33–59 for discussion.

[151] Oberman, *Harvest of Medieval Theology*, 369–75. For criticisms of this approach, see Alister E. McGrath, *The Intellectual Origins of the European Reformation*. Oxford: Blackwell, 1987, 142–8.

[152] Council of Trent, 'Decree on Scripture and Tradition', in H. Denzinger (ed.), *Enchiridion Symbolorum*, 24–25 edn. Barcelona: Herder, 1948, 279.

mouth, or by the Holy Spirit, and preserved in the Catholic Church by a continuous succession.

The Council of Trent, responding to the challenge to the authority of the church posed by the Protestant Reformation, thus reaffirmed a double-source theory of revelation, arguing that the deposit of revelation was dispersed between the written text of Scripture and unwritten tradition.[153] The mainline Reformation, however, may be regarded as continuing the single-source theory of tradition, arguing for the coinherence of Scripture and tradition.[154] It is within the Radical Reformation that the rejection of tradition is encountered; the individual reader is free to interpret Scripture as she or he pleases, without the necessity of taking the past history of interpretation or the *consensus fidelium* into account. In that the church is understood to have defected from its true identity and mission at an early stage in its history, tradition cannot be considered to be anything other than the musings of an apostate community.[155]

The approach adopted in this work is to reaffirm the coinherence of Scripture and tradition, a seminal notion which is found in one form in the writings of Calvin and Luther, and in another in *Verbum Dei*, the Second Vatican Council's 'Dogmatic Constitution on Revelation'.[156] While continuing many of the characteristic emphases of the Tridentine position, *Verbum Dei* nevertheless constitutes a significant modification of the Tridentine understanding of the role of tradition. Scripture is properly interpreted within the context of sacred tradition and of the *magisterium* of the church; all three together, though in different manners, are to be recognized as reflecting the work of the same Holy Spirit. Alongside this, however, is a new emphasis upon the priority of Scripture, which is evident in the revised liturgy, in the education of

---

[153] See Ratzinger, 'On the Interpretation of the Tridentine Decree on Tradition'. For further reflection, see J. R. Geiselmann, 'Scripture, Tradition, and the Church: An Ecumenical Problem', in D. J. Callahan, H. A. Oberman and D. J. O'Hanlon (eds), *Christianity Divided: Protestant and Roman Catholic Theological Issues*. London: Sheed & Ward, 1962, 39–72.

[154] McGrath, *Intellectual Origins of the European Reformation*, 148–51.

[155] This is best seen from the 1531 letter of Sebastian Franck to John Campanus, 1531; text in B. Becker, 'Fragment van Francks latijnse brief aan Campanus', *Nederlands Archief voor Kerkgeschiedenis* 46 (1964–5), 197–205. For radical views on the church in general, see Franklin H. Littell, *The Origins of Sectarian Protestantism: A Study of the Anabaptist View of the Church*. New York: Macmillan, 1964.

[156] See here Avery Dulles, 'Vatican II and the Recovery of Tradition', in *The Reshaping of Catholicism*. San Francisco: Harper & Row, 1988, 75–92. René Latourelle argues that Vatican II's understanding of revelation is significantly more personalist, Trinitarian and Christocentric than earlier dogmatic statements, especially those of Vatican I: René Latourelle, *Théologie de la révélation*, 2nd edn. Bruges: Desclée de Brouwer, 1966.

clergy, in the exposition of the council's teachings, and in the insistence that all persons be given full and easy access to Scripture. The results were immediately experienced most dramatically in the transformation of parish worship into the vernacular languages throughout the world, with a new emphasis on the reading of Scripture in public worship and private devotion.

The dogmatic constitution *Verbum Dei* distinguishes a number of 'strata' of revelation, such as the preaching of the apostles,[157] which was subsequently institutionalized in the church and its bishops: 'in order to keep the Gospel forever whole and alive within the Church, the Apostles left bishops as their successors, "handing over" to them "the authority to teach in their own place"'. This critical process of institutionalization is not restricted to the verbal transmission of ideas, but includes practices and social embodiment in the form of worship: 'the Church, in her teaching, life and worship, perpetuates and hands on to all generations all that she herself is, all that she believes'.[158] The 'practice and life of the believing and praying Church' is thus seen as essential to the practice of *tradition*, as much as to the substance of what is actually passed on. The 'Dogmatic Constitution on Divine Revelation' stressed the necessity of the *magisterium* of the church functioning within the ongoing sacred tradition 'which comes from the apostles [and] develops in the Church with the help of the Holy Spirit'. A particularly important role is thus attached 'to the living teaching office of the Church',[159] which is understood to be coinherent with Scripture and tradition on account of the common influence of the Holy Spirit. On this view of the church, the community of faith has developed in response to its foundational revelation, its strata reflecting in appropriately adapted manners the reality to which it bears witness.

In attempting to clarify the nature of revelation on the one hand, and ensure that the Christian community continues to embody, proclaim and honour this foundational heritage, it is clearly important to identify the means by which this revelation is transmitted and preserved. It is not my intention to act as mediator between the various dynamic understandings of tradition embodied in the magisterial Reformation, the Second Vatican Council, or contemporary Orthodoxy,[160] but simply

---

[157] *Verbum Dei*, 7.
[158] *Verbum Dei*, 8.
[159] *Verbum Dei*, 10.
[160] For useful reflections, see Jaroslav Pelikan, *The Vindication of Tradition*. New Haven: Yale University Press, 1984; Bernard Hoose, *Received Wisdom? Reviewing the Role of Tradition in Christian Ethics*. London: Geoffrey Chapman, 1994; Timothy McCarthy, *The Catholic Tradition Before and After Vatican II, 1878–1993*. Chicago: Loyola University Press, 1994.

to note the manner in which all emphasize the importance of continuity with the identity-giving past through its critical appropriation.[161]

To clarify the role of tradition – both as an organic body of ideas and as a defining activity of a socially embedded community – in the historical transmission of faith, we may turn to consider how the issue emerged as significant in the writings of Martin Kähler (1835–1912) and Rudolf Bultmann (1884–1976), and the approaches they developed in articulating the contemporary theological significance of the *kerygma*.

The kerygma: *on rereading Martin Kähler and Rudolf Bultmann*

The related approaches to the *kerygma* developed by Kähler and Bultmann are best understood as arising out of the Christological dead end of historical positivism – the approach to history which holds that facts may be 'read off' the historical record, and thus duly assembled for interpretation. The possibility of precisely such a process of assemblage is presupposed by the *Leben-Jesu-Forschung* (or 'Life of Jesus' movement) of the nineteenth century.[162] For both theological and philosophical reasons,[163] however, the plausibility of this simplistic empiricist account of the historical task became discredited. Bultmann's theology can be seen, in part, as a response to this historical *aporia*.

The leading themes of Bultmann's approach can be seen foreshadowed in Martin Kähler's 1892 treatise *Der sogenannte historische Jesus und der geschichtliche, biblische Christus* ('The So-Called Historical Jesus and the Historic, Biblical Christ'). The work, a mere 45 pages in length, represented an attempt to establish an 'invulnerable area' for faith in the midst of the crisis which he correctly perceived to be developing in the final decade of the nineteenth century over the historical reconstruction of the person of Jesus Christ through the 'Life of Jesus' movement. Kähler believed that the dispassionate and provisional Jesus of the academic historian cannot become the object of faith. Yet how can Jesus Christ be the authentic basis and content of Christian faith, when historical science can never establish certain knowledge concerning the historical Jesus? How can faith be based upon an historical event without being vulnerable to the charge of historical relativism?

---

[161] See especially Walter Kasper, 'Tradition als theologisches Erkenntnisprinzip', in W. Löser, K. Lehmann and M. Lutz-Bachmann (eds), *Dogmengeschichte und katholische Theologie*. Würzburg: Echter Verlag, 1985, 376–403.

[162] For something of the background, see Franz Courth, *Das Leben Jesu von David Friedrich Strauss in der Kritik Johann Evangelist Kuhns*. Göttingen: Vandenhoeck & Ruprecht, 1975.

[163] See, for example, the huge literature resulting from Albert Schweitzer, *The Quest of the Historical Jesus*, 3rd edn. London: A&C Black, 1954.

Kähler states his two objectives in this work as follows: first, to criticize and reject the errors of the 'Life of Jesus' movement; and second, to establish the validity of an alternative approach. The attempt to reconstruct Jesus through historical research was, he believed, fundamentally flawed, both theologically and methodologically, in that the intrusion of preconceived notions of who Jesus ought to be inevitably determined who he was found to be.[164]

> The historical Jesus of modern writers conceals the living Christ from us. The Jesus of the 'life of Jesus' movement is merely a modern example of a brain-child of the human imagination (*eine moderne Abart von Erzeugnissen menschlicher erfindlicher Kunst*), no better than the notorious dogmatic Christ of Byzantine Christology. They are both equally far removed from the real Christ. In this respect, historicism is just as arbitrary, just as humanly arrogant, just as speculative and 'faithlessly Gnostic', as that dogmatism which was itself considered modern in its own day.

While Kähler concedes that the 'Life of Jesus' movement was completely correct in so far as it contrasted the biblical witness to Christ with the abstract theological dogmatics of Protestant orthodoxy, he nevertheless insists that there were severe limits placed upon the historical reconstruction of the person of Jesus – a view summarized in his well-known statement that the entire 'Life of Jesus' movement was a blind alley. The most fundamental reason for levelling this charge against *Leben-Jesu-Forschung* is that Christ must be regarded as a 'supra-historical' (*übergeschichtlich*) rather than a merely 'historical' (*geschichtlich*) figure, whose influence includes his ongoing aftermath. The critical-historical method, Kähler argues, could not deal with the supra-historical characteristics of the impact of Jesus, and hence could lead only to an Arian or Ebionite Christology, on account of its latent dogmatic presuppositions.

What is important for Kähler is not who Christ was, but what he presently is and does for believers. The 'Jesus of history' lacks the soteriological significance of the 'Christ of faith'. The thorny problems of Christology may therefore be left behind in order to develop 'soterology' – note the spelling; this is not a misprint for 'soteriology' – a term which Kähler introduces to designate 'the knowledge of faith concerning the person of the saviour'. For Kähler, 'the real Christ is the preached Christ (*der wirkliche Christus ist der gepredigte Christus*)'.

---

[164] Martin Kähler, *The So-Called Historical Jesus and the Historic, Biblical Christ.* Philadelphia: Fortress Press, 1964, 21. For details of the background to Kähler's work, see Johann Heinrich Schmid, *Erkenntnis des geschichtlichen Christus bei Martin Kähler und bei Adolf Schlatter.* Basel: Reinhardt, 1978.

Kähler argues that the New Testament proclamation of Christ does not presuppose or necessitate a distinction between 'the memory of the days of his flesh and the confession of his eternal significance (*Erinnerung an die Tage seines Fleisches und Bekenntnis zu seiner ewigen Deutung*)'. This means that the New Testament itself contains an irreducible dogmatic element, which cannot be eliminated without gross historical distortion. It is for this reason that Kähler feels able to assert that, even in those circles in which 'apostolic dogma' is depreciated, 'one finds a dim reflection of that dogma, namely the knowledge of a certain incomparable evaluation of Jesus within the church, and the mediation of his portrait for attention and approval'. The *biblische, geschichtliche Christus* is thus the total Christ, rather than the fictitious and soteriologically deficient *historische Jesus*.

By accepting the distinction between the 'Jesus of history' and the 'Christ of faith', Kähler is thus able to argue that, as a matter of fact, Christian faith is based upon the latter, rather than the former. The 'Life of Jesus' movement has thus little significance for faith, in that the *geschichtliche Christus* cannot be reduced to a mere biography or intellectual analysis of the *historische Jesus*. For Kähler, the historical method cannot objectively demonstrate (or, indeed, negate) the revelation upon which faith stands – and as such, has little ultimate significance for faith. The saving significance of the historical figure of Jesus of Nazareth is encapsulated in the biblical portrait of Christ, which is immeasurably richer, and which alone evokes and sustains faith. It is this biblical portrait of Christ as saviour which, for Kähler, constitutes the invulnerable foundation of faith.

There are some serious weaknesses associated with this approach, as both his contemporaries and successors pointed out. In the same year as the publication of Kähler's essay, Wilhelm Herrmann argued that Kähler's approach made it utterly impossible to ascertain whether the 'historical Christ (*geschichtliche Christus*)' – supposedly the *basis* of faith – was not, in fact, a product of faith rather than an historical actuality.[165] In the following year, Otto Ritschl (1860–1944) argued that Kähler had misunderstood and unnecessarily depreciated the results of the application of the critical-historical method.[166] More recently, Ernst Käsemann

---

[165] Wilhelm Herrmann, 'Der geschichtliche Christus der Grund unseres Glaubens', *Zeitschrift für Theologie und Kirche* 2 (1892), 232–73.

[166] Otto Ritschl, 'Der historische Christus, der christliche Glaube und die theologische Wissenschaft', *Zeitschrift für Theologie und Kirche* 3 (1893), 371–426.

has called into question some of the historical assumptions underlying Kähler's position.[167]

While Kähler's attempts at a solution to the historical difficulties attending Christology are open to justifiable criticism, his identification of the trans-historical imprint of Jesus as being an integral aspect of his significance remains a seminal contribution to modern theology. The perceived significance of Jesus is transmitted by and within the community of faith, as a means both of preserving and maintaining its own identity, and of confronting others with the Christian proclamation. The most celebrated theological exploitation of this point is associated with Rudolf Bultmann, who argued that the New Testament *kerygma* transmitted the existence-changing potential of Christ, which demanded a response from its hearers.

Bultmann's idiosyncratic use of the term *kerygma* requires further explanation. For Bultmann, the *kerygma* is the word of proclamation through which the Christ-event confronts the individual here and now. The *kerygma* both *interprets* and *transmits* the significance of Jesus throughout the historical process, concentrating and compressing the interpreted history of salvation into an eschatological demand. Through his controversial programme of demythologization, Bultmann attempts to extract the significance of the history of Jesus of Nazareth – which he formulates in existential terms – through removing the mythical 'husk' from the cosmic apocalyptic drama narrated by the New Testament, thus revealing the 'kernel' of the proclamation of the permanent significance of Jesus Christ for human existence throughout the ages.[168]

The cross and the resurrection are linked in the *kerygma* as the divine acts of judgement and salvation. It is this divine act, pregnant with existential significance, which is of continuing significance, and not the historical phenomenon which acted as its bearer. The *kerygma* is thus not concerned with matters of historical fact, but with conveying the necessity of a decision on the part of its hearers, and thus transferring the

[167] Ernst Käsemann, 'The Problem of the Historical Jesus', in *Essays on New Testament Themes*. London: SCM Press, 1964, 15–47. For related concerns in Gerhard Ebeling, see René Marlé, 'Foi et parole: la théologie de Gerhard Ebeling', *Recherches de sciences religieuses* 49 (1976), 27–48; Wolfgang Grieve, 'Jesus und Glaube: Das Problem der Christologie Gerhard Ebelings', *Kerygma und Dogma* 22 (1976), 163–80.
[168] This approach to the relation between the historical Jesus and the *kerygma* is particularly well expressed in an essay of 1929 dealing with the relation between Jesus and Paul: Rudolf Bultmann, 'The Significance of the Historical Jesus for the Theology of Paul', in *Faith and Understanding*. London: SCM Press, 1966, 220–46.

eschatological moment from the past to the here and now of the proclamation itself:[169]

> This means that Jesus Christ encounters us in the *kerygma* and nowhere
> else, just as he confronted Paul himself and forced him to a decision. The
> *kerygma* does not proclaim universal truths or a timeless idea – whether it
> is an idea of God or of the redeemer – but an historical fact . . . Therefore
> the *kerygma* is neither a vehicle for timeless ideas nor the mediator of his-
> torical information: what is of decisive importance is that the *kerygma* is
> Christ's 'that', his 'here and now', a 'here and now' which becomes present
> in the address itself.
>
> One cannot therefore go behind the *kerygma*, using it as a source in
> order to reconstruct an 'historical Jesus' with his 'messianic consciousness',
> his 'inner life', or his 'heroism'. That would merely be 'Christ according
> to the flesh', who no longer exists. It is not the historical Jesus, but Jesus
> Christ, the one who is preached, who is the Lord.[170]

Bultmann may thus be regarded as developing the insights of Martin
Kähler in relation to the correlation between the historical Jesus and the
Christ of faith – or, as we might describe him in this context, the Christ
of the *kerygma*. The existentially significant Christ is not 'Christ according to the flesh', but the 'preached Christ', the Christ who is present in
the *kerygma*. Although Bultmann does not reduce the theological significance of the resurrection to a single point, it is certainly true to
suggest that, in Bultmann's view, the theological significance of the resurrection relates primarily to the presence of Christ in the faith and
preaching of his disciples – that is, in the *kerygma*. Thus Bultmann has
no hesitation in asserting that the Easter faith consists of faith that 'Jesus
Christ is present in the *kerygma*'. The contemporary experience of the
truth of Christ may be regarded as identical with the confrontation by
the *kerygma*, and the existential decision it occasions.[171]

Faith comes into being through an encounter with an historical event
– the 'event of Christ', as it is evoked by the *kerygma* itself. Although that
kerygma is based upon the history of Jesus of Nazareth, it now transcends
it. Bultmann thus has no time for critical questions concerning the
nature of the historical Jesus, and his relation to the Christ of faith,
insisting that it is, in principle, both impossible and illegitimate to go
behind the Christ of the *kerygma* to its historical foundations. All that

---

[169] Bultmann, 'Significance of the Historical Jesus', 241.
[170] See John Painter, *Theology as Hermeneutics: Rudolf Bultmann's Interpretation of the History of Jesus*. Sheffield: Almond, 1987, for an extended discussion of this point.
[171] On these points, here made in a very compressed manner, see James F. Kay, *Christus prae-sens: A Reconsideration of Rudolf Bultmann's Christology*. Grand Rapids, MI: Eerdmans, 1994.

it is necessary to state about Jesus is the fact that he has come, and that he is present in the *kerygma*.[172]

While it is important not to overstate the extent to which Bultmann draws upon the writings of Martin Heidegger,[173] it is clear that Bultmann's construal of the *kerygma* reflects an existentialist analysis of the structures of human existence. According to Bultmann, the New Testament recognizes two modes of human existence: unbelieving and unredeemed existence, and believing and redeemed existence. The former is characterized by the delusion of self-sufficiency, and by the adhesion to (and hence the dependence upon) the visible and transitory world. Although the goal of human endeavours (to attain our essential and authentic existence) is appropriate, the means which human beings adopt towards this end are inappropriate and, ultimately, self-defeating: they attempt to find themselves through their own unaided efforts, and, by doing so, merely become more and more deeply embedded in the transitory world of death and despair.

Believing and redeemed existence, however, arises through our abandoning every hope that we may attain this authentic existence through our own efforts or on the basis of the visible and transitory world in which we exist: we recognize that our life is given to us as a gift, and in an act of 'desecularization (*Entweltlichung*)' choose to base our existence upon what is invisible and intangible. Although we continue to exist in the world, our attitude to it is now one of freedom from it. Although we are in the world, we are no longer of the world (John 17:15–16). This approach to the New Testament may be illustrated from Bultmann's 1928 essay on the eschatology of the Fourth Gospel.

In this essay, Bultmann identifies existentialist categories as underlying what he terms the 'Johannine dualism' in which concepts such as light and darkness, truth and falsehood, life and death, are set in permanent antithesis. These antitheses serve to express the double possibility in human existence, and derive their meaning both from the threat which is perceived to be posed to human existence by the world, and from the means by which the threat may be overcome. Thus we find Bultmann interpreting the key Johannine term *kosmos* ('world') in the

---

[172] For this central theme in Bultmann's approach to the *kerygma*, see Kay, *Christus praesens*.

[173] For the best study, see Glaude Ozankom, *Gott und Gegenstand: Martin Heideggers Objektivierungsverdikt und seine theologische Rezeption bei Rudolf Bultmann und Heinrich Ott.* Paderborn: Schöningh, 1994. The older study of John Macquarrie, *An Existentialist Theology: A Comparison of Heidegger and Bultmann.* London: SCM Press, 1955, still repays study, although in need of modification at points – see, for example, Gareth Jones, 'Phenomenology and Theology: A Note on Bultmann and Heidegger', *Modern Theology* 5 (1989), 161–80.

twofold manner indicated by Heidegger – the world as the sphere of existence, and the world as the threat to existence:[174]

> Through the event of revelation, two possibilities are actualized for the world: 1. 'To be world' (*Weltsein*) in the new sense of 'remaining world' (*Weltbleiben*) – to set the seal on one's fallenness (*Verfallenheit*), to hold fast to it, to hold fast to one's self. 2. 'Not to be world' (*Nicht-Welt-sein*), not to be 'of the world', and thus to be 'of the world' in the new sense of being 'out of' the world, namely, 'outside' it, no longer belonging to it.

For Bultmann, the New Testament in general asserts that our true nature is no longer to be attained by our own efforts, which merely serve further to enmesh and embed us in our existential alienation. We cannot liberate ourselves from this existential alienation by our own effort: such liberation must come from without. The most fundamental difference between Heidegger and Bultmann is that the former regards authentic existence as a possibility which we may achieve for ourselves, whereas the latter regards it as a possibility which comes about only by a gratuitous act of God. It is here that Bultmann's soteriology demonstrates its distinctive Christological concentration, in that this act of God is identified with the 'Christ-event' (*Christusereignis*) – the cross and resurrection of Jesus Christ.[175]

So what are the implications of this approach? For our purposes, the most important point to note is that it is not necessary to be able to reconstruct the original revelatory events in order to be affected and shaped by them. For Bultmann, continuity with the identity-giving past can be maintained through its impact upon the present – namely, through the *kerygma*. It is not my intention to defend Bultmann at the many points at which he has been criticized – for example, the somewhat skewed manner in which he developed David Friedrich Strauss's notion of *Entmythologisierung*,[176] nor the alarming retreat from history

---

[174] Rudolf Bultmann, 'The Eschatology of the Gospel of John', in *Faith and Understanding*. London: SCM Press, 1966, 165–83, quote at 170.

[175] On which see José Ewaldo Scheid, *Die Heilstat Gottes in Christus: Eine Studie zu Rudolf Bultmanns Auffassung von der Erlösung in Jesu Tod und Auferstehung*. Hamburg-Bergstedt: Reich, 1962.

[176] See especially Gunther Backhaus, *Kerygma und Mythos bei David Friedrich Strauss und Rudolf Bultmann*. Hamburg-Bergstedt: Herbert Reich Evangelischer Verlag, 1956. Bultmann's strategy may also be challenged at a more fundamental level. As Richardson points out, the biblical language about God's mighty acts in history 'does not need demythologizing, because it is not a myth. It does not speak in mythological terms of an existential meaning disclosed in a certain situation, but of how God intervened in the stream of events and altered the course of history.' Richardson, *History, Sacred and Profane*, 253.

which is so characteristic a feature of his mature writings.[177] Rather, I wish to note that Bultmann identified a point which many of his critics and supporters fail to have appreciated – namely, that there exists a means by which the perceived significance of Christ is transmitted *to* history and *through* history through the *kerygma*. Bultmann's analysis of this *kerygma* is deficient in two respects:

1. It offers too sharp a distinction between proclamation and teaching, failing to note, for example, how the New Testament can use the term 'teaching' to refer to the content of the *kerygma*.[178]

2. It fails to do justice to the role of the church as the bearer of the *kerygma*, tending to detach the *kerygma* from its historical modes of transmission as much as from its historical origins.[179]

Yet while these shortcomings must be acknowledged, Bultmann's emphasis upon the importance of the transmission of the perceived significance of Jesus Christ, both in the New Testament and beyond, must not be deemed to be discredited on account of the vulnerability of the ancillary hypotheses which he unwisely links to it. While Bultmann's disinterest in history extends to glossing over the precise historical means by which the *kerygma* is transmitted, and the different levels of reality at which this process of transmission takes place, these can easily be built in to his basic approach. Revelation may be taken to embrace both the foundational events of the Christian faith (now inaccessible to us in their fullness and totality) *and* their perceived significance for the generation and nourishment of faith. What Bultmann failed to appreciate is that revelation is transmitted intergenerationally through a nexus of modalities, located at different levels of reality – and each of these can be regarded as part of the 'economy of salvation', of which theology seeks to offer a coherent account.

Theology and the economy of salvation

We are now in a position to offer a fuller statement concerning the proper subject of theology. We have seen how Bultmann's anti-historical approach offers an account of theology which relates tolerably well to the present-day proclamation of the church, while failing to address both the

---

[177] The displacement of Bultmann's hegemony by more Marxist approaches in 1967–8 reflects the latter's more substantial engagement with history.

[178] The best discussion of this point is to be found in James I. H. McDonald, *Kerygma and Didache: The Articulation and Structure of the Earliest Christian Message.* Cambridge: Cambridge University Press, 1980.

[179] See Hermann Häring, *Kirche und Kerygma: das Kirchenbild in der Bultmannschule.* Freiburg: Herder, 1972.

historical aspects of this matter, as well as the full range of social embodiments of the Christian proclamation. A convenient point of transition between Bultmann's historically deficient account of theology and a more robust understanding of its parameters is provided by Luther's insistence that the proper object of theology is the saving work of God, and its implications for a right understanding of humanity.[180] This viewpoint was severely criticized by Karl Barth, not least on account of the deficiencies which it exposed in his own understanding of the theological task.[181] Luther's insight is that the dynamics of salvation – which, in his view, embrace the actuality of revelation as a means to that end – offers the theologian the most appropriate standpoint for theological reflection. Yet Luther's approach is vulnerable, both historically and sociologically, in that it fails to take proper account of the theologian's own location within both the historical process and the Christian community as a social entity. Yet both these can be remedied. In what follows, I shall set out a model for the object of theology which recognizes the stratified nature of reality, and the historical location of the theologian.

A proper starting point for theology is the economy of salvation – that is, the recognition that theology seeks to respond to the revelation of God in all its fullness – that is to say, at every moment in history and at every level of reality. It embraces the divine acts of creation, redemption and consummation, as well as the faithful and obedient human attempts to apprehend and embrace these realities, and represent them under the limiting conditions of human language. Theology is the outcome of the community of faith's corporate beholding of the vision of God as creator, redeemer and sustainer. It will therefore be clear that a scientific theology is as relentlessly Trinitarian in its outlook as it is Christological in its focus and biblical in its foundations, in that this most difficult of all Christian doctrines represents the attempt to preserve and proclaim the glory, wonder and mystery of the living God.[182] Four points are of especial importance from the perspective of a scientific theology.

---

[180] See Ernst Wolf, 'Die Rechtfertigungslehre als Mitte und Grenze reformatorischer Theologie', *Evangelische Theologie* 9 (1949), 298–308.

[181] Alister E. McGrath, 'Karl Barth and the *Articulus Iustificationis*. The Significance of His Critique of Ernst Wolf within the Context of His Theological Method', *Theologische Zeitschrift* 39 (1983), 349–61. I develop these criticisms more fully elsewhere: 'Karl Barth als Aufklärer? Der Zusammenhang seiner Lehre vom Werke Christi mit der Erwählungslehre', *Kerygma und Dogma* 81 (1984), 383–94.

[182] See, for example, Robert W. Jenson, *The Triune Identity*. Philadelphia, Fortress Press, 1982; Thomas G. Weinandy, *The Father's Spirit of Sonship: Reconceiving the Trinity*. Edinburgh: T&T Clark, 1995; Colin E. Gunton, *The Triune Creator: A Historical and Systematic Study*. Edinburgh: Edinburgh University Press, 1998.

1. The economy of salvation embraces the past, present and future. Its scope extends to all that has happened, what is now happening, and what is yet to come. The theologian therefore cannot rest content with an engagement with the past alone (Pannenberg's engagement with the historical Jesus), nor with the present alone (Bultmann's *kerygma*). Equally, the theologian cannot overlook the fundamental themes of a 'theology of hope', which looks to the future for the final revelation of the glory of God (as in Jonathan Edwards' affirmation of the 'great and last end of God's works' as the 'emanation and true eternal expression of God's internal glory and fullness'[183]).

2. The community of faith is itself part of that economy of salvation. The entire theological enterprise is undertaken *in via* (to use the classic imagery of medieval theology), or, borrowing a more recent image from Otto Neurath, from within a ship that is presently at sea. The economy of salvation thus cannot be conceived as reflection purely and simply on what is past, in that the present voyage is itself part of that process. There is no 'view from nowhere'; the theology is undertaken from within the economy of salvation itself.

3. Both Scripture itself and the church's process of reflection upon Scripture are part of the same economy of salvation. While Barth's notion of the 'three-fold form of the word of God' is sociologically defective (vol. 2, 232–4), it nevertheless affirms the critically important theological point that Scripture and proclamation are interlocked and interrelated. A scientific theology must thus engage with a series of layers of reality, which are differentiated both synchronically and diachronically. The stratification of reality extends across the present and throughout the historical process of the economy of salvation.

4. Historical theology has a genuine and significant role to play in a scientific theology. To understand this point, we may revert to a comparison with the biological sciences – namely, the role of fossils in clarifying the nature of the evolutionary process (see 154–5). A fossil, providing it can be dated, offers a snapshot of the

[183] Jonathan Edwards, 'Dissertation Concerning the End for which God Created the World', in *Works*, 2 vols. London: Tegg, 1834, vol. 1, 94–121, 119–20. See further W. J. Wainwright, 'Jonathan Edwards, William Rowe and the Necessity of Creation', in J. Jordan and D. Howard-Snyder (eds), *Faith, Freedom and Rationality*. London: Rowman & Littlefield, 1996, 119–33.

biological process at a given moment, allowing us to understand something of the origins and development of life. Similarly, historical theology allows us a series of specific insights into the manner in which the Christian revelation has been apprehended and understood at any given moment, thus allowing us insights into the nature of the precipitating and directive factors in the development of theology.

A scientific theology and the explanation of reality

Christian theology offers an explanation of the internal structures and dynamics of the Christian tradition, without in any sense legitimating the theologically destructive notion that such a tradition need not have any external transcendent referent in order to account for its existence, or by means of which it may be judged and reformed. While some theologians argue that the explanatory aspects of Christian theology are limited to religious experience or the specifics of the Christian tradition, a scientific theology – with its emphasis upon a unitary yet stratified reality – will insist that its explanatory competence extends to every aspect of reality. In the present section, we shall explore some aspects of this wider explanatory role of Christian doctrine.

Clifford Geertz points out that, from the standpoint of cultural anthropology, there is a clear explanatory aspect to religious life. Religious beliefs fulfil some kind of explanatory role for believers by integrating, and thus rendering 'comprehensible', phenomena and events that appear at first sight inexplicable.[184]

> It does appear to be a fact that at least some men – in all probability, most men – are unable to leave unclarified problems of analysis merely unclarified . . . Any chronic failure of one's explanatory apparatus, the complex of received culture patterns (common sense, science, philosophical speculation, myth) one has for mapping the empirical world, to explain things which cry out for explanation tends to lead to a deep disquiet.

From a phenomenological perspective, Geertz suggests that religious belief systems can be demonstrated to play a role in facilitating understanding of the world for the believer. One of the functions of religion is to render intelligible things that 'cry out for explanation'.

In one sense, the success of such explanations is not the primary issue.

---

[184] Clifford Geertz, 'Religion as a Cultural System', in D. R. Cutler (ed.), *The Religious Situation*. Boston: Beacon Press, 1968, 639–88.

The point is that a scientific theology is impelled, by its vision of reality, to attempt to offer an account of the totality of all things, believing that the Christian tradition both encourages such an enterprise in the first place, and in the second, makes the necessary resources available through its understanding of the economy of salvation, particularly its doctrine of creation. Shivesh Chandra Thakur makes a useful distinction between 'trying' and 'succeeding' in the context of explanation: '"Does religion explain?" is not the same question as "Does it succeed in explaining whatever it purports to explain?"'[185] The question of the plausibility of such explanations remains to be addressed; at this stage, our concern is to note that a theologically grounded compulsion to offer such explanations is to be seen as an integral component of the Christian view of reality.

We have already seen how a scientific theology engages with the complex multilayered reality of the Christian tradition itself. So how does it engage with what lies beyond this? The trajectory of the argument deployed throughout the three volumes of this work is such that we have already covered some of these themes already; nevertheless, others remain to be addressed. We begin by considering the question of how the existence of other traditions, each in its turn making explanatory claims, may be addressed.

The explanation of other traditions

We have already noted in great detail the critical role played by a responsible natural theology in offering an explanation of other traditions (vol. 2, 55–120), and it would be pointless to repeat that discussion here. Again, it is essential to appreciate that this new role for natural theology arises from the collapse of any notion that there exists a tradition-independent standpoint from which each tradition may be judged. There is no neutral transcendent vantage point from which the claims of competing traditions may be evaluated. As Alasdair MacIntyre stresses, this does not mean that any attempt to adjudicate between traditions collapses into *relativism* ('a denial that rational debate between and rational choice among traditions is possible') or *perspectivism* (which 'puts in question the possibility of making truth claims from within any one tradition').[186] Rather, traditions may be judged by their success in explaining both their own existence and distinctive features, and at least something of their rivals'.

---

[185] Shivesh Chandra Thakur, *Religion and Rational Choice*. London: Macmillan, 1981, 47.
[186] Alasdair MacIntyre, *Whose Justice? Which Rationality?* London: Duckworth, 1988, 352.

The kind of natural theology which a scientific theology seeks to justify and commend offers an account of the trans-traditional quest for truth, beauty and goodness which does not require the interposition of an additional tradition, or the imposition of a supratraditional device, in order to offer an explanation of some of the most fundamental impulses of the human mind. A Christian natural theology is a tradition-specific construal with universal applicability, thus both offering an explanation of other traditions, while at the same time reinforcing its own plausibility.

The explanation of the world

The explanatory potential of the Christian tradition is immense. As we argued earlier (vol. 1, 193–240), a Christian doctrine of creation offers an explanatory window into both the ordering of the natural world, and the capacity of the human mind to discern and represent this ordering. While it would be injudicious to suggest that there is a firmly established connection between the historical development of the natural sciences and a Christian worldview which encouraged and affirmed engagement with the natural order as a means of enhancing an appreciation of the wisdom of its creator, it is nevertheless essential to observe that some such connection – however muted – is regularly affirmed to exist.

Richard Swinburne's classic *The Existence of God* may be regarded as one of the most important twentieth-century affirmations of the explanatory capacity of theism. An important aspect of his argument concerns the potential of the Christian understanding of God to make sense of the ordering of the world.[187] The older habit of positing a 'God of the gaps' has now been generally discarded as useless. Rather than suggesting that God offers an explanation of what the natural sciences are currently unable to explain, more recent theistic writers have stressed the importance of belief in God in explaining the 'big picture' – that is to say, the overall patterns of ordering which are discerned within the universe. Swinburne thus insists that the explanatory aspects of theism are not limited to the fine details of reality, but extend far beyond these to embrace the great questions of life – those things that are either 'too big' or 'too odd' for science to explain.[188] Theism embraces the totality of reality, which it embraces and explains.[189]

---

[187] Richard Swinburne, *The Existence of God*. Oxford: Clarendon Press, 1979, 136.
[188] Swinburne, *The Existence of God*, 71.
[189] Swinburne, *The Existence of God*, 252–3.

> For many people life is one vast religious experience. Many people view almost all the events of their life not merely under their ordinary description, but also as God's handiwork. For many people, that is, very many of the public phenomena of life are viewed religiously and so constitute religious experiences . . . . What is seen by one man as simply a wet day is seen by another as God's reminding us of his bounty in constantly providing us with food by means of his watering plants.

The reliability of such explanations is open to challenge; there is, however, no doubt that such explanations are being offered, and are seen as important.

One single example may be cited to illustrate the capacity of theism to illuminate the world – namely, the apparent 'fine-tuning' of the universe to permit carbon-based life forms to emerge and survive. The term 'anthropic principle' is now widely used to refer to this remarkable degree of 'fine-tuning' uncovered by the natural sciences within the natural order. Paul Davies has argued that the remarkable convergence of certain fundamental constants is laden with religious significance. 'The seemingly miraculous concurrence of numerical values that nature has assigned to her fundamental constants must remain the most compelling evidence for an element of cosmic design.'[190] In their useful study *The Anthropic Cosmological Principle*, John D. Barrow and Frank J. Tipler set out some issues that seem to them to require explanation.[191]

> One of the most important results of twentieth-century physics has been the gradual realization that there exist invariant properties of the natural world and its elementary components which render the gross size and structure of virtually all its constituents quite inevitable. The size of stars and planets, and even people, is neither random nor the result of any Darwinian selection process from a myriad of possibilities. These, and other gross features of the Universe are the consequences of necessity; they are manifestations of the possible equilibrium states between competing forces of attraction and compulsion. The intrinsic strengths of these controlling forces of Nature are determined by a mysterious collection of pure numbers that we call the *constants of Nature*.

Examples of the alleged 'fine-tuning' of fundamental cosmological constants include the following:[192]

---

[190] Paul Davies, *God and the New Physics*. New York: Penguin, 1984, 189.
[191] John D. Barrow and Frank J. Tipler, *The Anthropic Cosmological Principle*. Oxford: Oxford University Press, 1986, 5.
[192] B. J. Carr and M. J. Rees, 'The Anthropic Principle and the Structure of the Physical World', *Nature* 278 (1979), 605–12. More generally, see Barrow and Tipler, *The Anthropic Cosmological Principle*.

1. If the strong coupling constant was slightly smaller, hydrogen would be the only element in the universe. Since the evolution of life as we know it is fundamentally dependent on the chemical properties of carbon, that life could not have come into being without some hydrogen being converted to carbon by fusion. On the other hand, if the strong coupling constant were slightly larger (even by as much as 2 per cent), the hydrogen would have been converted to helium, with the result that no long-lived stars would have been formed. In that such stars are regarded as essential to the emergence of life, such a conversion would have led to life as we know it failing to emerge.

2. If the weak fine constant was slightly smaller, no hydrogen would have formed during the early history of the universe. Consequently, no stars would have been formed. On the other hand, if it was slightly larger, supernovae would have been unable to eject the heavier elements necessary for life. In either case, life as we know it could not have emerged.

3. If the electromagnetic fine structure constant was slightly larger, the stars would not be hot enough to warm planets to a temperature sufficient to maintain life in the form in which we know it. If smaller, the stars would have burned out too quickly to allow life to evolve on these planets.

4. If the gravitational fine structure constant were slightly smaller, stars and planets would not have been able to form, on account of the gravitational constraints necessary for coalescence of their constituent material. If stronger, the stars thus formed would have burned out too quickly to allow the evolution of life (as with the electromagnetic fine structure constant).

This (disputed) evidence of 'fine-tuning' has been the subject of considerable discussion among scientists, philosophers and theologians.[193] A constant theme to emerge from this discussion is that the anthropic principle, whether stated in a weak or strong form,[194] is strongly consistent with a theistic perspective. A theist (for example, a Christian) with a firm commitment to a doctrine of creation will find the 'fine-tuning'

---

[193] Richard Swinburne, 'The Argument from the Fine-Tuning of the Universe', in John Leslie (ed.), *Physical Cosmology and Philosophy*. New York: Macmillan, 1990, 154–73; Errol Harris, *Cosmos as Anthropos: A Philosophical Interpretation of the Anthropic Cosmological Principle*. New Jersey: Humanities Press, 1990.

[194] For the distinction, see Michael Redhead, *From Physics to Metaphysics*. Cambridge: Cambridge University Press, 1995, 39.

of the universe to be an anticipated and pleasant confirmation of his religious beliefs. This would not constitute a 'proof' of the existence of God, but would be a further element in a cumulative series of considerations which is at the very least consistent with the existence of a creator God. This is the kind of argument set forth by F. R. Tennant in his important study *Philosophical Theology*, in which the term 'anthropic' is thought to have been used for the first time to designate this specific type of teleological argument.[195]

> The forcibleness of Nature's suggestion that she is the outcome of intelligent design lies not in particular cases of adaptedness in the world, nor even in the multiplicity of them . . . [but] consists rather in the conspiration of innumerable causes to produce, by their united and reciprocal action, and to maintain, a general order of Nature. Narrower kinds of teleological arguments, based on surveys of restricted spheres of fact, are much more precarious than that for which the name of 'the wider teleology' may be appropriated in that the comprehensive design-argument is the outcome of synopsis or conspection of the knowable world.

This does not mean that the factors noted above constitute irrefutable evidence for the existence or character of a creator God; few religious thinkers would suggest that this is the case, and I am certainly not among them. What would be affirmed, however, is that they are consistent with a theistic worldview; that they can be accommodated with the greatest of ease within such a worldview; and that they reinforce the plausibility of such a worldview for those who are already committed to it.[196] While a Christian doctrine of creation would not presume to fill in the fine detail of such an argument, it nevertheless affirms the broad principle that these details appear to confirm.

But what of those observations which appear to be disconfirming of the Christian worldview? How are these to be included in any account of explanation? In what follows, we shall consider some issues which arise from tensions which arise between theory and observation in both the natural sciences and Christian theology.

Explanation and anomaly in the sciences: Pierre Duhem

As we have seen, both the sciences and religion may therefore be described as offering interpretations of experience. This is not to say that both or either may be reduced to such interpretations, but simply to

---

[195] F. R. Tennant, *Philosophical Theology*, 2 vols. Cambridge: Cambridge University Press, 1930, vol. 2, 79.

[196] Keith Ward, *God, Chance and Necessity*. Oxford: One World, 1996, 50–60.

note that both possess explanatory elements. This being the case, a comparison of the way in which the two disciplines deal with the complexities of experience is of considerable interest to our study, offering the potential to illuminate the place of explanation in a scientific theology. We may begin by considering the contribution of the French philosopher of science Pierre Duhem (1861–1916) to the interaction of theory and experience, considering particularly the place of 'anomalies' in theoretical explanation of the world.

Interest in the ideas of Pierre Duhem has been catalysed considerably by Anglo-American discussions of empiricism since about 1955, especially through the influence of Willard van Orman Quine's seminal essay 'Two Dogmas of Empiricism'. The doctrine traditionally, yet misleadingly, known as the 'Duhem–Quine thesis' asserts that, if incompatible data and theory are seen to be in conflict, one cannot draw the conclusion that any particular theoretical statement is responsible for this tension, and must therefore be rejected. The root of the problem may lie in an auxiliary assumption used in the theoretical analysis, or the manner of observation which leads to the suggestion that such a conflict does in fact exist. The Duhem–Quine thesis is of fundamental importance to any attempt to correlate theory and experience, whether in science or religion. It also indicates a significant degree of convergence in relation to the problems which both the natural sciences and religions are forced to engage with.

Quine has provided us with what is undoubtedly one of the finest and most influential accounts of the way belief systems or worldviews relate to experience.[197]

> The totality of our so-called knowledge or beliefs, from the most casual matters of geography and history to the profoundest laws of atomic physics . . . is a man-made fabric which impinges on experience only along the edges . . . A conflict with experience at the periphery occasions adjustments in the interior of the field . . . But the total field is so underdetermined by its boundary conditions, experience, that there is much latitude of choice as to what statements to reevaluate in the light of any single contrary experience.

In other words, experience often has relatively little impact upon worldviews. (Imre Lakatos made a related point in connection with his discussion of the 'protective belt' of auxiliary hypotheses in scientific reasoning.[198]) Where experience seems to contradict a worldview or

---

[197] W. V. O. Quine, *From a Logical Point of View*. Cambridge, MA: Harvard University Press, 1953, 42–3.

[198] Imre Lakatos, 'Falsification and the Methodology of Scientific Research Programmes', in I. Lakatos and A. Musgrave (eds), *Criticism and the Growth of Knowledge*. Cambridge: Cambridge University Press, 1970, 91–195.

system of beliefs, the most likely outcome is an internal readjustment of the system, rather than its rejection. Quine thus points to some of the difficulties in refuting a theory on the basis of experience, which must be addressed by any empirical approach.[199]

Quine's most succinct summary of Duhem's position – which, incidentally, he bases on secondary English language sources – can be found in his 'Two Dogmas of Empiricism'. One of Quine's objectives in this seminal essay is to demonstrate the weakness of the 'empiricist dogma' that each theoretical statement, considered in isolation, can be confirmed or falsified. Quine asserts that this view has been effectively countered by Duhem, who demonstrated that 'our statements about the external world face the tribunal of sense experience not individually, but only as a corporate body'.[200] Adolf Grünbaum mounted a powerful challenge to what he termed 'Duhem's thesis', demonstrating that it is either empirically false or trivially true. Yet this is actually a criticism of Quine's presentation of the thesis, which introduces ideas which cannot be attributed to Duhem himself.[201]

Since then, there has been a growing awareness of the divergence between Quine and Duhem at a number of critical junctures.[202] In general terms, Quine's interpretation of Duhem must be recognized as being much stronger than Duhem himself would allow. For example, Duhem explicitly distinguishes a number of different sciences, arguing that his thesis has greater applicability, for example, in physics than in physiology.[203] In making this distinction, it is clear that Duhem was responding to a series of crucial experiments by Claude Bernard. Quine, however, appears to extend Duhem's thesis to embrace 'the whole body of our knowledge'.[204] Rather than attempt to disentangle the complex question of the extent to which Quine misunderstood Duhem, and subsequently diverged from this misinterpretation, I propose to engage directly with Duhem, with a view to clarifying his relevance to our themes.

---

[199] This point has given rise to the influential 'underdetermination' thesis: see Larry Laudan and Jarrett Leplin, 'Empirical Equivalence and Underdetermination', *Journal of Philosophy* 88 (1991), 449–72.

[200] Quine, *From a Logical Point of View*, 41.

[201] Adolf Grünbaum, 'The Duhemian Argument', *Philosophy of Science* 27 (1960), 75–87.

[202] Nancy Tuana, 'Quine on Duhem: An Emendation', *Philosophy of Science* 45 (1978), 456–62; J. Vuillemin, 'On Duhem's and Quine's Theses', *Grazer Philosophische Studien* 9 (1979), 69–96.

[203] Pierre Duhem, *La théorie physique: son objet – sa structure*, 2nd edn. Paris: Vrin, 1997, 249–72.

[204] Vuillemin, 'On Duhem's and Quine's Theses'.

Duhem's most fundamental assertion could be stated in terms of 'the thesis of inseparability'. According to Duhem, the physicist simply is not in a position to submit an isolated hypothesis to experimental test. 'An experiment in physics can never condemn an isolated hypothesis but only a whole theoretical group (*une ensemble théoretique*).'[205]

> En résumé, le physicien ne peut jamais soumettre au contrôle de l'expérience une hypothèse isolée, mais seulement tout un ensemble d'hypothèses; lorsque l'expérience est en disaccord avec ses prévisions, elle lui apprend que l'une au moins des hypothèses qui constituent cet ensemble est inacceptable et doit être modifiée; *mais elle ne lui désigne pas celle qui doit être changée.*

The physicist cannot subject an individual hypothesis to an experimental test, in that the experiment can only indicate that one hypothesis within a larger group of hypotheses requires revision. The experiment does not itself indicate which of the hypotheses requires modification. Even when a strict deductive consequence of a theory is shown to be false (assuming, of course, that a 'crucial experiment' can be devised which allows such an unequivocal conclusion to be drawn), that falsity cannot be attributed (for example, by *modus tollens*) to any specific site in the theory itself or its ancillary assumptions.[206]

Yet can such a 'crucial experiment' be devised? Duhem argues that this is simply impossible, in that we do not have access to the full list of hypotheses which underlie our thinking.[207] It might at first seem that we could enumerate all the hypotheses that can be made to account for a phenomenon, and then eliminate all of these hypotheses except one by experimental contradiction. However, the physicist is never in a position to be sure that all the hypotheses have been identified and checked. More significantly, Duhem insists that no theoretical hypothesis, considered in isolation, has observational consequences. An experiment is not simply about the observation of phenomena; it is about their interpretation. There is no direct logical bridge between concepts and experience.

Duhem's fundamental point concerns how observation statements are related to hypotheses within a given theory. Consider a given theory *T*,

---

[205] Duhem, *La théorie physique*, 278–85. Citation at 284; my emphasis.
[206] The 'Laudan–Leplin' thesis may be noted here, particularly on account of its emphasis upon the 'instability of auxiliary assumptions' (while conceding that such assumptions are necessary): Larry Laudan and Jarrett Leplin, 'Empirical Equivalence and Underdetermination', *Journal of Philosophy* 88 (1991), 449–72.
[207] Duhem, *La théorie physique*, 286–9.

which consists of an aggregate of hypotheses, H_1, H_2, H_3 . . . H_n. An example of such a theory might be Darwin's theory of natural selection, Einstein's theory of general relativity, or Newton's model of the solar system. Each theory consists of such a group of explicitly stated inter-related hypotheses. It also consists of a number of auxiliary hypotheses, A_1, A_2, A_3 . . . A_n, which are sometimes not formulated explicitly, but are nevertheless significant influences on the theory in question.

Duhem's point is simple: an observation statement O, which is inconsistent with the theory, may require the modification or even abandonment of a fundamental hypothesis of the theory, H_1, H_2, H_3 . . . H_n. It may equally require that similar action be taken in relation to an auxiliary hypothesis, A_1, A_2, A_3 . . . A_n. Yet the experiment will not be able to identify whether it is the theory which requires modification, or merely one of its hypotheses. Nor can the observation statement O by itself determine which of the hypotheses requires adjustment.

We have already noted (vol. 2, 166–8) how an excellent example of this general issue is provided by Newton's theory of planetary motion, as it was understood around the year 1800. The question under consideration is whether the observation statement $O =$ 'the observed orbit of the planet Uranus is not consistent with its predicted theoretical values', which seems inconsistent with this theory,[208] requires a fundamental or ancillary hypothesis of the Newtonian model to be modified. In this specific case, it was an auxiliary assumption which proved to be incorrect – namely, the assumption that the planet Uranus determined the outer limits of the solar system. If a transuranic planet were to be postulated, the anomalous orbital parameters of Uranus could be explained by the gravitational pull of this hypothetical planet on Uranus. In the event this proved to be the correct interpretation. But for some time, it was unclear how the anomalous behaviour of Uranus was to be explained.

A similar situation arose through the anomalous behaviour of the innermost planet Mercury. Urbain Le Verrier, who had been involved in the prediction of the existence of the transuranic planet Neptune, first noticed the anomalies in the motion in the perihelion of Mercury in 1855, shortly after he was appointed director of the Paris Observatory. Once more, the issue was which aspect of the received Newtonian model of the solar system required modification. Le Verrier took the view that

[208] N. R. Hanson, *Patterns of Discovery: An Inquiry into the Conceptual Foundations of Science.* Cambridge: Cambridge University Press, 1961. Duhem illustrates his point with reference to a somewhat different aspect of Newtonian mechanics: Duhem, *La théorie physique,* 289–96.

the anomalies once more required that certain auxiliary hypotheses of the prevailing model be modified, but not the fundamental model itself. The anomalies could be explained by postulating a new planet, Vulcan, closer to the Sun than Mercury or a second asteroid belt so close to the Sun as to be invisible.[209] In this case, however, the solution to the anomaly did not lie with unobserved planets, but with a vulnerability within Newtonian mechanics itself, which could only be resolved through Einstein's general theory of relativity.[210]

Duhem's thesis is also of considerable importance to Karl Popper's theory of falsifiability.[211] In his 1983 work *Realism and the Aim of Science*, Popper pointed out that Duhem's work made it impossible to falsify individual hypotheses within a group.[212]

> [I here note a serious] objection closely connected with the problem of *context*, and the fact that my criterion of demarcation applies to *systems of theories* rather than to statements out of context. This objection may be put as follows. No single hypothesis, it may be said, is falsifiable, because every refutation of a conclusion may hit any single premise of the set of all premises used in deriving the refuted conclusion. The attribution to the falsity to some particular hypothesis that belongs to this set of premises is therefore risky, especially if we consider the great number of assumptions which enter into every experiment . . . The answer is that we can indeed falsify only *systems of theories* and that attribution of falsity to any particular statement within such a system is always highly uncertain.

Duhem was quite clear that his thesis did not apply to all sciences, but only to those that 'require an interpretative chunk of theory in order for their theoretical hypotheses to confront observation'.[213] Physics thus represents a case in point. Yet it will be clear that Duhem's thesis can also be applied to other disciplines which seek to approach experience by means of a complex raft of theoretical assumptions – such as Christian theology. If any form of 'critical realism', such as that which we espoused in the second volume of this work, is an appropriate means of

[209] For something of the story, see Richard Baum and William Sheehan, *In Search of Planet Vulcan: The Ghost in Newton's Clockwork Universe*. New York: Plenum Press, 1997.

[210] Albrecht Fölsing, *Albert Einstein: A Biography*. New York: Viking Books, 1997, 369–77. For Einstein's critical paper, see Albert Einstein, 'Die Grundlage der allgemeinen Relativitätstheorie', *Annalen der Physik* 49 (1916), 769–822.

[211] Adolf Grünbaum, 'Is Falsifiability the Touchstone of Scientific Rationality? Karl Popper versus Inductivism', in R. S. Cohen, P. K. Feyerabend and M. W. Wartofsky (eds), *Essays in Memory of Imre Lakatos*. Dordrecht: Reidel, 1976, 213–52.

[212] Karl R. Popper, *Realism and the Aim of Science*. London: Hutchinson, 1983, 187.

[213] Roger Ariew, 'The Duhem Thesis', *British Journal for the Philosophy of Science* 35 (1984), 313–25.

understanding how we apprehend reality, it follows immediately that there is a significant theoretical and imaginative interface between the reality of God and human reflection upon God. We shall therefore turn to explore the potential of Duhem's approach for theology.

A theological anomaly: the problem of suffering

It is widely agreed that, if there exists an explanatory deficit in a Christian worldview, it relates to the problem of suffering in the world. This is often taken to imply a fundamental deficiency in Christian theology, calling into question some essential doctrine, such as the goodness or omnipotence of God.[214] Yet Pierre Duhem's analysis raises a significant question: does an anomaly necessitate the abandonment or modification of the central teachings of the Christian faith, or merely one of its many subsidiary aspects? And if the latter, what conceivable means exist for the identification of the deficient subsidiary hypothesis?

We may begin by considering how the problem of evil bears upon the issue of theoretical explanation in theology. William P. Alston has noted that two fundamentally different approaches to the problem of evil can be discerned in the writings of the twentieth century:[215]

1. A *logical* approach, which attempts to show that the existence of evil in the world is logically incompatible with the existence of God. Alston reports that it 'is now acknowledged on (almost) all sides' that this particular argument is bankrupt.

2. An *empirical* approach, which asserts that the observable evidence of evil – that is to say, that evil may be observed to exist in the world – is incompatible with the existence of God.

The *logical* aspects of the problem of evil, as it is traditionally formulated, can be set out as follows. Consider the following three hypotheses:

H_1 God is omnipotent and omniscient;

---

[214] F. J. Fitzpatrick, 'The Onus of Proof in Arguments about the Problem of Evil', *Religious Studies* 17 (1981), 19–38; Paul Draper, 'Pain and Pleasure: An Evidential Problem for Theists', *Nous* 23 (1989), 331–50; Marilyn McCord Adams, 'Horrendous Evils and the Goodness of God', in Marilyn McCord Adams and Robert Merrihew Adams (eds), *The Problem of Evil.* Oxford: Oxford University Press, 1990, 209–21.

[215] William P. Alston, 'The Inductive Argument from Evil and the Human Cognitive Condition', *Philosophical Perspectives* 5 (1991), 30–67. Stephen J. Wykstra had earlier suggested that these two approaches might be designated as 'logical' and 'evidential': Stephen J. Wykstra, 'The Humean Objection to Evidential Arguments from Suffering: On Avoiding the Evils of "Appearance"', *International Journal for Philosophy of Religion* 16 (1984), 73–93.

H_2 God is completely good;

H_3 The world contains instances of suffering and evil.

In the traditional logical formulation of the problem of suffering, the third of these propositions is held to be inconsistent with the first two by critics of theism.[216] If God is both loving and all-powerful, the existence of evil is argued to constitute a *prima facie* disconfirmation of either or both of these assertions, rendering the postulation of the existence of God as an explanatory device at least problematic, and probably incoherent.

A closer examination of the situation indicates that this stern judgement is more than a little premature. At least one further substantial hypothesis needs to be added before the possibility of evil can be regarded as constituting a potential logical difficulty for the theory.[217] An obvious example of such a hypothesis would be:

H_4 A good omnipotent God would eliminate suffering and evil.

This assumption is actually implicit in the crude analysis just considered, but was not made explicit. If some such assumption is not present, the dilemma loses its force. It might easily be countered, for example, that there is a 'greater good' that is somehow brought about by suffering, which therefore blunts the force of the objection.

Yet the issue is not entirely logical. As Alston rightly points out, the four propositions do not possess the same logical status, making it impossible to set them out in terms of a pure logical syllogism. Whereas three of the propositions (H_1, H_2, and H_4) could reasonably be defined as 'logical ideas' or 'propositions', the fourth (H_3) is actually an *observation statement*, making an empirical rather than theoretical affirmation. The three propositions H_1, H_2, and H_4 all make affirmations concerning the attributes of a (putative and hypothetical) god. The remaining statement H_3 takes the form of a report, based on experience and observation, of the way things are. Three are logical, concerned with the interconnection of ideas; the fourth is a report on what is to be observed in the external world. The conceptual bridge between experience and logic is fragile at the best of times, and is simply incapable of bearing the epistemic weight that is here being placed upon it.

---

[216] For an excellent account, see John Hick, *Evil and the God of Love*, 2nd edn. London: Macmillan, 1985.

[217] Stewart R. Sutherland, *God, Jesus and Belief: The Legacy of Theism*. Oxford: Blackwell, 1984, 22.

The fundamental question concerns the relation between theory and observation. A logical riddle, stated or conceived in terms of propositions, can give rise to an inconsistency through the manner in which those propositions are related (as, for example, in the statements 'I propose to draw a three-sided square' or 'Everything stated in this sentence is false'). The issues involved in the problem of suffering are rather more complex than this, in that they involve the attempted correlation of the world of ideas and empirical observations concerning the external world. The observational component of the problem would have to be stated in a purely logical manner, in order for the deductive objection to have force. Yet this turns out to be intensely problematic.

The problem can therefore be reformulated in a more inductive and empirical manner, as follows. Consider the following hypotheses, which we shall group together:

H_1 God is omnipotent and omniscient;

H_2 God is completely good.

Now add the following observation statement:

$O =$ The world contains instances of suffering and evil

The epistemological issues are now not purely logical, but concern the ability of a theory to accommodate observations which appear to be anomalous. The fundamental question which must be addressed in the problem of evil can be formulated, in a Duhemian manner, as follows. Does the observation statement O require that the group of hypotheses (H_1 and H_2) be abandoned? Or that just one of them should be revised? And if so, which one? Or is there a problem with a yet unidentified auxiliary hypothesis?

That there are problems with some of the hypotheses is obvious. For example, it could be argued that both H_1 and H_2 rest, at least to some extent, on Cartesian rather than Christian foundations.[218] The Cartesian emphasis upon the perfection of God is subverted by the existence of evil, which may clearly be viewed as a defect. The issue of suffering thus constitutes the grounds for disconfirmation of the Cartesian God, whereas in the Middle Ages – which was generally innocent of such assumptions – the same problem was seen as a riddle or puzzle, but most emphatically not the grounds for abandoning faith. As

---

[218] See the full analysis in Michael J. Buckley, _At the Origins of Modern Atheism_. New Haven, CT: Yale University Press, 1987.

Alasdair MacIntyre remarked, 'the God in whom the nineteenth and twentieth centuries came to disbelieve had been invented only in the seventeenth century'.[219]

One of the most careful statements of an inductive or empirical approach to the problem of evil can be found in the writings of William Rowe.[220] In what follows, we shall set out his formulation of the problem as it is found in his 1979 essay 'The Problem of Evil and Some Varieties of Atheism'.[221] In this essay, Rowe sets out his argument as follows.

1. There exist instances of intense suffering which an omnipotent, omniscient being could have prevented without thereby losing some greater good or permitting some evil which is equally bad, if not worse.

2. An omniscient, wholly good being would prevent the occurrence of any intense suffering it could, unless it could not do so without thereby losing some greater good or permitting some evil which is equally bad or worse.

3. There does not exist an omnipotent, omniscient, wholly good being.

This third statement is held to be entailed by the first two. Yet, on the basis of Duhem's analysis, such a conclusion simply cannot be drawn. There is a problem within the *ensemble théoretique*. But where? And is it fatal? Or is it merely an anomaly, which will be resolved through theoretical or observational advances?

Duhemian objections can easily be raised against each of Rowe's assertions. For example, note how his first assertion combines an observation statement with a hypothesis. We can disentangle them by suggesting that the first statement could more properly be expressed as an empirical observation statement O and a hypothesis H:

O = There exist instances of intense suffering;

H = An omnipotent, omniscient being could have prevented instances of intense suffering without thereby losing some

[219] Alasdair MacIntyre and Paul Ricœur, *The Religious Significance of Atheism*. New York: Columbia University Press, 1969, 14.

[220] See, for example, William L. Rowe, 'Evil and the Theistic Hypothesis: A Response to Wykstra', *International Journal for Philosophy of Religion* 16 (1984), 95–100; idem, 'The Empirical Argument from Evil', in R. Audi and W. J. Wainwright (eds), *Rationality, Religious Belief and Moral Commitment*. Ithaca: Cornell University Press, 1986, 227–47.

[221] William L. Rowe, 'The Problem of Evil and Some Varieties of Atheism', *American Philosophical Quarterly* 16 (1979), 335–41.

greater good or permitting some evil which is equally bad, if not worse.

How, we might reasonably ask, can Rowe know *H*? A number of writers have pointed out that the force of Rowe's objection would seem to be vitiated by an unwarranted confidence in a human ability to determine that God has (or could have) no good reason to allow some of the suffering we experience in the world.[222]

As Alston points out, one of Rowe's difficulties is that he is obliged to rely on inference in establishing his case against God. Arguments from experience must be accompanied by an acceptance of the cognitive limits which are imposed upon us – limits which Rowe seems unwilling to concede. Alston notes three areas of limitation: a lack of data (such as the nature of the universe, the reasons behind divine behaviour, and the nature of the afterlife); complexity beyond human capacity (in that the factors involved are too complex and nuanced to permit easy analysis); and difficulty in determining what is metaphysically possible or necessary (in that we are in no position to determine what can and cannot be the case). Alston concludes that:[223]

> we are simply not in a position to justifiably assert, with respect to . . . suffering that God, if he exists, would have no sufficient reason for permitting it. And if that is right, the inductive argument from evil is in no better shape than its late lamented deductive cousin.

The kind of considerations that Alston and others bring forward point to the present existence of evil and suffering as being an anomaly within the Christian worldview, rather than constituting its formal disconfirmation. On the basis of a naive falsificationism, any such *prima facie* contradiction between theory and observation is adequate grounds for the rejection of the theory; however, history suggests that many alleged contradictions are subsequently accommodated within expanded versions of theories, as the process of scientific advance continues. On the basis of his survey of the development of the natural sciences, Thomas Kuhn comments that 'if any and every failure to fit were ground for theory rejection, all theories ought to be rejected at all times'.[224] A more realistic approach is to recognize that even the best explanations are attended

---

[222] See Wykstra, 'The Humean Objection to Evidential Arguments from Suffering'.

[223] Alston, 'The Inductive Argument from Evil and the Human Cognitive Condition', 61.

[224] Thomas S. Kuhn, *The Structure of Scientific Revolutions*, 2nd edn. Chicago: University of Chicago Press, 1970, 146.

by anomalies and difficulties.[225] The difficulty lies in knowing which anomalies will eventually *be accommodated within* a theory, and which will eventually lead to the *discrediting* of a theory. Only time will tell.

The issue is familiar from the history of science. Charles Darwin, in closing his *Origin of Species*, made it clear that he was aware that his theory had many loose ends, and that there were many observations which did not fit with his proposed understanding of the evolutionary process. Yet the theory was sufficiently coherent, in his view, to encourage him to believe that it would, in the end, see them all resolved.[226]

> A crowd of difficulties will have occurred to the reader. Some of them are so grave that to this day I can never reflect on them without being staggered; but, to the best of my judgement, the greater number are only apparent, and those that are real are not, I think, fatal to my theory.

In the end, Darwin's theory is generally regarded as having triumphed, the anomalies and difficulties being explained by the general advancement of understanding of both the evolutionary process and its molecular basis.[227] Darwin himself took what might be called an eschatological perspective, arguing that observers would one day stand at a location at which his 'crowd of difficulties' would be seen for what he anticipated it would be – namely, a set of presently explicable observations. A change of historical and social perspective, he believed, would lead to anomalies being resolved, or even becoming evidence for his theory, rather than, as at present, counting against it.

Christian theology takes a similar stand, holding that its explanatory potency allows the many puzzles and anomalies of life – such as suffering – to be seen as noetic rather than ontic, resulting from limitations on our perception of the situation, rather than from the situation itself. Those puzzles or anomalies, it is argued, will ultimately only be resolved at the end of time, when all is finally revealed. There exist anomalies in our theoretical grasp of the world which must be considered to arise from our social and historical location, which limit our vision and our access to clearer perspectives.

---

[225] See Dorit A. Ganson, *The Explanationist Defense of Scientific Realism*. New York: Garland, 2001, 11–21.

[226] Charles Darwin, *The Origin of Species*. Harmondsworth: Penguin, 1968, 205.

[227] On which see R. J. Berry, *Neo-Darwinism*. London: Edward Arnold, 1982. Some important 'loose ends' of his theory were tied up through the discovery of the physical basis of heredity through the cytological work of A. F. L. Weissmann in the 1880s and 1890s, and the rediscovery of Gregor Mendel's work by Carl Correns in 1900: Lindley Darden, *Theory Change in Science: Strategies from Mendelian Genetics*. Oxford: Oxford University Press, 1991, 49–64, 80–3.

Yet this raises a question: how may the believer learn to live with the ambiguity of such anomalies, which presently seem to undermine faith, yet may one day serve to confirm it? In what follows, we shall consider a Duhemian approach, and develop it in a more explicitly Christian direction.

Duhem and le bon sens*: faith, hope and the resolution of theoretical anomalies*

In the course of his analysis of the physicist's predicament in resolving theoretical anomalies, Duhem considers the situation in which conflicting theoretical claims simply cannot be resolved. There are problems with the theory, but it is not clear quite what must be done as a result.[228]

> Lorsque l'expérience frappe de contradiction certaines conséquences d'une théorie, elle nous enseigne que cette théorie doit être modifiée, mais elle ne nous dit pas ce qu'il y faut changer. Elle laisse à la sagacité du physicien le soin de rechercher la tare qui rend boîteux tout le système. Aucun principe absolu ne guide cette recherche.

As Duhem points out, this must lead to at least the possibility that two physicists might interpret evidence in different manners, the fundamental distinction between them lying in what they regard as anomalous and what as of fundamental importance to the theory. So how may a decision be made, when a decision cannot be made? How can a conclusion be reached, when the evidence is such that a firm conclusion cannot be attained? How can a physicist live with the idea of provisionality, arising from uncertainty over whether a theory is correct, while possessing certain anomalies, or is instead fundamentally flawed?

There is no answer to these questions. Yet Duhem does not believe that this means that the physicist is condemned to silence, or haunted by the ambiguities of the situation. An appeal may be made to *le bon sens*.[229] 'Logic does not determine with strict precision the time when an inadequate hypothesis should give way to a more fruitful assumption . . . recognizing this moment belongs to good sense.' This 'good sense' is a communal intuition, a sense of what works and what does not work, which is generated within the scientific community as a consequence of its inherited experience of engaging with nature. It is a living notion, grounded in the corporate wisdom of the scientific community. *Le bon sens* is neither subjective, nor is it purely logical. It is something deeper,

---

[228] Duhem, *La théorie physique*, 329.
[229] Duhem, *La théorie physique*, 329–32.

shaped by a long engagement with nature, designating 'motives which do not proceed from logic and yet direct our choices'.

Duhem's notion of *le bon sens* is, when all is said and done, frustratingly vague, making it difficult to offer a critical account of its plausibility. Yet while Duhem has ultimately failed to solve the problem of theory choice in the faith of multiple options and anomalous evidence, he nevertheless points to two factors which are integral to the problematics of theory choice:

1. It is often impossible to choose between competing theories on the basis of the evidence available.

2. A choice must nevertheless be made.

An excellent example of this difficulty concerns the rival claims of the Copenhagen and Bohmian models of quantum mechanics, which are empirically equivalent, and equally elegant in terms of their simplicity and so forth. Yet a choice must be made between them.[230] Maybe one day physicists will be in a position to make such a choice; yet that point has not yet arrived.

The degree of confirmation of, or warrant for, a theory is limited by the perspective of the theoretician. With the demise of foundationalism, any idea that theoretical perspectives may be justified on the basis of a universal rationality have been abandoned. A new appreciation of the limits placed upon the thinker by social and historical factors has raised new questions for the whole issue of epistemic warrant. It must be conceded that there is at least a possibility that anomalies arise through the observer's perception of the situation, rather than the situation itself. On the basis of a very modest Kantianism, it may be argued that it is impossible to experience the *Ding-an-sich*. Anomalies may thus be argued to arise at the level of phenomena, rather than noumena – in other words, to reflect the observer's limited perspective, rather than a full vision of the reality which lies behind it. Hume's empiricism leads him to demand epistemic warrant for theories in terms of presently accessible experience;[231] he fails, however, to appreciate the limiting effect of the location of the thinker, which limits the 'available believable' (Paul Ricoeur).

Duhem's concept of *le bon sens* articulates the notion that such theoretical choices are not irrational or arbitrary, but represent the best

[230] James T. Cushing, *Quantum Mechanics: Historical Contingency and the Copenhagen Hegemony.* Chicago: University of Chicago Press, 1994, especially 199–215.
[231] Christopher Norris, *Against Relativism: Philosophy of Science, Deconstruction and Critical Theory.* Oxford: Blackwell, 1997, 211.

judgement of the scientific community, in the light of its past experience and accumulated experience of engaging with nature. The community, perhaps intuitively as much as cognitively, sets out its sense as to what the best option might be, recognizing that the decision is not being made on rigorously logical or empirical criteria. Although Duhem does not make this point, *le bon sens* can thus be said to belong to the category of *sapientia* rather than *scientia*.

Duhem's dilemma, which is stated rather than resolved in the notion of *le bon sens*, is shared by the theological community, as it wrestles with the anomalies thrown up by experience, and their implications for the Christian view of reality. An integral aspect of the Christian vision of the economy of salvation is that the past and present may one day be viewed from the perspective of the end of history, in which the limitations of sin, finitude and historical location will be eliminated. Perhaps just as importantly, the Christian tradition holds that at least something of this final disclosure of all things may be anticipated in the present. This vision of a future beholding of the fullness of all things carries with it the promise of seeing things in their proper perspective, when what is presently apparently incoherent or anomalous within a theory may be seen to be a result of the limitations imposed upon us by virtue of our finite existence, and our specific location within the flux of history. Such an idea can be discerned in the writings of St Paul, most notably his famous assertion that 'we now see through a mirror darkly; then we shall see face to face' (1 Corinthians 13:12).

This notion of 'eschatological verification' was developed by the Oxford philosopher of religion I. M. Crombie at the height of the 'falsification' debate of the 1950s. Noting some of the conceptual difficulties raised by the problem of suffering, Crombie remarked that[232]

> There is a *prima facie* incompatibility between the love of God, and pain and suffering. The Christian maintains that it is *prima facie* only; others maintain that it is not. They may argue about it, and the issue cannot be decided; but it cannot be decided, not because (as in the case of e.g. moral or mathematical judgments) the appeal to facts is *logically* the wrong way of trying to decide the issue, and shows that you have not understood the judgment; *but* because, since our experience is limited in the way it is, we cannot get into a position to decide it . . . For the Christian the operation

---

[232] I. M. Crombie, 'Theology and Falsification', in Anthony Flew and Alasdair MacIntyre (eds), *New Essays in Philosophical Theology*. London: SCM Press, 1955, 109–30, 126. For a slightly different rendering of the idea, see John Hick, 'Theology and Verification', in John Hick (ed.), *The Existence of God*. London: Macmillan, 1964, 252–74.

of getting into position to decide it is called dying; and though we can all do that, we cannot return to report what we find.

This is not to be seen as an evasion of the issues. Rightly understood, Christian doctrine is an attempt to behold the vision of God, a vision which can only be fully apprehended once the limiting conditions of time, space and sin have been transcended. This notion is better apprehended by the theological category of hope, rather than faith, on account of its future orientation.

As noted earlier (149), the biblical term ἀποκάλυψις is specifically associated with a *future* divine self-revelation – that is to say, with an event of revelation, understood as divine unveiling, marking the end of the historical process itself, rather than an act or series of acts of divine self-disclosure within that historical process. The theological enterprise does not in any way displace that final revelation; it does, however, aim to anticipate it, by mediating its transformative potential for humanity and the way of beholding the world it legitimates. In its light, suffering is to be seen as an anomaly within a mystery, rather than as a scandal within an incoherency, just as faith will give way to sight, so that what is presently held on trust will be seen and known to be true.

The evolution of explanation: heresy, orthodoxy and the development of doctrine

One of the most problematical areas of theological explanation concerns disagreements within the church over what is 'orthodox' and 'heretical', and the attending issue of the 'development of doctrine', which is often held to point to a non-realist understanding of the true object of Christian theology. Yet the recognition that there are significant parallels between both theories and the process of theory construction and evaluation in theology and the natural sciences allows the development of new theoretical models, capable of offering at least partial explanations of the complex history of Christian doctrine. In this concluding section of the present chapter, we propose to note some new models, and briefly explore their potential. A full statement and exploration will follow in two larger books devoted to these themes; for the present, limits of space permit only a brief engagement with the issues.

The question of the development of doctrine has been of no small importance within Roman Catholicism since the nineteenth century, when it became increasingly clear that Jacques Benigne Bossuet's insistence that catholic dogma never changed – *semper eadem!* – could not be maintained. It is a commonplace of the history and philosophy of science that scientific theories have been subject to development and radical revision throughout the modern period. Yet such development does not entail the attenuation of the fundamental scientific belief that theories represent a response to an extra-systemic reality, so that the sciences may be said to possess a 'tightening grasp of an actual reality'.[233] So might the development of scientific theories offer a model for understanding the development of Christian doctrine, thus illuminating what otherwise occasionally seems to be a complex and slightly incoherent process?

The second question concerns the much-debated relationship between orthodoxy and heresy. How are these concepts to be related to each other? The prevailing view tends to incline towards the popular, yet theologically problematic, notion that orthodoxy represents the political triumph of a particular faction within the church, with the result that hitherto accepted theories were rebranded as heresies. A scientific theology offers an account of the plurality of theory and the mode of its reception which allows some sense to be made of the historical evidence at our disposal, while at the same time offering a more rigorous theoretical account of the relation between orthodoxy and heresy, in some ways allowing the classical theological notions of 'orthodoxy' and 'heresy' to be revalidated.

Scientific theorizing as a model for doctrinal development

There is no doubt that scientific theories have undergone development, including the displacement of those which were once widely accepted and regarded as the best available explanation of the known evidence. Newton's theory of mechanics, for example, was widely accepted in the eighteenth and nineteenth centuries, and was widely regarded as one of the most firmly established of all scientific theories. Although involving the once counter-intuitive notion of action-at-a-distance in relation to gravitational forces,[234] Newton's approach achieved such a high degree of explanatory success, both retrodictive and predictive, that it seemed to be the ultimate paradigm of a triumphant scientific theory. Today, Newton's theories have been displaced by Einstein's general theory of relativity. Newtonian kinematics can now be seen as a limiting case of a

---

[233] John Polkinghorne, *One World: The Interaction of Science and Theology.* Princeton: Princeton University Press, 1986, 22.

[234] Ernan McMullin, 'The Explanation of Distant Action: Historical Notes', in J. T. Cushing and E. McMullin (eds), *Philosophical Consequences of Quantum Theory: Reflections on Bell's Theorem.* Notre Dame, IN: University of Notre Dame Press, 1989, 272–302.

more general theory. Where objects are moving with a sufficiently small velocity in comparison with that of light, the relativistic dimensions of the situation are such that the Newtonian account of their motion is a good approximation to the truth. But it is now seen as only an approximation. What was once thought to be an unassailable theory is now seen as a special instance of a more general theory. At one level, Newton is simply wrong. Similarly, Newtonian mechanics offers an excellent approximation to the truth in the case of relatively large (by quantum standards) bodies, now being seen as a limiting case of quantum mechanics. Once more, Newton's approach is seen as a special instance of a more general approach. It is possible to speak of Newtonian mechanics as being 'true within its own domain' (meaning 'when dealing with macroscopic entities moving at low velocities').[235]

Other examples of apparently firmly established theories which have been subject to radical historical erosion can be drawn from the field of optics. In the eighteenth century, the Newtonian corpuscular theory was widely accepted; by the nineteenth, Fresnel's elastic solid ether theory had largely displaced it. Both attempted to give an account of substantially the same observations; they did so, however, in rather different – and ultimately incommensurable – manners.[236] On the basis of such considerations, Larry Laudan argues that the history of science offers a 'plethora of theories which were both successful and (so far as we can judge) non-referential with respect to many of their central explanatory concepts'.[237] Further examples of theories which were once widely accepted but have long since been abandoned or drastically modified include the crystalline spheres of ancient and medieval astronomy, the humoral theory of medicine, the caloric theory of heat, and the electromagnetic ether.[238] Each of these theories was once judged to be successful

---

[235] This raises the question of the point at which classical approaches must give way to their quantum counterparts – an issue addressed by the 'Ehrenfest theorem', which deals with the question of the 'classical limit' in quantum mechanics: Albert Messiah, *Quantum Mechanics*, 2 vols. Amsterdam: North-Holland, 1976, vol. 1, 216–28.

[236] For full documentation, see the superb study of Jed Z. Buchwald, *The Rise of the Wave Theory of Light: Optical Theory and Experiment in the Early Nineteenth Century*. Chicago: University of Chicago Press, 1989.

[237] Larry Laudan, 'A Confutation of Convergent Realism', *Philosophy of Science* 48 (1981), 19–49. For a criticism of this approach, see Clyde L. Hardin and Alexander Rosenberg, 'In Defense of Convergent Realism', *Philosophy of Science* 49 (1982), 604–15.

[238] On which see Tetu Hirosige, 'The Ether Problem, the Mechanistic World View, and the Origins of the Theory of Relativity', *Historical Studies in the Physical Sciences* 7 (1976), 3–82; Andrew Warwick, 'The Sturdy Protestants of Science: Larmor, Trouton and the Earth's Motion through the Ether', in Jed Z. Buchwald (ed.), *Scientific Practice: Theories and Stories of Doing Physics*. Chicago: University of Chicago Press, 1995, 300–43.

by the criteria of their contemporaries; they have now been abandoned. Yet as we argued earlier, this does not entail the abandonment of the central realist thesis that the natural sciences offer an increasingly tight representation and explanation of an external reality (vol. 2, 161–6).

While there are many criticisms that may be directed against Thomas Kuhn's *Structure of Scientific Revolutions*,[239] the work dealt a mortal blow to the simplistic notion of a linear advance in scientific theorizing. Kuhn's observations of 'radical theory change' and 'paradigm shifts' in the history of the natural sciences do not, as he appears to believe, entail the rejection of realism; rather, the patterns he observes in the development of scientific theories clarify how a scientific realism does not necessarily lead to a linear development of theories. The authenticity of theoretical advance is determined not by the linearity of the process, but by the empirical adequacy and intratheoretical excellence of the outcome of that process. The process is subject to all the constraints of history; the validity of the ensuing theories is dependent not upon the process by which they evolved, but upon their empirical credentials.

The non-linear development of scientific theories raises questions concerning those more simplistic models of the development of Christian doctrine, which suggest that doctrines may be regarded as emerging in an essentially direct manner from a central core – for example, as in a seed germinating into a plant, or a plant developing growth. In stressing the continuity within doctrinal development, such approaches are unduly insensitive to the effects of the complex environment within which doctrinal development takes place, and the apparently erratic directions in which the process leads.

The noted Dominican theologian Ambroise Gardeil (1859–1931) argued that this theory is found at its purest in the writings of John Henry Newman.[240] The church can here be seen as the 'gardener', nurturing the development of a Spirit-led process of growth and development. But why should doctrine develop at all? Gardeil finds the organic model of doctrinal development wanting precisely because it fails to identify and account for the fundamental impulse which drives the process of evolution. For this reason, Gardeil argued that the natural sciences offer a much more appropriate model for an authentic understanding of doctrinal development. While the object which the

---

[239] See, for example, Paul Hoyningen-Huene, *Reconstructing Scientific Revolutions: Thomas S. Kuhn's Philosophy of Science.* Chicago: University of Chicago Press, 1993.

[240] See Ambroise Gardeil, *Le donné révélé et la théologie.* Paris: Editions Du Cerf, 1932. For comment, see Aidan Nichols, *From Newman to Congar: The Idea of Doctrinal Development from the Victorians to the Second Vatican Council.* Edinburgh: T&T Clark, 1990, 155–76.

natural sciences aim to investigate does not change, development does indeed take place at the level of understanding the internal relations of the constituent elements of the reality which is being investigated.

Gardeil then argues that the theological equivalent of this reality is *le donné* – the original 'gift' of faith, which has been entrusted to the church. The church intuitively grasps something of this *donné*, but has yet to give a full account of its identity and interrelationships. The task of theology is to explicate this complexity and richness by a process of 'intellectual fermentation', already begun by the apostles, but entrusted to the church for its development and ultimate perfection.

There are difficulties with Gardeil's approach, which are not of great significance for our purposes. What is of interest is his recognition of the deficiencies of an 'organic' approach – which are further evidenced by the non-linear mode of doctrinal evolution disclosed through a study of the history of doctrine – and his appeal to the natural sciences for models of theoretical development. It is my intention to pursue this approach.

The development of Christian doctrine: a new model

One of the most fertile models of the church compares it to a ship, which carries the faithful safely across the tempestuous seas of life, until finally arriving at the safe harbour of the heavenly city. The imagery is based on 1 Peter 3:20–1, which appears to draw a comparison between the church and Noah's ark; both offer salvation through water.[241] This ecclesiological iconography was developed during the patristic period by Gregory the Great and others,[242] but would find a special resonance with seafaring nations, such as the Danish. Having been converted to Christianity, the erstwhile Vikings continued their maritime emphasis through the 'church boat (*Kirkeskibe*)', now traditionally hung from the roof of the church naves of the Baltic region.[243]

This traditional imagery for the Christian community has become increasingly significant after the collapse of foundationalism, in that one of the most powerful and productive images deployed in contemporary philosophy for the exploration of a tradition-mediated rationality is

---

[241] Other New Testament passages of relevance include Matthew 14:22–33; Mark 6:45–52; Luke 8:22–5; John 6:16–21. On Noah's ark in Christian exegesis, see Hartmut Boblitz, 'Die Allegorese der Arche Noahs in der frühen Bibelauslegung', *Frühmittelalterliche Studien* 6 (1972), 159–70.

[242] For a full discussion, see H. S. Benjamins, 'Noah, the Ark and the Flood in Early Christianity: The Ship of the Church in the Making', in Florentino García Martínez and Gerard P. Luttikhuizen (eds), *Interpretations of the Flood*. Leiden: Brill, 1998, 134–49.

[243] For examples and illustrations, see Henning Henningsen, *Kirkeskibe og kirkeskibsfester*. Copenhagen: Host, 1950; Jens Petersen, *Kirkeskibe i Thisted Amt*. Nykobing Mors: Jul pa Mors, 1978.

Neurath's ship. The Christian tradition may, in several respects, be likened to one of Otto Neurath's ships, already constructed and under sail.[244] For example, the entire theological enterprise, as medieval writers never tired of reminding us, is undertaken *in via*; it is not something which can be constructed *de novo* or *ab initio* in some hypothetical dry dock, in that the historical trajectory of the Christian tradition is such that a return to origins is impossible. We are unable to step outside the boat, or return to port. The business of theological explanation must take place while the journey is under way.

The comparison of the Christian tradition to Neurath's boat carries with it the recognition of the multilevelled structure of this complex social reality. The image of a ship under way on the seas offers an admirable model for the task of theology. But more importantly for our present purposes, it offers a model for the development of doctrine which is vastly superior to those currently advocated. Here is the image in Neurath's own words:[245]

> We cannot start from a *tabula rasa* as Descartes thought we could. We have to make do with words and concepts that we find when our reflections begin. [Pierre] Duhem has shown with special emphasis that every statement about any happening is saturated with hypotheses of all sorts and that these in the end are derived from our whole worldview. We are like sailors who on the open sea must reconstruct their ship (*wie Schiffer sind wir, die ihr Schiff auf offener See umbauen müssen*) but are never able to start afresh from the bottom. Where a beam is taken away a new one must at once be put there, and for this the rest of the ship is used as support. In this way, by using the old beams and driftwood, the ship can be shaped entirely anew, but only by gradual reconstruction.

Neurath's metaphor offers a means of making sense of the empirical development of doctrine, rather than forcing the material into a preconceived dogmatic pattern, determined by the needs of a specific theory of development on the one hand, or a constraining ecclesiological agenda on the other.[246]

---

[244] This image occurs at several points in Neurath's writings: see, for example, Otto Neurath, 'Protokollsätze', *Erkenntnis* 3 (1932), 204–14.

[245] Otto Neurath, *Empiricism and Sociology*. Dordrecht: Reidel, 1973, 198. For an earlier formulation of the image, see Otto Neurath, 'Protokollsätze', *Erkenntnis* 3 (1932), 204–14, 209: 'Es gibt keine tabula rasa. Wie Schiffer sind wir, die ihr Schiff auf offener See umbauen müssen, ohne es jemals in einem Dock zerlegen und aus besten Bestandteilen neu errichten zu können.'

[246] For approaches which I must confess I find deficient in one or other respects, see R. Garrigou-Lagrange, 'Le relativisme et l'immutabilité du dogme', *Angelicum* 27 (1950), 219–46; Pierre Rousselot, 'Petit théorie du développement du dogme', *Recherches de science religieuse* 53 (1965), 355–90.

In what follows, I shall explore how this metaphor allows some of the major themes of doctrinal development to be rationalized. Such an approach has four distinguishing features:

1. It will be descriptive, not prescriptive – that is, it will be based on the historical study of Christian theology without reference to any preconceived notions of what form that development ought to have taken.

2. It will acknowledge the parallels between the episodic and discontinuous development of scientific theories, and the development of Christian doctrine, thus avoiding the notion of the continuous development of doctrine – such as a seed sprouting – which is difficult to reconcile with the actual historical evidence.

3. It avoids foundationalist assumptions which have so often found their way into alternative accounts of the process of the genesis, development and reception of doctrine.

4. It recognizes that the developmental pressures which may be identified can point in different directions, sometimes leading to differing local outcomes, or occasional appearances of stagnation or retrogression.

Neurath's metaphor of the boat offers an important framework by which the factors implicated in doctrinal development may be identified and their impact explored. It identifies the fundamental pressure which leads to doctrinal development as the need to remain afloat in response to a series of challenges and threats it faces *in via*. Three specific pressures may be noted, all of which are implicit in Neurath's original metaphor.

Unpacking – a process of learning to live within the boat's confines, and understanding what is already incorporated within its structures.

Reconstruction – the rebuilding of parts of the ship from what is already present, in response to damage caused by adverse conditions (such as storms) which threaten to capsize or swamp the ship.

Incorporating driftwood – using material which is to hand in the environment to strengthen the boat.

In what follows, we shall explore each of these in a little more detail.

1. *The unpacking of resources*

The process of inhabiting the Christian tradition entails becoming acquainted with its basic features, and establishing certain connections. The image of 'unpacking' conveys the notion of identifying what is already present within the Christian tradition, and establishing connections between the various resources that are found to be present. In some ways, this aspect of the metaphor of boat corresponds to certain aspects of the 'organic' model of doctrinal development, in that it proposes a simple unfolding of what is already present, through the establishment of interrelationships.

2. *The reconstruction of the boat*

The ship exists in the sea; if the sea penetrates the ship, it will sink. The defence of the ship against internal and external threats is of paramount importance to its continuing existence. Holes require to be plugged; broken masts require to be repaired. As Neurath points out, this task is to be undertaken *in via*, using materials already present within the boat. Retrogression in doctrinal development is thus easily understood as a process of reassembling resources, with a view to improving the overall structure and coherence of the ship. The sixteenth-century Reformation can be seen as a particularly luminous example of this process of reconstruction. The mainline reformers were clear that they were not attempting to construct a new church, but to renew an existing church. Nor did they see themselves as introducing any new ideas or methods to the Christian theological tradition. The fundamental intention of reformers such as Luther was to reconstruct the church on the basis of its fundamental theological resources, in response to developments and accretions during the later Middle Ages which he regarded as prejudicial to the future existence and integrity of the church. Luther's agenda was renovation, not innovation.

3. *The incorporation of driftwood into the structure of the boat*

Neurath points out that his hypothetical sailors were able to reconstruct the boat using material to hand within the boat, or driftwood around them. The history of the Christian tradition demonstrates a marked propensity to avail itself of intellectual and cultural resources it encountered around it, floating in the water of history. These may be incorporated into the fabric of the boat. Once worn out, they may be replaced by new driftwood, scooped up from another historical location. Such driftwood is not part of the original fabric of the boat, and its incorporation must be seen as temporary, not permanent. Medieval theology incorporated the Ptolemaic model of the solar system into its deliberations; today, a Copernican model has displaced it. Both are driftwood. Various ancillary hypotheses and working methods – including those of the natural sciences – may be adopted and incorporated, until such time as their utility has been exhausted, and new material needs to be incorporated.

The revalidation of the categories of orthodoxy and heresy

In a review of Jaroslav Pelikan's excellent student textbook *The Emergence of the Catholic Tradition, 100–600*,[247] James S. Preus raises some questions concerning what he regards as the uncritical approach to the emergence of both orthodoxy and heresy underlying Pelikan's analysis.[248] Preus argues that the scholarly undertakings of Walter Bauer, Martin Werner, and more recently, Helmut Koester, call into question these traditional categories. The church chose to define what it would believe in an act of institutional authority, so that the category of 'orthodoxy' represents those ideas that the church authorized.

> Pelikan's superb description leaves the reader groping for an historical understanding of the very meaning of doctrinal orthodoxy itself. Did the church confess certain doctrines because they were orthodox? Or are some doctrines orthodox because the church confessed them? The weight of Pelikan's historical account points decisively to the second alternative, while the substance of his own commitment seems to embrace the first as well.

Preus's comments raise the question of the interplay of historical and theoretical factors in Pelikan's account of the development of doctrine. For Preus, Pelikan has failed to disentangle his own theoretical precommitments from his account of the origins and development of both orthodoxy and heresy, and hence presents a biased account of the subject.

> An institution in the very process of defining itself cannot be presupposed until that formative process and definition is farther along. Orthodoxy and heresy cannot be presupposed when describing the very conflicts out of which these categories assumed concrete identification. The definition of doctrine as 'the church's' confession on the basis of the 'Word of God' demands, in a genuinely *historical* account, some clarity about who speaks for 'the church' at each given moment, how that body is so identified, and what is meant by 'Word of God' (other than what the church is confessing) in the absence of a universally accepted canon of Christian Scripture, creed, or teaching *magisterium*.

[247] Jaroslav Pelikan, *The Emergence of the Catholic Tradition, 100–600*. Chicago: University of Chicago Press, 1971.
[248] *Theology Today* 29 (1972), 225–9.

Preus's comments are insightful and significant, and point to the serious difficulties which are encountered in any allegedly 'neutral', 'objective' or 'scholarly' attempt to define orthodoxy or heresy in purely historical or theoretical terms. We shall explore this problem further in what follows.

The first major difficulty faced by any attempt to offer a purely theoretical account of heresy is that the term is itself possessed of a conceptual fluidity, no doubt reflecting its polemical associations, which results in a constant process of reinterpretation throughout the Christian tradition. It is manifestly obvious that the term 'heresy' has changed its meaning over the years, causing no small difficulties for those who would seek to determine its essence or structure on the basis of purely historical considerations. The etymology of the term is not especially helpful;[249] the term has come to have developed associations which, though clearly related to its original meaning, incorporate additional nuances.

Strictly speaking, the use of the term 'heresy' must be restricted to the patristic period. The term was extensively used throughout the Middle Ages, but with overtones which distance the medieval usage of the term from its original associations. The case against the continuing use of the term 'heresy' to designate religious movements in the Middle Ages was first made in 1935 by Herbert Grundmann,[250] who argued that the notion was defined from an inquisitional, rather than theological, perspective. 'Heresy' was defined in terms of challenges posed to the authority of the church, from the perspective of those who were thus challenged. A purely historical account of the notion of heresy in the Middle Ages is thus obliged to define orthodoxy in terms of papal teaching, and heresy in terms of dissent from such teaching.[251] Heresy increasingly became a juridical notion.[252] Where the patristic period conceived

[249] Marcel Simon, 'From Greek Hairesis to Christian Heresy', in William R. Schoedel and Robert L. Wilken (eds), *Early Christian Literature and the Classical Intellectual Tradition*. Paris: Beauchesne, 1979, 101–16.

[250] Herbert Grundmann, *Religiöse Bewegungen im Mittelalter: Untersuchungen über die geschichtlichen Zusammenhänge zwischen der Ketzerei, den Bettelorden und der religiösen Frauenbewegung um 12. und 13. Jahrhundert und über die geschichtlichen Grundlagen der deutschen Mystik*. Berlin: Emil Ebering, 1935. For his later analysis, see Herbert Grundmann, *Ketzergeschichte des Mittelalters*. Göttingen: Vandenhoeck & Ruprecht, 1963.

[251] Malcolm Lambert, *Medieval Heresy: Popular Movements from the Gregorian Reform to the Reformation*. Oxford: Blackwell, 2002, xi. 'I have written as a historian, not a theologian. I have taken "heresy" to mean whatever the papacy explicitly or implicitly condemned during the period.'

[252] As demonstrated by Othmar Hageneder, 'Der Häresiebegriff bei den Juristen des 12. und 13. Jahrhunderts', in W. Lourdaux and D. Verhelst (eds), *The Concept of Heresy in the Middle Ages*. Louvain: Louvain University Press, 1978, 42–103.

heresy in terms of a deviation from the Catholic faith, the Jurists of the twelfth and thirteenth centuries succeeded in redefining the notion in terms of the rejection of ecclesiastical authority, especially papal authority. There is thus no theological contradiction involved in the Reformation's insistence that many of those stigmatized as 'heretics' by the medieval church were, in fact, orthodox Christians. As Robert Moore has argued, the extension of the category of heresy was an important instrument of social control.[253] The medieval redefinition of heresy locates its essence in challenging papal power, rather than in deviating from Christian orthodoxy. Heresy became the means by which a society subsumed its endemic tensions under a notionally religious category. It ceased to be a theological notion, and was now defined legally or sociologically.[254]

Yet a theoretical account of 'heresy' must also confront the fact that it is not only the general idea of heresy which has been subjected to a process of revision in the course of its reception within the Christian tradition; individual heresies have also been viewed in the light of the contemporary situations of their interpreters, and cast in a series of often imaginative theological and political roles. An excellent example of this process of reinterpretation and redefinition is provided by Arianism, which has been presented in an astonishing series of guises, particularly in more recent Christian history.[255] For French Catholic writers of the seventeenth century, Arianism was the prototype and historical occasion for the malicious Protestant heresy of Socinianism.[256] For John Henry Newman, Arianism was the baleful precursor of the kind of evangelicalism he so detested;[257] for Adolf von Harnack, it was the eccentric embodiment of the excesses of Hellenism to which the development of dogma bore such a disturbing witness.

Recent studies have made the succinct definition of Arianism increasingly problematic, by drawing attention to the manner in which the heresy was increasingly presented and interpreted within the framework

---

[253] Robert I. Moore, *The Formation of a Persecuting Society: Power and Deviance in Western Europe, 950–1250*. Oxford: Basil Blackwell, 1990.

[254] For the exploration of this point with reference to the continuity between medieval heresy and the Reformation, see René Bornert, *La réforme protestante du culte à Strasbourg au XVIe siècle (1523–1598): approche sociologique et interprétation théologique*. Leiden: Brill, 1981.

[255] Rowan Williams, *Arius: Heresy and Tradition*, 2nd edn. London: SCM Press, 2001, 1–25, 247–67.

[256] I have in mind the interesting work of the Jesuit historian Louis Maimbourg, *Histoire de l'arianisme depuis sa naissance jusqu'à sa fin*. Paris: Sébastian Mabre-Cramoisy, 1673.

[257] John Henry Newman, *The Arians of the Fourth Century*. London: Rivington, 1833. For perceptive criticisms of this puzzling work, see Stephen Thomas, *Newman and Heresy: The Anglican Years*. Cambridge: Cambridge University Press, 1991.

of the Enlightenment project.[258] Whereas it might plausibly be argued that Arianism is best to be understood as a serious rival to the orthodox construal of the biblical witness to Christ,[259] concerns within traditional Christian circles over the impact of the anti-transcendental aspects of the Enlightenment agenda led to the heresy being recast as primarily, if not essentially, a rationalist Unitarianism, divested of any sense of a transcendent reality.

A purely theoretical account of heresy in general thus faces formidable difficulties. This is evident in the case of F. D. E. Schleiermacher's interesting and suggestive theoretical account of the 'four natural heresies' of the Christian faith (vol. 2, 302–6), where four historically abstracted, deficient accounts of the person and work are described, and mapped against the specific historical actualities of Ebionitism, Docetism, Pelagianism and Manichaeism.[260] The process of historical abstraction necessitated by any purely theoretical account of heresy fails to take into account such critical questions as the social dimensions of the heresy (consider, for example, the importance of the tension between indigenous Berbers and Roman colonists as background to the Donatist controversy),[261] or the manner in which it is received within the Christian tradition itself.

Yet a purely historical approach to the issue is also problematical. The simplest historical approach to defining both orthodoxy and heresy can be summarized in the slogan *primum est verum*. According to this rather neat formula, the earliest doctrinal formulations must be regarded as the most authentic – whether a later generation would consider them to be orthodox or heretical. One school of thought would argue that the earliest Christian understandings of the best interpretation of the Christian witness to – for example – the person of Christ constitute orthodoxy, whereas later deviations represent heresy; another would argue that the earliest (and hence most authentic) ideas were subsequently suppressed by the church, as it attempted to enforce its rather restrictive vision of orthodoxy. These two views share a flawed approach to the constitution of theological reality, resting upon the apparently self-evident assumption that the earliest ideas are the most authentic, with later developments representing distortions.

[258] The best study of this development is Maurice Wiles, *Archetypal Heresy: Arianism through the Centuries*. Oxford: Clarendon Press, 1996.

[259] See, for example, the study of T. E. Pollard, *Johannine Christology and the Early Church*. Cambridge: Cambridge University Press, 1970.

[260] On which see Klaus M. Beckmann, *Der Begriff der Häresie bei Schleiermacher*. Munich: Kaiser Verlag, 1959.

[261] A point stressed by W. H. C. Frend, *The Donatist Church: A Movement of Protest in Roman North Africa*. Oxford: Clarendon Press, 1971.

One of the most able accounts of the emergence of orthodoxy in the early church is also an attempt to clarify the relation of the Reformation (especially its Lutheran constituency) to the theological heritage of the early church.[262] In his magisterial study of Philip Melanchthon's understanding of the *testimonia patrum*,[263] Peter Fraenkel demonstrates the intense difficulties faced by Melanchthon as he sought to clarify the means by which the 'primum et verum' emerged historically, was distorted and confused by the medieval church, and was successfully recovered through the theological endeavours of the evangelical Reformers. 'Ancient doctrine, original doctrine and true doctrine are thus one and the same thing.'[264] Theological orthodoxy may be determined by an extrapolation to the earliest teachings of the church. The complex notion of *purior antiquitas* came to function for Melanchthon as a theological criterion against which heretical developments may be identified and purged.[265]

Melanchthon's agenda has both polemical and constructive aspects. His appeal to antiquity resonates with the values and norms of the later Renaissance, of which he was such a distinguished representative, allowing him to locate the Reformation conceptually within the greater cultural movements of his day.[266] More significantly, Melanchthon was able to defend the catholicity of the Lutheran Reformation through the implicit equation of 'catholicity' with 'antiquity', implying that disagreements between the reformers and their Catholic opponents was due to medieval doctrinal innovations or distortions: *ecclesiae catholicae doctrinam renovamus et illustramus.*[267]

Yet Melanchthon's successors found themselves in something of a quandary over the approach he adopted. Perhaps benefiting from a less than thorough knowledge of the patristic *corpus* on the part of both his supporters and opponents, Melanchthon was able to get away with some sweeping historical statements of rather dubious validity. His successors were less fortunate, not least on account of the substantial expansion in

---

[262] On the importance of the theological heritage of the early church to the theological method of the Reformation, see Alister E. McGrath, *The Intellectual Origins of the European Reformation.* Oxford: Blackwell, 1987, 175–90.

[263] Peter Fraenkel, *Testimonia Patrum: The Function of the Patristic Argument in the Theology of Philip Melanchthon.* Geneva: Droz, 1961.

[264] Fraenkel, *Testimonia Patrum*, 162.

[265] Fraenkel, *Testimonia Patrum*, 170–1.

[266] For the general issues, see Christine Treml, *Humanistische Gemeinschaftsbildung: soziokulturelle Untersuchung zur Entstehung eines neuen Gelehrtenstandes in der frühen Neuzeit.* Hildesheim: Olms, 1989.

[267] Fraenkel, *Testimonia Patrum*, 171.

patristic scholarship within the post-Tridentine Roman Catholic church, which raised some very difficult questions for many of Melanchthon's assertions.[268] Many early patristic writers adopted views which were at odds with those of the Reformation, leaving Melanchthon's attempts to define orthodoxy and present the Reformation as its recovery looking more than a little implausible. A much more nuanced model was clearly required.

For Melanchthon, orthodoxy was defined as the earliest, and hence most authentic form of belief; for Walter Bauer (1877–1960), the earliest and most authentic form of belief was likely to be heretical, not orthodox. The publication of Bauer's *Rechtgläubigkeit und Ketzerei im ältesten Christentum* (1934) caused no small stir in the world of early Christian studies. Bauer argued that the shared sense of fellowship within the early Christian churches did not seem to be located at the level of doctrines, but lay primarily in the worship of the same Lord, rather than in any formal statement of doctrine (which is how 'orthodoxy' tends to be defined). Bauer went on to argue that a variety of views which were tolerated in the early church gradually began to be regarded with suspicion by the later church. Teachings which were accepted in the earliest decades of the church's existence were later condemned, particularly from the end of the second century onwards, as an orthodox consensus began to emerge. Bauer's hostility to the idea of doctrinal norms can be seen particularly clearly in his conviction that these were a late development within Christianity. Opinions that had once been tolerated were now discarded as inadequate.

But how was this distinction between heresy and orthodoxy drawn? Bauer argued that the notion of 'orthodoxy' was a direct result of the growing political power of Rome, which increasingly came to impose its own views upon others, using the term 'heresy' to designate and disparage those views it rejected. For Bauer, the distinction between orthodoxy and heresy often seemed arbitrary. These ideas were taken up and devel-

---

[268] Owen Chadwick, *From Bossuet to Newman: The Idea of Doctrinal Development.* Cambridge: Cambridge University Press, 1957, 1–20. For some of the general issues attending the patristic testimony within the Reformation, see Luchesius Smits, *Saint Augustin dans l'oeuvre de Jean Calvin.* Assen: Van Gorcum, 1957, 265–70; Leif Grane, 'Divus Paulus et S. Augustinus, interpres eius fidelissimus: Über Luthers Verhältnis zu Augustin', in G. Ebeling, E. Jüngel and G. Schunack (eds), *Festschrift für Ernst Fuchs.* Tübingen: Mohr, 1973, 133–46; J. Marius J. Lange van Ravenswaay, *Augustinus totus noster: das Augustinverständnis bei Johannes Calvin.* Göttingen: Vandenhoeck & Ruprecht, 1990. There is much valuable material in Leif Grane, Alfred Schindler and Markus Wriedt (eds), *Auctoritas patrum: zur Rezeption der Kirchenväter im 15. und 16. Jahrhundert.* Mainz: Verlag Philipp von Zabern, 1993.

oped in the writings of the Harvard scholar Helmut Koester,[269] and enjoyed at least a degree of acceptance within the scholarly community until as late as the 1960s.[270]

Today, Bauer's thesis looks decidedly shaky.[271] While fully conceding that Bauer has demonstrated that early 'orthodoxy' was a more fluid and less rigidly defined notion than some had supposed, his critics have called most of his conclusions into question, expressing particular concern over his extensive argumentation from silence.[272] Bauer's assertion that, in most geographical regions, what would later be stigmatized as 'heresy' was actually the earliest form of Christianity has been firmly rebutted on the basis of both literary and archaeological evidence.[273] A growing awareness of the ease of communication within the Roman empire has led to an increasing understanding of how relatively easy it was for a widely flung faith to sustain a network of interlocking and interrelating communities, with a shared sense of identity and purpose.[274]

Perhaps one of the most unsatisfactory approaches to the question of the development of heresy is set out by J. M. Robinson and Helmut Koester. In their study *Trajectories through Early Christianity*, these writers argue that Christianity represents a series of highly diverse ideas, each with their distinctive 'trajectory', which makes any attempt to adjudicate between them intensely problematic. The *kerygma* itself was thus 'subject to a plurality of understandings', including the heretical ideas described in the Corinthian correspondence.[275] As E. P. Sanders pointed out in a decisive refutation of this simplistic model, a 'trajectory' implies

[269] See, for example, Helmut Koester, 'Gnomai Diaphorai: The Origin and Nature of Diversification in the History of Early Christianity', *Harvard Theological Review* 58 (1965), 279–318.

[270] The shift in mood can be discerned in the excellent essay of Hans Dieter Betz, 'Orthodoxy and Heresy in Primitive Christianity: Some Critical Remarks on Georg Strecker's Republication of Walter Bauer's *Rechtgläubigkeit und Ketzerei im ältesten Christentum*', *Interpretation* 19 (1965), 299–311.

[271] For magisterial surveys of the issue, see Robert M. Grant, *Heresy and Criticism: The Search for Authenticity in Early Christian Literature*. Louisville, KY: Westminster/John Knox Press, 1993; Arland J. Hultgren, *The Rise of Normative Christianity*. Minneapolis: Fortress Press, 1994. For comments on some specific issues, see Daniel J. Harrington, 'The Reception of Walter Bauer's *Orthodoxy and Heresy in Earliest Christianity* during the Last Decade', *Harvard Theological Review* 73 (1980), 289–98.

[272] Hultgren, *The Rise of Normative Christianity*, 10.

[273] See especially Thomas A. Robinson, *The Bauer Thesis Examined: The Geography of Heresy in the Early Christian Church*. Lewiston, NY: Edwin Mellen Press, 1988, 35–91.

[274] Robert Wilken, 'Diversity and Unity in Early Christianity', *The Second Century* 1 (1981), 101–10.

[275] James M. Robinson and Helmut Koester, *Trajectories through Early Christianity*. Philadelphia: Fortress Press, 1971, 1–19, 26–34.

'sequential development and implicit goal'.[276] Thus Robinson rather naively presupposes that one can distinguish two streams of 'Paulinism', one of which leads on to orthodoxy and the other to heresy. Paul's thought thus leads directly to both 'orthodox' and 'heretical' movements within an emerging Christianity. Against this, it may be pointed out that even the development of scientific theories does not show the linear trajectory of progress that one might expect over a period of time; rather, a series of theories exist in competition, with the communal process of adjudication proceeding in a complex manner which is difficult to fit to any single model of 'scientific progress', and is most certainly not consistent with a simplistic 'trajectory' model of scientific advance.

As Robin Lane Fox, who has no vested interest in the traditional understanding of 'orthodoxy', makes clear, Bauer's historical approach to heresy fails on the grounds of precisely those historical criteria which he chooses to deploy in its support. While it is difficult to make firm historical judgements on many issues relating to the history of early Christianity, on one a clear verdict is possible:[277]

> An older view that heretical types of Christianity arrived in many places before the orthodox faith has nothing in its favour, except perhaps in the one Syrian city of Edessa. In Lyons and North Africa, there is no evidence of this first heretical phase and the likelier origins are all against it. In Egypt, the argument has been decisively refuted from the evidence of the papyri. Details of practice and leadership did differ widely, but the later existence of so many heresies must not obscure the common core of history and basic teaching throughout the Christian world.

Instead, there has been a renewed appreciation of the merits of a more traditional view, which holds that second-century Christianity ought to be viewed essentially as an orthodox core surrounded by a *penumbra* within which the borderline between 'orthodoxy' and 'heresy' was still somewhat blurred, and open to further clarification through controversy and debate.[278] It has also been pointed out that the historical observation that heresy existed prior to orthodoxy in some given location

[276] E. P. Sanders, *Paul and Palestinian Judaism: A Comparison of Patterns of Religion.* Philadelphia: Fortress Press, 1977, 20–4.

[277] Robin Lane Fox, *Pagans and Christians in the Mediterranean World from the Second Century AD to the Conversion of Constantine.* London: Penguin, 1988, 276. Fox draws particular attention to the critical evidence assembled in the 1977 Schweich Lectures of the British Academy: Colin H. Roberts, *Manuscript, Society and Belief in Early Christian Egypt.* London: Oxford University Press, 1979.

[278] This is the position developed in the classic study of H. E. W. Turner, *The Pattern of Christian Truth: A Study in the Relations between Orthodoxy and Heresy in the Early Church.* London: Mowbray, 1954, 81–94.

cannot legitimately be used to justify the rather more ambitious theory that heresy is to be seen as existing on historically equal terms as orthodoxy.[279]

Orthodoxy and heresy: a new model

This section sets out to offer a theoretical account of the origins and nature of heresy, based on the fundamental principles of a scientific theology. In view of the central importance of Jesus Christ to the Christian tradition, we shall focus our attention on the problems associated with theoretical accounts of his identity and significance. There are compelling similarities between the manners in which the scientific community generates and evaluates theories and the Christian community receives doctrines, which require close and extended analysis. Two fundamental theoretical issues make the notion of 'heresy' an inevitability:

1. The *underdetermination of theory by evidence*, which means that any given event is open to a number of interpretations, with the evidence often not being sufficient to secure closure of the issue.

2. The *dynamics of the reception of theory*, which account for the manner in which certain theories may enjoy a temporary degree of popularity or acceptance, before being discarded in favour of another as the process of evaluation and reception continues.

Taken together, these two factors determine that there are likely to be divergent interpretations of the person of Jesus Christ, in that interpretations of his identity and significance are at least to some extent underdetermined by the evidence; and that the process of evaluating these alternatives within the community through a process of 'reception' takes some time. In what follows, we shall explore these two issues in a little more detail.

In many cases, the empirical evidence discriminates between theoretical possibilities, indicating that one is to be preferred over another. Nevertheless, there are limits to such discriminatory potential, often giving rise to the situation in which, for a given set of observation statements, a number of potential explanations may be offered. Such explanations are empirically equivalent, in that they each offer equally satisfactory accounts of what may be observed; they are, however, different explanations. The Copenhagen and Bohm versions of quantum mechanics are currently observationally equivalent, forcing the choice

[279] Hultgren, *The Rise of Normative Christianity*, 11.

between them to be made on other grounds.[280] Such observations give rise to what is usually referred to as the 'underdetermination thesis' – the view that there exist rival theories which are empirically equivalent but logically incompatible. This approach has proved especially attractive to those committed to primarily sociological approaches to the natural sciences, which hold that there are, in principle, an indefinite number of theories that are capable of fitting observed facts more or less adequately.[281]

If there exist any number of equivalent explanations of a given set of observations, it follows that the actual choice of theory is to be explained on the basis of *sociological* factors, such as vested interests, power structures, or race or gender issues. As Mary Hesse has rightly pointed out, some form of relativism seems to be the inescapable consequence of more radical forms of the thesis of the underdetermination of theory by evidence[282] – a conclusion which has admirably suited certain sociological interpretations of the natural sciences. The strongest form of this approach ('maximal underdetermination') would take the following form:[283]

> For any theoretical statement S and acceptable theory T essentially containing S, there is an acceptable theory T' with the same testable consequences but which contains, essentially, the negation of S.

In its stronger form, the 'underdetermination theory' is highly vulnerable.[284] In particular, Adolf Grünbaum mounted a powerful challenge to what he unhelpfully termed 'the Duhemian argument', demonstrating that it is either empirically false or trivially true.[285]

While the idea that every theory has at least one equally well supported rival, making theory choice an impossibility or the consequence of non-scientific considerations, has been widely criticized, the difficul-

---

[280] A point developed by James T. Cushing, *Quantum Mechanics: Historical Contingency and the Copenhagen Hegemony*. Chicago: University of Chicago Press, 1994.

[281] See, for example, Richard Boyd, 'Realism, Underdetermination, and a Causal Theory of Evidence', *Nous* 7 (1973), 1–12; W. Newton-Smith and Steven Lukes, 'The Underdetermination of Theory by Data', *Proceedings of the Aristotelian Society* 52 (1978), 71–91; Larry Laudan and Jarrett Leplin, 'Empirical Equivalence and Underdetermination', *Journal of Philosophy* 88 (1991), 449–72.

[282] Mary Hesse, 'What is the Best Way to Assess Evidential Support for Scientific Theories?' in L. Jonathan Cohen and Mary Hesse (eds), *Applications of Inductive Logic*. Oxford: Clarendon Press, 1980, 202–17. See further Paul Horwich, 'How to Choose Between Empirically Indistinguishable Theories', *Journal of Philosophy* 79 (1982), 61–77.

[283] Crispin Wright, *Realism, Meaning and Truth*, 2nd edn. Oxford: Blackwell, 1993, 287.

[284] See the points made by Clark Glymour, *Theory and Evidence*. Princeton, NJ: Princeton University Press, 1980.

[285] Adolf Grünbaum, 'The Duhemian Argument', *Philosophy of Science* 27 (1960), 75–87.

ties in securing theoretical closure in many experimental contexts is widely conceded. In such cases, the evidence cannot be used to make a decisive discrimination between two rival positions. The outcome of such a situation is to precipitate a discussion within the scientific community over the merits of the theories in question, which may continue for an extended period of time. In effect, this raises the issue of the 'reception' of theories, to which we may turn immediately.

The term 'reception' designates the process by which an idea, perhaps originally associated with or generated by an individual or group, becomes generally accepted and adopted by a community. The term refers to the manner in which a broad range of ideas – religious, philosophical, scientific and literary – are understood, appropriated and modified by receptor communities.[286] The term has recently been given a new significance in the field of literary studies through the work of Hans Robert Jauss and others, who have stressed the importance of literary scholarship going beyond mere textual analysis, and extending to include the manner in which text and public interact – in short, the process of reception (*Rezeptionsprozess*).[287] It is, however, in the field of scientific and theological reflection that the notion of 'reception' has proved to be of especial importance.

Within the natural sciences, it is instructive to note the way in which certain theories were initially associated with individuals or small groups, before gradually finding wider acceptance within the scientific community as a whole. This process can be seen at work in the reception of Copernican theory in various parts of Europe in the later sixteenth century,[288] the gradual acceptance of a wave theory of light in Britain,[289] or the growing endorsement of Darwinian theory within popular scientific culture in the Victorian period.[290] In each case, an

---

[286] For some basic considerations, see Enzo Caramaschi, 'Histoire de la critique, sociologie du public et théorie de la réception', in Rien T. Segers (ed.), *Etudes de réception*. Bern: Peter Lang, 1993, 31–9.

[287] Hans Robert Jauss, *Toward an Aesthetic Reception*. Minneapolis: University of Minnesota Press, 1982. For comments, see Heinrich Anz, 'Erwartungshorizont: Ein Diskussionsbeitrag zu H. R. Jauß' Begründung einer Rezeptionsästhetik der Literatur', *Euphorion* 70 (1970), 398–408.

[288] Victor Navarro Brotóns, 'The Reception of Copernicus in Sixteenth-Century Spain: The Case of Diego de Zúñiga', *Isis* 86 (1995), 52–78. Additional case studies are easily adduced: see, for example, Robert S. Westman, 'Three Responses to the Copernican Theory: Johannes Praetorius, Tycho Brahe, and Michael Maestlin', in Robert S. Westman (ed.), *The Copernican Achievement*. London: University of California Press, 1975, 285–345.

[289] Geoffrey Cantor, 'The Reception of the Wave Theory of Light in Britain: A Case Study Illustrating the Role of Methodology in Scientific Debate', *Historical Studies in the Physical Sciences* 6 (1975), 109–32.

[290] Alvar Ellegård, *Darwin and the General Reader: The Reception of Darwin's Theory of Evolution in the British Periodical Press, 1859–1872*. Chicago: University of Chicago Press, 1990.

extended process of critical reflection within influential communities was of critical importance in determining how a scientific theory was evaluated and 'received' within culture as a whole.

In that reception is a social process, the importance of social factors in determining the reception of a theory can be of critical importance. While the assertion (typically associated with the 'strong programme' in the sociology of knowledge) that 'scientific truth' is a purely social construct is widely rejected,[291] there are excellent reasons for suggesting that the plausibility of certain theories – and hence the manner and extent of their acceptance – can be accounted for, to some limited extent, by social factors. Thus in their richly documented study of the controversy between Richard Boyle and Thomas Hobbes over the role of experimental evidence, Shapin and Schaffer argue that social factors helped Boyle win acceptance for his distinctive approach. In particular, Boyle's (non-scientific) argument that the experimental programme was a potential guarantor of civil stability and peace is argued to have been particularly attractive to a society which had all too recent memories of a destructive civil war. Shapin and Schaffer thus suggest that non-scientific factors played a leading role in determining how this specific approach was received by its public.[292]

> There was nothing self-evident or inevitable about the series of historical judgements in that context which yielded a natural philosophical consensus in favour of the experimental programme. Given other circumstances bearing upon that philosophical community, Hobbes's views might well have found a different reception. They were not widely credited or believed – but they were *believeable*; they were not counted to be correct – but there was nothing inherent in them that prevented a different evaluation.

Perhaps there is a blurring here of the critical distinction between the intellectual foundations of a theory and the factors which influence its reception, so that the latter is somehow elided with the former. Yet the point made is fair: non-scientific factors affect the reception of scientific theories.

[291] Christopher Norris, *Against Relativism: Philosophy of Science, Deconstruction and Critical Theory*. Oxford: Blackwell, 1997, 218–47, 265–94. On the 'strong programme', see Peter T. Manicas and Alan Rosenberg, 'Naturalism, Epistemological Individualism and "The Strong Programme" in the Sociology of Knowledge', *Journal for the Theory of Social Behaviour* 15 (1985), 76–101.

[292] Steven Shapin and Simon Schaffer, *Leviathan and the Air-Pump: Hobbes, Boyle and the Experimental Life*. Princeton, NJ: Princeton University Press, 1985, 13. For an important criticism of this work, see Cassandra L. Pinnick, 'What is Wrong with the Strong Programme's Case Study of the "Hobbes–Boyle Dispute"?' in Noretta Koertge (ed.), *A House Built on Sand: Exposing Postmodernist Myths about Science*. New York: Oxford University Press, 1998, 227–39.

A careful study of the reception of Darwinism in nineteenth-century France casts considerable light on this process of evaluation and appropriation.[293] Yvette Conry demonstrated that 'reception' was not to be conceived as a general process by which French society as a whole came to regard Darwin in a certain manner; rather, specific interest groups developed different 'takes' on Darwin, reflecting their particular vested interests and precommitments. While marine biologists were generally favourable towards Darwinism, other groups were more negative, with each group having a specific concern. Thus botanists tended to read Darwin through an interpretative grid derived from Bernardian physiology, which simultaneously enhanced their interest in Darwin and predisposed them to reject his specific approach.[294] Conry's approach indicates that 'Darwinism' was approached, understood and evaluated in different manners by different groupings, making it difficult to maintain an 'essentialist' approach to the theory.[295] The reception of Darwinism in England also owed much to economic, political, social and religious factors.[296]

In the case of scientific theories, it could be argued that, in the end, an accumulation of evidence is ultimately of decisive importance in how a theory is received. What of theories where the criteria of evaluation are more tenuous? Or where those criteria are tradition-specific? The same general *Rezeptionsprozess* can be seen in the process of doctrinal development within Christianity, in which an interpretative and evaluative community plays a critical role. There are clear parallels between the development of doctrine and the emergence of new paradigms within the scientific community.[297]

In Christian theology, as we have seen, an important distinction must be drawn between a 'theological opinion' and a 'doctrine' or 'dogma', in that the latter represents opinions which are received by the community of faith (see the analysis at 24–9). A theological opinion may be understood to be an idea associated with and advocated by an individual theologian or a school of opinion. It has no authority within the

[293] Yvette Conry, *L'introduction du Darwinisme en France au XIXe siècle*. Paris: Vrin, 1974.

[294] Conry, *L'introduction du Darwinisme*, 188.

[295] See the important study of David Hull, 'Darwinism as a Historical Entity: A Historiographic Proposal', in David Kohn (ed.), *The Darwinian Heritage*. Princeton: Princeton University Press, 1985, 773–812.

[296] For an example of the influence of individuals on the shaping of this process within the Reformed theological community, see David N. Livingstone, 'Darwinism and Calvinism: The Belfast–Princeton Connection', *Isis* 83 (1992), 408–28.

[297] See the suggestions of Christopher Knight, 'An Authentic Theological Revolution? Scientific Perspectives on the Development of Doctrine', *Journal of Religion* 74 (1994), 524–41. I am not entirely persuaded of Knight's appeal to Kuhn, but believe he is right to note the general parallels which emerge from this comparison.

ecclesiastical community. Yet that community may, by an often long and complex process of 'reception', come to accept that opinion as authoritative, so that a teaching originally associated with an individual or small group comes to have authority within the community.[298] This can be illustrated by the manner in which the medieval western church 'received' the theological notion of transubstantiation,[299] or Protestant churches accepted the concept of forensic justification as representing the distinctive evangelical position on this issue.[300] Most critically for our purposes, the same issues can be seen at work in the manner in which the early church committed itself to a 'two natures' Christology.

The application of the model: classic Christological heresies

Christology aims to offer an account of the significance of the person of Jesus Christ. There is no doubt that one of the most formidable tasks facing the early church was the clarification of the complex biblical witness to the identity of Christ. The process of Christological clarification cannot be conceived simply as a linear trajectory from the New Testament to Chalcedon, involving organic metaphors such as a seed growing to maturity. The pattern of development which emerges can, however, be understood satisfactorily if two complex interactive processes are recognized to have been in operation during the first five centuries of Christian reflection on the matter.

1. A process of *interpretation* of a complex biblical witness to the identity and significance of Jesus Christ, which was open to more than one interpretation. The underdetermination of theory by evidence led to the realization that the biblical witness did not decisively discriminate between the various models of the person of Christ. A series of approaches was proposed and evaluated, some involving 'ready-to-hand Jewish models',[301] others involving models borrowed from Hellenistic culture. To use Gilbert Harmann's phrase, the Christian community was attempting to 'infer to the best explanation' of Jesus Christ on the basis of a body of evidence which seemed to be capable of multiple interpretations. But which was the best?

---

[298] Roger Greenacre, 'Two Aspects of Reception', in Gillian R. Evans (ed.), *Christian Authority*. Oxford: Clarendon Press, 1988, 40–58.

[299] Kenneth Plotnik, *Hervaeus Natalis OP and the Controversies over the Real Presence and Transubstantiation*. Munich: Schöningh, 1970.

[300] Alister E. McGrath, *Iustitia Dei. A History of the Christian Doctrine of Justification*, 2nd edn. Cambridge: Cambridge University Press, 1998, 207–40.

[301] Edward Schillebeeckx, *Jesus: An Experiment in Christology*. London: Collins, 1979, 439–515.

2. A process of *reception*, in which the community of faith explored and assessed the proposed models, testing them against the testimony of Scripture, and the tradition and worship of the church. This process of testing cannot be regarded as universal throughout the church, in that it was clearly catalysed by local factors, such as certain key individuals and debates, and crystallized by certain events, not least ecumenical councils.[302] This process can be regarded as being shaped to some extent by a theological or ecclesiological equivalent of Pierre Duhem's *le bon sens* (discussed earlier in this chapter: see 210–13), often framed in terms of a doctrine of divine providence or the guidance of the Holy Spirit.

To the external observer, these two processes – especially when interlocked – appear decidedly non-linear, involving what seems to be backtracking, digression and stagnation. To attempt to 'freeze' this process at any one time, particularly in its earlier stages, would be to disclose a complex pattern of variations, rather than a uniform picture, representing a debate which was proceeding at different paces in different ways at different locations. Yet the overall process is recognizable to anyone concerned with the reception of ideas – namely, a communal attempt to explore, evaluate and appropriate, which is catalysed by individuals and institutions. In one sense, it is not really possible to speak of 'pre-Nicene orthodoxy' – only of the existence of the processes which would lead to the final emergence of orthodoxy as a consequence of Nicea.[303] The process is specific to the community of faith, even if factors from outside that community – such as those noted earlier in our discussion of the development of doctrine in general – may play a role in shaping the manner in which such models of Christ are received.

These new models for explaining doctrinal development and the nature of orthodoxy and heresy have been set out with extreme brevity. Both require (and, it need not surprise the reader, both are receiving) full book-length treatment, in which the basic models are developed at much greater length, and set alongside the complex historical evidence they are required to explain, and the contemporary theological concerns which they illuminate. However, it would have been unthinkable to

---

[302] For assessments of the process involved, see works such as Aloys Grillmeier, *Christ in Christian Tradition*, 2nd edn. London: Mowbrays, 1975; James D. G. Dunn, *Christology in the Making: A New Testament Inquiry into the Origins of the Doctrine of the Incarnation*, 2nd edn. London: SCM Press, 1989.

[303] See the excellent analysis provided by Rowan Williams, 'Does it Make Sense to Speak of Pre-Nicene Orthodoxy?' in Rowan Williams (ed.), *The Making of Orthodoxy*. Cambridge: Cambridge University Press, 1989, 1–23.

exclude these brief reflections, as they represent an integral element of a scientific theology as it seeks to explain its own history, and cast light on its continuing tasks. These brief reflections indicate work in progress, which will publish in much more extended form in due course.

But other questions must now claim our attention. One concern which has been implicit throughout this entire project is whether a scientific theology is limited to a purely naturalist account of reality, restricting its statements and its scope to what may be perceived and experienced, thus leaving no place for metaphysics in the theological enterprise. In what follows, we shall offer a defence of metaphysics within a scientific theology, arguing that there exists a real and significant role for metaphysics in articulating the Christian vision of God.

Chapter 15

The Place of Metaphysics in a Scientific Theology

In 1936, a hard-hitting work appeared, declaring war on philosophical 'non-sense' with the stirring assertion that 'the traditional disputes of philosophers are, for the most part, as unwarranted as they are unfruitful'.[1] The opening page of A. J. Ayer's *Language, Truth and Logic* plunged directly into a sustained criticism of 'the metaphysical thesis that philosophy affords us knowledge of a reality transcending the world of science and common sense'. It was a bold statement, reflecting both the author's youth and his hostility towards the prevailing political and intellectual establishment. Although the contents of *Language, Truth and Logic* were neither original nor, in the long term, sustainable, it ignited a ferocious debate over the place of metaphysics in philosophy and theology. The classic affirmations of theology were declared to be non-sense, because they aspired to affirm truths about God without being able to specify how these might be verified, or under what circumstances they might be shown to be true.[2]

Ayer proposed *the criterion of verifiability* as a test for meaningful statements. 'We say that a sentence is factually significant to any given person, if, and only if, he knows how to verify the proposition which it purports to express.'[3] Only when we can specify exactly what conditions would make a statement true, and what conditions would make

[1] A. J. Ayer, *Language, Truth and Logic*, 2nd edn. London: Victor Gollancz, 1946, 45. For the background to this work, see Ben Rogers, *A. J. Ayer: A Life*. London: Chatto & Windus, 1999, 117–22.
[2] Ayer, *Language, Truth and Logic*, 151–8. Among the better responses to this line of argument, see Frederick Ferré, *Language, Logic and God*. New York: Harper & Row, 1961.
[3] Ayer, *Language, Truth and Logic*, 48.

it false, is a statement properly considered meaningful. This, it was argued, rendered specious any claim to 'knowledge of a transcendent reality'.

Time has been unkind to Ayer's position, leading to a growing awareness of the severe limitations placed upon the verification principle proposed by logical positivism. For example, consider the following statement: 'There were six geese sitting on the front lawn of Buckingham Palace at 5.15 p.m. on 18 June 1865.' This statement is clearly meaningful, in that it asserts something which could have been verified. But we – that is, observers located in the present – are not in a position to confirm the statement. For Ayer, these statements must be considered to be neither true nor false, in that they do not relate to the external world. Yet this clearly runs contrary to our basic intuition that such statements do indeed make meaningful affirmations. As is well known, Karl Popper felt that the verification principle associated with the Vienna Circle was far too rigid, and ended up excluding many valid scientific statements.[4]

> My criticism of the verifiability criterion has always been this: against the intention of its defenders, it did not exclude obvious metaphysical statements; but it did exclude the most important and interesting of all scientific statements, that is to say, the scientific theories, the universal laws of nature.

This naturally raises the question of the place of metaphysics in a scientific theology. Writers such as Ayer clearly believed that an appeal to the sciences eliminated metaphysics, even if their published writings witnessed a gradual erosion of confidence in this belief.[5] Such anti-metaphysical polemic, he believed, created a world in which humanity could feel at home without being distracted or disturbed by alleged mysteries, whether arising from religious affirmations or from unresolved questions in the natural sciences. Interesting and entertaining though Ayer's judgements concerning the ease and benefits of the elimination

---

[4] Karl R. Popper, *Conjectures and Refutations: The Growth of Scientific Knowledge*. London: Routledge & Kegan Paul, 1963, 281. For evaluations of Popper's critique of verificationism, and his falsificationist alternative, see Richard C. Jeffrey, 'Probability and Falsification: Critique of the Popper Program', *Synthese* 30 (1975), 95–117; Adolf Grünbaum, 'Is Falsifiability the Touchstone of Scientific Rationality? Karl Popper versus Inductivism,' in R. S. Cohen, P. K. Feyerabend and M. W. Wartofsky (eds), *Essays in Memory of Imre Lakatos*. Dordrecht: Reidel, 1976, 213–52.

[5] See Stephan Körner, 'On the Relation between Common Sense, Science and Metaphysics', in A. Phillips Griffiths (ed.), *A. J. Ayer: Memorial Essays*. Cambridge: Cambridge University Press, 1991, 89–103.

of metaphysics may be, they must ultimately be recognized as premature and unpersuasive.[6]

In its most rigorous form, Ayer's approach entails the highly problematic *a priori* denial of the *a posteriori* possibility of metaphysics. Far from opening the way to a rigorous scientific assessment of the issues, in which the legitimacy of any form of metaphysical speculation will be judged on the basis of the nature and extent of its grounding in observation and experience, Ayer proposes to declare the entire metaphysical enterprise to be invalid in advance of any such engagement, on the basis of a methodologically confused reading of the traditions and tasks of the natural sciences.

A critical reading of those writers who are most disposed towards a 'naturalist' reading of reality raises some uncomfortable questions for those inclined to accept Ayer's ejection of metaphysics from the categories of responsible human reflection on the world.[7] Whatever the exaggerations of its achievements, the naturalist appraisal of the epistemic implications of the natural world in reality leads to the chastening, not the abandoning, of metaphysics.[8]

So what is the place of metaphysics in a scientific theology? Should such a theology share the twentieth century's reaction against metaphysics, often held to be grounded in the natural sciences themselves? To begin to explore these issues, we must first establish how the contentious term 'metaphysics' is to be used.

---

[6] For a useful survey, see C. J. Misak, *Verificationism: Its History and Prospects*. London: Routledge, 1995, 58–96. In particular, severe criticism has been directed against the positivist assumption that the natural sciences are possessed of a formal deductive structure: Misak, *Verificationism*, 85. Some individual contributions of interest to the debate include David Wiggins, 'Truth, Invention and the Meaning of Life', *Proceedings of the British Academy* 62 (1976), 331–78; Christopher Peacocke, *Thoughts: An Essay on Content*. Oxford: Basil Blackwell, 1986.

[7] For a basic overview of this approach, see Arthur C. Danto, 'Naturalism', in P. Edwards (ed.), *Encyclopaedia of Philosophy*. New York: Macmillan, 1967, vol. 5, 448–50. For significant individual contributions, see Arthur Murphy, 'Naturalism and the Human Spirit', *Journal of Philosophy* 42 (1945), 400–17; John H. Randall, 'The Nature of Naturalism', in Yervant H. Krikorian (ed.), *Naturalism and the Human Spirit*. New York: Columbia University Press, 1945, 354–82; Oliver Martin, 'An Examination of Contemporary Naturalism and Materialism', in John Wild (ed.), *The Return to Reason: Essays in Realistic Philosophy*. Chicago: Henry Regnery, 1953, 68–91; Abner Shimony, *Search for a Naturalistic World View*, 2 vols. Cambridge: Cambridge University Press, 1993; Kai Nielsen, *Naturalism without Foundations*. Amherst, NY: Prometheus Books, 1996.

[8] William M. Shea, *The Naturalists and the Supernatural: Studies in Horizon and an American Philosophy of Religion*. Macon, GA: Mercer University Press, 1984, 79–80; Paul Kurtz, *Philosophical Essays in Pragmatic Naturalism*. Buffalo, NY: Prometheus Books, 1990, 97–120; Kevin Schilbrack, 'Problems for a Complete Naturalism', *American Journal of Theology and Philosophy* 15 (1994), 269–91.

Metaphysics: some preliminary reflections

What is to be understood by the term 'metaphysics'? Recent discussions of the matter have been somewhat hesitant to offer firm definitions, reflecting a widespread lack of agreement on what the term denotes. Peter van Inwagen suggests that the most helpful understanding of the term is the study of 'ultimate reality', including such questions as why the world exists, and what place humanity has within it.[9] It will be clear that, on this broad definition of the term, metaphysics denotes the knowledge of entities or matters which transcend the realm of empirically grounded sciences, including the idea of 'God'. This may be contrasted with a more stipulative and narrow reading of the term, which holds that it designates a *specific* type of metaphysic – such as Plato's theory of Forms, Leibniz's monadology, or Hegel's theory of the Absolute.

Perhaps the opponents of metaphysics have offered its most illuminating definitions. In a series of comments added to the 1959 English translation of his famous 1932 essay 'Überwindung der Metaphysik durch logische Analyse der Sprache',[10] Carnap offered an explanation of how he interpreted the term. 'Metaphysics' refers to[11]

> the field of alleged knowledge of the essence of things, which transcends the realm of empirically founded, inductive science. Metaphysics in this sense includes systems like those of Fichte, Schelling, Hegel, Bergson, Heidegger. But it does not include endeavours towards a synthesis and generalization of the results of the various sciences.

This suggests that Carnap understands metaphysics in a specific sense – namely, as the post-Kantian German idealism, which he clearly regards as dominating European thought in the opening decades of the twentieth century, not least through the writings of Martin Heidegger.

On this broad reading of the term as 'alleged knowledge of the essence of things, which transcends the realm of empirically founded, inductive science', both a philosophical and a theological evasion of metaphysics becomes slightly problematic. Despite certain reservations concerning the concept, Immanuel Kant held that metaphysics was central to the

---

[9] See, for example, Peter van Inwagen, *Metaphysics*. Oxford: Oxford University Press, 1993, 4–5.

[10] Rudolf Carnap, 'Überwindung der Metaphysik durch logische Analyse der Sprache', *Erkenntnis* 2 (1932), 219–41.

[11] Rudolf Carnap, 'The Elimination of Metaphysics through Logical Analysis', in A. J. Ayer (ed.), *Logical Positivism*. New York: Free Press, 1959, 60–81, quotation at 80. This English translation, as noted above, represents an expansion of the original essay of 1932 (see previous note).

philosophical task, and identified its three central questions as: What can I know? What ought I to do? What may I hope?[12] Kant's task was rendered both complex and necessary through the rise of the mechanical Newtonian worldview, which made the correlation of moral value and scientific fact problematic. For Kant, metaphysics was the only arena in which a reconciliation might be achieved between the new mechanical view of the world and the traditional Christian values to which Kant (more or less) adhered. While many have rejected Kant's metaphysics, for reasons we shall consider presently, this is by no means a universal trend within recent philosophy. The writings of the neglected philosopher and novelist Ayn Rand (1905–82) – to which we shall return presently – show a clear commitment to the importance of metaphysics.[13] For Rand, metaphysics is essential to the philosophical enterprise, precisely because it offers a unitary worldview that cannot be attained by any other means.[14] As the 'basic branch of philosophy', metaphysics deals with 'the study of existence', including how we might know whether what we observe is real or merely an illusion.[15]

Metaphysics in the classical period

The origins of the term 'metaphysics' lie in the classical period. An exploration of the root of the term, however, casts little light on its proper meaning. In the first century before Christ, the works of Aristotle were brought together by Andronicus of Rhodes as an ordered corpus of writings, including the *Physics,* the *Nicomachean Ethics* and *Eudemian Ethics,* the *Poetics* and *Rhetoric.* What proved problematic, however, were fourteen loosely connected treatises, dealing with subjects such as first principles and causes, theology, and the nature of being. It was clear that these treatises had some connection with those dealing with nature in general, yet dealt with more fundamental themes. Unable to find a suitable collective name for these fourteen works, the editor placed them after the *Physics,* and named them τὰ μετὰ τὰ φυσικά – 'the [books placed] after the [books dealing with] nature'. And so the term *metaphysics* – unknown, incidentally, to Plato or Aristotle – entered the

[12] Immanuel Kant, *Kritik der reinen Vernunft,* 14th edn, 2 vols. Frankfurt am Main: Suhrkamp, 2000, vol. 2, 676–7.

[13] For an introduction to this neglected figure, see Allan Gotthelf, *On Ayn Rand.* Belmont: Wadsworth, 2000. For more detail, see Leonard Peikoff, *Objectivism: The Philosophy of Ayn Rand.* New York: Dutton, 1991, and especially Christopher M. Sciabarra, *Ayn Rand: The Russian Radical.* University Park, PA: Pennsylvania State University Press, 1995.

[14] Sciabarra, *Ayn Rand,* 154–60.

[15] Ayn Rand, *Philosophy: Who Needs It?* New York: Bobbs-Merrill, 1982, 3.

vocabulary of philosophy. Given the diversity of the writings thus gathered together – not to mention the inconsistencies that appear to exist between them[16] – it is perhaps not surprising that the term 'metaphysics' proved to be somewhat elastic, being interpreted in significantly different manners by Aristotle's later interpreters.

As far as can be seen, Aristotle's general understanding of 'metaphysics' seems to focus primarily upon objects which actually exist in the world, particularly the question of what gives these objects their specific identity.[17] Aristotle placed particular emphasis on the importance of the concept of substance as a means of accounting for the continuities and changes observed in the natural world.[18] Perhaps most famously, in *Metaphysics* IV Aristotle argued for the need to 'save the phenomena' – that is, to ensure that all observations of the world are accurately recorded, and that these form the basis of human attempts to explain and categorize reality. In dealing with such questions, however, Aristotle is obliged to interact with earlier reflections on such issues, particularly the Platonic theory of Forms.

Despite Aristotle's concern to account for what may be observed in the world, the origins of the concept of metaphysics – as opposed to the specific term – can plausibly be argued to lie in the sphere of ethics and politics. Plato's *Republic* bears witness to the fundamental impulse to seek a ground for political judgements which lies outside the mere conventions of local human communities. Justice is based upon 'the good', something existing above and beyond human prejudice and convention, but which true human knowledge seeks to identify and reflect.[19] The task of philosophy is to provide a transcendental ground for political judgements, enabling humanity to avoid political debate degenerating into local squabbles over existing beliefs, irrespective of their origins and validity. To think and speak metaphysically is thus to speak confidently about something that is other than the observable state of affairs.[20] For Plato, there is an overarch-

[16] See, for example, Lynne Spellman, 'Specimens of Natural Kinds and the Apparent Inconsistency of Metaphysics Z', *Ancient Philosophy* 9 (1989), 49–65.

[17] See Joseph Owens, *The Doctrine of Being in the Aristotelian Metaphysics*, 3rd edn. Toronto: Pontifical Institute of Medieval Studies, 1978; Frank Lewis, *Substance and Predication in Aristotle*. Cambridge: Cambridge University Press, 1991.

[18] Charlotte Witt, *Substance and Essence in Aristotle: An Interpretation of Metaphysics VII–IX*. Ithaca, NY: Cornell University Press, 1989; John J. Cleary, *Aristotle and Mathematics: Aporetic Method in Cosmology and Metaphysics*. Leiden: Brill, 1995.

[19] For a sustained engagement with this idea, see Iris Murdoch, *Metaphysics as a Guide to Morals*. London: Penguin, 1992, especially 1–147.

[20] Jörg Peter Disse, 'Platons Ideenlehre als Metaphysik. Eine Auseinandersetzung mit der sprachanalytischen Philosophie', *Philosophisches Jahrbuch* 105 (1998), 267–82.

ing, fully objective reality that cannot entirely be captured by sense perception, which is therefore intuited rather than known. As Iris Murdoch has it: 'Something is apprehended as *there* which is not yet *known*.'[21]

Plato's views on metaphysics cannot be isolated from his epistemology.[22] If knowledge – as opposed to mere opinion – is a genuine possibility for humanity, there must be something about the world which permits that knowledge to come into existence. In his polemic against the so-called 'Sophists', particularly Protagoras, Plato insists upon three fundamental principles of knowledge:

1. that humanity is capable of gaining knowledge and avoiding error;
2. that there are objective facts about which different people may agree to disagree;
3. that humanity is capable of conceiving the notion of such objective facts.

The most satisfactory explanation of how human knowledge arises is that there exist non-perceptible 'Forms', which create the possibility of both the justification and the ultimate intelligibility of our judgements. The possibility of metaphysics is thus explicitly linked with a specifically realist understanding of the world. For Plato and his successors, metaphysics is an essential foundation for political morality.

There is thus a natural link between an epistemological realism and the affirmation of metaphysics. In that a scientific theology affirms such a realism, the formulation of a theological metaphysics consequent to an engagement with reality – but most emphatically not as a *precondition* for such an engagement – is to be viewed as a legitimate and proper task. In his careful exploration of the theme of rationality in science, the British philosopher Roger Trigg argues that the successes of the natural sciences are to be accounted for on the basis of both a realist approach to the natural world, and a recognition of the positive role of metaphysics in articulating the nature of that world, as uncovered by the sciences. 'Science has to depend on metaphysics if it is not itself to be discredited.'[23] Trigg is aware of the trend within twentieth-century phi-

---

[21] Murdoch, *Metaphysics as a Guide to Morals*, 505.

[22] Nicholas White, 'Plato's Epistemological Metaphysics', in R. Kraut (ed.), *Cambridge Companion to Plato*. Cambridge: Cambridge University Press, 1991, 277–310; Gregory Vlastos, 'Degrees of Reality in Plato', in R. Bambrough (ed.), *New Essays on Plato and Aristotle*. New York: Humanities Press, 1965, 1–18.

[23] Roger Trigg, *Rationality and Science: Can Science Explain Everything?* Oxford: Blackwell, 1993, 225.

losophy of science to insist that a 'scientific worldview rejects metaphysical philosophy'; he believes, however, that such a conclusion is both premature and ultimately unsustainable.[24] What happens if the scientific evidence appears to demand, or strongly suggest, the existence of unobservable entities? As we shall see, such lines of thought are profoundly subversive to the anti-metaphysical drift of twentieth-century thought, and lead in some very interesting directions.

Yet it must be pointed out that the ambiguity of the term 'metaphysics' makes clarification of the place of metaphysics in a scientific theology rather more complex than might at first be appreciated. In what follows, we shall reflect on the diversity of viewpoints represented by the term, and their implications for any attempt to lay down in advance what metaphysical positions may legitimately be held by those committed to the working methods and assumptions of the natural sciences.

The ambiguity of 'metaphysics': Ayn Rand and Iris Murdoch

The ambivalence of the term 'metaphysics' appears to have been lost to some of its more recent critics. Gordon Kaufman and John Milbank appear to believe that the notion is relatively well-defined, and represents something which theology should avoid, not least because of its autonomous pretensions or anti-theistic presuppositions. The problem, for Milbank, is not metaphysics absolutely; rather, it is its claims to autonomy that must be eliminated. Yet this seems to foreclose the critically important debate over whether metaphysical claims are *a priori* (and thus restrict and limit theology) or are *a posteriori* responses to an engagement with reality, and thus represent an integral aspect of the theological task. Where both the nature and provenance of 'metaphysics' are contested, clarification of the options and their warrants would seem an essential prerequisite to a meaningful discussion of theological method. Yet Milbank's perception of the issues seems to rest on a closure of an ongoing discussion concerning what might reasonably be understood by the term.

To illuminate the various meanings that the term 'metaphysics' might bear – and also to enter a preemptive challenge to Jacques Derrida's ludicrous dismissal of metaphysics as the peculiar tribal language of white males – we shall explore the metaphysical writings of two of the most distinguished women novelists of the twentieth century, Ayn Rand and Iris Murdoch, and note how two 'atheist' metaphysics actually look

[24] Trigg, *Rationality and Science*, 13–16.

rather different on closer examination.[25] Although this study will focus on two specific metaphysics, the point being made is that there exist any number of such metaphysics – including Christian, Jewish, Islamic and atheist options – precluding the premature dismissal of the metaphysical enterprise in general on account of the untenable belief that metaphysics is necessarily *a priori* in character.

Ayn Rand is one of the most widely read philosophers of the twentieth century, yet is virtually unknown outside a relatively small group of admirers, based largely in the United States.[26] Rand was born Alissa Zinovievna Rosenbaum in 1905 in St Petersburg. She attended its leading university during the last flowering of its intelligentsia before the Russian Revolution brought in a series of purges of students and academics in the early 1920s. Having relatives in Chicago, Rosenbaum was able to secure a passport, and emigrated to the United States in February 1926. At this point, she changed her name to 'Ayn Rand'.

Her rise to fame began in 1935, when her novel *The Fountainhead* was published. The work is best seen as a defence of the individual in the face of mass culture, reflecting a particular distaste for Soviet collectivism. Its successor, *Atlas Shrugged*, appeared in 1957; it can be understood as a development of the earlier themes of *The Fountainhead*, while pursuing them at an altogether deeper level. A metaphysical dualism, which demands that human nature be separated into 'body' and 'soul', and sets 'matter' and 'spirit' in opposition to one another, is identified as underlying the errors of the past.[27]

Rand's novels, along with her nonfictional works, are dominated by the theme of the 'metaphysically given'.[28] A critical distinction must be made between what is 'given' in nature (such as the solar system, including the natural satellites of the planets) and what is to be regarded as 'man-made' (such as artificial satellites).

---

[25] There would have been no difficulties in adding additional woman metaphysicians to this list – for example, Gillian Rose. See, for example, Gillian Rose, *Mourning Becomes the Law: Philosophy and Representation*. Cambridge: Cambridge University Press, 1996. On the theological relevance of Rose, see Rowan D. Williams, 'Between Politics and Metaphysics: Reflections in the Wake of Gillian Rose', *Modern Theology* 11 (1995), 3–22. Her Oxford University D.Phil. thesis of 1977 merits study: Gillian Rose, *Reification as a Sociological Category: Theodor W. Adorno's Concept of Reification and the Possibility of a Critical Theory of Society*. Edith Stein is also an obvious candidate for inclusion: for an assessment, see Mary Catherine Baseheart, *Person in the World: Introduction to the Philosophy of Edith Stein*. Dordrecht: Kluwer Academic, 1997.

[26] Her writings are estimated to have sold 30 million copies, although it is difficult to confirm this figure: Sciabarra, *Ayn Rand*, 1.

[27] For comments, see Sciabarra, *Ayn Rand*, 106–12, 113–16.

[28] Sciabarra, *Ayn Rand*, 147–9; Leonard Peikoff, *Objectivism: The Philosophy of Ayn Rand*. New York: Penguin, 1993, 23–30.

The metaphysically given cannot be true or false; it simply *is* – and man determines the truth or falsehood of his judgements by whether they correspond to or contradict the facts of reality. The metaphysically given cannot be right or wrong – it is the standard of right or wrong, by which a (rational) man judges his goals, his values, his choices.[29]

It is therefore necessary to draw a clear distinction between what is 'metaphysically given' and what is 'constructed'. The former is part of the world we inherit; the latter is something that we choose to create. While the 'metaphysically given is, was, will be and has to be . . . nothing made by man *had* to be; it was made by choice'. This allows Rand to develop a social philosophy which identifies those aspects of the world which cannot be changed, and those which are open to revision.[30]

It is the metaphysically given that must be accepted: it cannot be changed. It is the man-made that must never be accepted uncritically: it must be judged, then accepted or rejected and changed when necessary. Man is not omniscient or infallible.

We can see here a line of thought which parallels Aristotle's distinction between τέχνη (any action or product which results from a human mind acting upon reality) and φύσις ('that which is given' – those aspects of the world which cannot be accounted for by human actions or chance).[31] Metaphysical enquiry, she argues, is essential in clarifying and sustaining such a distinction, and teasing out its ethical and philosophical implications.

Rand takes it as evident that there is no God. Religion is merely an atrophied form of idealism, leading to a dualism which separates faith and reason, this life and the (imaginary) life to come. While Rand's assessment of religion is disappointingly superficial, often creating the impression that atheism is self-evidently true and hence requiring little in the way of defence or demonstration, there is no doubting its central importance to her thought. For Rand, God is most emphatically not part of the 'metaphysically given'; it is a human construction, which can and should be eliminated as part of a constructive social agenda. It will thus be clear that Rand's novels and writings are unquestionably 'metaphysical' in tone and substance. Yet that bald and potentially misleading statement must be qualified immediately, in that it is a *specific style of metaphysics* (rather than an interest in the discipline in general) which

---

[29] Rand, *Philosophy: Who Needs It?*, 1982, 25–7.
[30] Rand, *Philosophy: Who Needs It?*, 33.
[31] On which see Helen S. Lang, *The Order of Nature in Aristotle's Physics: Place and the Elements.* Cambridge: Cambridge University Press, 1998.

Rand assumes and commends. And this is by no means the only 'meta-physical' option which may be entertained, as is evident from the writings of Iris Murdoch – to which we now turn.

Iris Murdoch was born in Dublin in 1919, and went on to study Classical Moderations and *Literae Humaniores* at Somerville College, Oxford, from 1938 to 1942. In 1948, she became a fellow of the Society of Oxford Home Students, which became St Anne's College in 1952. She died in Oxford in 1999.[32] She is best known for her 26 novels and some works of philosophy, particularly *The Sovereignty of Good* (1970) and *Metaphysics as a Guide to Morals* (1992), which represents an expanded version of her Gifford Lectures of 1982. Both her novels and her more explicitly philosophical writings can be regarded as an attempt to retrieve the central themes and images of Platonism, thus opening up possibilities of dialogue between secular moral philosophy and religious ethics which parallel those afforded to the church during the patristic period.[33]

Murdoch designated herself as an 'atheist',[34] assuming that the existence of God 'in the traditional sense of that term' could not be demonstrated, and thus could not function as the basis of morality.[35] Murdoch, however, was quite clear that some metaphysical basis for morality was required, and was critical of philosophical trends prevailing within British philosophy during the 1960s, which she held to be morally inadequate on a numbers of counts.[36] An essentially *utilitarian* view of moral goodness is flawed, in that it fails to provide substance to the conception of 'the Good'. 'Oxford philosophy' – a term she understands to embrace writers such as A. J. Ayer, Stuart Hampshire and R. M. Hare – fails to develop an adequate theory of moral motivation, which takes seriously the notion of 'attending to the Good'. Metaphysics is thus the proper ground of morality.

In suggesting that Murdoch's metaphysics is 'atheistic', I have chosen to read her in a certain manner, which I hold to be justified on the basis of Murdoch's writings. Yet while Murdoch herself was hesitant over explicitly

[32] The best biography is currently Peter Conradi, *Iris Murdoch: A Life*. London: HarperCollins, 2001.

[33] On Murdoch's novels, see Peter J. Conradi, *The Saint and the Artist: A Study of the Fiction of Iris Murdoch*. London: HarperCollins, 2001.

[34] For useful reflections on how this 'atheism' should be understood, see Stanley Hauerwas, 'Murdochian Muddles: Can We Get through them if God Does not Exist?' in Maria Antonaccio and William Schweiker (eds), *Iris Murdoch and the Search for Human Goodness*. Chicago: University of Chicago Press, 1996, 190–208.

[35] Iris Murdoch, *The Sovereignty of Good*. London: Macmillan, 1970, 75–8.

[36] Murdoch, *The Sovereignty of Good*, 1–74.

theistic statements, the metaphysics she commends may reasonably be considered to be theistic in orientation, particularly if seen through a Plotinian-
Augustinian-Anselmian lens which allows a sense of goodness to be
construed as an inchoate sense of the divine presence. 'Our general awareness of good, or goodness, is with us unreflectively all the time, as a sense
of God's presence, or at least existence, used to be for all sorts of believers.'[37]

Murdoch herself was cautious over a simplistic identification of 'the
Good' with 'God', noting how this identification rested on the assumptions of Plato's heirs, rather than of Plato himself.[38]

> Plato illumines with stories which are deliberately cast as explanatory
> myths and must not be taken for anything else. Plato's 'sun' is separate and
> perfect, yet also immanent in the world as the life-giving magnetic genesis
> of all our struggles for truth and virtue. Plato never identified his Form of
> the Good with God (the use of *theos* in the *Republic* 579B is a *façon de
> parler*), and this separation is for him an essential one. Religion is above
> the level of the 'gods'. There are no gods and no God either. Neo-Platonic
> thinkers made the *identification* (of God with good) possible; and the
> Judaeo-Christian tradition has made it easy and natural for us to gather
> together the aesthetic and consoling impression of Good as a person.

Murdoch sees this Neoplatonist line of thought developed in the writings of Augustine and Anselm of Canterbury, leading to the transformation of the Platonic form of the Good into a supreme spiritual being
('God'), and thus to a metaphysical conception of the Christian God.[39]
Murdoch deplores Kant's rationalization of the so-called 'ontological
argument', holding that this reduces to a matter of logic what is properly a matter of experience – of intuition of the real.[40]

> We 'see' God through the morally good things of the world, through our
> (mortal) perception of what is beautiful and holy, through our just God-
> fearing understanding of what is not good. So we find God both, and
> inextricably both, in the world and in our own soul . . . We conceive of
> [God] by noticing *degrees of goodness*, which we see in ourselves and in all
> the world which is a shadow of God. These are aspects of the Proof
> wherein the definition of God as non-contingent is given body by our
> most general perceptions and *experience* of the fundamental and omni-
> present (uniquely necessary) nature of moral value, thought of in a
> Christian context as God.

---

[37] Murdoch, *Metaphysics as a Guide to Morals*, 509.

[38] Murdoch, *Metaphysics as a Guide to Morals*, 38.

[39] For comment on this development, see G. R. Evans, *Philosophy and Theology in the Middle
Ages*. London: Routledge, 1993, 51–66.

[40] Murdoch, *Metaphysics as a Guide to Morals*, 396.

It is hardly surprising that many Christian moral theologians have found Murdoch a highly congenial dialogue partner, whose metaphysics may be reappropriated and reconfigured in a more explicitly Christian manner. Such a process of adoption is catalysed to no small extent by Murdoch's obvious interest in Simone Weil, which often results in a form of Christ-mysticism which appears to provide the personal element to ethics which is absent from Plato's more austere account of the faceless form of the Good.[41] Yet it is also possible to see how Murdoch's metaphysic can be related to some of the themes of the classic theological tradition, especially the Cappadocian fathers. For example, Gregory of Nyssa's fourth-century sermons on the Beatitudes indicate the potential theological fecundity of an engagement with the category of 'the Good', even as Murdoch conceives it, in that Gregory is able to define the object of human longing as 'the Good', while at the same time developing a theological framework which holds that this 'Good' is, on account of a Christian doctrine of creation, specifically linked with God.[42]

The point of our digression into the writings of two leading female novelists of the twentieth century will be clear. Both insist upon the importance of metaphysics, and both would designate themselves as 'atheist'. Yet a world of difference exists between their respective understandings of how atheism is to be understood, and its implications for ethics – not to mention the manner in which their metaphysics may be appropriated and developed for the theological tasks. If our range of writers were to be extended to include G. K. Chesterton and C. S. Lewis, both of whom represent novelists with clear metaphysical convictions which are not merely commensurate with, but are grounded in, classical Christian theology,[43] the difficulty of following Milbank or Kaufman in

---

[41] Note the extensive references to Weil throughout *Metaphysics as a Guide to Morals*. For some thoughtful reflections on this theme, see David Tracy, 'Iris Murdoch and the Many Faces of Platonism', in Maria Antonaccio and William Schweiker (eds), *Iris Murdoch and the Search for Human Goodness*. Chicago: University of Chicago Press, 1996, 54–75.

[42] Gregory of Nyssa, *Commentary on the Beatitudes*, 3. We have already explored this passage in dealing with the importance of natural theology in transcending traditions: see vol. 2, 72–4.

[43] The following should be consulted to appreciate this point. On Chesterton, see Max Ribstein, *G. K. Chesterton (1874–1936): création romanesque et imagination*. Paris: Klincksieck, 1981; Matthias Wörther, *G. K. Chesterton, das unterhaltsame Dogma: Begriffe des Glaubens als Entdeckungskategorien*. Frankfurt am Main: Peter Lang, 1984; Joseph Chilton Pearce, *Wisdom and Innocence: A Life of G. K. Chesterton*. London: Hodder & Stoughton, 1996. On Lewis, see Michael D. Aeschliman, *The Restitution of Man: C. S. Lewis and the Case against Scientism*. Grand Rapids, MI: Eerdmans, 1998; Corbin Scott Carnell, *Bright Shadow of Reality: Spiritual Longing in C. S. Lewis*. Grand Rapids, MI: Eerdmans, 1999; Gilbert Meilander, *The Taste for the Other: The Social and Ethical Thought of C. S. Lewis*. Grand Rapids, MI: Eerdmans, 1998.

making global generalizations about 'theology and metaphysics' becomes painfully obvious.

The twentieth-century revolt against metaphysics

In a thoughtful and often provocative study of Jean-Paul Sartre, Iris Murdoch suggests that the nineteenth century's growing confidence in the application of the scientific method, and the mathematical symbolism which accompanied its application, led to the philosopher reappraising the relation of symbols, including words, to reality. Language was suddenly construed on the model of the scientific definition: the meaning of a sentence could be determined precisely by an explanation of the particular sensible observations which would determine its truth. Language was no longer thought of as naming things, even empirical things; rather, it was seen as a way of delineating, interpreting and predicting sense experience. Metaphysical objects were thus eliminated, and physical objects transformed into their phenomena, which justified statements about them.[44] As Murdoch stresses, in its formative early phase, linguistic philosophy took as real the facts of science and everyday life; it regarded as unreal the world of art, politics and religion, emotion, fantasy and dream. Value, failing to be physically observable and located in the world, was best left to behaviourist psychology.[45] It was thus inevitable that metaphysics should be excluded from this view of the world.

Murdoch's comments are a particularly apposite preface to any engagement with the ideas of the Vienna Circle. The complex story of the twentieth-century rejection of metaphysics is best told by focusing on the 'Vienna Circle', which brought together some of the most intriguing intellectual figures of central Europe in the years between the First and Second World Wars. In what follows, we shall explore some of the basic themes to emerge from this grouping, and their implications for the theological development of metaphysics. But first, we must consider the background to these developments in Humean metaphysical scepticism and beyond.

For many today – despite vigorous counterblasts from writers such as Iris Murdoch – any interest in metaphysics now seems out of place in a totally changed intellectual landscape, whether we are considering literary, philosophical or scientific writings. This is not to say that western

---

[44] Iris Murdoch, *Sartre: Romantic Rationalist.* London: Collins, 1967, 39.
[45] Murdoch, *Sartre*, 48.

literature has in any way abandoned an interest in questions which might legitimately be described as 'metaphysical'. The exploration of such questions as the place of humanity in the universe, the ultimate purpose of human life, and the mysterious operation of such forces as destiny, continue to be explored in novels, dramas and poetry.[46] It is that such questions are often discussed on the basis of the assumption that no reference need be made to any correlation with a 'real' world beyond what is known to the senses. The harbingers of this trend are not difficult to identify.

Misgivings concerning the potentially inflationist claims of metaphysics may be discerned during the seventeenth century. John Milton (1608–74), arguably one of the most significant Christian writers of the seventeenth century, had serious misgivings concerning the place of metaphysics in Christian theology. These were perhaps most trenchantly expressed in a manuscript entitled *de doctrina christiana*, probably written during the period 1658–60, but never published on account of its somewhat heterodox ideas. The manuscript was rediscovered in November 1823 by Robert Lemon, Deputy Keeper of His Majesty's State Papers, and was translated and published in 1825. Milton makes his distrust of the theological use of metaphysics, doubtless heightened by the uncritical deployment of such notions in some of the more speculative theological reflections of his age, absolutely clear:[47]

> Through what madness is it, then, that even members of the reformed church persist in explaining and illustrating and interpreting the most holy truths of religion, as if they were conveyed obscurely in the Holy Scriptures? Why do they shroud them in the thick darkness of metaphysics . . . as if the sense of the divine truth, itself absolutely plain, needed to be brought out more clearly or more fully, or otherwise explained, by means of terms imported from the most abstruse of human sciences?

Milton's censure of the 'thick darkness of metaphysics' was reflected in the works of other literary figures of this period. The explicit interest in questions of metaphysics evident in the poetry of John Donne (1571/2–1631) and Andrew Marvell (1621–78) was the subject of much

---

[46] See, for example, Roy Roussel, *The Metaphysics of Darkness: A Study in the Unity and Development of Conrad's Fiction*. Baltimore, MD: Johns Hopkins University Press, 1971; Sarah Pratt, *Russian Metaphysical Romanticism: The Poetry of Tiutchev and Boratynskii*. Stanford, CA: Stanford University Press, 1984; Eyal Amiran, *Wandering and Home: Beckett's Metaphysical Narrative*. University Park, PA: Pennsylvania State University Press, 1993.

[47] John Milton, *de doctrina christiana* I.30, translated by John Carey, in *Complete Prose Works of John Milton*, ed. Maurice Kelley. New Haven, CT: Yale University Press, 1973, 580.

criticism by their successors, such as John Dryden (1631–1700).[48] For Dryden, Donne 'affects the Metaphysics . . . in his amorous verses, where nature only should reign; and perplexes the minds of the fair sex with nice speculations of philosophy, when he should engage their hearts'. While Dryden's point primarily concerns the task of poetry, rather than the intellectual legitimacy of metaphysics, there is no doubt that at least something of a growing discontent with the increasingly vague and unsubstantiated claims of the discipline can be discerned within the literary classes on the eve of the Enlightenment.

It is, however, in the writings of David Hume (1711–76) that we find a sustained critique of metaphysics, which has had a decisive impact on modern reflection on the place of metaphysics in theological reflection. In the final paragraph of his *Enquiry concerning Human Understanding,* entitled 'Of the Academical or Sceptical Philosophy', Hume set out limits to human knowledge which vitiated many of the traditional metaphysical beliefs. While rejecting a Pyrrhonian scepticism which calls into question all reasoning about the external world, abstract reasoning about space and time, or causal reasoning about matters of fact since 'no durable good can ever result from it', Hume nevertheless commends a more moderate (or 'Academic') scepticism that tempers Pyrrhonism by, first, exercising caution and modesty, and, second, restricting our speculations to abstract reasoning and matters of fact.[49]

> When we run over libraries, persuaded of these principles, what havoc must we make? If we take in our hand any volume; of divinity or school metaphysics, for instance; let us ask, *Does it contain any abstract reasoning concerning quantity or number?* No. *Does it contain any experimental reasoning concerning matter of fact and existence?* No. Commit it then to the flames: for it can contain nothing but sophistry and illusion.

While it is important to avoid reading Hume through the lens of his later interpreters, this closing paragraph clearly restricts meaningful statements to the fields of formal logic ('abstract reasoning concerning quantity or number') or empirical investigation ('experimental reasoning concerning matter of fact and existence').

Hume's critique of metaphysics is not entirely convincing, and rests on the prioritization of logical consistency and empirical verification as the cornerstones of a common-sense philosophy. 'When we analyse our

---

[48] Robert Lathrop Sharp, *From Donne to Dryden: The Revolt Against Metaphysical Poetry.* Hamden, CT: Archon Books, 1965.

[49] David Hume, *Enquiries concerning Human Understanding and concerning the Principles of Morals,* 3rd edn. Oxford: Clarendon Press, 1975, 165.

thoughts or ideas, however compounded or sublime, we always find that they resolve themselves into such simple ideas as were copied from a precedent feeling or sentiment.'[50] Hume challenges his readers to adduce a simple idea which is not preceded by a correspondent impression.[51] While this argument is not without its difficulties, it has the merit – at least, in Hume's eyes – of eliminating any appeal to transcendent categories.

These ideas were developed further in the writings of Auguste Comte (1798–1857). The complex history of human thought could, in Comte's view, be seen as an irreversible progression, initially from the theological to the metaphysical, and finally from the metaphysical to the positive. In his massive *Cours de philosophie positive* (1830–42), Comte argued that the early history of humanity was dominated by the idea of gods, responsible for the complexities of the natural world. Polytheism gradually gave way to monotheism, which Comte identified as the underlying principle of modern western culture. Through the inexorable upward development of human thought, these personal divinities were then displaced by impersonal metaphysical forces, which in turn gave way to a 'positive' or 'scientific' understanding of the world.[52] Metaphysics is thus seen as a temporary (and inherently unstable and unsustainable) phase in the history of human thought, representing a transition from a primitive theology (appealing to supernatural agencies as a means of natural explanation) to a sophisticated positivism (which is grounded on the scientific laws which govern nature). This third and final phase involved scientific exploration and the objective collection and judgements of facts in order that humankind might arrive at 'positive' truth, as distinct from theological or metaphysical truths. The final triumph of scientific thinking would thus eliminate the need for metaphysics, as well as destroy its intellectual plausibility.

Comte's ideas were taken up enthusiastically by many clergy and theologians in the United Kingdom and United States during the second half of the nineteenth century.[53] Jeremiah Lewis Diman (1831–81) argued that there was an ineluctable progression from Hume's recognition that human knowledge was limited to the natural world to the elimination of metaphysics: 'This, in fact, is the grand characteristic of the

---

[50] Hume, *Enquiries concerning Human Understanding*, 19.

[51] For some of the problems with this approach, see Jonathan Bennett, *Locke, Berkeley, Hume: Central Themes*. Oxford: Oxford University Press, 1977, 225–30.

[52] Robert C. Scharff, *Comte after Positivism*. Cambridge: Cambridge University Press, 1995.

[53] Charles D. Cashdollar, *The Transformation of Theology, 1830–1890: Positivism and Protestant Thought in Britain and America*. Princeton, NJ: Princeton University Press, 1989.

speculative thought of the present time. Metaphysics has been transmuted into science.'[54]

The inexorable rise of the scientific method in the eighteenth and nineteenth centuries thus sets the background for a sustained assault on metaphysics. While the rise of the Newtonian worldview was initially seen as confirmatory of the basic themes of Christian theology (as is evident from the growing interest in natural theology), the advances of the natural sciences seemed to many to confirm the existence of a radical gulf between empirically based scientific beliefs and rather more tenuously grounded religious beliefs.[55] Hume's jibe that 'metaphysics' was basically 'nothing but sophistry and illusion' reflects this growing hostility to religion and metaphysics (the two often being merged), and an increasing interest in grounding beliefs in the relative security offered by logic and empirical investigation.

Earlier, we noted Hume's double criterion for the investigation of the truthfulness or meaningfulness of statements: 'Does it contain any abstract reasoning concerning quantity or number? . . . Does it contain any experimental reasoning concerning matter of fact and existence?' Following Hume at this point, it would be possible to argue for two criteria for meaningfulness: logical analysis, and empirical investigation (in addition to a system of logic which establishes under what circumstances one sentence is deducible from another):

1. The meaning of the term *verification* must be established, so that there is an agreed understanding of what logical relation must hold between two sentences in order for one to verify, or confirm, the other.

2. The elusive term 'empirical' requires clarification, so that there is agreement concerning what it means to say that a 'statement is observational'.

To be cognitively significant, therefore, a sentence must either be a statement of a logical truth, or possess an empirical basis which allows its content to be confirmed. A sentence is thus meaningful only if it is *verifiable* by either logical or empirical means. One way of avoiding 'meaningless' metaphysical statements was to construct a scientific language

---

54 J. Lewis Diman, *The Theistic Argument as Affected by Recent Theories*. Boston: Houghton Mifflin, 1882, 11.

55 James E. Force, 'The Breakdown of the Newtonian Synthesis of Science and Religion: Hume, Newton and the Royal Society', in R. H. Popkin and J. E. Force (eds), *Essays on the Context, Nature and Influence of Isaac Newton's Theology*. Dordrecht: Kluwer Academic, 1990, 143–63.

grounded in experience, which restricted itself to an account of what could be verified. This appeal to 'observation statements' would prove to be of decisive importance to the development of twentieth-century philosophy. In what follows, we shall explore the development of this theme in the 1930s, and establish the issues which this raised.

Observation statements: the evasion of metaphysics

One of the most vigorous critiques of metaphysics in the early twentieth century was due to the physicist and philosopher Ernst Mach (1838–1916). For Mach, the natural sciences are radically empirical, concerning only that which is immediately given by the senses. Science can thus be nothing more and nothing other than the investigation of the dependence of phenomena on one another. The only thing we know directly is experience, and all experience consists of sensations or sense impressions (*Empfindungen*).[56] Mach's hostility towards assuming or postulating (even in a heuristic manner) the existence of something that cannot be seen is evidenced by his rejection of Newton's concepts of absolute space and time. Mach also adopted a strongly negative view of the atomic hypothesis, arguing that atoms were merely theoretical constructs which cannot be perceived.[57] Nevertheless, Mach allows the use of 'auxiliary concepts' which serve as bridges linking one set of observations with another. These 'concepts' have no real existence, and must therefore not be thought of as actual or existing entities. They are 'products of thought' which 'exist only in our imagination and understanding'. The natural scientist can only evade the 'apparently inextricable tangle of metaphysical difficulties' by insisting that the natural sciences are concerned only with 'the establishment of functions and relations' and the clarification of 'the mutual dependence of experiences'.[58]

Mach's views had a very significant impact on the Vienna Circle (which initially styled itself the 'Verein Ernst Mach'), as it reflected on how metaphysics might systematically be eliminated from both the natural sciences and philosophy. One of the most significant developments in twentieth-century philosophy to emanate from the Vienna Circle was the notion of the 'observation statement' or 'protocol

[56] Ernst Mach, *Die Analyse der Empfindungen und das Verhältnis des Physischen zum Psychischen*, 2nd edn. Jena: Gustav Fischer, 1919, 10.

[57] On which see Erwin Hiebert, 'The Genesis of Mach's Early Views on Atomism', in R. Cohen and R. Seeger (eds), *Ernst Mach: Physicist and Philosopher*. Dordrecht: Reidel, 1970, 79–106.

[58] Mach, *Die Analyse der Empfindungen*, 28.

statements',[59] which were seen as a highly promising means of bypassing metaphysical claims. These concepts have been of no small significance in relation to the sustained revolt against metaphysics within logical positivism and related movements. Yet recent studies have raised significant questions as to whether earlier accounts of the 'protocol dispute' have really penetrated to the core of the matter, overlooking, for example, the general context in which they were formulated and its broader implications for the agenda of the Vienna Circle.[60]

Otto Neurath developed a deeply anti-foundationalist naturalism which vigorously rejected any concept of *a priori* truth. Neurath's concept of the 'protocol statement', which reflects this viewpoint, emerged from his discussions with other members of the Vienna Circle, particularly Rudolf Carnap and Moritz Schlick. As Thomas Oberdan has stressed, the entire debate about protocol statements must be set against the Vienna Circle's preoccupation with the question of how language relates to experience.[61] The 'protocol statement' consists only of observable predicates and spatio-temporal coordinates; these are embedded in a threefold manner which allows the observer and the general conditions of the process of observation to be established. This leads to the rather complex formulation of a protocol statement as follows:[62]

> A complete protocol statement might, for example, read: 'Otto's protocol at 3:17 o'clock [at 3:16 o'clock Otto said to himself: (at 3:15 o'clock there was a table in the room perceived by Otto)].'

This complexly embedded statement is intended to convey information concerning the circumstances of the observation, including the identity of the observer and the conditions of the observation.

> For a protocol statement to be complete, it is essential that the name of some person occurs in it. 'Now joy' or 'now red circle' or 'a red die is lying on the table' are not complete protocol statements. They are not even candidates for a position within the innermost set of brackets. On the basis of our analysis, for this they would have to read 'Otto now joy' or 'Otto now sees a red circle' or 'Otto now sees a red die lying on the table.'

---

[59] The German term *Satz* is rendered as both 'sentence' and 'statement' in the English-language literature. I prefer the latter translation.

[60] See J. Alberto Coffa, *The Semantic Tradition from Kant to Carnap: To the Vienna Station*. Cambridge: Cambridge University Press, 1991; Thomas E. Uebel, *Overcoming Logical Positivism from Within: The Emergence of Neurath's Naturalism in the Vienna Circle's Protocol Sentence Debate*. Amsterdam: Rodopi, 1992.

[61] Thomas Oberdan, *Protocols, Truth and Convention*. Amsterdam: Rodopi, 1993.

[62] Otto Neurath, 'Protokollsätze', *Erkenntnis* 3 (1932), 204–14, quotations at 207–8.

Scientific progress takes place through the accumulation of protocol statements, in which a process of comparison allows the gradual elimination of such statements which are to be regarded as unreliable (Neurath offers, as an example of such a statement, 'In Africa, lions sing only in major scales').

The key point is that no metaphysical statements are included or implied in these statements. They relate to the 'immediately given'. Although Carnap diverged from Neurath on some significant issues, he was in absolute agreement with him over the role of protocols.[63]

> Of first importance for epistemological analyses are the protocol language, in which the primitive protocol statements (in the material mode of speech – the sentences about the immediately given) of a particular person are formulated, and the system language in which the statements of the system of science are formulated . . . If the physical language, on the grounds of its universality, were adopted as the system language of science, all science would become physics. Metaphysics would be discarded as meaningless.

Carnap's analysis of the process of observation is ultimately based on the assumption that the syntactic analysis of protocols can reveal their salient epistemic features.

Yet, as has often been pointed out, this approach leads to the conclusion that the question of the 'warrant' or 'truth' of protocol statements lies beyond the realm of proper philosophical investigation. The origins and foundations of the protocols are relegated to the world of the natural sciences, especially behavioural psychology.[64] Now a protocol statement is not self-authenticating, and requires evaluation. The observation process itself may be flawed, skewed or distorted. The question of how an individual would come to *confirm* or *accept* a given protocol statement is not adequately analysed by either Neurath or Carnap; indeed, at points, Carnap offers purely sociological accounts of the reception of protocols.[65] The vulnerability of this position was quickly pointed out by Karl Popper in his *Logic of Scientific Discovery* (1934), in which Popper noted the need for established agreed norms by which protocol statements could be accepted or rejected. By failing to provide any rules for

---

[63] Rudolf Carnap, 'Psychologie im physikalischer Sprache', *Erkenntnis* 3 (1932), 107–42, quotation at 107–8.

[64] See the important discussion in Thomas Oberdan, 'Postscript to Protocols: Reflections on Empiricism', in Ronald N. Giere and Alan W. Richardson (eds), *Origins of Logical Empiricism*. Minneapolis: University of Minnesota Press, 1996, 269–91, especially 272–4.

[65] See, for example, Carnap, 'Psychologie im physikalischer Sprache', 107–42.

accepting or rejecting protocol statements, he argues, Neurath has undermined the entire empiricist project.[66]

The reception of 'protocol statements' since the Second World War has seen a growing recognition of their radical limitations, and a deepening awareness of the problems of the forms of empiricism which espoused them. Of particular concern to this critical debate is the issue of unobservable theoretical entities – such as subatomic particles – in the natural sciences. These cannot strictly be 'observed', yet cannot be regarded as 'non-existent' for that reason. This raises significant difficulties for logical positivism, and led some of its leading advocates to modify their position on the matter. Thus in a 1938 paper entitled 'Procedures of Empirical Science', V. F. Lenzen argued that certain entities had to be *inferred* from experimental observation.[67] For example, the behaviour of oil droplets in an electric field leads one to infer the existence of electrons as negatively charged particles of a certain mass. They cannot be seen (and hence cannot be 'verified') – yet their existence is a reasonable inference from the observational evidence. This represented a very significant dilution of the original verification principle. Later positivists – such as A. N. Flew[68] and others – were careful to formulate their criteria of meaning to permit some non-sensible entities, and hence to avoid the cold equation of 'existence' with 'the sensorily perceivable'. Yet this distinction is to be compared to a Trojan horse, allowing the 'metaphysical' to be deemed potentially meaningful on the basis of at least one influential construal of the notion.[69]

It is thus perhaps unsurprising that the early twentieth-century dismissal of metaphysics is now seen as somewhat hasty in its formulation, and unduly dogmatic in its methods, particularly in that it appears to assume the possibility (indeed, necessity) of an *a priori* rejection of metaphysics. We may therefore turn to consider the new interest in these issues, particularly as we see it reflected in the debate over Heidegger's legacy in this matter.

---

[66] K. R. Popper, *The Logic of Scientific Discovery*. New York: Science Editions, 1961, 97.

[67] V. F. Lenzen, 'Procedures of Empirical Science', in O. Neurath, R. Carnap and C. Morris (eds), *Foundations of the Unity of Science: Toward an International Encyclopedia of Unified Science*, 2 vols. Chicago: University of Chicago Press, 1955, vol. 1, 279–339.

[68] See especially Antony Flew, 'Theology and Falsification', in A. Flew and A. MacIntyre (eds), *New Essays in Philosophical Theology*. London: SCM Press, 1955, 96–9. For further comments on this essay, see Larry J. Churchill, 'Flew, Wisdom and Polanyi: The Falsification Challenge Revisited', *International Journal for Philosophy of Religion* 3 (1972), 185–94.

[69] Frederick Copleston, 'Ayer and World Views', in A. Phillips Griffiths (ed.), *A. J. Ayer: Memorial Essays*. Cambridge: Cambridge University Press, 1991, 63–75.

The critique of Heidegger: Carnap and Derrida

An example of the sort of scholastic or mystical nonsense (as he saw it) that Hume so excoriated in the eighteenth century may be found in Meister Eckhart's famous assertion 'Alle Kreaturen sind reines Nichts.'[70] Yet modern critics of metaphysical claims have turned their attention to Martin Heidegger, rather than scholastic theologians or philosophers. In his important essay 'Overcoming Metaphysics through the Logical Analysis of Language', Rudolf Carnap set out a series of metaphysical statements which he regarded as constituting pseudo-sentences.[71] This paper was first written in November 1930, and was originally delivered as a lecture at the University of Warsaw, and criticized a series of metaphysical statements taken from Heidegger's inaugural address on assuming the chair of philosophy at the University of Freiburg in July 1929. Perhaps the most important of these statements is the famous assertion: 'Das Nichts selbst nichtet.'

It is widely agreed that Heidegger has probably done more than any writer of the twentieth century to rehabilitate metaphysics. In his 1938 essay 'Die Zeit des Weltbildes', Heidegger made it clear that metaphysics remained of central importance to the human quest for truth.[72]

> In metaphysics, meditation on the essence of beings and a decision concerning the nature of truth are brought to completion. Metaphysics grounds an age in that it gives the ground of the form of its essence via a determinate interpretation of beings and a determinate comprehension of truth. This ground thoroughly dominates all the phenomena that distinguish the age.

Heidegger's views on metaphysics are best studied from his inaugural lecture at the University of Freiburg, which he, perhaps somewhat misleadingly, entitled 'What Is Metaphysics?'[73] In the opening pages of this work, he makes it clear that he does not propose to consider the general issue of 'metaphysics' as such, but rather to focus on the general metaphysical question of how 'being' (*das Sein*) is to be investigated. Heidegger asserts that, as a matter of historical fact, metaphysics has

---

[70] Meister Eckhart, *Deutsche Predigten und Traktate*. Munich: Carl Hanser, 1955, 171.

[71] Rudolf Carnap, 'Überwindung der Metaphysik durch logische Analyse der Sprache', *Erkenntnis* 2 (1932), 219–41.

[72] Martin Heidegger, *The Question concerning Technology, and Other Essays*. New York: Harper & Row, 1977, 115.

[73] Martin Heidegger, *Was ist Metaphysik?*, 15th edn. Frankfurt am Main: Vittorio Klosterman, 1998. Note that this edition includes the prefatory material of 1949, and the 'Afterword' of 1943.

approached the issue of 'substance' or 'being' through an engagement with entities (*das Seiende*).

> In all the sciences (*Wissenschaften*), following their specific intentions, we relate ourselves to entities themselves. From the standpoint of the sciences, no field takes precedence over another, neither nature over history nor vice versa. No particular way of treating objects of inquiry dominates the others. Mathematical knowledge is no more rigorous than philological-historical knowledge. It merely has the character of 'exactness,' which does not coincide with rigor. To demand exactness in the study of history is to violate the idea of the specific rigor of the humanities. The relation to the world that pervades all the sciences as such lets them – each according to its particular content and mode of being – seek beings themselves in order to make them objects of investigation and to determine their grounds.

Yet Heidegger's bold metaphysical statements seemed to his critics to demonstrate the pointlessness of the discipline – evident in the statement 'Das Nichts selbst nichtet', which might loosely be translated as 'nothingness negates itself'. For Carnap, this opaque sentence represents metaphysics in its most repellent and pointless form. First of all, the phrase does not make sense, if taken simply as a short piece of German prose. The verb *vernichten* certainly exists, having the general sense of 'to destroy' or 'to annihilate'. Yet Heidegger has coined a new word to express a metaphysical notion, thus achieving the highly dubious distinction of inventing a word without any meaning.[74] The English translation 'nothingness negates itself' – or perhaps 'nothingness nothings itself' – conveys at least something of the apparent absurdity of this statement. Carnap observes that Heidegger is obliged to use essentially the same idea both as a substantive notion and as a verb, which at the least violates the rules of logic. Metaphysics is just a series of cognitively meaningless pseudo-sentences, which is to be distinguished in the strongest possible terms from logic and the exact sciences.

This reaction against metaphysics has, if anything, been intensified with the rise of postmodernity. Postmodern writers have generally been hostile to the notion of metaphysics, (correctly) seeing the ideas of 'reality' and 'metaphysics' as correlated, and (rather more questionably) viewing an interest in metaphysics as representing a throwback to a pre-critical phase in intellectual history. That postmodernity should react

---

[74] Carnap, 'Überwindung der Metaphysik', 230–1. For the passages which Carnap cites, see Martin Heidegger, *Was ist Metaphysik?* Bonn: Friedrich Cohen Verlag, 1929, 14, 18. In a 'Nachwort', added to the 1940 edition of his work, Heidegger responded to Carnap's critique: *Was ist Metaphysik?*, 4th edn. Frankfurt: Klostermann Verlag, 1940, 104.

against realism is entirely understandable, given its intellectual and moral precommitments. The general trajectory of postmodernity can be considered – in the words of Roy Bhaskar – as 'a succession of poems, all marginally different; and a succession of paradigm shifts, for which no overarching criteria can be given'.[75] Instead of seeing the natural world as a something whose truths are uncovered through the procedures of the sciences, that world is to be seen as open; 'closure' is secured through the human agent, not on account of that world itself.[76]

For many postmodern writers, there is a link between metaphysics and a plethora of social, political and economic evils. In part, this is linked with the vigorous espousal of metaphysical interests by Martin Heidegger, whose Nazi political sympathies were regarded with intense distaste by his critics. Emmanuel Lévinas argued that Heidegger's use of the 'language of Being' perpetuates patterns of power and domination, deeply embedded in the Greek philosophical tradition, which leads to the effacement of the 'other'.[77] This point is developed more provocatively in Jacques Derrida's analysis of Heidegger, in which he argues for the ineluctable contamination of Heidegger's thought by a metaphysics of violence. Although focusing especially on Heidegger's rectoral address of 1934, Derrida regards this metaphysical complicity with violence and oppression as pervading Heidegger's works.[78]

> Because one cannot demarcate oneself from biologism, from naturalism, from racism in its genetic form, one cannot be opposed to them except by re-inscribing spirit in an oppositional determination, by once again making it a unilaterality of subjectivity, even if in its voluntarist form. The constraint of this program remains very strong, it reigns over the majority of discourses which, today and for a long time to come, state their opposition to racism, to totalitarianism, to nazism, to fascism etc., and do this in the name of spirit, and even of the freedom of the spirit in the name of an axiomatic, for example, that of democracy or 'human rights' – which, directly or not, comes back to this metaphysics of subjectivity . . .

[75] Roy Bhaskar, *Philosophy and the Idea of Freedom*. Oxford: Blackwell, 1991, 135.

[76] See the analysis in Hilary Lawson, *Closure: A Story of Everything*. London: Routledge, 2001.

[77] Emmanuel Lévinas, *Totalité et infini: essai sur l'extériorité*. The Hague: Martinus Nijhoff, 1984.

[78] Jacques Derrida, *Of Spirit: Heidegger and the Question*. Chicago: University of Chicago Press, 1989, 39–40. For comment, see Dominique Janicaud, *The Shadow of that Thought: Heidegger and the Question of Politics*. Evanston, IL: Northwestern University Press, 1996. For Derrida's defence of his interpretation of Heidegger, see 'Nietzsche and the Machine', *Journal of Nietzsche Studies* 7 (1994), 7–66. Derrida's theme of 'metaphysics and violence' is discussed in Leonard Lawlor, *Derrida and Husserl: The Basic Problem of Phenomenology*. Bloomington, IN: University of Indiana Press, 2002.

> If [the program set out in the rectoral address] seems diabolical, it is
> because, without there being anything fortuitous in this, it capitalizes on
> the worst, that is on both evils at once: the sanctioning of Nazism, and the
> gesture that is still metaphysical.

Metaphysics is thus implicated in the sanctioning of violence and
oppression, and is to be eliminated.

Derrida, of course, does not limit his critique of metaphysics to an
engagement with Heidegger. As we noted earlier (vol. 2, 178–80),
Derrida's sustained attack on Plato in his 1971 essay 'La pharmacie de
Platon' represents one of the most significant postmodern deconstruc-
tions of Plato's philosophical enterprise.[79] The ambiguity of the Greek
term φάρμακον, designating both 'poison' and 'cure', is to be seen as a
telling indication of the failure of language to deliver what it promises.
Far from being a natural account of reality, it is an essentially arbitrary
construction. 'Writing is both poison *and* cure, on the one hand a threat
to the living presence of authentic (spoken) language, on the other an
indispensable means for anyone who wants to record, transmit or
somehow commemorate that presence.'[80] Both writing and the structures of thought which it embodies and reflects are to be seen as arbitrary. Plato's metaphysics cannot conceivably be taken as having an
'eternal' or 'necessary' character, as if this is how reality must be depicted.
While it is entirely possible that Plato may think that he possesses significant rational insights into the eternal order of being, his arguments
owe their success to rhetoric, rather than reason – that is to say, to Plato's
ability to persuade his readers that his ideas resonate with their culture.
Metaphysics is essentially a 'white mythology', the tribal language preferred by white European males from Plato to Heidegger.[81]

Yet the postmodern critique of metaphysics extends beyond this association of metaphysics with oppression and violence to include the issue
of privilege. To suggest that there exists an external reality which may be
known or represented through a complex series of engagements and
negotiations on the part of the human knowing agent is to raise the (at
least, for postmodernity) spectre of claims of privilege on the part of the
knower. Those who are less troubled by this issue point out, not entirely
unreasonably, that the issue is not *privilege* but *accountability*, in that the

---

[79] For an English translation, see Jacques Derrida, *Dissemination*. Chicago: University of
Chicago Press, 1981, 63–171. There is a useful study of this work in Andrew J. McKenna, *Violence
and Difference: Girard, Derrida and Deconstruction*. Urbana, IL: University of Illinois Press, 1992.
[80] Christopher Norris, *Derrida*. London: Fontana, 1987, 37–8.
[81] Jacques Derrida, 'White Mythology: Metaphor in the Text of Philosophy', *New Literary
History* 6 (1974), 11–74.

knower is under a legitimate obligation to give an account of what she believes and why. Knowledge is a matter of public concern and debate; some of the forms of 'post-realism' to emerge in recent years are so sensitized to issues of power, privilege and presence that the quest for knowledge is increasingly construed as the solitary and essentially ahistorical pursuit of individual self-determination.

Doubts about this individualism have been expressed, even within the postmodern philosophical community. Richard Rorty and Stanley Fish, however, offer an important correction to this seriously deficient individualist account of the origins and validation of knowledge. For both, knowledge is essentially *communitarian* – a settled consensus within a society, such as Aristotle's πόλις. This knowledge is not to be taken as a response to reality, but simply as an expression of the existing values and beliefs of that community. As Rorty argues, a consequence of this communitarian or pragmatic approach to truth must be the recognition that 'there is nothing deep down inside us except what we have put there ourselves, no criterion that we have not created in the course of creating a practice, no standard of rationality that is not an appeal to such a criterion, no rigorous argumentation that is not obedience to our own conventions'.[82] Truth and morality are thus to be seen as matters of social convention, created by human communities, rather than as considered responses to an external reality.

Given Derrida's strictures, it is entirely to be expected that metaphysics would have no place, privileged or otherwise, in postmodernism. We are often told that we live in a 'post-realist' age, in which it has become pointless to suggest that language can have any 'substance' or 'matter' other than itself. There is nothing outside the text. Yet it is important to ask precisely *who* is telling us these things. The continuing predictive and explanatory successes of the natural sciences, which have persisted unabated since the advent of postmodernity, pose a powerful challenge to the second of these bland assertions. Might not the first be equally untenable? Might metaphysics have a lingering place, however reluctantly conceded or carefully disguised, in the postmodern world?

The incoherence of the postmodern rejection of metaphysics

The force of this point is best seen through a close reading of Carl Rapp's difficult recent essay on the 'post-rational' turn in philosophy.[83]

---

[82] Richard Rorty, *Consequences of Pragmatism*. Minneapolis, MN: University of Minneapolis Press, 1982, xlii.

[83] Carl Rapp, *Fleeing the Universal: The Critique of Post-Rational Criticism*. Albany, NY: State University of New York Press, 1998.

Rapp's complex work in its turn takes the form of a series of close readings of seminal postmodern texts, which allegedly abandon or reject any attempt to 'tell the truth' about reality, holding that human reason is such that it simply cannot undertake this task, not least on account of the contamination of knowledge by such issues as power. Yet, as Rapp points out, there is a long and tortuous path leading from the recognition that knowledge is tainted or skewed to the totalizing assertion that knowledge is impossible. While many postmodern writers seem to suggest that – in Rapp's words – 'we are the only ones who are willing to admit that all knowledge is contaminated, including even our own',[84] the simple fact is that some such recognition underlies most theories of knowledge, traditional and otherwise. Many Christian theologians, for example, argue that true knowledge is distorted by sin (vol. 1, 286–94).

Rapp, however, is not prepared to leave matters here. He notes that the postmodern admission that knowledge is contaminated, leading to the forced conclusion that truth is unattainable, merely raises another much more problematic question, which renders the entire postmodernist project suspect. Given the self-referentiality of the postmodern understanding of truth, how is it that one can arrive at such a deep insight as an awareness that truth is unattainable? A consistently sceptical position is simply an impossibility, since the truth of such a position requires to be affirmed or presupposed in order to be applied. Yet how is this insight to be explained? Or, perhaps more tellingly, to be *justified*? As Rapp observes, there is an inevitable circularity to the postmodern position on this matter.[85]

> The discovery that knowledge has been skewed by a variety of factors or circumstances that one has come to know of cannot be used as evidence that knowledge per se is unachievable. To do so would be to rely on the knowledge one has acquired concerning the factors or circumstances.

Rapp's basic argument is that, while postmodernity has eschewed the vocabulary and traditional concepts of metaphysics, that much-critiqued discipline has made an unacknowledged reentry into postmodern thinking under another guise. To illustrate this point, Rapp considers the pragmatism of Richard Rorty and Stanley Fish. Where traditional metaphysics considers itself as offering an account of reality, Fish holds that contemporary philosophy sees itself as elucidating and confirming the ideas and values of 'communities of interpretation'.

---

[84] Rapp, *Fleeing the Universal*, 10.
[85] Rapp, *Fleeing the Universal*, 8.

When Fish's arguments are stripped of their exiguous anti-metaphysical rhetoric, Rapp observes that some surprisingly metaphysical notions remain embedded in his thinking.[86]

> In reducing ethics and politics to the actual behaviors of individuals and communities, the pragmatists arrived at their own set of 'first principles,' without realizing, or at least without admitting, that anything metaphysical had happened.

There is a clear parallel here with Foucault's polemic against the notion of 'truth', partly on the grounds that claims to be 'telling the truth' are often disguised claims to power, authority and oppression. According to Foucault, the very idea of 'truth' grows out of the interests of the powerful. Lying behind this can be discerned a direct engagement with the Nietzschean notion of 'will to power', with its implications for the concept of 'truth'.[87] For Foucault, there is a direct line of connection between truth and power. 'Truth' can support systems of repression, by identifying standards to which people can be forced to conform. Thus what is 'mad' or 'criminal' does not depend upon some objective criterion, but upon the standards and interests of those in authority. Each society has its 'general politics of truth', which serves its vested interests.

'Truth' thus serves the interests of the powerful in a society, by perpetuating its ideas and values, and providing a rational justification for the imprisonment or elimination of those who are opposed to the prevailing ideology. Philosophy can too easily become an accomplice in this repression, by providing the oppressors with rational arguments to justify their practices. *Knowledge* is inextricably linked with *power*. Philosophers have allowed society to believe that it was persecuting its marginal elements on the basis of 'truth' or 'morality' – universal and objective standards of morality, of what is right and wrong – rather than on the basis of its own vested interests. The basic Enlightenment belief in the goodness of knowledge is thus called into question. Knowledge can enslave as much as it can liberate. The task of philosophy is therefore to criticize, in order to achieve emancipation from covert patterns of domination and oppression.[88]

> Philosophy is precisely the challenging of all phenomena of domination at whatever level or under whatever form they present themselves – political,

[86] Rapp, *Fleeing the Universal*, 14.

[87] Michael Mahon, *Foucault's Nietzschean Genealogy: Truth, Power, and the Subject*. Albany, NY: State University of New York Press, 1992.

[88] This citation is taken from a late interview, published as 'The Ethic of Care for the Self as a Practice of Freedom', in James Bernauer and David Rasmussen (eds), *The Final Foucault*. Cambridge, MA: MIT Press, 1988, 20.

economic, sexual, institutional, and so on. This critical function of philosophy, up to a certain point, emerges right from the Socratic imperative: 'Be concerned with yourself', i.e., ground yourself in liberty, through the mastery of self.

The very idea of objective truth or morality must be challenged, in that it lends support to the legitimation or perpetuation of repression.

The difficulty here is the inherent self-referentiality of Foucault's position. Foucault's criticism of 'truth' rests upon a set of quite definite beliefs about what is right and what is wrong – that is to say, what is *true* and what is *right*. Foucault's passionate belief that repression is wrong can be instanced at point after point – but is never subject to the critical analysis which its pivotal role would seem to demand.[89] Foucault's attitude here appears to be determined by what is, in effect, an objective moral value – namely, that freedom is to be preferred to repression. Foucault's critique of morality thus covertly presupposes certain moral values. Beneath his critique of conventional ethics lies a hidden set of moral values, and an unacknowledged commitment to them. As Ben Meyer shrewdly observed:[90]

> The followers of Nietzsche and Foucault are passionately persuaded that truth is a mere rhetorical device employed in the service of oppression, and say so at length. What, then, is the status of their saying so? We should give them their choice. Is it false? Or in the service of oppression?

In effect, Foucault has arrived at his own set of moral values, his own truths, without apparently realizing – and certainly without admitting – that any such claims to truth or objectivity were being made.

The suggestion that we may simply dispense with metaphysics might therefore prove to be more problematic than might at first seem to be the case. Metaphysical assumptions are actually implicit within the ideologies of those who oppose the notion. To explore this in more detail, we shall turn to consider one of the most remarkable themes in twentieth-century western philosophy – the massive revolt against metaphysics. We shall attempt to trace its roots and development, before asking why it has ultimately failed, and what the implications of this failure must be for a scientific theology, before moving on to deal with more specifically theological reflections on the theme.

---

[89] Michel Foucault, *Ethics: Subjectivity and Truth*. London: Penguin, 2000. For comment, see John Rajchman and Oristelle Bonis, *Érotique de la vérité: Foucault, Lacan et la question de l'éthique*. Paris: Presses Universitaires de France, 1994.

[90] Ben F. Meyer, 'The Philosophical Crusher', *First Things* (12 April 1991), 9–11. See also Bernard Bergonzi, *Exploding English: Criticism, Theory, Culture*. Oxford: Clarendon Press, 1990.

As is well known, the same issue arises within the natural sciences, where metaphysical conclusions are regularly drawn consequent to an encounter with experience, although with varying degrees of confidence, by those anxious to demonstrate the relevance of those sciences to human life and thought. We shall explore this further in what follows.

The metaphysical implications of the natural sciences

In one sense, the natural sciences could be argued to be methodologically anti-metaphysical, in that the sustained engagement with the natural world is not shaped or determined by metaphysical assumptions. In fact, of course, this statement is problematic, not least because the complex array of implicit metaphysical assumptions brought to the scientific task has an impact both on the motivation for the scientific quest in the first place, and on the manner in which it is undertaken. For example: the metaphysical belief that God created the natural order, and that something of the divine wisdom and beauty may be apprehended by a rigorous engagement with nature, clearly lends both impetus and direction to a certain approach to the scientific task, whereas the view that the universe is a matter of happenstance might lead to another.[91]

A related difficulty concerns the awkward historical observation that a number of leading scientific theories, each regarded as 'objective' in its own day, actually reflect certain metaphysical assumptions, whether these are explicitly recognized or not, on the part of their proponents. This is particularly clear in the case of the nineteenth-century British debate on human evolution. The doctrine of 'special creation', as set out in the writings of William Paley and his successors, is clearly shaped by quite specific metaphysical precommitments.[92] Yet it is also important to note the covert influence exercised over nineteenth-century biological evolutionary theories by contemporary theories of progress.[93] Yet it

[91] For discussion of these issues, see works such as Richard Dawkins, *Unweaving the Rainbow: Science, Delusion and the Appetite for Wonder*. London: Penguin Books, 1998; Michael D. Aeschliman, *The Restitution of Man: C. S. Lewis and the Case against Scientism*. Grand Rapids, MI: Eerdmans, 1998; Mary Midgley, *Evolution as a Religion: Strange Hopes and Stranger Fears*, 2nd edn. London: Routledge, 2002; Alister McGrath, *The Reenchantment of Nature: The Denial of Religion and the Ecological Crisis*. New York: Doubleday, 2002.

[92] Richard P. Aulie, 'Evolution and Special Creation: Historical Aspects of the Controversy', *Proceedings of the American Philosophical Society* 127 (1983), 418–62; Neal C. Gillespie, 'Divine Design and the Industrial Revolution: William Paley's Abortive Reform of Natural Theology', *Isis* 81 (1990), 214–29.

[93] For the best study of this important theme, see Michael Ruse, *Monad to Man: The Concept of Progress in Evolutionary Biology*. Cambridge, MA: Harvard University Press, 1996.

would be perfectly reasonable to counter both these points by insisting that, whatever motivations are brought to the scientific task, and whatever metaphysical assumptions these may entail, the actual business of *investigating* nature on the basis of publicly accessible and agreed criteria proceeds without reference to such assumptions.

Our concern in this section, however, is with the metaphysical consequences rather than the presuppositions of scientific theories. For many in the public arena, the natural sciences only start to get interesting when they have implications for the wider sphere of human knowledge and understanding. One of the most significant aspects of the contemporary discussion of the natural sciences concerns precisely the question of the implications of their ideas for the greater questions of life – such as who we are, what our destiny might be, and how fundamental values are to be derived.[94] The transition from the natural sciences to metaphysics may be problematic; it is, nevertheless, a remarkably well-travelled road.

Perhaps the most familiar of those metaphysical roads is the debate over realism, widely held within the natural sciences to lead to a view of the world which 'exists independently of us human beings and which stands before us like a great, eternal riddle, at least partially accessible to our inspection' (Albert Einstein).[95] Yet there are other metaphysical issues on which the natural sciences are widely held to have a bearing, even if these can be argued to possess considerably weaker evidential force than the theories which gave rise to them. To illustrate this point, we shall consider some metaphysical questions which arise from quantum theory and sociobiology.

From physics to metaphysics: quantum theory and indeterminacy

'Physics and metaphysics blend into a seamless whole, each enriching the other.'[96] In thus concluding his 1993 Tanner Lectures at Cambridge University, Michael Redhead makes the point that physics cannot help but address metaphysical issues, whether its practitioners regard

---

[94] For reflections on these themes, see works such as Mary Midgley, *Science as Salvation: A Modern Myth and its Meaning*. London: Routledge, 1992; Daniel C. Dennett, *Darwin's Dangerous Idea: Evolution and the Meaning of Life*. New York: Simon & Schuster, 1995; Ursula Goodenough, *The Sacred Depths of Nature*. New York: Oxford University Press, 1998.

[95] See Albert Einstein, 'Quanten-Mechanik und Wirklichkeit', *Dialectica* 2 (1948), 320–4; Arthur Fine, *The Shaky Game: Einstein, Realism and the Quantum Theory*. Chicago: University of Chicago Press, 1986; Azaria Polikarov, 'On the Nature of Einstein's Realism', *Epistemologia* 12 (1989), 277–304.

[96] Michael Redhead, *From Physics to Metaphysics*. Cambridge: Cambridge University Press, 1995, 87.

themselves as qualified to do so or not. The area in which such issues emerge with particular force is that of quantum theory, which we shall explore in the present section.

The questions of whether the natural world is to be regarded as deterministic (that is, as predetermined by certain fundamental principles and parameters) or indeterministic (that is, as lying beyond prediction, in that it is subject to random or indeterminable influences)[97] are important metaphysical questions, which are of no small importance in contemporary debates concerning biological evolution. Thus Barbara Horan and Alexander Rosenberg have argued that the evolutionary process (as opposed to evolutionary *theory*) is essentially deterministic.[98] This has been countered by Roberta Millstein, who insists that the influence of essentially random factors on that process is such that it must be regarded as indeterministic.[99] Historically, the discipline which has provoked the most discussion over indeterminism is quantum theory. It is widely argued that the standard Copenhagen approach is strongly supportive of an indeterministic account of reality, with the Heisenberg 'Uncertainty Principle' often being elevated beyond its original context to become a general statement concerning limitations on human knowledge.[100]

Yet as Erwin Schrödinger emphasized in his inaugural oration at the University of Zurich in 1922, it is empirically impossible to determine whether the world is deterministic or indeterministic; the matter simply cannot be settled on the basis of observation.[101] This is not to deny the importance of the question; it is to point out that it cannot be resolved by the working methods of the natural sciences. It lies beyond their proper scope. It might be objected that since the Copenhagen version of quantum theory is widely accepted as the standard account, the

[97] For an excellent introduction to the issue, see Ernst Cassirer, *Determinism and Indeterminism in Modern Physics: Historical and Systematic Studies of the Problem of Causality.* New Haven and London: Yale University Press, 1956.

[98] Alexander Rosenberg, 'Is the Theory of Natural Selection a Statistical Theory?' *Canadian Journal of Philosophy* 14 (1988), 187–207; Barbara L. Horan, 'The Statistical Character of Evolutionary Theory', *Philosophy of Science* 61 (1994), 76–95.

[99] Roberta L. Millstein, 'Random Drift and the Omniscient Viewpoint', *Philosophy of Science* 63 (1996), 10–18. See also Robert Brandon and Scott Carson, 'The Indeterministic Character of Evolutionary Theory', *Philosophy of Science* 63 (1996), 315–37.

[100] For the principle itself, see Werner Heisenberg, 'Über den anschaulichen Inhalt der quantentheoretischen Kinematik und Mechanik', *Zeitschrift für Physik* 43 (1927), 172–98. There is an excellent discussion of the origins of the principle in David C. Cassidy, *Uncertainty: The Life and Science of Werner Heisenberg.* New York: Freeman, 1992, 226–46.

[101] Erwin Schrödinger, *Science, Theory and Man.* London: George Allen & Unwin, 1957, 147. See also Yemima Ben-Menahem, 'Struggling with Causality: Schrödinger's Case', *Studies in History and Philosophy of Science* 23 (1989), 147–80.

metaphysical implications of its explicit indeterminism must be conceded to be well founded.

Yet the situation is far from simple. The Copenhagen version is not the only available account of quantum mechanics. Instead of representing microentities as waves or particles (as in the Copenhagen theory), it is perfectly possible to represent them as particles guided by a quantum potential. This is the approach pioneered by David Bohm in 1952, when he took the nonrelativistic Schrödinger equation, and expressed its basic ideas in what could be thought of as a 'Newtonian' form.[102] The dynamics of this particle of mass and momentum p can thus be expressed in terms of the combination of a classical potential energy V and a 'quantum potential' U as follows:

$$\frac{dp}{dt} = -\nabla(V + U)$$

Where U is small, this reduces immediately to the standard Newtonian equation describing the Second Law of Motion. The 'quantum potential' can be expressed as

$$U \equiv -\frac{\hbar^2}{2m} \frac{\nabla^2 R}{R}$$

Two significant points must be made concerning Bohm's quantum theory. First, it is empirically equivalent to the Copenhagen interpretation. In other words, it is just as good at accounting for the observed phenomena as its better-known rival.[103] Second, in common with the Copenhagen interpretation, Bohm's theory implies an ontology.[104] These two ontologies, however, are incompatible. Broadly speaking, the Copenhagen interpretation excludes realism as forcefully as the Bohmian position affirms it.[105] While both theories are rich in potentially inflationary metaphysical implications, these are radically divergent and ultimately incommensurate. It is therefore unwise to speak of 'the metaphysics of quantum theory', in that this implies a uniformity

---

[102] David Bohm, 'A Suggested Interpretation of the Quantum Theory in Terms of "Hidden" Variables', *Physical Review* 85 (1952), 166–93.

[103] A point stressed by James T. Cushing, *Quantum Mechanics: Historical Contingency and the Copenhagen Hegemony*. Chicago: University of Chicago Press, 1994.

[104] Bohm did not pay much attention to this aspect of his theory in earlier publications, particularly during the 1950s. For his later reflections, see David Bohm and Basil J. Hiley, *The Undivided Universe: An Ontological Interpretation of Quantum Theory*. London and New York: Routledge, 1993.

[105] Cushing, *Quantum Mechanics*, 204–5.

of approach which studiously ignores the diversity within the field.[106] One can speak, although perhaps less confidently than some seem to appreciate, of 'the metaphysics of the Copenhagen approach to quantum theory'.

So what are the implications of this brief foray into the development of quantum theory for a scientific theology? The trajectory which links reflection on the observable world with metaphysics can be represented as follows:

Empirical observation ⇒ theory ⇒ metaphysics

Theory here functions as a bridge between experience and metaphysics. Yet, as the radical convergence of the Copenhagen and Bohmian theories makes clear, in this case the same basic observations give rise to two empirically indistinguishable approaches, rendering a choice between them problematic. Nevertheless, many would argue that a choice must ultimately be made.[107] This leads to two possible outcomes, which are metaphysically incompatible:

1. Empirical observation ⇒ Bohmian theory ⇒ determinist realist metaphysics
2. Empirical observation ⇒ Copenhagen theory ⇒ indeterminist nonrealist metaphysics

The ontological implications of the same set of empirical observations are thus both mediated and modulated by the choice of the interposed theoretical prism. A similar issue emerges from the field of evolutionary biology, to which we may now turn.

From biology to theology: evolutionary theory and belief in God

The rise of evolutionary theory in the nineteenth century illustrates once more how theories compete to account for the available evidence. Charles Darwin's *Origin of Species* sets out a substantial array of observational data which can be explained on the basis of natural selection, but which caused some difficulties for the then-prevailing theory of the special creation of individual species.[108] There are good reasons for believing that Darwin was influenced at this point by William

---

[106] See the approach adopted by Henry Krips, *The Metaphysics of Quantum Theory*. Oxford: Clarendon Press, 1987.

[107] Cushing, *Quantum Mechanics*, 213–14.

[108] Paul R. Thagard, 'The Best Explanation: Criteria for Theory Choice', *Journal of Philosophy* 75 (1976), 76–92; Michael C. Banner, *The Justification of Science and the Rationality of Religious Belief*. Oxford and New York: Oxford University Press, 1990, 125–30.

Whewell's notion of 'consilience' as a measure of the explanatory power of explanations.[109] On the basis of a number of criteria, the doctrine of special creation was now viewed as a less satisfactory explanation of the observed features of the natural world than the posited process of natural selection.[110] The metaphysical implications of this transition will be clear: the observational data concerning flora and fauna leads to very different metaphysical conclusions if viewed through the prism of a doctrine of special creation on the one hand, and natural selection on the other.

But is the theory of natural selection necessarily linked with a *specific* metaphysic? Writers such as Richard Dawkins and Daniel Dennett have argued that Darwinism is intrinsically atheistic.[111] In his important work *Consilience* (1998), Edward O. Wilson suggests that Darwin's theories may be extended beyond their original application, to include aspects of human culture, such as ethics and religious belief. The origins of these need not be grounded in any metaphysical entity – such as God – but are to be traced back to the complex process of human evolution, which determined which ideas would survive and which would not. Thus religious beliefs and ethical principles are not 'ordained by God or plucked from the air as self-evident truth'. Rather, they are to be seen as having evolved 'as a necessary device of survival in social organisms', and have been 'selected' precisely because they proved most adapted to ensuring the survival of those social groupings who adopted them.[112] Wilson's argument, at first sight, certainly seems to lead to an atheist position; or at least to the view that God does not play a significant role in human concept-formation. For Wilson, Darwinism eliminates God, and the evolutionary process will eventually lead to the secularization of religion.[113]

---

[109] See especially Michael Ruse, 'Darwin's Debt to Philosophy: An Examination of the Influence of the Philosophical Ideas of John F. Herschel and William Whewell on the Development of Charles Darwin's Theory of Evolution', *Studies in the History and Philosophy of Science* 66 (1975), 159–81. For further reflections on Whewell, see Richard R. Yeo, 'William Whewell's Philosophy of Knowledge and its Reception', in Menachem Fisch and Simon Schaffer (eds), *William Whewell: A Composite Portrait*. Oxford: Clarendon Press, 1991, 175–99; idem, *Defining Science: William Whewell, Natural Knowledge, and Public Debate in Early Victorian Britain*. Cambridge: Cambridge University Press, 1993.

[110] The gradual erosion of Darwin's belief in 'special creationism' has been documented by Neal C. Gillespie, *Charles Darwin and Special Creation*. Chicago: University of Chicago Press, 1979. See further Phillip R. Sloan, 'Darwin on Nature and Divinity', *Osiris* 16 (2001), 251–69.

[111] Richard Dawkins, *The Blind Watchmaker: Why the Evidence of Evolution Reveals a Universe Without Design*. New York: Norton, 1986; Dennett, *Darwin's Dangerous Idea*, 511–20.

[112] Edward O. Wilson, *Consilience: The Unity of Knowledge*. New York: Knopf, 1998, 273.

[113] Wilson, *Consilience*, 296.

Yet it is far from evident that this is actually the case. The Oxford Neo-Darwinian school, which flourished in the first decade of the twentieth century, was prepared to acknowledge that a modest doctrine of divine providence, or a more developed notion of the indwelling of the divine *Logos* within creation, allowed Darwin's theory to be viewed in a positive theistic context.[114] Similarly, a group of significant conservative Protestant writers based at Princeton Theological Seminary during the later nineteenth century believed that Darwinism could be accommodated within a Christian worldview. While Charles Hodge (1797–1878) held that Darwinism was simply a form of atheism, this rested on his belief that the Darwinian viewpoint was unacceptable on account of its apparent rejection or elimination of the notion of divine design.[115] For Hodge, it was possible to accept the idea of biological evolution, without being committed to an atheist interpretation of the phenomenon, by seeing divine providence (rather than random events) as guiding the evolutionary process. In an 1888 essay on Darwin, Hodge's colleague Benjamin B. Warfield argued that the Darwinian doctrine of natural selection could easily be seen as a natural law operating under the aegis of the general providence of God.[116]

Furthermore, Wilson argues that there is ample empirical evidence to suggest that people 'flourish within certain belief systems, and wither under others'.[117] He regards it as being important to determine why this might be the case. It would seem to be important at this point to bring forward the theological considerations set out earlier in this work, which stress the importance of a Christian doctrine of creation in offering an explanation of why the human mind seems adapted to belief in God (vol. 1, 196–218). Taken together, the Christian doctrines of creation and providence offer an alternative way of understanding the remarkable adaptation of humanity towards religious belief, which must not be overlooked in such discussions.

[114] Richard England, 'Natural Selection, Teleology, and the Logos: From Darwin to the Oxford Neo-Darwinists, 1859–1909', *Osiris* 16 (2001), 270–87. For a general overview of Darwin's theistic defenders and interpreters, see James R. Moore, *The Post-Darwinian Controversies: A Study of the Protestant Struggle to Come to Terms with Darwin in Great Britain and America, 1870–1900*. Cambridge: Cambridge University Press, 1979.

[115] Charles Hodge, *What is Darwinism?* New York: Scribner, Armstrong & Co., 1874, 174–7. See David N. Livingstone, *Darwin's Forgotten Defenders: The Encounter between Evangelical Theology and Evolutionary Thought*. Grand Rapids, MI: Eerdmans, 1987, 100–5.

[116] David N. Livingstone, 'B. B. Warfield, the Theory of Evolution and Early Fundamentalism', *Evangelical Quarterly* 58 (1986), 69–83. A central issue concerned how the notion of 'design' was interpreted: David N. Livingstone, 'The Idea of Design: The Vicissitudes of a Key Concept in the Princeton Response to Darwin', *Scottish Journal of Theology* 37 (1984), 329–57.

[117] Wilson, *Consilience*, 294.

The concept of biological evolution through natural selection is thus amenable to a number of metaphysical interpretations. It is consistent with a number of metaphysical precommitments, and can endorse a number of metaphysical conclusions. What must be appreciated is that there is no direct, unambiguous and unproblematic transition from the affirmation of an evolutionary worldview to a specific metaphysic, allegedly based upon that worldview. As Wilson himself points out, both atheism and theism are to be regarded as 'transcendent' or 'metaphysical' outlooks.[118] Yet the notion of any 'embargo' on metaphysical standpoints as a result of evolutionary theory – or any such theory – cannot be sustained.

On reaffirming the metaphysical dimensions of theology

It will be clear that the curt dismissal of metaphysics by the Vienna Circle and their associates is now seen as premature and unsatisfactory. In both the natural sciences and theology, the question of metaphysics is increasingly being recognized as legitimate and proper.[119] The issue could be framed in terms of the issue of observability: What must be true or exist that is *unobservable* if what is *observable* is to be explained?

A. J. Ayer vigorously rejected 'the metaphysical thesis that philosophy affords us knowledge of a reality transcending the world of science and common sense'. A similar stance permeates the earlier writings of Bas van Fraassen, who clearly echoes Ayer's concerns.[120]

> To be an empiricist is to withhold belief in anything that goes beyond the actual, observable phenomena, and to recognize no objective modality in nature. To develop an empiricist account of science is to depict it as involving a search for truth only about the empirical world, about what is

---

[118] Wilson, *Consilience*, 265–7.

[119] There is a huge literature. Some typical representatives to focus on affirming the place of metaphysics and ontology in the natural sciences include James Maffie, 'Naturalism, Scientism and the Independence of Epistemology', *Erkenntnis* 43 (1995), 1–27; Murray Code, 'On the Poverty of Scientism, or: The Ineluctable Roughness of Rationality', *Metaphilosophy* 28 (1997), 102–22; Mikael Stenmark, *Scientism: Science, Ethics and Religion*. Aldershot: Ashgate, 2001, especially 4–17; Frederick A. Olafson, *Naturalism and the Human Condition: Against Scientism*. London: Routledge, 2001. Even some of those inclined to a more naturalist perspective – such as Willem Drees, who argues that 'science does not need a great deal of metaphysics' – make the highly significant concession that 'our understanding of reality' may be considered as 'pointing beyond science to metaphysical issues, without, however, pointing to one particular metaphysical view', Willem B. Drees, *Religion, Science and Naturalism*. Cambridge: Cambridge University Press, 1995, 11, 152.

[120] Bas C. van Fraassen, *The Scientific Image*. Oxford: Oxford University Press, 1980, 202–3. See our discussion of the difficulties encountered by Fraassen in this respect (vol. 2, 146–60).

actual and observable . . . it must invoke throughout a resolute rejection of the demand for an explanation of the regularities in the observable course of nature, by means of truths concerning a reality beyond what is actual and observable, as a demand which plays no role in the scientific enterprise.

Yet Ayer and his followers were obliged to qualify, modify and amplify this bald statement to such an extent that it is doubtful whether anything of great significance remains amidst its wreckage. What was once a simple, no-nonsense assertion has suffered a slow and lingering 'death of a thousand qualifications'. When all is said and done, Ayer's criticism of metaphysics has now been reduced to the recommendation that we offer good warrant for any metaphysical entities we posit. Heidegger's early bold assertions that metaphysics must be 'overcome' or 'destroyed' has given way to the more placid request that the metaphysical enterprise takes place within certain limits.[121] Metaphysics lives on; the debate concerns its warrant and limits – especially within a scientific theology.

Some sections of Christian theology remain intensely distrustful of metaphysics, of any kind. Earlier, we noted John Milton's misgivings about the role of metaphysics. His distaste for the 'thick darkness of metaphysics' is echoed by many twentieth-century theologians. Indeed, such is the force of this reaction that Christian theology appears to have reached something of a rare consensus that metaphysics has no real place within the field of systematic theology. Gordon Kaufman's assertion that 'there is an inescapable rivalry between metaphysics and theology'[122] both reflects and sustains this general consensus, even if he fails to cast much light on what he means by this notoriously elusive term, arguably rejecting metaphysics *as a genre* through conveniently reducing it to one specific metaphysic, unrepresentatively anti-Christian in its tone. On Kaufman's skewed misconstrual of metaphysics, it is quite impossible to understand why such a thoroughly Christian writer as Thomas Aquinas should hold metaphysics in such high regard, and incorporate so much metaphysical material in his dogmatics.[123]

---

[121] For a useful account of these shifts in Heidegger's thinking, see Dominique Janicaud and Jean-François Mattéi, *Métaphysique à la limite: cinq études sur Heidegger*. Paris: Presses Universitaires de France, 1983.

[122] Gordon D. Kaufman, 'Metaphysics and Theology', *Cross Currents* 28 (1978), 325–41. The quotation constitutes the opening sentence of the article.

[123] See the now classic studies of Norman Kretzmann, *The Metaphysics of Theism: Aquinas's Natural Theology in Summa contra Gentiles I*. Oxford: Clarendon Press, 1997; idem, *The Metaphysics of Creation: Aquinas's Natural Theology in Summa contra Gentiles II*. Oxford: Clarendon Press, 1999.

In his somewhat overheated essay 'Only Theology Overcomes Metaphysics', John Milbank argues that metaphysics is to be rejected on account of its pretensions to theological autonomy, in that it[124]

> claims to be able fully to define the conditions of finite knowability, or to arrive at possible being as something 'in itself.' . . . Modernity is metaphysical, for since it cannot refer the flux of time to the ungraspable infinite, it is forced to seek a graspable *immanent* security . . . By contrast, the Christian thought which flowed from Gregory of Nyssa and Augustine was able fully to concede the utter unknowability of creatures which continually alter and have no ground within themselves, for it derived them from the infinity of God which is unchanging and yet circumscribable, even in itself.

Milbank thus argues for the elimination of metaphysics from a radically orthodox theology, holding that metaphysics is in the first place theologically *unnecessary* (in that the Christian revelation of God is epistemologically autonomous), and in the second place *degrading* (in that metaphysics is intellectually contaminated by the presuppositions of a secular world). Once more, it is necessary to express a considerable degree of puzzlement here, in that many of the theologians who Milbank clearly regards as exemplary in their orthodoxy – such as Dionysius and Gregory of Nyssa – were enthusiastic in their appropriation of metaphysics for apologetic and eidetic purposes.[125] Milbank appears to endorse a deployment of metaphysics by his favoured surrogates, even if he declares the procedure to be illegitimate for others.

This theological revolt against metaphysics reflects a broader discontent with the discipline, especially evident within the Vienna Circle, but now widely distributed within the philosophy of science. The natural sciences are widely regarded – and, if the truth is told, regard themselves – as being strongly anti-metaphysical in character. Metaphysics arises from a faulty grasp of the natural sciences which, when remedied, eliminates the need for any such meaningless statements. The situation is nicely captured in Lord Kelvin's famous pillorying of Hegel's somewhat

---

[124] John Milbank, *The Word made Strange: Theology, Language, Culture*. Oxford: Blackwell, 1997, 44.

[125] Douglas Hedley, 'Should Divinity Overcome Metaphysics? Reflections on John Milbank's *Theology Beyond Secular Reason* and *Confessions of a Cambridge Platonist*', *Journal of Religion* 80 (2000), 271–98. For the rather limited place of metaphysics in Milbank's Cambridge colleague Nicholas Lash, see Gale Z. Heide, 'The Nascent Noeticism of Narrative Theology: An Examination of the Relationship between Narrative and Metaphysics in Nicholas Lash', *Modern Theology* 12 (1996), 459–81.

tenuous grasp of Newtonian physics, which he held to be the ground of his pointless metaphysical speculations: 'If, gentlemen, these be his physics, think what his metaphysics must be!'[126]

At first sight, it might therefore be expected that a scientific theology would reflect this anti-metaphysical trend. In fact, it opposes it, arguing for the reinvigoration of a theological metaphysics under conditions that safeguard the discipline from the intellectual inflationism which so discredited it in previous generations. There are a number of factors which point to this conclusion, which will be discussed in detail in the present chapter, and it may be helpful to identify them at this early stage, while postponing their full exposition until later.

First, we must note how a careful study of *history* subverts some of the more simplistic accounts of the erosion or rejection of metaphysics through the steady advance of the sciences. Those who read the history of scientific advance in terms of an increasingly unbridgeable gulf between scientific and religious or metaphysical beliefs must come to terms with the awkwardness of the historical record, which indicates that the scientific, religious and metaphysical beliefs of leading natural scientists interlock and interact, making it quite unrealistic to speak of the 'elimination' of metaphysics from scientific advance.[127] Again, a more careful study of the early views of the Vienna Circle suggests that the origins and concerns of this group of thinkers were rather more complex and subtle than has hitherto been appreciated, with important implications for our understanding of the complex motivations for developing *eine wissenschaftliche Weltauffassung*, and assessing its significance for both the scientific and philosophical enterprises.[128] This historical revisionism, which is reflected in this chapter, leads to a more restrained and historically sensitive assessment of the challenge to metaphysics posed by the natural sciences, and hence to a more realistic

---

[126] Silvanus P. Thompson, *The Life of William Thomson, Baron Kelvin of Largs*, 2 vols. London: Macmillan, 1910, vol. 2, 1124.

[127] Stephen J. Wykstra, 'Religious Beliefs, Metaphysical Beliefs and Historiography of Science', *Osiris* 16 (2001), 29–46.

[128] This revision was prompted by Jolle Proust, *Questions de forme: logique et proposition analytique de Kant à Carnap*. Paris: Librairie Arthème Fayard, 1986. For its further development, see J. Alberto Coffa, *The Semantic Tradition from Kant to Carnap: To the Vienna Station*. Cambridge: Cambridge University Press, 1991; Thomas E. Uebel, *Overcoming Logical Positivism from Within: The Emergence of Neurath's Naturalism in the Vienna Circle's Protocol Sentence Debate*. Studien zur Österreichischen Philosophie 17. Amsterdam: Rodopi, 1992; Thomas Oberdan, *Protocols, Truth and Convention*. Studien zur Österreichischen Philosophie 19. Amsterdam: Rodopi, 1993; Michael Friedman, *A Parting of the Ways: Carnap, Cassirer, and Heidegger*. Chicago: Open Court, 2000.

positive approach to the place of metaphysics in any *wissenschaftliche Weltauffassung* – including a *naturwissenschaftliche Weltauffassung*.

Second, a close reading of a representative range of Christian theologians suggests that the *theological* case for the elimination of metaphysics from theology simply has not been made. For example, Martin Luther's critique of metaphysics is actually directed against those who import preconceived metaphysical notions of God from outside the Christian tradition, and demand that theology adjust its ideas accordingly; it is not strictly a criticism of the development of a metaphysics within Christian theology itself.[129] Luther opposes those who smuggle an *a priori* metaphysical system into theology, not those who derive such a system *a posteriori* on the basis of an engagement with Scripture. Nor has the inner propensity of the Christian tradition to *generate* a metaphysic been fully appreciated, particularly by John Milbank, who commends writers such as Augustine of Hippo and Gregory of Nyssa for defending an 'anti-metaphysical tradition',[130] yet puzzlingly fails to concede that both engaged positively and constructively – some might even say 'uncritically' – with Neoplatonic metaphysics in developing that tradition.

On my reading of the Christian tradition, its inner dynamic is such that the emergence of some form of metaphysics within its theology is to be expected. Attempts to embargo metaphysical discussions are doomed to failure. Thus while both participants to the debate between Martin Luther and Huldrych Zwingli over the nature of the real presence had no enthusiasm for metaphysical issues, believing that the central questions concerned biblical exegesis, it soon became clear that both a defence and a criticism of the notion of the 'ubiquity of Christ' demanded an engagement with metaphysical issues. Equally, the remarkable re-emergence of metaphysics within both Lutheran and Reformed theology during the period 1590–1620 rested partly on the realization that debates between the two styles of theology could not be conducted without at least some degree of engagement with metaphysical questions.[131] Considerations such as the above suggest that it is decidedly premature to declare that theology can do – or has done – without metaphysics.

---

[129] Alister E. McGrath, *Luther's Theology of the Cross: Martin Luther's Theological Breakthrough.* Oxford: Blackwell, 1985, 136–41, with particular reference to Aristotle.

[130] Milbank, *The Word made Strange*, 44–5.

[131] See the careful study of Kristian Jensen, 'Protestant Rivalry: Metaphysics and Rhetoric in Germany, c. 1590–1620', *Journal of Ecclesiastical History* 41 (1990), 24–43.

The next two sections will therefore engage with the views of some leading theological critics of metaphysics, attempting to identify their points of concern and offer responses to them. We may begin with one of the most significant theological schools to express anxieties over the theological deployment of metaphysics – German liberal Protestantism.

A. B. Ritschl and Adolf von Harnack

The most significant theological assault on metaphysics is generally regarded to have its beginnings in German liberal Protestantism, originating with Albrecht Benjamin Ritschl and culminating in the works of Adolf von Harnack. Ritschl's *Gemeindetheologie*, though now generally regarded as of little more than antiquarian interest, must be regarded as an essential element in the overall trajectory of the development of German liberal Protestant theology from Schleiermacher through to Harnack. As even a casual reading of Ritschl's *Theologie und Metaphysik* (1881) makes clear, that theology is markedly anti-metaphysical in its orientation. Schleiermacher had earlier remarked that religion did not concern itself with the 'nature of things, but with their operation upon us'.[132] Yet Ritschl appears to regard Philip Melanchthon and Schleiermacher as developing doctrines of God which rested on a natural theology rather than the specifics of the Christian faith. This judgement is more than a little puzzling, and appears to rest on a failure to distinguish the related notions of 'natural religion' and 'natural theology'.[133]

Ritschl's *Theologie und Metaphysik* is a highly polemical work, perhaps written in haste, which at times appears to be internally incoherent. It is therefore difficult to know quite what to make of Ritschl's repeated insistence that theology must concern itself with actual appearances and relations, and eschew any attempt to know things as they actually are. This radical empiricism can be seen as the logical outcome of a Kantian reserve concerning the possibility of knowing anything other than phenomena; indeed, it might reasonably be argued that Ritschl's hostility to metaphysics is determined by his covert neo-Kantian presuppositions.[134]

---

[132] Friedrich Schleiermacher, *On Religion: Speeches to its Cultured Despisers.* New York: Harper & Row, 1958, 48.

[133] H. J. Birkner, 'Natürliche Theologie und Offenbarungstheologie: Ein theologiegeschichtlicher Überblick', *Neue Zeitschrift für systematische Theologie und Religionsphilosophie* 3 (1961), 279–95, especially 289–91. Ritschl's importance for the modern articulation of the concept of revelation has been explored in Stephan Weyer-Menkhoff, *Aufklärung und Offenbarung: Zur Systematik Albrecht Ritschls.* Göttingen: Vandenhoek & Ruprecht, 1988.

[134] See especially Paul Wrzecionko, *Die philosophischen Wurzeln der Theologie Albrecht Ritschls. Ein Beitrag zum Problem des Verhältnisses von Theologie und Philosophie im 19. Jahrhundert.* Berlin: De Gruyter, 1964.

The implications of the Kantian reserve concerning the possibility of knowing the *Ding-an-sich* would have been well known to Ritschl, not least through the influence of Hermann Lotze, who stressed that the realm of the logical possesses a domain of validity (*Geltung*) which is distinct from that of actual spatio-temporal entities.[135] (Indeed, such is Lotze's influence at points that Ritschl appears generally unable to make the critical distinction between a Platonic form and a Lotzean *Erinnerungsbild*.) Yet the critical importance of Kant's moral philosophy must also be acknowledged at this point: Ritschl's aversion to metaphysics can be argued to lie, at least in part, on Kant's critique of metaphysics and affirmation of a moralistic conception of God.[136] Ritschl develops a deontological conception of God which is essentially moral in nature, to be construed according to its impact upon humanity rather than its intrinsic metaphysical properties.[137]

Ritschl's concerns at this point are best understood as religious, rather than philosophical. Standing in a Lutheran tradition, Ritschl echoes Luther's longstanding concern over any attempt to know God *in se*; theology must rather know God *pro nobis*.[138] Yet Ritschl's position cannot be regarded as a legitimate extension of Luther's theological concerns. While at times there are clear resonances with Luther's agenda, Ritschl's vigorous empiricist assault on metaphysics is generally regarded as reflecting a marked prejudice against the use of Hellenistic ideas by the early church, particularly during the first four centuries. Ritschl's radically empiricist programme, if carried through, could only lead to the forced separation of theology and metaphysics.[139]

Ritschl lacked the historical and philosophical competence to develop his critique of metaphysics beyond the often unsubstantiated assertions of his polemical tract of 1881. It fell to his more distinguished successor

---

[135] Hermann Lotze, *Metaphysik: Drei Bücher der Ontologie, Kosmologie und Psychologie.* Leipzig: Hirzel Verlag, 1879.

[136] This has been well documented by Ralf Geisler, *Kants moralischer Gottesbeweis im protestantischen Positivismus.* Göttingen: Vandenhoeck & Ruprecht, 1992, 21–110. Geisler explores the impact of Kant's critique of metaphysics in the writings of Ritschl, Wilhelm Herrmann (1846–1922), Julius Kaftan (1846–1926) and Georg Wobbermin (1869–1943).

[137] Geisler, *Kants moralischer Gottesbeweis,* 111–77.

[138] For an excellent account of this principle, see Ernst Wolf, 'Die Rechtfertigungslehre als Mitte und Grenze reformatorischer Theologie', *Evangelische Theologie* 9 (1949), 298–308.

[139] Wolfhart Pannenberg's excellent study of the use of Hellenistic philosophy in the patristic period can be seen as an attempt to counter this trend: Wolfhart Pannenberg, 'The Appropriation of the Philosophical Concept of God as a Dogmatic Problem of Early Christian Theology', in *Basic Questions in Theology II.* London: SCM Press, 1971, 119–83. For Pannenberg's evaluation of Ritschl's critique of metaphysics, see Wolfhart Pannenberg, *Systematic Theology,* 3 vols. Grand Rapids, MI: Eerdmans, 1991–8, vol. 1, 98–101.

Adolf von Harnack to set in place a sustained critique of metaphysics, based largely on a critical study of the emergence of early Christianity.[140] On the basis of his studies of the emergence of early Christianity – as reflected, for example, in his massive *Dogmengeschichte* – Harnack argued forcefully that the transition of the gospel from its original Palestinian milieu, dominated by Hebraic modes of thought and rationality, to a Hellenistic milieu characterized by radically different modes of thinking, represented a decisive turning point in the history of Christian thought. The notion of dogma, Harnack argues, is metaphysically determined, in that it is characterized by the distinctively Hellenistic modes of thought and patterns of discourse within which the dogmatic statements of the early church were formulated.[141]

> What Protestants and Catholics call 'dogmas' are not only ecclesiastical teachings, but also (1) conceptually expressed theses which, taken collectively, form a unity. These theses establish the contents of the Christian religion as knowledge of God, of the world, and of sacred history as demonstrated truths. Furthermore, (2) these theses have emerged at a definite stage in the history of the Christian religion. Both in the manner in which they are conceived and in many of their details, they demonstrate the influence of this stage (the Greek period), and they have preserved this character in all subsequent epochs, despite qualifications and additions.

Harnack's critique of the theological deployment of metaphysics is most evident in the field of Christology. For Harnack, the gospel is nothing other than Jesus Christ himself.[142] 'Jesus does not belong to the gospel as one of its elements, but was the personal realization and power of the gospel, and we still perceive him as such.'[143] Jesus himself *is* Christianity. In making this assertion, however, Harnack implies no *doctrine* of Jesus; the basis of the assertion is partly historical (based on an analysis of the genesis of Christianity), and partly a consequence of Harnack's personalist religious assumption that Jesus' significance resides primarily in the impact he has upon individuals. Nevertheless, the transmission of the

---

[140] For an excellent study of Ritschl's influence on Harnack's programme, see E. J. Meijering, *Theologische Urteile über die Dogmengeschichte: Ritschls Einfluss auf von Harnack*. Leiden: Brill, 1978.

[141] Adolf von Harnack, *Lehrbuch der Dogmengeschichte*, 3rd edn. Freiburg: Mohr, 1894, vol. 1, 69–70.

[142] Harnack, *Lehrbuch der Dogmengeschichte*, 79.

[143] Adolf von Harnack, *Das Wesen des Christentums: sechzehn Vorlesungen vor Studierenden aller Facultäten im Wintersemester 1899/1900 an der Universität Berlin gehalten*. Leipzig: Hinrichs, 1906, 92.

gospel within a Hellenistic milieu, with its distinct patterns of rationality and modes of discourse, led to the attempt to conceptualize and give metaphysical substance to the significance of Jesus. In the first edition of his *Dogmengeschichte*, Harnack illustrates this trend with particular reference to Gnosticism, the Apologists, and particularly the *logos*-Christology of Origen.[144] To a certain extent, the development of doctrine may be likened, in Harnack's view, to a chronic degenerative illness.[145] In the case of Christology, for example, Harnack detects in the shift from soteriology (an analysis of the personal impact of Jesus) to speculative metaphysics a classical instance of the Greek tendency to retreat into the abstract.[146]

Harnack does not regard this as an historically irreversible process: Athanasius is viewed as correcting the Hellenistic excesses of Origen; Augustine is seen as a reformer of Greek speculative theology in general; and Luther is declared to be the reformer of the post-Augustinian western theological tradition. The role assigned to Luther by Harnack is of particular interest, in that the German reformer is viewed as directing fundamental criticism against speculative and moral conceptions of God, Christ and faith.[147] Harnack clearly saw the science of the history of dogma as performing a comparable task in the modern period. In a letter of March 1879, Harnack stated the object of his programme of historical investigation as the reversal of the trend towards 'philosophical evaporation (*philosophische Verflüchtigung*) of our saviour'.[148] Metaphysics may thus be eliminated by critical historical analysis.

Many criticisms have been directed against the anti-metaphysical 'history of dogma' movement, in terms of both its historical methods and its unstated philosophical presuppositions. For example, the notion of 'Hellenization' can persuasively be argued to be a polemical and anti-metaphysical construct, rather than a valid historical cat-

[144] E. J. Meijering, *Die Hellenisierung des Christentums im Urteil Adolf von Harnack*. Amsterdam: Kampen, 1985, 19–48.

[145] Meijering, *Hellenisierung des Christentums*, 99–102 for an analysis of the main passages.

[146] The best discussion of this point is to be found in Hermann-Josef Schmitz, *Frühkatholizismus bei Adolf von Harnack, Rudolph Sohm und Ernst Käsemann*. Düsseldorf: Patmos Verlag, 1977, 50–93.

[147] See E. P. Meijering, *Der 'ganze' und der 'wahre' Luther: Hintergrund und Bedeutung der Lutherinterpretation Adolf von Harnacks*. Amsterdam: Noord-Hollandsche Uitgevers Maatschappij, 1983, 17. Early concerns about Harnack's representation of Luther are expressed in D. R. Kübel, 'Über die Darstellung des Christentums und der Theologie Luthers in Harnacks Dogmengeschichte III', *Neue kirchliche Zeitschrift* 2 (1891), 13–51.

[148] Karl H. Neufeld, *Adolf von Harnack: Theologie als Suche nach der Kirche*. Paderborn: Verlag Bonifacius-Druckerei, 1977, 109.

egory.[149] Yet our concern here is primarily with the theological outcome of Harnack's anti-metaphysical programme. Granted his concern to avoid a 'philosophical evaporation' of Jesus Christ, does his programme actually ensure such an outcome?

The positive intention of Ritschl's programme (and subsequently that of Harnack) must be appreciated.[150] For Ritschl, there was a serious risk of making Christianity dependent upon what was seen as an outdated metaphysic, which would have been totally out of place within a culture which was embracing a more positivist outlook on such issues. More generally, Ritschl was convinced that the growing concern about the moral dimensions of faith, catalysed by the Kantian philosophy, required a growing emphasis to be placed on the moral impact of Christianity, with a corresponding disinclination to indulge in what was increasingly seen as the irrelevance of metaphysics. Harnack can be seen as supplementing this concern through identifying the historical occasion for the introduction of what he regarded as alien elements within the Christian worldview through the improper absorption of Hellenistic ideas within an essentially Hebraic faith, and thus further identifying the means by which these unwelcome ideas might be eliminated – namely, through the 'history of dogma', understood both as an explanation of the origins of theological metaphysics, and as a means by which it could be criticized.

Harnack's historical analysis implies that such metaphysical explorations were all very well for the metaphysically inclined Greek patristic writers, but have no place in a modern theology from Luther onwards. Yet this viewpoint, readily accepted by a liberal Protestant readership wearied through a surfeit of metaphysical speculation, cannot be sustained historically or theologically. The procedures advocated by Ritschl and Harnack lead to a functional, rather than ontological, approach to Christology – that is to say, to an interpretation of the significance of Jesus Christ in terms of his perceived impact upon the individual believer or the Christian community. Yet this approach merely defers – for it cannot entirely evade – the central question of

[149] Aloys Grillmeier, 'Hellenisierung-Judaisierung des Christentums als Deuteprinzipien der Geschichte des kirchlichen Dogmas', *Scholastik* 33 (1958), 321–55, 528–55; Bernhard Lohse, 'Theorien der Dogmengeschichte im evangelische Raum heute', in W. Löser, K. Lehmann and M. Lutz-Bachmann (eds), *Dogmengeschichte und katholische Theologie*. Würzburg: Echter Verlag, 1985, 97–109.

[150] For a very sympathetic reading of Ritschl at this point, see James Richmond, *Ritschl: A Reappraisal*. London: Collins, 1978, 48–77. For a much more critical reading, see A. E. Garvie, *The Ritschlian Theology, Critical and Constructive: An Exposition and an Estimate*. Edinburgh: T&T Clark, 1899.

Christology: who must Jesus Christ *be* if he is able to have this impact? As John Macquarrie points out in his careful assessment of the Christological issues confronting contemporary theology, a belief that the metaphysical beliefs and terminology which undergird the patristic understanding of Christ are outmoded does *not* lead to the conclusion that all metaphysical understandings of Christ are to be abandoned or declared illegitimate. The question concerns which metaphysics is legitimate for the contemporary philosophical task. 'Metaphysics or ontology is indispensable if one is going to give an account of Jesus Christ that is intellectually well-founded.'[151] Functional statements entail ontological commitments, which demand to be evaluated critically. It is part of the task of a scientific theology to assess which set of ontological commitments is most appropriate, in the light of the evidence available.

The task of determining the metaphysical corollaries of a positive theology is thus an integral aspect of a scientific theology. Yet further caution must be exercised in this matter. It is one thing to argue that metaphysics has a genuine place in the theological task. Yet the risk of excessive theological deference to metaphysics must be acknowledged and respected. To explore this issue, we may turn to consider two significant writers to have commented on this theme – Martin Luther and Eberhard Jüngel.

Martin Luther and Eberhard Jüngel

Luther's 'theology of the cross' is perhaps one of the most theologically acute accounts of the relation of theology and metaphysics.[152] Luther's theology is often incorrectly described as 'anti-metaphysical', which has led to a cluster of unhistorical judgements concerning his theology. Luther's fundamental point, however, is that the biblical narrative of the crucified Christ must be interpreted on the basis of a conceptual framework established by that narrative itself, rather than upon the basis of an imposed alien framework. For Luther, metaphysics is to be seen as appropriate when it represents a considered *a posteriori* response to the biblical narrative; what is unacceptable, according to Luther, is the theological deployment of an *a priori* metaphysical framework which is determined in advance of and independent of that narrative. Luther's hostility towards Aristotelian metaphysics is based on his con-

---

[151] John Macquarrie, *Jesus Christ in Modern Thought*. London: SCM Press, 1990, 344.
[152] For the emergence and distinctive themes of this theology, see Alister E. McGrath, *Luther's Theology of the Cross: Martin Luther's Theological Breakthrough*. Oxford: Blackwell, 1985.

viction that it imposes an alien interpretative framework upon the scriptural narrative, resulting in an inauthentic reading of that narrative.[153]

Historically, it is easy to demonstrate that Luther's particular concern centres upon a cluster of divine attributes, such as the 'glory of God', the 'power of God', and the 'righteousness of God'. If these attributes are defined on the basis of prior metaphysical presuppositions (including an uncritical use of the principle of analogy), the gospel is distorted. How can the revelation of the 'righteousness of God (*iustitia Dei*)' (Romans 1:16–17) be good news for sinful humanity, when – on the basis of an Aristotelian construal of *iustitia* as *reddens uniqueque quod suum est* – this revelation can only imply condemnation?[154] Luther's theological breakthrough (to be dated at some point in 1515) centred upon his realization that it is the narrative of Jesus of Nazareth, centring upon the crucified Christ, which defines the meaning of such terms as the 'righteousness of God'. The 'theologian of the cross' is one who generates a conceptual framework on the basis of the scriptural narrative; a 'theologian of glory' is one who interprets the scriptural narrative on the basis of a predetermined conceptual framework.

Luther thus has no objection to metaphysics, as even a cursory reading of his writings in the period 1515–21 demonstrates; his concern is to allow the scriptural narrative of Jesus of Nazareth, as it is focused upon the crucified Christ, to generate its own framework of conceptualities. Luther's assertion of the autonomy of the scriptural narrative does not involve the rejection of metaphysics; it merely denies to any preconceived metaphysics the right to impose its interpretative framework upon Scripture. For Luther, conceptualities such as 'the righteousness of God' are defined by the scriptural narrative.[155] Even 'God' is defined in this manner, as may be seen from Luther's celebrated reference to the 'crucified and hidden God (*Deus crucifixus et absconditus*)'. Aristotle's definition of 'God'[156] has, according to Luther, no direct bearing upon the interpretation of Scripture, which identified a somewhat different God as its chief agent. It is possible to regard Luther's

---

[153] Adolar Zumkeller, 'Die Augustinertheologen Simon Fidati von Cascia und Hugolin von Orvieto und Martin Luthers Kritik an Aristoteles', *Archiv für Reformationsgeschichte* 54 (1963), 13–37.

[154] On which see Alister E. McGrath, '*Mira et Nova Diffinitio Iustitiae*. Luther and Scholastic Doctrines of Justification', *Archiv für Reformationsgeschichte* 74 (1983), 37–60.

[155] For Luther's critique of Aristotle, see McGrath, *Luther's Theology of the Cross*, 136–41.

[156] On which see David W. Hamlyn, 'Aristotle's God', in G. J. Hughes (ed.), *The Philosophical Assessment of Theology*. Washington, DC: Georgetown University Press, 1987, 15–33.

axiom '*crux sola nostra theologia*'[157] as a sophisticated statement of the *sola scriptura* principle, which asserts the priority of a historically based narrative – rather than *a priori* concepts of divinity – in theological reflection. Metaphysical reflection follows engagement with the biblical narrative, and can neither precede nor predetermine this engagement.

Luther's concern to allow the Christian notion of God to be determined biblically, rather than through precommitment to metaphysical concepts, has been echoed in many works of twentieth-century theology. Karl Barth's emphasis on revelation can be construed as the assertion of the priority of God's act of self-revelation over any existing human understandings of how revelation may take place, what form it should take, or what information it should convey. Jürgen Moltmann's *Crucified God* – whose title is taken directly from Luther's writings – can be seen as a principled attempt to determine the concept of God which arises from allowing the cross of Christ to be the foundation and criterion of Christian theology.[158] Yet it is in the works of Eberhard Jüngel's *Gott als Geheimnis der Welt* that we find the most sustained engagement with the place of metaphysics in a Christian theology.

Jüngel's difficult work first appeared in 1976, and is deeply embedded in the intellectual concerns and engagements of that time. Jüngel's theological programme relates fundamentally to the question of how it is possible to speak of God in a responsible manner in a world in which people live *etsi Deus non daretur* ('as if God were not given').[159] In an age still influenced by the characteristic Enlightenment anthropocentrism (which occasionally verges on a Feuerbachian-legitimated anthropotheism), Jüngel may be regarded as having developed a theological programme whose chief concern is to distinguish between God and humanity.

Like Moltmann, Jüngel stresses that God identifies himself with the crucified Christ,[160] so that faith recognizes the crucified human being

---

[157] *WA* 5.176.32–3.

[158] For some reflection on the relation of Moltmann to Luther, see Pierre Böhler, *Kreuz und Eschatologie: Eine Auseinandersetzung mit der politischen Theologie, im Anschluss an Luthers Theologia Crucis.* Tübingen: Mohr, 1981.

[159] This phrase is used regularly in the writings of Dietrich Bonhoeffer, and is to be traced back to the legal theorist Hugo Grotius, who argued for the validity of human laws *etsi Deus non daretus* – thus decoupling human law from any necessary foundation in the will of God. See Heimo Hoffmeister, '"Etsi Deus non daretur": Zum Verhaltnis von Philosophie und Theologie', *Neue Zeitschrift für Systematische Theologie und Religionsphilosophie* 21 (1979), 272–85. The Latin phrase is puzzling; perhaps it ought to have been *acsi Deus non daretur*.

[160] Eberhard Jüngel, 'Das Sein Jesu Christi als Ereignis der Versöhnung Gottes mit einer gottlosen Welt: Die Hingabe der Gekreuzigten', *Evangelische Theologie* 38 (1978), 510–17.

Jesus of Nazareth as identical to God. This insight is of central importance in *Gott als Geheimnis der Welt*, in which Jüngel addresses the question of how it is meaningful to speak of God in a world from which he has been displaced. Like Moltmann, Jüngel firmly anchors the Christian understanding of God – which he sharply distinguishes from that of theism – in the crucified Christ:[161]

> The Christian tradition of speaking (*die christliche Sprachüberlieferung*) insists that we *must be told* what we are to *think* of the word 'God'. It is thus presupposed that only the God who speaks can himself finally tell us what we are to understand by the word 'God'. Theology expresses this subject area under the category of revelation . . . Therefore, in our attempt to think of God as the one who is communicated and expressed in the human being Jesus, we must remember that, in fact, this human being was *crucified*, that he was killed in the name of the law of God. The one who was crucified is thus precisely the concrete definition (*Realdefinition*) of what is meant by the word 'God', for responsible Christian use of the word. Christianity is thus fundamentally a 'theology of the one who was crucified (*Theologie der Gekreuzigten*)'.

The basis of all heresy, according to Jüngel, is to be located in a refusal or reluctance to recognize God in Jesus Christ.[162]

Jüngel then moves on to make the cross the centre of the trinitarian history of God.[163] A proper interpretation of the crucifixion of Christ leads decisively away from the undifferentiated monotheism of classical theism, towards the distinctively and authentically *Christian* doctrine of the Trinity. The cross reveals a differentiation between Father and Son. (A similar point had been made by Moltmann, who disentangles the different manners in which Father and Son experience suffering, and draws out their trinitarian implications.) The resurrection, however, affirms the unity of Father and Son, God and Jesus. How is this to be interpreted? Jüngel maps out a road which leads to the doctrine of the Trinity with his declaration that 'the knowledge of the identification of God with Jesus necessitates the distinction of God from God'.[164] The New Testament itself makes such a distinction, when it distinguishes

---

[161] Eberhard Jüngel, *Gott als Geheimnis der Welt: Zur Begründung der Theologie des Gekreuzigten im Streit zwischen Theismus und Atheismus*, 4th edn. Tübingen: Mohr, 1982, 14–15.

[162] Eberhard Jüngel, 'Thesen zur Grundlegung der Christologie', in *Unterwegs zur Sache: Theologsiche Bemerkungen*. Munich: Kaiser Verlag, 1972, 274–95, 283: 'Die Ursache aller Häresien ist die Unfähigkeit (die Unlust), Gott in Jesus Christus ausreden zu lassen.'

[163] For reflection, see Claude Royon, *Dieu, l'homme et la croix: Stanislas Breton et Eberhard Jüngel*. Paris: Éditions du Cerf, 1998; Paul J. DeHart, *Beyond the Necessary God: Trinitarian Faith and Philosophy in the Thought of Eberhard Jüngel*. Atlanta, GA: Scholars Press, 1999.

[164] Jüngel, 'Thesen zur Grundlegung der Christologie', 293.

God the Son (the crucified Jesus) from God the Father (who raised him from the dead).[165]

This 'self-differentiation' (*Selbstdifferenzierung* or *Selbstunterscheidung*) within God, recognized on the basis of the relation between the resurrection and crucifixion of Christ, constitutes the basis of the doctrine of the Trinity. It also forms the basis of the Christian critique of both monotheism and metaphysical theism, as well as the types of atheism which correspond to these forms of theism.[166] Jüngel develops his insights in a vigorously polemical manner, demonstrating their destructive impact upon the whole Cartesian theological enterprise upon which the Enlightenment was ultimately grounded. Yet Jüngel is not primarily concerned about the development of a theological metaphysic; indeed, his own reflections on the doctrine of the Trinity constitute precisely such a metaphysical extension of theology. His concern is that a specific strand of metaphysics – which he traces back to Descartes – makes certain imperialistic claims which, if conceded, lead to the erosion of an authentically Christian conception of God.[167] Thus Jüngel notes how J. G. Fichte, Ludwig Feuerbach and Friedrich Nietzsche derive their understanding of God (and hence, it may also be pointed out, their antithetically conceived atheisms) from the metaphysical tradition, not from the Christian tradition.[168] Making much the same point, Alasdair MacIntyre remarks that 'the God in whom the nineteenth and twentieth centuries came to disbelieve had been invented only in the seventeenth century'.[169] In particular, Jüngel stresses the negative consequences of the separation of the essence and existence of God, which he takes to be the inevitable outcome of such a metaphysically preconceived and predetermined approach to the question of God. Thus for Feuerbach, the motivation for 'the preservation of the metaphysically defined divine (*der Wahrung des metaphysisch bestimmten Göttlichen*)' lies in its function as the basis of his divinization of humanity.[170] The category of the divine remains; it has, however, been transposed from what was mistakenly termed 'God' to humanity itself.

---

[165] Jüngel, 'Thesen zur Grundlegung der Christologie', 293.

[166] Jüngel, 'Thesen zur Grundlegung der Christologie', 294.

[167] Jüngel, *Gott als Geheimnis der Welt*, 146–67. For a fuller historical analysis of this, see Michael J. Buckley, *At the Origins of Modern Atheism*. New Haven, CT: Yale University Press, 1987. While conceding the importance of Descartes, Buckley traces the origins of this metaphysical autonomy to the later Middle Ages.

[168] Jüngel, *Gott als Geheimnis der Welt*, 200.

[169] Alasdair MacIntyre and Paul Ricoeur, *The Religious Significance of Atheism*. New York: Columbia University Press, 1969, 14.

[170] Jüngel, *Gott als Geheimnis der Welt*, 201.

Yet Jüngel has another distinctive contribution to make to the issue of metaphysics in theology. Even in his earlier writings, Jüngel brings together a powerful combination of a traditional Lutheran approach to the doctrine of justification, a Christocentric understanding of theology that owes much to Karl Barth, and the German hermeneutical school of Ernst Fuchs and Gerhard Ebeling, to yield an ontology which is determined by the event of the word.[171] Following Fuchs, Jüngel locates the point of divine determination of reality in the speech-event (*Sprachereignis*) which constitutes an 'interruptive newness' by which God restores and renews the world. It is through the word that God creates and sustains the world on the one hand, and enters into it in the incarnation and atonement. A theological ontology is thus determined by the divine word.

The concerns expressed here can easily be accommodated with a scientific theology, especially through insisting that any associated metaphysics is understood to be *a posteriori*, generated and governed by the act of revelation (as here understood, for example, as narrative or word-event). The notion that theology should be submissive to a metaphysics which has been arrived at in advance, determined on *a priori* grounds, is to be rejected as inauthentic. The plausibility of the metaphysical entities derived from the envisaged process of analysis will be a matter for discussion; the process of arriving at such metaphysical conclusions, however, is entirely legitimate.

The theological affirmation of metaphysics

We have considered some serious theological objections to the involvement of metaphysics in theological discourse. Many will feel sympathy with the concerns articulated by the many theological critics of metaphysics. Joseph O'Leary's plea to adopt a theological 'counter-metaphysical reading which frees faith from the morose, introspective provincialism characteristic of the metaphysical theology which is still dominant'[172] will resonate with many who are anxious concerning the erosion of confidence in metaphysics in general, and especially the specific form of metaphysics which seems to attend the Christological formulations of the patristic era.[173] O'Leary has no interest in abandoning

---

[171] For a critical discussion of this point, see Roland Spjuth, 'Redemption without Actuality: A Critical Interrelation between Eberhard Jüngel's and John Milbank's Ontological Endeavours', *Modern Theology* 14 (1998), 505–22, especially 506–9.

[172] Joseph Stephen O'Leary, *Questioning Back: The Overcoming of Metaphysics in Christian Tradition*. Chicago: Winston Press, 1985, 225.

[173] On which see O'Leary, *Questioning Back: The Overcoming of Metaphysics in Christian Tradition*, 73–87, 212–21.

the church's dogmatic concerns, or even rejecting the dogmatic tradition; rather, he pleads for 'a new deconstructive relationship to it, wherein it is reinterpreted as the history of the Church's witness to its faith rather than the building up of a dogmatic system'.[174] Yet even a modest natural theology is declared to be 'the tip of the metaphysical iceberg' which can only be overcome 'through a critique of the metaphysical thought-forms which inevitably produce it'.[175]

Yet it is far from being as simple as O'Leary and others suggest. Metaphysics can only be eliminated from Christology – to deal merely with this one area of theology – by an absolute prior refusal to entertain metaphysical possibilities. Any theology which chooses to see itself as dealing with a self-revealing God, rather than with investigating human religiosity and its social manifestations, is already committed to an inchoate metaphysics. Jüngel rightly protests against allowing any metaphysically predetermined notions of divinity to shape the norms of Christian language and reflection about God. Yet the moment the notion of a self-revealing God is conceded, the metaphysical agenda has been significantly advanced. Jüngel's approach demands that we speak of the metaphysical implications of divine self-revelation, rather than its presuppositions, treating the metaphysical enterprise as possessing a fundamentally *a posteriori* character. If there is any value in John Milbank's protests against metaphysics, this lies in his concerns about the subversive consequences of permitting theological reflection to be predicated on *a priori* metaphysical notions – such as a preconceived idea of God.

A scientific character issues no embargo against metaphysical concepts; it merely demands that such concepts be warranted by evidence, rather than presupposed by convention. Metaphysical entities ultimately lie beyond such proofs as empirical demonstration. A scientific theology thus conjectures how things are – yet not in a fanciful or purely speculative manner. Metaphysical reflection is subject to evidential control by observation – by demanding warrant for its metaphysical postulates. Yet such metaphysical entities cannot be ruled in or ruled out in advance; they are to be postulated and warranted by the available evidence.

It may suit O'Leary's limited purposes to ban metaphysical formula-

[174] O'Leary, *Questioning Back: The Overcoming of Metaphysics in Christian Tradition*, 76.
[175] O'Leary, *Questioning Back: The Overcoming of Metaphysics in Christian Tradition*, 105. His analysis here is set within the context of a discussion of Karl Barth's critique of natural theology.

tions from theological reflection. But what happens if they arise naturally? What happens if a Newton postulates a metaphysical force of 'gravity', which cannot be seen, and is known only through its effects?[176] Or if a Darwin, observing patterns in the natural world, postulates a metaphysical process called 'natural selection', which cannot be seen, and is known only by its effects?[177] Or if a Thompson postulates an unobservable metaphysical entity called an 'electron', which cannot be seen, yet whose existence appears to be warranted by a series of electrodynamic experiments? Or if the New Testament postulates an unobservable metaphysical entity called 'God', who cannot be seen, but whose characteristics are disclosed in the history of Jesus of Nazareth? 'God is whoever raised Jesus from the dead, having before raised Israel from Egypt.'[178]

The only manner in which Christian theology can excuse itself from an engagement with metaphysical questions is by declaring itself to be concerned only with what is observable of the church as an empirical and social entity, including those approaches to theology which regard the church as a sociolinguistic community. The moment the question of God is acknowledged to be legitimate, the clarification of metaphysical options becomes imperative.

The theological evasion of metaphysics is perhaps most evident in Christological debates. There has been no shortage of those urging the elimination of such metaphysical categories as static and outdated, insisting instead on an ontological atheism.[179] A functional approach to Christology is seen by some as legitimating a focus on what Jesus Christ can be said to have done or achieved, without entailing any awkward metaphysical questions. From a historical perspective, this distinction involves contrasting an essentially Jewish approach to the identity of Christ (which readily attributed certain specific functions to him) and a Greek approach (which sought to define his identity using categories of

---

[176] In fact, of course, Newton was wary of positing any such metaphysical entity, preferring to merely describe, in kinematic terms, an observed regularity of behaviour. But this was merely a postponement of the metaphysical discussion of the nature of the posited force of 'gravity'.

[177] L. T. Evans, 'Darwin's Use of the Analogy between Artificial and Natural Selection', *Journal of the History of Biology* 17 (1984), 113–40.

[178] Robert W. Jenson, *Systematic Theology*, 2 vols. New York: Oxford University Press, 1997–9, vol. 1, 63.

[179] This is the position of the Canadian philosopher Leslie Dewart. See his *The Future of Belief: Theism in a World Come of Age*. London: Burns & Oates, 1967; idem, *The Foundations of Belief*. London: Burns & Oates, 1969. For a useful survey of his views, see Desmond Connell, 'Professor Dewart and Dogmatic Development', *Irish Theological Quarterly* 34 (1967), 309–28; 35 (1968), 33–57, 117–40.

divinity and being borrowed, rather uncritically, from Hellenistic philosophy). Yet as Richard Bauckham has shown, on the basis of a detailed examination of critical passages, this simple model really will not do.[180]

> The dominance of the distinction between 'functional' and 'ontic' Christology has made it seem unproblematic to say that for early Christology Jesus exercises the 'functions' of Lordship without being regarded as 'ontologically' divine. In fact, such a distinction is highly problematic from the point of view of early Jewish monotheism, for in this understanding of the unique divine identity, the unique sovereignty of God was not a mere 'function' which God could delegate to someone else. It was one of the key identifying characteristics of the unique divine identity, which distinguishes the one God from all other reality.

For Bauckham, the New Testament 'identifies Jesus as intrinsic to who God is'.[181] The New Testament may not make significant use of the language of metaphysics; it nevertheless prepared the ground for those who realized that such categories would be needed to contain the new wine of the gospel proclamation. This naturally leads to the view that the New Testament contains the fundamental themes and pointers, in embryonic form, which would eventually lead to the Nicene theology of the fourth century. This theology thus brings to full and conscious articulation the somewhat more tentative metaphysical hints of the New Testament, developing – not distorting – them in doing so.[182]

Yet such an evolutionary view of the development of doctrine only requires that the validity of the theological use of metaphysical categories should be conceded; it does not stipulate which specific categories are appropriate or necessary. The considerations we have here noted certainly point to the propriety of conceptualizing the significance of Christ using the categories of metaphysics; nevertheless, it could be argued with some persuasiveness that the decision to adopt the specific metaphysical categories associated with the Nicene theology was linked with a specific social and historical location.[183] This would leave the church in subsequent eras free to choose which metaphysical categories

---

[180] Richard Bauckham, *God Crucified: Monotheism and Christology in the New Testament*. Grand Rapids, MI: Eerdmans, 1998, 41.

[181] Bauckham, *God Crucified*, 42.

[182] The basic issues and some of the concerns they raise are set out fully in Winfried Schulz, *Dogmenentwicklung als Problem der Geschichtlichkeit der Wahrheitserkenntnis. Eine erkenntnis-theoretisch-theologische Studie zum Problemkreis der Dogmenentwicklung*. Roma: Libreria Editrice dell'Università Gregoriana, 1969.

[183] Avery Dulles, *The Survival of Dogma: Faith, Authority and Dogma in a Changing World*. New York: Crossroad, 1982.

were best adapted to the contingencies of their periods, rather than limiting them to those definitively set out at Nicea. Karl Rahner, for example, argued for the recognition of corrective replacements of historically conditioned theological formulations, and in his later writings pressed for the translation of traditional formulae into contemporary thought forms and modes of expression.[184]

A commitment to the metaphysical dimensions of the Christian faith – for example, in giving an account of the significance of Jesus Christ – can thus be seen to have metaphysical implications – but not necessarily that these should be set out in the terms of the Greek philosophical tradition of the third and fourth centuries. The question of the metaphysical languages and conceptualities best adapted for the specifics of the Christian revelation must be left open. In this sense, Chalcedon initiated an important discussion, offering its definitive response using the *standortsgebunden* metaphysical concepts at its disposal. But we who do not share their historical location are not bound to develop our Christology using their historically located categories. Chalcedon demands that we develop its fundamental insights in terms of the best metaphysical categories at our disposal for this purpose. In this sense, Chalcedon marks the beginning, not the end, of Christological reflection, as it entrusts to us the fundamental parameters which must govern our reflections, while inviting us to explore how its insights might be stated afresh in our own specific historical location.

It is not my intention to address this issue of the *Standortsgebundenheit* of metaphysical categories at this point; my concern has been merely to indicate that there is an ongoing legitimate place for metaphysics in Christian theology, where the nature and style of that metaphysic is determined *a posteriori*, in the light of the specific nature and characteristics of the gospel proclamation. While some will hold this to represent the recognition of a chastened metaphysics, I would regard it as the recognition of a *responsible* metaphysics, grounded in and determined by an engagement with reality, rather than predetermined in advance, and shaped by the 'vision of God', which is the *Kern und Stern* of a scientific theology. A scientific theology does not endorse a metaphysically inflationary account of reality, but insists that whatever account of reality we offer must represent a proper response to our encounter with reality, and the categories which that reality itself

---

[184] Karl Rahner, 'Zur Frage der Dogmenentwicklung', in *Schriften zur Theologie*, vol. 1. Einsiedeln: Benziger Verlag, 1954, 49–90; idem, 'Überlegungen zur Dogmenentwicklung', in *Schriften zur Theologie*, vol. 4. Einsiedeln: Benziger Verlag, 1960, 11–50.

imposes upon us as we seek to represent and explain it. Metaphysics is not the precondition of any engagement with the world, but its legitimate inferred consequence.

Karl Barth suggested that we must speak of the 'fundamentally non-foundational character of the dogmatic method (*das grundsätzlich Ungründsatzliche der dogmatischen Methode*)', recognizing that theology ensues from a revelation which both 'presupposes and proves itself by the power of its contents'. Neither a specific metaphysic nor epistemology is presupposed by such an approach. Theology is a response to its distinctive object, whose character cannot be determined in advance of an engagement with that object. Both the natural sciences and a scientific theology recognize the impossibility of separating out the way in which knowledge arises from the actual knowledge that ensues. But this does not in any way preclude a specific metaphysic or epistemology from arising as a consequence of an engagement with reality. We must keep an open mind as to what the intellectual consequences of revelation might be.

So what are those consequences? Having demonstrated that a scientific theological method may indeed lead to legitimate metaphysical conclusions, we have finally completed the groundwork for its application. This three-volume prolegomenon to a future scientific dogmatics is now complete; it remains now to apply it, and develop that scientific dogmatics. At this point, therefore, our discussion of the possibility and legitimacy of what we have styled 'a scientific theology' must end. Yet in another sense, it has only begun.

Conclusion: Anticipating a Scientific Dogmatics

'Every book is the wreck of a perfect idea' (Iris Murdoch).[1] Bringing this work to an end is both a relief and a matter of some frustration. The process of unfolding what seemed like a bright idea back in 1976 has proved to be far more difficult than I had imagined, and its execution less satisfactory than I had hoped. Initially, it seemed to me that the vast spaciousness afforded by these three volumes would be more than adequate to deal with the issues I knew had to be addressed in articulating a coherent and plausible vision of 'a scientific theology'. My frustration is partly due to the obvious fact that this has turned out to be signally less than adequate for my purposes. What I had hoped might be extensive discussions of central methodological questions have ended up being rather shallow; what I had hoped to be close readings of seminal texts seem to have turned out to be little more than superficial engagements.[2]

A further cause of frustration is my realization that, in bringing this work to its conclusion, I have certainly not achieved real closure on the issues which it aimed to address. As far as I can see, what I have managed to do is chart a potentially interesting and productive theological trajectory, identifying navigable channels for one of Otto von Neurath's interesting conceptual boats, and avoiding what are now recognized to be philosophical and theological dead ends (although earlier generations

---

[1] Iris Murdoch, *The Black Prince*. London: Vintage, 1999, 172.
[2] My personal research habits probably compound this problem. Over the years, I have written a number of unpublished 'working papers in scientific theology', which represent various stages in my thinking on how a scientific theology might be constructed, and include close readings of central texts and reflections on issues of method.

entertained what can now be seen as unrealistically high hopes concerning them). Yet it is one thing to plot a trajectory, and another to traverse it and explore where it leads – for example, in terms of the development of a coherent systematic theology. This latter task has not even been attempted, even if defending its *possibility* has been the ultimate goal of this work.

As the Princeton ethical philosopher Jeffrey Stout once commented, writing on method is a bit like clearing your throat before beginning a lecture. You can only go on for so long before the audience starts to get a little restless. These three volumes on the theme of a 'scientific theology' will have made excessive demands upon their readers' patience. The work to date has focused on issues of *theological method* – more precisely, on the intellectual viability of a specific approach to Christian theology – yet it has not yet initiated or applied the approach in question. While there has been some modest degree of interaction with a few issues of Christian doctrine – most notably, the doctrine of creation – the entire work to date has been dominated by concerns relating to theological method, rather than the traditional agenda of Christian dogmatics. After more than 400,000 words of rather dense English prose, I have still to engage with the great themes of Christian doctrine as these are traditionally understood.

At one level, I suspect that it is not really necessary for me to apologize to my readers for this shortcoming. The enterprise of Christian theology is like civilization itself, characterized by Arnold Toynbee as 'a movement and not a condition, a voyage and not a harbour'. In that theology is, when rightly understood, a dynamic and living process of intellectual celebration and exploration, rather than a static and wooden repetition of yesterday's certainties (so often shown to be yesterday's idiosyncrasies), it is essential to deal with the issue of how theology learns and validates its ideas. Systematic theology simply cannot be done without a preliminary engagement with issues of method. Before dealing with the classic themes of Christian dogmatics, it is thus entirely proper to reassure the intended audience of the intellectual viability of Christian theology as a serious participant in the long human search for wisdom and enlightenment.

The distinctive feature of this work has been its critical yet positive use of the natural sciences as both comparator and helpmate for the theological task, seen against the backdrop of the intellectual engagement with reality as a whole. While this work has trodden a delicate and at times somewhat fuzzy line between a treatise on the relation of Christian theology and the natural sciences and a full-blown work on theological methodology, there is a third way in which these three volumes may be read – perhaps the most significant, even if it has not been uppermost in the author's mind as he wrote them – namely, as an apologia for the entire theological enterprise itself. Christian theology is here conceived and presented as a legitimate intellectual discipline, with its own sense of identity and purpose, linked with an appreciation of its own limitations and distinctive emphases within the human quest for wisdom as a whole. A unitary understanding of reality, such as that mandated by a Christian doctrine of creation, thus does not demand that each human intellectual discipline should adopt identical methods for their tasks, but that they should accommodate themselves to the distinctive natures of those aspects of reality which they attempt to represent and depict.

The approach to Christian theology which is mapped out in these pages is innovative and, I believe, constructive, with genuine potential for the task of developing a systematic theology. It is inevitable that this exploration should primarily concern itself with the question of how theology is to be done, rather than with the actual outcome of that activity. The 'scientific theology' project has therefore concerned issues of method rather than of substance, and it is inevitable that this will leave many readers dissatisfied. What, they might reasonably ask, are the implications of adopting the working methods and assumptions of the natural sciences as the *ancilla theologiae* for the doctrine of the Trinity? Or the person of Christ? The development of a systematic theology on the basis of the approach charted in these volumes remains a future task, which the present work cannot be considered to have in any way achieved.

It would be manifestly unfair to those readers who have followed my arguments thus far to leave them stranded on this methodological sandbank, rather than try to navigate into the harbour which lies beyond. Having explored the potential of a specific approach to theology, it is entirely reasonable to demand that I should go on and explore the application of that approach myself, rather than leave others to guess where this approach might lead us.

So, patient reader, I must leave you for a while. I trust, however, that we shall meet again soon.

Alister McGrath
Oxford, December 2002

Bibliography

ABRAHAM, WILLIAM J., *Divine Revelation and the Limits of Historical Criticism*. Oxford: Oxford University Press, 1982.

ACHINSTEIN, PETER, 'Scientific Discovery and Maxwell's Kinetic Theory', *Philosophy of Science* 54 (1987), 409–34.

ADAM, GOTTFRIED, *Der Streit die Prädestination im ausgehenden 16. Jahrhundert: Eine Untersuchung zu den Entwürfen von Samuel Huber und Aegidius Hunnius*. Neukirchen: Neukirchener Verlag, 1970.

ADAMS, MARILYN MCCORD, 'Horrendous Evils and the Goodness of God', in Marilyn McCord Adams and Robert Merrihew Adams (eds), *The Problem of Evil*. Oxford: Oxford University Press, 1990, 209–21.

AESCHLIMAN, MICHAEL D., *The Restitution of Man: C. S. Lewis and the Case against Scientism*. Grand Rapids, MI: Eerdmans, 1998.

ALBERIGO, GIUSEPPE, *I Vescovi Italiani al Concilio di Trento (1545–1547)*. Florence: Sansoni, 1959.

ALFORD, JOHN A., 'Jesus the Jouster: The Christ-Knight and Medieval Theories of Atonement in Piers Plowman and the "Round Table" Sermons', *Yearbook of Langland Studies* 10 (1996), 129–43.

ALSTON, WILLIAM P., 'Functionalism and Theological Language', *American Philosophical Quarterly* 22 (1985), 221–30.

ALTHAUS, PAUL, 'Offenbarung als Geschichte und Glaube', *Theologische Literaturzeitung* 87 (1962), 321–80.

ANDERSON, MARGARET J., *Carl Linnaeus: Father of Classification*. Springfield, NJ: Enslow, 1997.

APEL, KARL-OTTO, *Die Erklären-Verstehen Kontroverse in transzendental-pragmatischer Sicht*. Frankfurt am Main: Suhrkamp, 1979.

——, 'The Erklären-Verstehen Controversy in the Philosophy of the Natural and Human Sciences', in G. Floistad (ed.), *Contemporary Philosophy: A New Survey*. The Hague: Nijhof, 1982, 19–49.

ARIEW, ROGER, 'The Duhem Thesis', *British Journal for the Philosophy of Science* 35 (1984), 313–25.

ASCH, RONALD G., *The Thirty Years War: The Holy Roman Empire and Europe, 1618–1648*. New York: St Martin's Press, 1997.

ASHLEY, KATHLEEN M., 'The Guiler Beguiled: Christ and Satan as Theological Tricksters in Medieval Religious Literature', *Criticism* 24 (1982), 126–37.

ASHWORTH, E. J., 'Analogical Concepts: The Fourteenth-Century Background to Cajetan', *Dialogue* 31 (1992), 399–413.

——, 'Signification and Modes of Signifying in Thirteenth-Century Logic: A Preface to Aquinas on Analogy', *Medieval Philosophy and Theology* 1 (1991), 39–67.

AUBENQUE, PIERRE, *Le problème de l'être chez Aristote: essai sur la problèmatique aristotélicienne*. Paris: Presses Universitaires de France, 1977.

AUERBACH, ERICH, *Dante als Dichter der irdischen Welt*. Berlin: Walter de Gruyter, 1929.

——, 'Figura', in *Gesammelte Aufsätze zur romanischen Philologie*. Bern: Francke, 1998, 55–92.

——, *Mimesis: Dargestelle Wirklichkeit in der abendländischen Literatur*, 10th edn. Tübingen: Francke Verlag, 2001.

AYER, A. J., *Language, Truth and Logic*, 2nd edn. London: Victor Gollancz, 1946.

AYRES, LEWIS, 'Representation, Theology and Faith', *Modern Theology* 11 (1995), 23–46.

BACKHAUS, GUNTHER, *Kerygma und Mythos bei David Friedrich Strauss und Rudolf Bultmann*. Hamburg-Bergstedt: Herbert Reich Evangelischer Verlag, 1956.

BACON, FRANCIS, *Novum organum scientiarum*. London: John Bill, 1620.

BALENTINE, SAMUEL E., *The Hidden God: The Hiding of the Face of God in the Old Testament*. Oxford: Oxford University Press, 1983.

BANDT, HELLMUT, *Luthers Lehre vom verborgenen Gott: Eine Unter-*

suchung zu dem offenbarungsgeschichtlichen Ansatz seiner Theologie. Berlin: Evangelische Verlagsanstalt, 1958.

BANNER, MICHAEL C., *The Justification of Science and the Rationality of Religious Belief.* Oxford and New York: Oxford University Press, 1990.

BARR, JAMES, 'Revelation through History in the Old Testament and in Modern Theology', *Interpretation* 17 (1963), 193–205.

BARTH, KARL, 'Schicksal und Idee in Theologie', in *Theologische Frage und Antworten.* Zurich: Evangelischer Verlag, 1957, 54–92.

BAUCKHAM, RICHARD, *God Crucified: Monotheism and Christology in the New Testament.* Grand Rapids, MI: Eerdmans, 1998.

BAUER, WALTER, *Rechtgläubigkeit und Ketzerei im ältesten Christentum.* Tübingen: Mohr, 1934.

BEARDSLEY, MONROE, *Practical Logic.* New York: Prentice-Hall, 1950.

BEER, GILLIAN, ' "The Face of Nature": Anthropomorphic Elements in the Language of *The Origin of Species*', in L. J. Jordanoca (ed.), *Languages of Nature.* New Brunswick, NJ: Rutgers University Press, 1986, 207–43.

BEINTKER, MICHAEL, *Die Dialektik in der 'dialektischen Theologie' Karl Barths.* Munich: Kaiser Verlag, 1987.

BELL, CLIVE, *Art.* London: Chatto and Windus, 1914.

BENIN, STEPHEN D., *The Footprints of God: Divine Accommodation in Jewish and Christian Thought.* Albany: State University of New York Press, 1993.

BENJAMINS, H. S., 'Noah, the Ark and the Flood in Early Christianity: The Ship of the Church in the Making', in Florentino García Martínez and Gerard P. Luttikhuizen (eds), *Interpretations of the Flood.* Leiden: Brill, 1998, 134–49.

BEN-MENAHEM, YEMIMA, 'Struggling with Causality: Schrödinger's Case', *Studies in History and Philosophy of Science* 23 (1989), 147–80.

BENNETT, JONATHAN, *Locke, Berkeley, Hume: Central Themes.* Oxford: Oxford University Press, 1977.

BERCOVITCH, SACVAN, 'The Problem of Ideology in American Literary History', *Critical Inquiry* 12 (1986), 631–53.

BERNSTEIN, RICHARD J., 'Judging: The Actor and the Spectator', in *Philosophical Profiles: Essays in a Pragmatic Mode.* Philadelphia: University of Pennsylvania Press, 1986, 221–38.

BERTI, ENRICO, 'L'analogia in Aristotele. Interpretazioni recenti e possibili sviluppi', in Enrico Berti and Giuseppe Casetta (eds), *Origini e sviluppi dell'analogia da Parmenide a S. Tommaso*. Roma: Edizioni Vallombrosa, 1987, 94–115.

BETZ, HANS DIETER, 'Orthodoxy and Heresy in Primitive Christianity: Some Critical Remarks on Georg Strecker's Republication of Walter Bauer's *Rechtgläubigkeit und Ketzerei im ältesten Christentum*', *Interpretation* 19 (1965), 299–311.

BEUMER, JOHANNES, *Theologie als Glaubensverständnis*. Würzburg: Echter-Verlag, 1953.

——, 'Die Regula Fidei Catholicae des Ph. N. Chrisman, O.F.M. und ihre Kritik durch J. Kleutgen, S.J.', *Franziskanische Studien* 46 (1964), 321–34.

BHASKAR, ROY, *A Realist Theory of Science*, 2nd edn. London: Verso, 1997.

——, *The Possibility of Naturalism: A Philosophical Critique of the Contemporary Human Sciences*, 3rd edn. London: Routledge, 1998.

BIELER, MARTIN, 'Karl Barths Auseinandersetzung mit der *analogia entis* und der Anfang der Theologie', *Catholica* 40 (1986), 229–45.

BIENERT, WOLFGANG A., 'Das vornicaenische ὁμοούσιος als Ausdruck der Rechtgläubigkeit', *Zeitschrift für Kirchengeschichte* 90 (1979), 5–29.

——, 'Zur Logos-Christologie des Athanasius von Alexandrien in *contra gentes* und *de incarnatione*', in E. A. Livingstone (ed.), *Papers presented to the Tenth International Conference on Patristic Studies*. Louvain: Peeters, 1989, 402–19.

——, 'Die Funktion des Dogmas für den christlichen Glauben', in *Vom Finden und Verkünden der Wahrheit in der Kirche. Beiträge zur theologischen Erkenntnislehre*. Freiburg and Basel: Herder, 1993, 92–115.

BIRKNER, H. J., 'Natürliche Theologie und Offenbarungstheologie: Ein theologiegeschichtlicher Überblick', *Neue Zeitschrift für systematische Theologie und Religionsphilosophie* 3 (1961), 279–95.

BLUM, GEORG GÜNTER, *Tradition und Sukzession: Studien zum Normbegriff des Apostolischen von Paulus bis Irenaeus*. Berlin: Lutherisches Verlagshaus, 1963.

BOBLITZ, HARTMUT, 'Die Allegorese der Arche Noahs in der frühen Bibelauslegung', *Frühmittelalterliche Studien* 6 (1972), 159–70.

BOCKMUEHL, M. N. A., *Revelation and Mystery*. Tübingen: Mohr, 1990.

BOHM, DAVID, 'A Suggested Interpretation of the Quantum Theory in Terms of "Hidden" Variables', *Physical Review* 85 (1952), 166–93.

BOHM, DAVID, AND BASIL J. HILEY, *The Undivided Universe: An Ontological Interpretation of Quantum Theory.* London and New York: Routledge, 1993.

BOHR, NIELS, *Niels Bohr: Collected Works*, ed. Leon Rosenfield and Erik Rudiger, 6 vols. Amsterdam: North Holland, 1972–85.

BORNERT, RENÉ, *La réforme protestante du culte à Strasbourg au XVIe siècle (1523–1598): approche sociologique et interprétation théologique.* Leiden: Brill, 1981.

BOULNOIS, OLIVIER, 'Duns Scot, théoricien de l'analogie de l'être', in Ludger Honnefelder, Rega Wood and Mechthild Dreye (eds), *John Duns Scotus: Metaphysics and Ethics.* Leiden: Brill, 1996, 293–315.

BOWKER, JOHN, *The Religious Imagination and the Sense of God.* Oxford: Clarendon, 1978.

BOYD, R., 'Realism, Underdetermination, and a Causal Theory of Evidence', *Nous* 7 (1973), 1–12.

BRANDON, ROBERT, AND SCOTT CARSON, 'The Indeterministic Character of Evolutionary Theory', *Philosophy of Science* 63 (1996), 315–37.

BREDELLA, LOTHAR, *Das Verstehen literarischer Texte.* Stuttgart: Kohlhammer, 1980.

——, *Literarisches und interkulturelles Verstehen.* Tübingen: Gunter Narr, 2002.

BRIGGS, JOHN C., *Francis Bacon and the Rhetoric of Nature.* Cambridge, MA: Harvard University Press, 1989.

BRINK, J. N. BAKHUIZEN VAN DEN, 'Tradition und Heilige Schrift am Anfang des dritten Jahrhunderts', *Catholica* 9 (1953), 105–14.

BROBERG, GUNNAR, *Homo Sapiens: Studier i Carl von Linnés naturuppfattning och människolära.* Uppsala: Almqvist & Wiksell, 1975.

BROTÓNS, VICTOR NAVARRO, 'The Reception of Copernicus in Sixteenth-Century Spain: The Case of Diego de Zúñiga', *Isis* 86 (1995), 52–78.

BRUNNER, EMIL, *Wahrheit als Begegnung.* Zurich: Zwingli-Verlag, 1963.

BUCHER, ALEXIUS J., *Martin Heidegger: Metaphysikkritik als Begriffsproblematik.* Bonn: Bouvier Verlag, 1972.

BUCHWALD, JED Z., *The Rise of the Wave Theory of Light: Optical Theory and Experiment in the Early Nineteenth Century.* Chicago: University of Chicago Press, 1989.

BULTMANN, RUDOLF, *Der Begriff der Offenbarung im Neuen Testament.* Tübingen: Mohr, 1929.

BURRELL, DAVID, *Analogy and Philosophical Language.* New Haven, CT: Yale University Press, 1973.

CAIRD, GEORGE B., *The Language and Imagery of the Bible.* London: Duckworth, 1980.

CALIN, WILLIAM, 'Ernst Robert Curtius: The Achievement of a Humanist', *Studies in Medievalism* 9 (1997), 218–27.

———, 'Makers of the Middle Ages: Leo Spitzer', *Journal of Medieval and Early Modern Studies* 27 (1997), 495–506.

CAMPBELL, ROBERT J., *The New Theology.* London: Chapman & Hall, 1907.

CANTOR, GEOFFREY, 'The Reception of the Wave Theory of Light in Britain: A Case Study Illustrating the Role of Methodology in Scientific Debate', *Historical Studies in the Physical Sciences* 6 (1975), 109–32.

CARAFIOL, PETER, 'The New Orthodoxy: Ideology and the Institution of American Literary History', *American Literature* 59 (1987), 628–38.

CARAMASCHI, ENZO, 'Histoire de la critique, sociologie du public et théorie de la réception', in Rien T. Segers (ed.), *Etudes de réception.* Bern: Peter Lang, 1993, 31–9.

CARNAP, RUDOLF, 'Psychologie im physikalischer Sprache', *Erkenntnis* 3 (1932), 107–42.

CASHDOLLAR, CHARLES D., *The Transformation of Theology, 1830–1890: Positivism and Protestant Thought in Britain and America.* Princeton, NJ: Princeton University Press, 1989.

CASSIDY, DAVID C., *Uncertainty: The Life and Science of Werner Heisenberg.* New York: W. H. Freeman, 1992.

CASSIRER, ERNST, *Determinism and Indeterminism in Modern Physics: Historical and Systematic studies of the Problem of Causality.* New Haven and London: Yale University Press, 1956.

CASTLE, W. E., 'Mendel's Law of Heredity', *Science* 18 (1903), 396–406.

CHADWICK, OWEN, *From Bossuet to Newman: The Idea of Doctrinal Development.* Cambridge: Cambridge University Press, 1957.

CHELINI, JEAN, AND HENRY BRANTHOMME, *Histoire des pélerinages non-chrétiens: entre magique et sacré – le chemin des dieux.* Paris: Hachette, 1987.

CHURCHILL, LARRY J., 'Flew, Wisdom and Polanyi: The Falsification Challenge Revisited', *International Journal for Philosophy of Religion* 3 (1972), 185–94.

CLARKE, W. NORRIS, *The Philosophical Approach to God: A Neo-Thomist Perspective*. Winston-Salem, NC: Wake Forest University Press, 1979.

COCK, A. G., 'William Bateson's Rejection and Eventual Acceptance of Chromosome Theory', *Annals of Science* 40 (1983), 19–60.

CODE, MURRAY, 'On the Poverty of Scientism, or: The Ineluctable Roughness of Rationality', *Metaphilosophy* 28 (1997), 102–22.

COFFA, J. ALBERTO, *The Semantic Tradition from Kant to Carnap: To the Vienna Station*. Cambridge: Cambridge University Press, 1991.

CONRY, YVETTE, *L'introduction du Darwinisme en France au XIXe siècle*. Paris: Vrin, 1974.

CONTI, CHARLES C., *Metaphysical Personalism: An Analysis of Austin Farrer's Metaphysics of Theism*. Oxford: Clarendon Press, 1995.

CORRENS, CARL, 'G. Mendels Regel über das Verhalten der Nachkommenschaft der Rassenbastarde', *Berichte der deutschen botanischen Gesellschaft* 18 (1900), 158–68.

COURTH, FRANZ, *Das Leben Jesu von David Friedrich Strauss in der Kritik Johann Evangelist Kuhns*. Göttingen: Vandenhoeck & Ruprecht, 1975.

CROUCH, WALTER B., *Death and Closure in Biblical Narrative*. New York: Peter Lang, 2000.

CUNNINGHAM, VALENTINE, *Reading after Theory*. Oxford: Blackwell, 2002.

CUSHING, JAMES T., 'Quantum Theory and Explanatory Discourse: Endgame for Understanding?' *Philosophy of Science* 58 (1991), 337–58.

DALMAIS, IRÉNÉE HENRI, 'The Liturgy and the Deposit of Faith', in Irénée Henri Dalmais, Pierre-Marie Gy and Pierre Jounel (eds), *Principles of the Liturgy*. London: Geoffrey Chapman, 1987, 272–80.

DANZ, CHRISTOPH, 'Dogmatik als Differenzhermeneutik. Überlegungen zur Funktion moderner Systematischer Theologie im Anschluß an Ernst Troeltsch', *Kerygma und Dogma* 47 (2001), 210–26.

DARDEN, LINDLEY, 'William Bateson and the Promise of Mendelism', *Journal of the History of Biology* 10 (1977), 87–106.

———, *Theory Change in Science: Strategies from Mendelian Genetics.* Oxford: Oxford University Press, 1991.

DARWIN, CHARLES, *A Monograph on the Fossil Lepadidae or Pedunculated Cirripedes of Great Britain.* London: Palaeontographical Society, 1851.

———, *A Monograph on the Fossil Balanidae and Verrucidae of Great Britain.* London: Palaeontographical Society, 1854.

———, *The Origin of Species.* Harmondsworth: Penguin, 1968.

DAWKINS, RICHARD, *The Blind Watchmaker: Why the Evidence of Evolution Reveals a Universe without Design.* New York: W. W. Norton, 1986.

———, *The Selfish Gene.* Oxford and New York: Oxford University Press, 1989.

———, *Unweaving the Rainbow: Science, Delusion and the Appetite for Wonder.* London: Penguin Books, 1998.

DE BROGLIE, LOUIS, 'Radiations – ondes et quanta', *Comptes Rendus* 177 (1923), 507–10.

DE LIBERA, ALAIN, 'Les sources gréco-arabes de la théorie médiévale de l'analogie de l'être', *Etudes philosophiques* 3–4 (1989), 319–45.

DE MAN, PAUL, 'Structure intentionnelle de l'image romantique', *Revue internationale de philosophie* 51 (1960), 68–84.

DE PURY, ALBERT, 'Sagesse et révélation dans l'Ancien Testament', *Review of Theology and Philosophy* 27 (1979), 1–50.

DE SOLAGES, BRUNO, *Dialogue sur l'analogie.* Paris: Aubier, 1966.

DEHART, PAUL J., *Beyond the Necessary God: Trinitarian Faith and Philosophy in the Thought of Eberhard Jüngel.* Atlanta, GA: Scholars Press, 1999.

DEL FRA, MARIO, 'La teoria dei "significato totale" delle propositione nel pensiero di Gregorio da Rimini', *Rivista critica di storia della filosofia* 11 (1956), 287–311.

DENEFFE, AUGUST, *Der Traditionsbegriff: Studie zur Theologie.* Münster in Westfalie: Aschendorff, 1931.

———, 'Dogma: Wort und Begriff', *Scholastik* 6 (1931), 381–400.

DENNETT, DANIEL C., *Darwin's Dangerous Idea: Evolution and the Meaning of Life.* New York: Simon & Schuster, 1995.

DERRIDA, JACQUES, 'White Mythology: Metaphor in the Text of Philosophy', *New Literary History* 6 (1974), 11–74.

——, *Of Spirit: Heidegger and the Question*. Chicago: University of Chicago Press, 1989.

DISSE, JÖRG PETER, *Metaphysik der Singularität: Eine Hinführung am Leitfaden der Philosophie Hans Urs von Balthasars*. Vienna: Passagen Verlag, 1996.

——, 'Platons Ideenlehre als Metaphysik. Eine Auseinandersetzung mit der sprachanalytischen Philosophie', *Philosophisches Jahrbuch* 105 (1998), 267–82.

DRAPER, PAUL, 'Pain and Pleasure: An Evidential Problem for Theists', *Nous* 23 (1989), 331–50.

DULLES, AVERY, 'Vatican II and the Recovery of Tradition', in *The Reshaping of Catholicism*. San Francisco: Harper & Row, 1988, 75–92.

——, 'Faith and Revelation', in Francis Schüssler Fiorenza and John P. Galvin (eds), *Systematic Theology: Roman Catholic Perspectives*. Minneapolis: Augsburg Fortress, 1992, 89–128.

DUNN, JAMES D. G., *Christology in the Making: A New Testament Inquiry into the Origins of the Doctrine of the Incarnation*, 2nd edn. London: SCM Press, 1989.

——, *Unity and Diversity in the New Testament: An Inquiry into the Character of Earliest Christianity*, 2nd edn. London: SCM Press, 1990.

EBELING, GERHARD, *Kirchengeschichte als Geschichte der Auslegung der Heiligen Schrift*. Tübingen: Mohr, 1947.

——, *Wort Gottes und Tradition: Studien zu einer Hermeneutik der Konfessionen*. Göttingen: Vandenhoeck & Ruprecht, 1964.

ECKERMANN, WILLIGIS, 'Christus als Gekreuzigter: Grundzüge einer Kreuzestheologie', in Joachim Kuropka (ed.), *Zur Sache – Das Kreuz! Untersuchungen zur Geschichte des Konflikts um Kreuz und Lutherbild in den Schulen Oldenburgs*. Vechta: Vechtaer Druckerei, 1986, 254–71.

EDWARDS, R. B., 'The Pagan Dogma of the Absolute Unchangeableness of God', *Religious Studies* 14 (1975), 305–13.

EGGINTON, WILLIAM, 'On Dante, Hyperspheres and the Curvature of the Medieval Cosmos', *Journal of the History of Ideas* 60 (1999), 195–216.

EHRHARDT, ARNOLD, 'Christianity before the Apostles' Creed', *Harvard Theological Review* 55 (1962), 73–119.

EIKHENBAUM, BORIS, 'The Theory of the "Formal Method"', in, *Russian Formalist Criticism: Four Essays*. Lincoln, NE: University of Nebraska Press, 1965, 99–139.

EINSTEIN, ALBERT, 'Quanten-Mechanik und Wirklichkeit', *Dialectica* 2 (1948), 320–4.

ELDREDGE, NILES, *Time Frames: The Rethinking of Darwinian Evolution and the Theory of Punctuated Equilibria*. London: Heinemann, 1986.

——, *The Pattern of Evolution*. New York: Freeman, 1999.

ELDRIDGE, RICHARD, 'Kant, Hölderlin, and the Experience of Longing', in *The Persistence of Romanticism: Essays in Philosophy and Literature*. Cambridge: Cambridge University Press, 2001, 31–51.

ELLEGÅRD, ALVAR, *Darwin and the General Reader: The Reception of Darwin's Theory of Evolution in the British Periodical Press, 1859–1872*. Chicago: University of Chicago Press, 1990.

ELSHTAIN, JEAN BETHKE, *Augustine and the Limits of Politics*. Notre Dame, IN: University of Notre Dame Press, 1995.

ELZE, MARTIN, 'Der Begriff des Dogmas in der Alten Kirche', *Zeitschrift für Theologie und Kirche* 61 (1964), 421–38.

ENGLAND, RICHARD, 'Natural Selection, Teleology, and the Logos: From Darwin to the Oxford Neo-Darwinists, 1859–1909', *Osiris* 16 (2001), 270–87.

ERESHEFSKY, MARC, *The Poverty of the Linnaean Hierarchy: A Philosophical Study of Biological Taxonomy*. Cambridge: Cambridge University Press, 2001.

EVANDER, R. L., 'Phylogeny of the family *Equidae*', in D. R. Prothero and R. M. Schoch (eds), *The Evolution of the Perissodactyls*. New York: Oxford University Press, 1989, 109–27.

EVANS, GILLIAN R., 'The Borrowed Meaning: Grammar, Logic and the Problem of Theological Language in Twelfth-Century Schools', *Downside Review* 96 (1978), 165–75.

——, *Alan of Lille: The Frontiers of Theology in the Later Twelfth Century*. Cambridge: Cambridge University Press, 1983.

——, *Problems of Authority in the Reformation Debates*. Cambridge: Cambridge University Press, 1992.

EVANS, L. T., 'Darwin's Use of the Analogy between Artificial and Natural Selection', *Journal of the History of Biology* 17 (1984), 113–40.

EVANS, RICHARD J., *In Defence of History*. London: Granta, 1997.

EVANS, ROBERT REES, *Pantheisticon: The Career of John Toland*. New York: Peter Lang, 1991.

EYNDE, DAMIEN VAN DEN, *Les normes de l'enseignement chrétien dans la littérature patristique des trois premiers siècles*. Gembloux: Duculot, 1933.

FARRER, AUSTIN, *The Glass of Vision*. London: Dacre Press, 1948.

FERGUSON, ANTHONY, 'Can Evolutionary Theory Predict?' *American Naturalist* 110 (1976), 1101–4.

FERMI, ENRICO, 'Tentativo di una theoria dell'emissione dei raggi "beta"', *Ricerca Scientifica* 4 (1933), 491–5.

FERRÉ, FREDERICK, *Language, Logic and God*. New York: Harper & Row, 1961.

FINE, ARTHUR, *The Shaky Game: Einstein, Realism and the Quantum Theory*. Chicago: University of Chicago Press, 1986.

FINE, GAIL, 'Knowledge and Belief in *Republic* V', *Archiv für Geschichte der Philosophie* 60 (1978), 121–39.

FISCHER, JOHANNES, 'Kann die Theologie der naturwissenschaftlichen Vernunft die Welt als Schöpfung verständlich machen?' *Freiburger Zeitschrift für Philosophie und Theologie* 41 (1994), 491–514.

FISHER, PHILIP, *Wonder, the Rainbow, and the Aesthetics of Rare Experiences*. Cambridge, MA: Harvard University Press, 1998.

FITZPATRICK, F. J., 'The Onus of Proof in Arguments about the Problem of Evil', *Religious Studies* 17 (1981), 19–38.

FOGELIN, ROBERT J., 'Three Platonic Analogies', *Philosophical Review* 80 (1971), 371–82.

FOLSE, HENRY J., *The Philosophy of Niels Bohr: The Framework of Complementarity*. Amsterdam: North Holland, 1985.

FORSYTH, P. T., *The Person and Place of Jesus Christ*. London: Independent Press, 1909.

——, *The Principle of Authority in Relation to Certainty, Sanctity, and Society: An Essay in the Philosophy of Experimental Religion*, 2nd edn. London: Independent Press, 1952.

FOUCAULT, MICHEL, *Ethics: Subjectivity and Truth*. London: Penguin, 2000.

FRAENKEL, PETER, *Testimonia Patrum: The Function of the Patristic Argument in the Theology of Philip Melanchthon*. Geneva: Droz, 1961.

FRÄNGSMYR, TORE, *Geologi och skapelsetro: Föreställningar om jordens historia från Hiärne till Bergman*. Stockholm: Almqvist & Wiksell, 1969.

FRIEDMAN, MICHAEL, *A Parting of the Ways: Carnap, Cassirer, and Heidegger*. Chicago: Open Court, 2000.

GALISON, PETER L., *How Experiments End*. Chicago: University of Chicago Press, 1987.

GANSON, DORIT A., *The Explanationist Defense of Scientific Realism*. New York: Garland, 2001.

GARDEIL, AMBROISE, *Le donné révélé et la théologie*. Paris: Editions Du Cerf, 1932.

GÄRDENFORS, PETER, 'Mental Representation, Conceptual Spaces and Metaphors', *Synthese* 106 (1996), 21–47.

GARRIGOU-LAGRANGE, R., 'Le relativisme et l'immutabilité du dogme', *Angelicum* 27 (1950), 219–46.

GARVIE, A. E., *The Ritschlian Theology, Critical and Constructive: An Exposition and an Estimate*. Edinburgh: T&T Clark, 1899.

GEISELMANN, J. R., 'Scripture, Tradition, and the Church: An Ecumenical Problem', in D. J. Callahan, H. A. Oberman and D. J. O'Hanlon (eds), *Christianity Divided: Protestant and Roman Catholic Theological Issues*. London: Sheed & Ward, 1962, 39–72.

GEISLER, RALF, *Kants moralischer Gottesbeweis im protestantischen Positivismus*. Göttingen: Vadenhoeck & Ruprecht, 1992.

GERTZ, BERNHARD, *Glaubenswelt als Analogie: Die theologische Analogie-Lehre Erich Przywaras und ihr Ort in der Auseinandersetzung um die analogia fidei*. Düsseldorf: Patmos-Verlag, 1969.

——, 'Was ist Analogia Fidei?' *Catholica* 26 (1972), 309–24.

GESSEL, WILHELM, 'Das "homoousios" als Testfall für die Frage nach der Geltung und dem Verhältnis von Schrift und Tradition auf dem Konzil von Nizäa', *Annuarium Historiae Conciliorum. Internationale Zeitschrift für Konziliengeschichtsforschung* 17 (1985), 1–7.

GILLESPIE, NEAL C., *Charles Darwin and Special Creation*. Chicago: University of Chicago Press, 1979.

——, 'Divine Design and the Industrial Revolution: William Paley's Abortive Reform of Natural Theology', *Isis* 81 (1990), 214–29.

GLICK, THOMAS F., *The Comparative Reception of Darwinism*. Austin: University of Texas Press, 1972.

GODZICH, WLAD, 'Foreword: The Tiger on the Paper Mat', in Paul de Man (ed.), *The Resistance to Theory*. Minneapolis: University of Minnesota Press, 1986, ix–xviii.

GOEWENS, DAVID J., 'Kierkegaard's Understanding of Doctrine', *Modern Theology* 5 (1988), 13–22.

GOEWENS, KENNETH, 'Ciceronianism and Collective Identity: Defining the Boundaries of the Roman Academy, 1525', *Journal of Medieval and Renaissance Studies* 23 (1993), 173–95.

GOMBRICH, E. H., '*Icones Symbolicae*: The Visual Image in Neoplatonic Thought' *Journal of the Courtauld and Warburg Institutes* 11 (1948), 163–92.

GOODENOUGH, URSULA, *The Sacred Depths of Nature*. New York: Oxford University Press, 1998.

GORE, CHARLES, *The New Theology and the Old Religion*. London: John Murray, 1907.

——, *The Incarnation of the Son of God*. London: John Murray, 1922.

GOULD, STEPHEN JAY, *The Structure of Evolutionary Theory*. Cambridge, MA: Belknap, 2002.

GRABNER-HAIDER, ANTON, *Semiotik und Theologie: religiöse Rede zwischen analytischer und hermeneutischer Philosophie*. Munich: Kösel, 1973.

GRANT, ROBERT M., *Heresy and Criticism: The Search for Authenticity in Early Christian Literature*. Louisville, KY: Westminster/John Knox Press, 1993.

GREEN, GEOFFREY, *Literary Criticism and the Structures of History: Erich Auerbach and Leo Spitzer*. Lincoln, NE: University of Nebraska Press, 1982.

GREENACRE, ROGER, 'Two Aspects of Reception', in Gillian R. Evans (ed.), *Christian Authority*. Oxford: Clarendon Press, 1988, 40–58.

GRILLMEIER, ALOYS, 'Hellenisierung-Judaisierung des Christentums als Deuteprinzipien der Geschichte des kirchlichen Dogmas', *Scholastik* 33 (1958), 321–55, 528–55.

——, *Christ in Christian Tradition*, 2nd edn. London: Mowbrays, 1975.

GRÜNBAUM, ADOLF, 'The Duhemian Argument', *Philosophy of Science* 27 (1960), 75–87.

——, 'Is Falsifiability the Touchstone of Scientific Rationality? Karl Popper versus Inductivism', in R. S. Cohen, P. K. Feyerabend and M. W. Wartofsky (eds), *Essays in Memory of Imre Lakatos*. Dordrecht: Reidel, 1976, 213–52.

GRUNDMANN, HERBERT, *Religiöse Bewegungen im Mittelalter: Untersuchungen über die geschichtlichen Zusammenhänge zwischen der Ketzerei, den Bettelorden und der religiösen Frauenbewegung um 12. und 13. Jahrhundert und über die geschichtlichen Grundlagen der deutschen Mystik.* Berlin: Emil Ebering, 1935.

——, *Ketzergeschichte des Mittelalters.* Göttingen: Vandenhoeck & Ruprecht, 1963.

GUNTON, COLIN E., *The Triune Creator: A Historical and Systematic Study.* Edinburgh: Edinburgh University Press, 1998.

——, *Trinity, Time, and Church: A Response to the Theology of Robert W. Jenson.* Grand Rapids, MI: Eerdmans, 2000.

HAEFFNER, GERD, *Heideggers Begriff der Metaphysik.* Munich: Berchmanskolleg, 1974.

HAGENEDER, OTHMAR, 'Der Häresiebegriff bei den Juristen des 12. und 13. Jahrhunderts', in W. Lourdaux and D. Verhelst (eds), *The Concept of Heresy in the Middle Ages.* Louvain: Louvain University Press, 1978, 42–103.

HÄGGLUND, BENGT, 'Die Bedeutung der "regula fidei" als Grundlage theologischer Aussagen', *Studia Theologica* 12 (1958), 1–44.

HAMLYN, DAVID W., 'Aristotle's God', in G. J. Hughes (ed.), *The Philosophical Assessment of Theology.* Washington, DC: Georgetown University Press, 1987, 15–33.

HAMMER, FELIX, *Genugtuung und Heil: Absicht, Sinn und Grenzen der Erlösungslehre Anselms von Canterbury.* Vienna: Herder, 1967.

HANSON, R. P. C., *Tradition in the Early Church.* London: SCM Press, 1962.

HÄRING, HERMANN, *Kirche und Kerygma: Das Kirchenbild in der Bultmannschule.* Freiburg: Herder, 1972.

HARMAN, GILBERT, 'The Inference to the Best Explanation', *Philosophical Review* 74 (1965), 88–95.

HARRINGTON, DANIEL J., 'The Reception of Walter Bauer's *Orthodoxy and Heresy in Earliest Christianity* during the Last Decade', *Harvard Theological Review* 73 (1980), 289–98.

HAUERWAS, STANLEY, *A Community of Character.* Notre Dame, IN: University of Notre Dame Press, 1981.

——, *In Good Company: The Church as Polis.* Notre Dame, IN: University of Notre Dame Press, 1995.

——, 'Murdochian Muddles: Can we get through them if God does not Exist?' in Maria Antonaccio and William Schweiker (eds), *Iris Murdoch and the Search for Human Goodness*. Chicago: University of Chicago Press, 1996, 190–208.

HAWKES, TERENCE, *Structuralism and Semiotics*. London: Methuen, 1977.

HAYS, RICHARD B., *The Moral Vision of the New Testament: Community, Cross, New Creation*. Edinburgh: T&T Clark, 1997.

HEDLEY, DOUGLAS, 'Should Divinity Overcome Metaphysics? Reflections on John Milbank's *Theology beyond Secular Reason* and *Confessions of a Cambridge Platonist*', *Journal of Religion* 80 (2000), 271–98.

HEDWIG, KLAUS, 'Edith Stein und die analogia entis', in R. L. Fetz, M. Rath and P. Schulz (eds), *Studien zur Philosophie Edith Stein*. Munich: Verlag Karl Alber, 1991, 320–52.

HEIDE, GALE Z., 'The Nascent Noeticism of Narrative Theology: An Examination of the Relationship between Narrative and Metaphysics in Nicholas Lash', *Modern Theology* 12 (1996), 459–81.

HEIDEGGER, MARTIN, *The Question concerning Technology, and Other Essays*. New York: Harper & Row, 1977.

——, *Was ist Metaphysik?* 15th edn. Frankfurt am Main: Vittorio Klosterman, 1998.

HEISENBERG, WERNER, 'Über den anschaulichen Inhalt der quanten-theoretischen Kinematik und Mechanik', *Zeitschrift für Physik* 43 (1927), 172–98.

HERRMANN, WILHELM, 'Der geschichtliche Christus der Grund unseres Glaubens', *Zeitschrift für Theologie und Kirche* 2 (1892), 232–73.

HESSE, MARY, 'What is the Best Way to Assess Evidential Support for Scientific Theories?' in L. Jonathan Cohen and Mary Hesse (eds), *Applications of Inductive Logic*. Oxford: Clarendon Press, 1980, 202–17.

HICK, JOHN, 'Theology and Verification', in John Hick (ed.), *The Existence of God*. London: Macmillan, 1964, 252–74.

HIEBERT, ERWIN, 'The Genesis of Mach's Early Views on Atomism', in R. Cohen and R. Seeger (eds), *Ernst Mach: Physicist and Philosopher*. Dordrecht: D. Reidel, 1970, 79–106.

HODGDON, BARBARA, *The End Crowns All: Closure and Contradiction in Shakespeare's History*. Princeton, NJ: Princeton University Press, 1991.

HOFFMANN, FRITZ, 'Der Satz als Zeichen der theologischen Aussage bei Holcot, Crathorn und Gregor von Rimini', in Albert Zimmermann (ed.), *Der Begriff der Repräsentatio im Mittelalter: Stellvertretung, Symbol, Zeichen, Bild*. Berlin: de Gruyter, 1971, 296–313.

HOFFMEISTER, HEIMO, '"Etsi Deus non daretur": Zum Verhaltnis von Philosophie und Theologie', *Neue Zeitschrift für Systematische Theologie und Religionsphilosophie* 21 (1979), 272–85.

HOLLADAY, G. WENDELL, 'The Nature of Particle–Wave Complementarity', *American Journal of Physics* 66 (1998), 27–33.

HOLLAND, D. L., 'History, Theology and the Kingdom of God: A Contribution of Johannes Weiss to Twentieth Century Theology', *Biblical Research* 13 (1968), 54–66.

HOLT, MACK P., *The French Wars of Religion, 1562–1629*. Cambridge: Cambridge University Press, 1995.

HOLYOAK, KEITH J., AND PAUL THAGARD, *Mental Leaps: Analogy in Creative Thought*. Cambridge, MA: MIT Press, 1995.

HONNER, JOHN, *The Description of Nature: Niels Bohr and the Philosophy of Quantum Physics*. Oxford: Clarendon Press, 1987.

HORAN, BARBARA L., 'The Statistical Character of Evolutionary Theory', *Philosophy of Science* 61 (1994), 76–95.

HORWICH, PAUL, 'How to Choose between Empirically Indistinguishable Theories', *Journal of Philosophy* 79 (1982), 61–77.

HULTGREN, ARLAND J., *The Rise of Normative Christianity*. Minneapolis: Fortress Press, 1994.

HUMPHRIES, JEFFERSON, 'On the Inevitability of Theory in Southern Literary Study', *Yale Journal of Criticism* 3 (1989), 175–86.

HÜNERMANN, PETER, *Offenbarung Gottes in der Zeit: Prolegomena zur Christologie*. Münster: Aschendorff, 1989.

HUNTER, ARCHIBALD MACBRIDE, *P. T. Forsyth: per crucem ad lucem*. London: SCM Press, 1974.

HUYSSTEEN, J. WENTZEL VAN, *Theology and the Justification of Faith: Constructing Theories in Systematic Theology*. Grand Rapids, MI: Eerdmans, 1989.

JALABERT, JACQUES, *La théorie leibnizienne de la substance*. Paris: Presses Universitaires de France, 1974.

JAMES, LAURENCE J., 'Pseudo-Dionysius' Metaphysics of Darkness and Chartres Cathedral', *Essays in Medieval Studies* 2 (1985), 182–206.

JAMMER, MAX, *The Conceptual Development of Quantum Mechanics.* New York: McGraw-Hill, 1966.

JANICAUD, DOMINIQUE, *The Shadow of that Thought: Heidegger and the Question of Politics.* Evanston, IL: Northwestern University Press, 1996.

——, AND JEAN-FRANÇOIS MATTÉI, *Métaphysique à la limite: cinq études sur Heidegger.* Paris: Presses Universitaires de France, 1983.

JAY, MARTIN, *Downcast Eyes: The Denigration of Vision in Twentieth-Century French Thought.* Berkeley, CA: University of California Press, 1993.

JEFFERSON, ANN, 'Russian Formalism', in Ann Jefferson and David Robey (eds), *Modern Literary Theory: A Comparative Introduction.* London: Batsford, 1986, 24–45.

JEFFREY, RICHARD C., 'Probability and Falsification: Critique of the Popper Program', *Synthese* 30 (1975), 95–117.

JENSEN, KRISTIAN, 'Protestant Rivalry: Metaphysics and Rhetoric in Germany, *c.*1590–1620', *Journal of Ecclesiastical History* 41 (1990), 24–43.

JENSON, ROBERT W., *Systematic Theology,* 2 vols. New York: Oxford University Press, 1997–9.

——, *The Triune Identity: God According to the Gospel.* Philadelphia: Fortress, 1982.

JOHNSON, WILLIAM STACY, *The Mystery of God: Karl Barth and the Postmodern Foundations of Theology.* Louisville, KY: Westminster John Knox Press, 1997.

JUNG, FRANZ, *Soter: Studien zur Rezeption eines hellenistischen Ehrentitels im Neuen Testament.* Münster: Aschendorff, 2002.

JÜNGEL, EBERHARD, 'Die Möglichkeit theologischer Anthropologie auf den Grunde der Analogie: Eine Untersuchung zum Analogieverständnis Karl Barths', *Evangelische Theologie* 22 (1962), 535–57.

——, *Zum Ursprung der Analogie bei Parmenides und Heraklit.* Berlin: De Gruyter, 1964.

——, 'Das Sein Jesu Christi als Ereignis der Versöhnung Gottes mit einer gottlosen Welt: Die Hingabe der Gekreuzigten', *Evangelische Theologie* 38 (1978), 510–17.

——, *Gott als Geheimnis der Welt: Zur Begründung der Theologie des Gekreuzigten im Streit zwischen Theismus und Atheismus,* 4th edn. Tübingen: Mohr, 1982.

——, 'Von der Dialektik zu Analogie: Die Schule Kierkegaards und der Einspruch Petersons', in Eberhard Jüngel (ed.), *Barth Studien*. Zurich: Benziger Verlag, 1982, 127–79.

——, *Das Evangelium von der Rechtfertigung des Gottlosen als Zentrum des christlichen Glaubens: Eine theologische Studie in ökumenischer Absicht*. Tübingen: Mohr, 1998.

JUNKER, MAUREEN, *Das Urbild des Gottesbewusstseins: Zur Entwicklung der Religionstheorie und Christologie Schleiermachers von der ersten zur zweiten Auflage der Glaubenslehre*. Berlin: De Gruyter, 1990.

KAISER, CHRISTOPHER B., 'Quantum Complementarity and Christological Dialectic', in W. Mark Richardson and Wesley J. Wildman (eds), *Religion and Science: History, Method, Dialogue*. New York: Routledge, 1996, 291–8.

KASPAR, WALTER, 'Tradition als theologisches Erkenntnisprinzip', in W. Löser, K. Lehmann and M. Lutz-Bachmann (eds), *Dogmengeschichte und katholische Theologie*. Würzburg: Echter Verlag, 1985, 376–403.

KAUFMAN, GORDON D., 'Metaphysics and Theology', *Cross Currents* 28 (1978), 325–41.

KAUFMANN, THOMAS, *Universität und lutherische Konfessionalisierung: Die Rostocker Theologieprofessoren und ihr Beitrag zur theologischen Bildung und kirchlichen Gestaltung im Herzogtum Mecklenburg zwischen 1550 und 1675*. Gütersloh: Gerd Mohn, 1997.

KAY, JAMES F., *Christus praesens: A Reconsideration of Rudolf Bultmann's Christology*. Grand Rapids, MI: Eerdmans, 1994.

KENNESON, PHILIP, 'Nicholas Lash on Doctrinal Development and Ecclesial Authority', *Modern Theology* 5 (1989), 271–300.

KERR, FERGUS, *Theology after Wittgenstein*. Oxford: Blackwell, 1988.

KITCHER, PHILIP, '1953 and All That: A Tale of Two Sciences', *Philosophical Review* 93 (1984), 335–73.

KLEINER, SCOTT A., 'Problem Solving and Discovery in the Growth of Darwin's Theories of Evolution', *Synthese* 62 (1981), 119–62.

——, 'A New Look at Kepler and Abductive Argument', *Studies in History and Philosophy of Science* 14 (1983), 279–313.

——, 'The Logic of Discovery and Darwin's Pre-Malthusian Researches', *Biology and Philosophy* 3 (1988), 293–315.

KNECHT, R. J., *The French Wars of Religion, 1559–1598*, 2nd edn. London: Longman, 1996.

KNIGHT, CHRISTOPHER, 'An Authentic Theological Revolution? Scientific Perspectives on the Development of Doctrine', *Journal of Religion* 74 (1994), 524–41.

KNÖPPLER, THOMAS, *Die theologia crucis des Johannesevangeliums: Das Verständnis des Todes Jesu im Rahmen der johanneischen Inkarnations- und Erhöhungschristologie.* Neukirchen-Vluyn: Neukirchener Verlag, 1994.

KOCH, TRAUGOTT, 'Dogmatik ohne Frömmigkeit? Zum Konstitutionsproblem protestantischer Theologie', *Neue Zeitschrift für systematische Theologie und Religionsphilosophie* 43 (2001), 300–29

KOESTER, HELMUT, 'Gnomai Diaphorai: The Origin and Nature of Diversification in the History of Early Christianity', *Harvard Theological Review* 58 (1965), 279–318.

KOHN, DAVID, 'Darwin's Ambiguity: The Secularization of Biological Meaning', *British Journal for the History of Science* 22 (1989), 215–39.

KÖNIG, F. EDUARD, *Der Offenbarungsbegriff des Alten Testamentes.* Leipzig: Hinrichs, 1882.

KÖRNER, STEPHAN, 'On the Relation between Common Sense, Science and Metaphysics', in A. Phillips Griffiths (ed.), *A. J. Ayer: Memorial Essays.* Cambridge: Cambridge University Press, 1991, 89–103.

KOTTLER, MALCOLM J., 'Charles Darwin's Biological Species Concept and Theory of Geographic Speciation: The Transmutation Notebooks', *Annals of Science* 35 (1978), 275–97.

KRAGH, HELGE, 'Erwin Schrödinger and the Wave Equation: The Crucial Phase', *Centaurus* 26 (1982), 154–97.

KRAUS, HANS-JOACHIM, *Theologie der Psalmen.* Neukirchen-Vluyn: Neukirchener Verlag, 1979.

KRETZMANN, NORMAN, *The Metaphysics of Creation: Aquinas's Natural Theology in Summa contra gentiles II.* Oxford: Clarendon Press, 1999.

KRIPS, HENRY, *The Metaphysics of Quantum Theory.* Oxford: Clarendon Press, 1987.

KRUMBIEGEL, INGO, *Die Rudimentation: Eine monographische Studie.* Stuttgart: Fischer, 1960.

KUHN, H. W., 'Jesus als Gekreuzigter in der frühchristlichen Verkündigung bis zur Mitte des 2. Jahrhunderts', *Zeitschrift für Theologie und Kirche* 72 (1975), 1–46.

KUHN, THOMAS S., *The Structure of Scientific Revolutions*, 2nd edn. Chicago: University of Chicago Press, 1970.

KUNTZ, PAUL G., 'The Analogy of Degrees of Being: A Critique of Cajetan's "Analogy of Names"', *New Scholasticism* 56 (1982), 51–79.

LAKATOS, IMRE, 'Falsification and the Methodology of Scientific Research Programmes', in I. Lakatos and A. Musgrave (eds), *Criticism and the Growth of Knowledge.* Cambridge: Cambridge University Press, 1970, 91–195.

LAMBERT, MALCOLM, *Medieval Heresy: Popular Movements from the Gregorian Reform to the Reformation.* Oxford: Blackwell, 2002.

LANE FOX, ROBIN, *Pagans and Christians in the Mediterranean World from the Second Century AD to the Conversion of Constantine.* London: Penguin, 1988.

LANG, ALBERT, 'Der Bedeutungswandel der Begriffe "fides" und "haeresis" von Vienne und Trient', *Münchener Theologische Zeitschrift* 4 (1953), 133–46.

LANG, HELEN S., *The Order of Nature in Aristotle's Physics: Place and the Elements.* Cambridge: Cambridge University Press, 1998.

LANG, U. M., 'The Christological Controversy at the Synod of Antioch in 268/9', *Journal of Theological Studies* 51 (2000), 54–80.

LANGE, DIETZ, *Historischer Jesus oder mythischer Christus: Untersuchungen zu dem Gegensatz zwischen Friedrich Schleiermacher und David Friedrich Strauss.* Gütersloh: Mohn, 1975.

LASH, NICHOLAS, *Change in Focus: A Study of Doctrinal Change and Continuity.* London: Sheed & Ward, 1973.

LATOUR, BRUNO, *We Have Never Been Modern.* Cambridge, MA: Harvard University Press, 1993.

LATOURELLE, RENÉ, 'L'idée de révélation chez les pères de l'église', *Sciences Ecclésiastiques* 11 (1959), 297–344.

——, *Théologie de la révélation*, 2nd edn. Bruges: Desclée de Brouwer, 1966.

LAUDAN, LARRY, AND JARRETT LEPLIN, 'Empirical Equivalence and Underdetermination', *Journal of Philosophy* 88 (1991), 449–72.

LAWLOR, LEONARD, *Derrida and Husserl: The Basic Problem of Phenomenology.* Bloomington, IN: University of Indiana Press, 2002.

LAWSON, HILARY, *Reflexivity: The Post-Modern Predicament.* London: Hutchinson, 1985.

——, *Closure: A Story of Everything.* London: Routledge, 2001.

LENTRICCHIA, FRANK, 'On Behalf of Theory', in Gerald Graff and Reginald Gibbons (eds), *Criticism in the University*. Evanston, IL: Northwestern University Press, 1985, 105–10.

LENZEN, V. F., 'Procedures of Empirical Science', in O. Neurath, R. Carnap and C. Morris (eds), *Foundations of the Unity of Science: Toward an International Encyclopedia of Unified Science*, vol. 1. Chicago: University of Chicago Press, 1955, 279–339.

LERER, SETH (ed.), *Literary History and the Challenge of Philology: The Legacy of Erich Auerbach*. Stanford, CA: Stanford University Press, 1996.

LEVIN, DAVID MICHAEL, *The Listening Self: Personal Growth, Social Change and the Closure of Metaphysics*. London: Routledge, 1989.

LÉVINAS, EMMANUEL, *Totalité et infini: essai sur l'extériorité*. The Hague: Martinus Nijhoff, 1984.

LIVINGSTONE, DAVID N., 'The Idea of Design: The Vicissitudes of a Key Concept in the Princeton Response to Darwin', *Scottish Journal of Theology* 37 (1984), 329–57.

——, 'B. B. Warfield, the Theory of Evolution and Early Fundamentalism', *Evangelical Quarterly* 58 (1986), 69–83.

——, *Darwin's Forgotten Defenders: The Encounter between Evangelical Theology and Evolutionary Thought*. Grand Rapids, MI: Eerdmans, 1987.

LOCHBRUNNER, MANFRED, *Analogia caritatis: Darstellung und Deutung der Theologie Hans Urs von Balthasars*. Freiburg: Herder, 1981.

LODER, JAMES E., AND W. JIM NEIDHARDT, 'Barth, Bohr and Dialectic', in W. Mark Richardson and Wesley J. Wildman (eds), *Religion and Science: History, Method, Dialogue*. New York: Routledge, 1996, 271–89.

LOHSE, BERNHARD, 'Theorien der Dogmengeschichte im evangelische Raum heute', in W. Löser, K. Lehmann and M. Lutz-Bachmann (eds), *Dogmengeschichte und katholische Theologie*. Würzburg: Echter Verlag, 1985, 97–109.

LONGEWAY, JOHN L., 'Nicholas of Cusa and Man's Knowledge of God', *Philosophy Research Archives* 13 (1987–8), 289–313.

LÖSEL, STEFFEN, 'Unapocalyptic Theology: History and Eschatology in Balthasar's Theo-Drama', *Modern Theology* 17 (2001), 201–25.

LOUTH, ANDREW, *Discerning the Mystery: An Essay on the Nature of Theology*. Oxford: Clarendon Press, 1983.

——, *The Origins of the Christian Mystical Tradition from Plato to Denys.* Oxford: Clarendon Press, 1983.

LUHMANN, NIKLAS, *Funktion der Religion.* Frankfurt am Main: Suhrkamp, 1982.

LUZ, ULRICH, '*Theologia crucis* als Mitte der Theologie im Neuen Testament', *Evangelische Theologie* 34 (1974), 141–75.

LYTTKENS, HAMPUS, *The Analogy between God and the World: An Investigation of its Background and Interpretation of its Use by Thomas of Aquino.* Uppsala: Almquist & Wiksells, 1952.

MACH, ERNST, *Die Analyse der Empfindungen und das Verhältnis des Physischen zum Psychischen,* 2nd edn. Jena: Gustav Fischer, 1919.

MACINTYRE, ALASDAIR C., AND PAUL RICOEUR, *The Religious Significance of Atheism.* New York: Columbia University Press, 1969.

MACKINNON, EDWARD, 'Heisenberg, Models and the Rise of Matrix Mechanics', *Historical Studies in the Physical Sciences* 8 (1979), 137–85.

MACKINTOSH, H. R., *The Doctrine of the Person of Jesus Christ.* Edinburgh: T&T Clark, 1913.

MACNAGHTEN, PHIL, AND JOHN URRY, *Contested Natures.* London: Sage, 1998.

MACQUARRIE, JOHN, *An Existentialist Theology: A Comparison of Heidegger and Bultmann.* London: SCM Press, 1955.

——, *Jesus Christ in Modern Thought.* London: SCM Press, 1990.

MAFFIE, JAMES, 'Naturalism, Scientism and the Independence of Epistemology', *Erkenntnis* 43 (1995), 1–27.

MANZA, JEFF, 'Classes, Status Groups, and Social Closure: A Critique of Neo-Weberian Social Theory', *Current Perspectives in Social Theory* 12 (1992), 275–302.

MARCEL, GABRIEL, *Être et avoir.* Paris: Aubier Éditions Montaigne, 1935.

——, *The Mystery of Being.* London: Harvill Press, 1950.

MARGOLIN, JEAN-CLAUDE, 'L'analogie dans la pensée d'Erasme', *Archiv für Reformationsgeschichte* 69 (1978), 24–50.

MARKSCHIES, CHRISTOPH, *Gibt es eine "Theologie der gotischen Kathedrale"? nochmals: Suger von Saint-Denis und Sankt Dionys vom Areopag.* Heidelberg: Universitätsverlag C. Winter, 1995.

MARSHALL, I. HOWARD, *The Origins of New Testament Christology,* 2nd edn. Downers Grove, IL: InterVarsity Press, 1992.

MASCALL, E. L., 'On from Chalcedon', in *Whatever happened to the Human Mind? Essays in Orthodoxy*. London: SPCK, 1980, 28–53.

McCARTHY, TIMOTHY, *The Catholic Tradition before and after Vatican II, 1878–1993*. Chicago: Loyola University Press, 1994.

McCORMACK, BRUCE L., *Karl Barth's Critically Realistic Dialectical Theology: Its Genesis and Development, 1909–1936*. Oxford: Clarendon Press, 1997.

McCUMBER, JOHN, *Metaphysics and Oppression: Heidegger's Challenge to Western Philosophy*. Bloomington, IN: Indiana University Press, 1999.

McDONALD, JAMES I. H., *Kerygma and Didache: The Articulation and Structure of the Earliest Christian Message*. Cambridge: Cambridge University Press, 1980.

McFADDEN, B. J., *Fossil Horses: Systematics, Paleobiology, and Evolution of the Family Equidae*. Cambridge: Cambridge University Press, 1992.

McFAGUE, SALLIE, *Metaphorical Theology: Models of God in Religious Language*. Philadelphia: Fortress, 1985.

McGRATH, ALISTER, 'Karl Barth and the Articulus Iustificationis. The Significance of His Critique of Ernst Wolf within the Context of his Theological Method', *Theologische Zeitschrift* 39 (1983), 349–61.

——, 'Karl Barth als Aufklärer? Der Zusammenhang seiner Lehre vom Werke Christi mit der Erwählungslehre', *Kerygma und Dogma* 81 (1984), 383–94.

——, *Luther's Theology of the Cross: Martin Luther's Theological Breakthrough*. Oxford: Blackwell, 1985.

——, *The Intellectual Origins of the European Reformation*. Oxford: Blackwell, 1987.

——, 'Dogma und Gemeinde: Zur soziologische Funktion des christlichen Dogmas', *Kerygma und Dogma* 36 (1990), 24–43.

——, *The Reenchantment of Nature: The Denial of Religion and the Ecological Crisis*. New York: Doubleday, 2002.

McINERNY, RALPH, 'Aquinas and Analogy: Where Cajetan Went Wrong', *Philosophical Topics* 20 (1992), 103–24.

McKENNA, ANDREW J., *Violence and Difference: Girard, Derrida and Deconstruction*. Urbana, IL: University of Illinois Press, 1992.

McLEAN, BRADLEY H., *The Cursed Christ: Mediterranean Expulsion Rituals and Pauline Soteriology*. Sheffield: Sheffield Academic Press, 1996.

McLelland, Joseph C., *God the Anonymous: A Study in Alexandrian Philosophical Theology*. Cambridge, MA: Philadelphia Patristic Foundation, 1976.

McMullin, Ernan, *Newton on Matter and Activity*. Notre Dame, IN: University of Notre Dame Press, 1978.

——, 'The Explanation of Distant Action: Historical Notes', in J. T. Cushing and E. McMullin (eds), *Philosophical Consequences of Quantum Theory: Reflections on Bell's Theorem*. Notre Dame, IN: University of Notre Dame Press, 1989, 272–302.

McNeill, William, *The Glance of the Eye: Heidegger, Aristotle, and the Ends of Theory*. Albany: State University of New York Press, 1999.

Meeks, Wayne A., *The First Urban Christians: The Social World of the Apostle Paul*. New Haven, CT: Yale University Press, 1983.

Meijering, E. J., *Theologische Urteile über die Dogmengeschichte: Ritschls Einfluss auf von Harnack*. Leiden: Brill, 1978.

——, *Der 'ganze' und der 'wahre' Luther: Hintergrund und Bedeutung der Lutherinterpretation A. von Harnacks*. Amsterdam: Noord-Hollandsche Uitgevers Maatschappij, 1983.

——, *Die Hellenisierung des Christentums im Urteil Adolf von Harnack*. Amsterdam: Kampen, 1985.

Melandri, Enzo, 'The Analogia Entis according to Franz Brentano: A Speculative-Grammatical Analysis of Aristotle's Metaphysics', *Topoi* 6 (1987), 51–8.

Melchiorre, Virgilio, 'L'analogia in Aristotele', *Rivista di Filosofia Neo-Scolastica* 85 (1998), 230–55.

Michelson, A. A., and E. W. Morley, 'On the Relative Motion of the Earth and Luminiferous Ether', *American Journal of Science* 34 (1887), 333–45.

Midgley, Mary, *Science as Salvation: A Modern Myth and its Meaning*. London: Routledge, 1992.

——, *Evolution as a Religion: Strange Hopes and Stranger Fears*, 2nd edn. London: Routledge, 2002.

Milbank, John, *Theology and Social Theory: Beyond Secular Reason*. Oxford: Blackwell, 1993.

——, *The Word made Strange: Theology, Language, Culture*. Oxford: Blackwell, 1997.

Miller, A. I., 'Redefining *Anschaulichkeit*', in A. Shimony and H.

Feshbach (eds), *Physics as Natural Philosophy: Essays in Honor of Laszlo Tisza.* Cambridge, MA: MIT Press, 1982, 376–411.

MILLER, ARTHUR I., *Imagery in Scientific Thought: Creating 20th-Century Physics.* Boston, Basel and Stuttgart: Birkhäuser, 1984.

MILLER, D. A., *Narrative and its Discontents: Problems of Closure in the Traditional Novel.* Princeton: Princeton University Press, 1981.

MILLER, J. HILLIS, 'The Triumph of Theory, the Resistance to Reading, and the Question of the Material Base', *Publications of the Modern Language Association* 102 (1987), 281–91.

MILLSTEIN, ROBERTA L., 'Random Drift and the Omniscient Viewpoint', *Philosophy of Science* 63 (1996), 10–18.

MILNE, PAMELA J., *Vladimir Propp and the Study of Structure in Hebrew Biblical Narrative.* Sheffield: Almond Press, 1988.

MISAK, C. J., *Verificationism: Its History and Prospects.* London: Routledge, 1995.

MITCHELL, BASIL, *The Justification of Religious Belief.* London: Macmillan, 1973.

MONTAGNES, BERNARD, *La doctrine de l'analogie de l'être d'après Saint Thomas d'Aquin.* Louvain: Publications Universitaires, 1963.

MOORE, JAMES, 'Deconstructing Darwinism: The Politics of Evolution in the 1860s', *Journal of the History of Biology* 24 (1991), 353–408.

MOORE, JAMES R., *The Post-Darwinian Controversies: A Study of the Protestant Struggle to Come to Terms with Darwin in Great Britain and America, 1870–1900.* Cambridge: Cambridge University Press, 1979.

MOORE, ROBERT I., *The Formation of a Persecuting Society: Power and Deviance in Western Europe, 950–1250.* Oxford: Basil Blackwell, 1990.

MORGAN, ALISON, *Dante and the Medieval Other World.* Cambridge: Cambridge University Press, 1990.

MÜLLER, MICHAEL G., *Zweite Reformation und städtische Autonomie im königlichen Preussen: Danzig, Elbing und Thorn in der Epoche der Konfessionalisierung (1557–1660).* Berlin: Akademie Verlag, 1997.

MULSOW, MARTIN, *Johann Lorenz Mosheim (1693–1755): Theologie im Spannungsfeld von Philosophie, Philologie und Geschichte.* Wiesbaden: Harrassowitz, 1997.

MURDOCH, DUGALD, *Niels Bohr's Philosophy of Physics.* Cambridge: Cambridge University Press, 1987.

MURDOCH, IRIS, 'Nostalgia for the Particular', *Proceedings of the Aristotelian Society* 52 (1952), 243–60.

——, 'A House of Theory', *Partisan Review* 26 (1959), 17–31.

——, *Sartre: Romantic Rationalist*. London: Collins, 1967.

——, *The Sovereignty of Good*. London: Macmillan, 1970.

——, *The Fire and the Sun: Why Plato Banished the Artists*. London: Chatto & Windus, 1990.

——, *Metaphysics as a Guide to Morals*. London: Penguin, 1992.

MURPHY, ANDREW R., *Conscience and Community: Revisiting Toleration and Religious Dissent in Early Modern England and America*. University Park, PA: Pennsylvania State University Press, 2001.

MURPHY, RAYMOND, *Social Closure: The Theory of Monopolization and Exclusion*. Oxford: Clarendon Press, 1988.

NAGEL, ERNEST, *Teleology Revisited and Other Essays in the Philosophy and History of Science*. New York: Columbia University Press, 1974.

NAVONE, JOHN J., *History and Faith in the Thought of Alan Richardson*. London: SCM Press, 1966.

NEUFELD, KARL H., *Adolf von Harnack: Theologie als Suche nach der Kirche*. Paderborn: Verlag Bonifacius-Druckerei, 1977.

——, *Adolf Harnacks Konflikt mit der Kirche: Weg-Stationen zum 'Wesen des Christentums'*. Innsbruck: Tyrolia-Verlag, 1979.

——, 'Gebundenheit und Freiheit: Liberal Dogmengeschichtser-forschung in der evangelischen Theologie', in W. Löser, K. Lehmann and M. Lutz-Bachmann (eds), *Dogmengeschichte und katholische Theologie*. Würzburg: Echter Verlag, 1985, 78–96.

NEURATH, OTTO, 'Protokollsätze', *Erkenntnis* 3 (1932), 204–14.

NEWMAN, JOHN HENRY, 'On the Introduction of Rationalistic Principles into Revealed Religion', in *Essays Critical and Historical*. London: Pickering, 1871, 30–101.

NEWTON-SMITH, W., AND STEVEN LUKES, 'The Underdetermination of Theory by Data', *Proceedings of the Aristotelian Society* 52 (1978), 71–91.

NICHOLS, AIDAN, *From Newman to Congar: The Idea of Doctrinal Development from the Victorians to the Second Vatican Council*. Edinburgh: T&T. Clark, 1990.

NICKLES, THOMAS, 'Two Concepts of Intertheoretic Reduction', *Journal of Philosophy* 70 (1975), 181–201.

NORRIS, CHRISTOPHER, *Against Relativism: Philosophy of Science, Deconstruction and Critical Theory.* Oxford: Blackwell, 1997.

NOZICK, ROBERT, *Invariances: The Structure of the Objective World.* Cambridge, MA: Harvard University Press, 2001.

OBERDAN, THOMAS, *Protocols, Truth and Convention.* Studien zur Österreichischen Philosophie 19. Amsterdam: Rodopi, 1993.

——, 'Postscript to Protocols: Reflections on Empiricism', in Ronald N. Giere and Alan W. Richardson (eds), *Origins of Logical Empiricism.* Minneapolis: University of Minnesota Press, 1996, 269–91.

OBERMAN, HEIKO A., *The Harvest of Medieval Theology: Gabriel Biel and Late Medieval Nominalism.* Cambridge, MA: Harvard University Press, 1963.

——, *Forerunners of the Reformation: The Shape of Late Medieval Thought.* Philadelphia: Fortress Press, 1981.

O'BRIEN, CHARLES H., *Ideas of Religious Toleration at the Time of Joseph II: A Study of the Enlightenment among Catholics in Austria.* Philadelphia: American Philosophical Society, 1969.

OLAFSON, FREDERICK A., *Naturalism and the Human Condition: Against Scientism.* London: Routledge, 2001.

O'LEARY, JOSEPH STEPHEN, *Questioning Back: The Overcoming of Metaphysics in Christian Tradition.* Chicago: Winston Press, 1985.

OLIVIER, PAUL, 'Metaphysique et religion: Kant, Hegel, Heidegger', *Recherches des Sciences Religieuses* 72 (1984), 219–42.

OSER, FRITZ K., AND K. HELMUT REICH, 'The Challenge of Competing Explanations: The Development of Thinking in Terms of Complementarity of Theories', *Human Development* 30 (1987), 178–86.

OTTO, WALTER F., *Theophania: der Geist der altgriechischen Religion.* Frankfurt am Main: Klostermann, 1975.

OZANKOM, CLAUDE, *Gott und Gegenstand: Martin Heideggers Objektivierungsverdikt und seine theologische Rezeption bei Rudolf Bultmann und Heinrich Ott.* Paderborn: Schöningh, 1994.

PAGLIA, CAMILLE, *Sex, Art, and American Culture: Essays.* New York: Vintage, 1993.

PAINTER, JOHN, *Theology as Hermeneutics: Rudolf Bultmann's Interpretation of the History of Jesus.* Sheffield: Almond, 1987.

PAIS, ABRAHAM, 'The Early History of the Theory of the Electron: 1897–1947', in A. Salam and E. P. Wigner (eds), *Aspects of Quantum Theory*. Cambridge: Cambridge University Press, 1972, 79–92.

——, *Niels Bohr's Times, in Physics, Philosophy and Polity*. Oxford: Clarendon Press, 1991.

PALMER, RICHARD E., 'Husserl's Debate with Heidegger in the Margins of "Kant and the Problem of Metaphysics"', *Man and World* 30 (1997), 5–33.

PANNENBERG, WOLFHART, 'Einsicht und Glaube: Antwort an Paul Althaus', *Theologische Literaturzeitung* 88 (1963), 81–92.

——, 'Dogmatic Theses on the Doctrine of Revelation', in W. Pannenberg (ed.), *Revelation as History*. New York: Macmillan, 1968, 123–58.

——, *Jesus – God and Man*. London: SCM Press, 1968.

——, 'The Appropriation of the Philosophical Concept of God as a Dogmatic Problem of Early Christian Theology', in, *Basic Questions in Theology II*. London: SCM Press, 1971, 119–83.

——, *Systematic Theology*, 3 vols. Grand Rapids, MI: Eerdmans, 1991–8.

PARKIN, FRANK, *Class Inequality and Political Order: Social Stratification in Capitalist and Communist societies*. London: Paladin, 1972.

PATTARO, GERMANO, 'De oecumenismi exercitio: indicazioni per una verifica post-conciliare', *Studi Ecumenici* 2 (1984), 485–515.

PEACOCKE, ARTHUR, *Intimations of Reality*. Notre Dame, IN: University of Notre Dame Press, 1984.

PEIKOFF, LEONARD, *Objectivism: The Philosophy of Ayn Rand*. New York: Penguin, 1993.

PELIKAN, JAROSLAV, *The Vindication of Tradition*. New Haven: Yale University Press, 1984.

PETRUCCIOLI, SANDRO, *Atoms, Metaphors and Paradoxes: Niels Bohr and the Construction of a New Physics*. Cambridge: Cambridge University Press, 1993.

PHILLIPS, D. Z., *Faith and Philosophical Enquiry*. London: Routledge & Kegan Paul, 1970.

——, *Religion without Explanation*. Oxford: Blackwell, 1976.

——, *Wittgenstein and Religion*. London: Macmillan, 1993.

PICHET, CLAUDE, 'Heidegger et Cohen, lecteurs de Kant', *Archives de Philosophie* 61 (1998), 603–28.

PINNICK, CASSANDRA L., 'What is Wrong with the Strong Programme's

Case Study of the "Hobbes–Boyle Dispute"?' in Noretta Koertge (ed.), *A House Built on Sand: Exposing Postmodernist Myths about Science*. New York: Oxford University Press, 1998, 227–39.

PLANTINGA, ALVIN, 'The Probabilistic Argument from Evil', *Philosophical Studies* 35 (1979), 1–53.

——, *Warranted Christian Belief*. Oxford: Oxford University Press, 2000.

PLOTNIK, KENNETH, *Hervaeus Natalis OP and the Controversies over the Real Presence and Transubstantiation*. Munich: Schöningh, 1970.

PÖHLMANN, H. G., *Analogia entis oder analogia fidei? Die Frage nach Analogie bei Karl Barth*. Göttingen: Vandenhoeck & Ruprecht, 1965.

POLIKAROV, AZARIA, 'On the Nature of Einstein's Realism' *Epistemologia* 12 (1989), 277–304.

POLLARD, T. E., *Johannine Christology and the Early Church*. Cambridge: Cambridge University Press, 1970.

POPPER, KARL R., *Conjectures and Refutations: The Growth of Scientific Knowledge*. London: Routledge & Kegan Paul, 1963.

——, *Unended Quest: An Intellectual Autobiography*. London: Fontana, 1976.

——, 'Natural Selection and the Emergence of Mind', *Dialectica* 32 (1978), 339–55.

PROPP, VLADIMIR I. A., *Morphology of the Folktale*, 2nd edn. Austin, TX: University of Texas Press, 1968.

PROUST, JOLLE, *Questions de forme: logique et proposition analytique de Kant à Carnap*. Paris: Librairie Arthème Fayard, 1986.

RABATÉ, JEAN-MICHEL, *The Future of Theory*. Oxford: Blackwell, 2002.

RABB, THEODORE K., *The Thirty Years' War*. Lanham, MD: University Press of America, 1981.

RADER, MELVIN, *Marx's Interpretation of History*. New York: Oxford University Press, 1979.

RADINSKY, L. B., 'The Early Evolution of the Perissodactyla', *Evolution* 23 (1979), 308–28.

RAHNER, KARL, 'Chalkedon – Ende oder Anfang?' in Alois Grillmeier and Heinrich Bacht (eds), *Das Konzil von Chalkedon: Geschichte und Gegenwart*, vol. 3. Würzburg: Echter-Verlag, 1951–4, 3–49.

——, 'Zur Frage der Dogmenentwicklung', in *Schriften zur Theologie*, vol. 1. Einsiedeln: Benziger Verlag, 1954, 49–90.

——, 'Überlegungen zur Dogmenentwicklung', in *Schriften zur Theologie*, vol. 4. Einsiedeln: Benziger Verlag, 1960, 11–50.

RAJCHMAN, JOHN, AND ORISTELLE BONIS, *Érotique de la vérité: Foucault, Lacan et la question de l'éthique*. Paris: Presses Universitaires de France, 1994.

RAMSEY, IAN T., *Religious Language: An Empirical Placing of Theological Phrases*. London: SCM Press, 1957.

——, *Models and Mystery*. London: Oxford University Press, 1964.

——, *Models for Divine Activity*. London: SCM Press, 1973.

RAPP, CARL, *Fleeing the Universal: The Critique of Post-Rational Criticism*. Albany, NY: State University of New York Press, 1998.

RASMUSSON, ARNE, *The Church as Polis: From Political Theology to Theological Politics as exemplified by Jürgen Moltmann and Stanley Hauerwas*. Lund: Lund University Press, 1994.

RATZINGER, JOSEPH, 'On the Interpretation of the Tridentine Decree on Tradition', in Karl Rahner and Joseph Ratzinger (eds), *Revelation and Tradition*. New York: Herder & Herder, 1966, 50–68.

REDHEAD, MICHAEL, *From Physics to Metaphysics*. Cambridge: Cambridge University Press, 1995.

RENDTORFF, ROLF, 'Offenbarung und Geschichte. Partikularismus und Universalismus im Offenbarungsverständnis Israels', in *Kanon und Theologie*. Neukirchen-Vluyn: Neukirchener Verlag, 1991, 113–22.

RICHARDSON, ALAN, *History, Sacred and Profane*. London: SCM Press, 1964.

RICHMOND, JAMES, *Ritschl: A Reappraisal*. London: Collins, 1978.

RINGLEBEN, JOACHIM, 'Luther zur Metapher', *Zeitschrift für Theologie und Kirche* 94 (1997), 336–69.

RITSCHL, OTTO, 'Der historische Christus, der christliche Glaube und die theologische Wissenschaft', *Zeitschrift für Theologie und Kirche* 3 (1893), 371–426.

RITTER, ADOLF M., *Das Konzil von Konstantinopel und sein Symbol: Studien zur Geschichte und Theologie des II. Ökumenischen Konzils*. Göttingen: Vandenhoeck & Ruprecht, 1965.

ROBERTS, DEBORAH H., FRANCIS M. DUNN, AND DON FOWLER (eds), *Classical Closure: Reading the End in Greek and Latin Literature*. Princeton, NJ: Princeton University Press, 1997.

ROBINSON, JAMES M., AND HELMUT KOESTER, *Trajectories through Early Christianity*. Philadelphia: Fortress Press, 1971.

ROBINSON, THOMAS A., *The Bauer Thesis Examined: The Geography of Heresy in the Early Christian Church.* Lewiston, NY: Edwin Mellen Press, 1988.

RODGERS, JOHN H., *The Theology of P.T. Forsyth: The Cross of Christ and the Revelation of God.* London: Independent Press, 1965.

ROSENBERG, ALEXANDER, 'Is the Theory of Natural Selection a Statistical Theory?' *Canadian Journal of Philosophy* 14 (1988), 187–207.

——, 'A Field Guide to Recent Species of Naturalism', *British Journal for the Philosophy of Science* 47 (1996), 1–29.

RÖSSLER, DIETRICH, *Gesetz und Geschichte: Untersuchungen zur Theologie der jüdischen Apokalyptik und der pharisäischen Orthodoxie.* Neukirchen: Neukirchener Verlag, 1960.

ROUSSELOT, PIERRE, 'Petit théorie du développement du dogme', *Recherches de science religieuse* 53 (1965), 355–90.

ROWE, WILLIAM L., 'The Problem of Evil and Some Varieties of Atheism', *American Philosophical Quarterly* 16 (1979), 335–41.

——, 'Evil and the Theistic Hypothesis: A Response to Wykstra', *International Journal for Philosophy of Religion* 16 (1984), 95–100.

——, 'The Empirical Argument from Evil', in R. Audi and W. J. Wainwright (eds), *Rationality, Religious Belief and Moral Commitment.* Ithaca: Cornell University Press, 1986, 227–47.

ROYON, CLAUDE, *Dieu, l'homme et la croix: Stanislas Breton et Eberhard Jüngel.* Paris: Éditions du Cerf, 1998.

RUSE, MICHAEL, 'Darwin's Debt to Philosophy: An Examination of the Influence of the Philosophical Ideas of John F. Herschel and William Whewell on the Development of Charles Darwin's Theory of Evolution', *Studies in the History and Philosophy of Science* 66 (1975), 159–81.

——, *Monad to Man: The Concept of Progress in Evolutionary Biology.* Cambridge, MA: Harvard University Press, 1996.

RUSSO, GIUSEPPE, *Gabriel Marcel: esistenza e partecipazione.* Battipaglia: Il Fedone, 1993.

RUTHERFORD, IAN, '*Theoria* and *Darsan*: Pilgrimage and Vision in Greece and India', *Classical Quarterly* 50 (2000), 133–46.

SAID, EDWARD W., *Culture and Imperialism.* London: Chatto & Windus, 1993.

SALMON, WESLEY C., 'Scientific Explanation: Three Basic Conceptions', *Philosophy of Science Association* 2 (1984), 293–305.

SANDERS, E. P., *Paul and Palestinian Judaism: A Comparison of Patterns of Religion*. Philadelphia: Fortress Press, 1977.

SAWYER, JOHN F. A., *Semantics in Biblical Research: New Methods of Defining Hebrew Words for Salvation*. London: SCM Press, 1972.

SCHÄFER, PHILIP, '"Dogmenfreies Christentum": Seine Anliegen in einer Dogmenauslegung', in Eberhard Schockenhoff, Peter Walter and Walter Kasper (eds), *Dogma und Glaube: Bausteine für eine theologische Erkenntnislehre*. Mainz: Matthias-Grunewald-Verlag, 1993, 9–27.

SCHÄFER, ROLF, 'Das Reich Gottes bei Albrecht Ritschl und Johannes Weiss', *Zeitschrift für Theologie und Kirche* 61 (1964), 68–88.

SCHARFF, ROBERT C., *Comte after Positivism*. Cambridge: Cambridge University Press, 1995.

SCHELLENBERG, J. L., *Divine Hiddenness and Human Reason*. Ithaca: Cornell University Press, 1993.

SCHMID, JOHANN HEINRICH, *Erkenntnis des geschichtlichen Christus bei Martin Kähler und bei Adolf Schlatter*. Basel: Reinhardt, 1978.

SCHMITZ, HERMANN-JOSEF, *Frühkatholizismus bei Adolf von Harnack, Rudolph Sohm und Ernst Käsemann*. Düsseldorf: Patmos Verlag, 1977.

SCHRIJVER, GEORGES DE, 'Die analogia entis in der Theologie Hans Urs von Balthasar: Eine genetisch-historische Studie', *Bijdragen* 38 (1977), 249–81.

SCHULTE, HANNELIS, *Der Begriff der Offenbarung im Neuen Testament*. Munich: Kaiser, 1949.

SCHULZ, WINFRIED, *Dogmenentwicklung als Problem der Geschichtlichkeit der Wahrheitserkenntnis. Eine erkenntnistheoretisch-theologische Studie zum Problemkreis der Dogmenentwicklung*. Rome: Libreria Editrice dell'Università Gregoriana, 1969.

SHAPIN, STEVEN, AND SIMON SCHAFFER, *Leviathan and the Air-Pump: Hobbes, Boyle and the Experimental Life*. Princeton, NJ: Princeton University Press, 1985.

SHAW, WILLIAM H., AND L. R. ASHLEY, 'Analogy and Inference', *Dialogue* 22 (1983), 415–32.

SHKLOVSKY, VICTOR, 'Art as Technique', in *Russian Formalist Criticism: Four Essays*. Lincoln, NE: University of Nebraska Press, 1965, 3–24.

SIMON, MARCEL, 'From Greek Hairesis to Christian Heresy', in William R. Schoedel and Robert L. Wilken (eds), *Early Christian Literature and the Classical Intellectual Tradition*. Paris: Beauchesne, 1979, 101–16.

SLOAN, PHILLIP R., 'The Buffon-Linnaeus Controversy', *Isis* 67 (1976), 356–75.

——, 'Buffon, German Biology and the Historical Interpretation of Biological Species', *British Journal for the History of Science* 12 (1979), 109–53.

——, 'Darwin on Nature and Divinity', *Osiris* 16 (2001), 251–69.

SMITH, BARRY, *Austrian Philosophy: The Legacy of Franz Brentano*. Chicago: Open Court, 1994.

SMITH, MARK S., *The Origins of Biblical Monotheism: Israel's Polytheistic Background and the Ugaritic Texts*. Oxford: Oxford University Press, 2001.

SÖHNGEN, GOTTLIEB, *Analogie und Metapher: Kleine Philosophie und Theologie der Sprache*. Freiburg: Alber, 1962.

SOKOLOWSKI, ROBERT, *The God of Faith and Reason: Foundations of Christian Theology*. Notre Dame, IN: University of Notre Dame Press, 1982.

STAMOS, DAVID N., 'Popper, Falsifiability, and Evolutionary Biology', *Biology and Philosophy* 11 (1996), 161–91.

STEIGER, LOTHAR, 'Offenbarungsgeschichte und theologische Vernunft', *Zeitschrift für Theologie und Kirche* 59 (1962), 88–113.

STENMARK, MIKAEL, *Scientism: Science, Ethics and Religion*. Aldershot: Ashgate, 2001.

STERELNY, KIM, *Dawkins vs. Gould: Survival of the Fittest*. Cambridge: Icon Books, 2001.

STERTENBRINK, RUDOLF, *Ein Weg zum Denken: Die Analogia entis bei Erich Przywara*. Salzburg: Verlag Anton Pustet, 1971.

STICKELBERGER, HANS, 'Bullingers bekanntester Satz und seine Interpretation bei Karl Barth', in Hans Ulrich Bächtold (ed.), *Von Cyprian zur Walzenprägung: Streiflichter auf Zürcher Geist und Kultur der Bullingerzeit*. Zug: Achius, 2001, 105–14.

STIVER, DAN R., *The Philosophy of Religious Language: Sign, Symbol and Story*. Oxford: Blackwell, 1996.

STUHLMACHER, PETER, 'Erwägungen zum Problem vom Gegenwart und Zukunft in der paulinischen Eschatologie', *Zeitschrift für Theologie und Kirche* 64 (1967), 423–50.

SULLIVAN, ROBERT E., *John Toland and the Deist Controversy: A Study in Adaptations*. Cambridge, MA: Harvard University Press, 1982.

SULLOWAY, FRANK J., 'Darwin and his Finches: The Evolution of a Legend', *Journal of the History of Biology* 15 (1982), 1–53.

SWINBURNE, RICHARD, *The Existence of God*. Oxford: Clarendon Press, 1979.

——, 'The Argument from the Fine-Tuning of the Universe', in John Leslie (ed.), *Physical Cosmology and Philosophy*. New York: Macmillan, 1990, 154–73.

SYKES, JOHN, 'Narrative Accounts of Biblical Authority: The Need for a Doctrine of Revelation', *Modern Theology* 5 (1989), 327–42.

SYKES, STEPHEN W., *The Identity of Christianity: Theologians and the Essence of Christianity from Schleiermacher to Barth*. Philadelphia: Fortress Press, 1984.

TAVARD, GEORGE H., *Holy Writ or Holy Church: The Crisis of the Protestant Reformation*. London: Burns & Oates, 1959.

TENNANT, F. R., *Philosophical Theology*, 2 vols. Cambridge: Cambridge University Press, 1930.

THAGARD, PAUL R., 'The Best Explanation: Criteria for Theory Choice', *Journal of Philosophy* 75 (1976), 76–92.

THISELTON, ANTHONY C., *The Two Horizons: New Testament hermeneutics and Philosophical Description with Special Reference to Heidegger, Bultmann, Gadamer, and Wittgenstein*. Exeter: Paternoster, 1980.

THOMAS, STEPHEN, *Newman and Heresy: The Anglican Years*. Cambridge: Cambridge University Press, 1991.

TILLEY, TERRENCE W., 'The Institutional Element in Religious Experience', *Modern Theology* 10 (1994), 185–212.

TILLICH, PAUL, 'The Religious Symbol', in Sidney Hook (ed.), *Religious Experience and Truth: A Symposium*. New York: New York University Press, 1961, 301–23.

TORRANCE, THOMAS F., *Theological Science*. London: Oxford University Press, 1969.

——, 'The Deposit of Faith', *Scottish Journal of Theology* 36 (1983), 1–28.

TRACY, DAVID, 'Iris Murdoch and the Many Faces of Platonism', in Maria Antonaccio and William Schweiker (eds), *Iris Murdoch and the Search for Human Goodness*. Chicago: University of Chicago Press, 1996, 54–75.

TREML, CHRISTINE, *Humanistische Gemeinschaftsbildung: sozio-kulturelle Untersuchung zur Entstehung eines neuen Gelehrtenstandes in der frühen Neuzeit*. Hildesheim: Olms, 1989.

TRIGG, ROGER, *Rationality and Science: Can Science Explain Everything?* Oxford: Blackwell, 1993.

TROISFONTAINES, ROGER, *De l'existence à l'être: la philosophie de Gabriel Marcel*, 2 vols. Louvain: Nauwelaerts, 1953.

TUANA, NANCY, 'Quine on Duhem: An Emendation', *Philosophy of Science* 45 (1978), 456–62.

TURNER, DENYS, *The Darkness of God: Negativity in Christian Mysticism*. Cambridge: Cambridge University Press, 1998.

TURNER, H. E. W., *The Patristic Doctrine of Redemption: A Study of the Development of Doctrine during the First Five Centuries*. London: Mowbray, 1952.

——, *The Pattern of Christian Truth: A Study in the Relations between Orthodoxy and Heresy in the Early Church*. London: Mowbray, 1954.

UEBEL, THOMAS E., *Overcoming Logical Positivism from Within: The Emergence of Neurath's Naturalism in the Vienna Circle's Protocol Sentence Debate*. Studien zur Österreichischen Philosophie 17. Amsterdam: Rodopi, 1992.

VAN INWAGEN, PETER, *Metaphysics*. Oxford: Oxford University Press, 1993.

VAUGHT, CARL G., 'Metaphor, Analogy and the Nature of Truth', in Robert C. Neville (ed.), *New Essays in Metaphysics*. Albany, NY: State University of New York Press, 1987, 217–36.

VLASTOS, GREGORY, 'Degrees of Reality in Plato', in R. Bambrough (ed.), *New Essays on Plato and Aristotle*. New York: Humanities Press, 1965, 1–18.

VON BALTHASAR, HANS URS, *Karl Barth: Darstellung und Deutung seiner Theologie*. Cologne: Hegner, 1951.

——, 'Die christliche Gestalt', in *Pneuma und Institution*. Einsiedeln: Johannes Verlag, 1974, 38–60.

——, *Herrlichkeit: Eine theologische Ästhetik: 1 – Schau der Gestalt*. Einsiedeln: Johannes Verlag, 1961.

VON HARNACK, ADOLF, *History of Dogma*, 7 vols. Edinburgh: Williams & Norgate, 1894–9.

HARNACK, ADOLF VON, *Lehrbuch der Dogmengeschichte*, 3rd edn. Freiburg: Mohr, 1894.

———, *Das Wesen des Christentums: sechzehn Vorlesungen vor Studierenden aller Facultäten im Wintersemester 1899/1900 an der Universität Berlin gehalten.* Leipzig: Hinrichs, 1906.

VON HOFTSEN, NILS, 'Skapelsetro och uralstringshypoteser före Darwin', *Uppsala Universiteits Årsskrift* 2 (1928), 31–6.

VUILLEMIN, J., 'On Duhem's and Quine's Theses', *Grazer Philosophische Studien* 9 (1979), 69–96.

WATSON, FRANCIS, 'Is Revelation an Event?' *Modern Theology* 10 (1994), 383–99.

WEIKART, RICHARD, 'A Recently Discovered Darwin Letter on Social Darwinism', *Isis* 86 (1995), 609–11.

WEINANDY, THOMAS G., *The Father's Spirit of Sonship: Reconceiving the Trinity.* Edinburgh: T&T Clark, 1995.

WEINBERG, STEVEN, *Facing Up: Science and Its Cultural Adversaries.* Cambridge, MA: Harvard University Press, 2001.

WEISER, ARTUR, 'Zur Frage nach den Beziehungen der Psalmen zum Kult: Die Darstellung der Theophanie in den Psalmen und im Festkult', in Walter Baumgartner (ed.), *Festschrift Alfred Bertholet zum 80. Geburtstag.* Göttingen: Mohr, 1950, 513–31.

WESSELS, LINDA, 'Schrödinger's Route to Wave Mechanics', *Studies in History and Philosophy of Science* 10 (1979), 311–40.

WESTCOTT, BROOKE FOSS, *The Gospel of the Resurrection: Thoughts on its Relation to Reason and History*, 8th edn. London: Macmillan, 1891.

———, 'The Gospel of Creation', in *The Epistles of St John.* London: Macmillan, 1892, 285–328.

WETHERLY, PAUL, *Marx's Theory of History: The Contemporary Debate.* Aldershot: Avebury, 1992.

WEYER-MENKHOFF, STEPHAN, *Aufklärung und Offenbarung: Zur Systematik Albrecht Ritschls.* Göttingen: Vandenhoek & Ruprecht, 1988.

WHALE, J. S., *Christian Doctrine.* Cambridge: Cambridge University Press, 1941.

WHITE, NICHOLAS, 'Plato's Epistemological Metaphysics', in R. Kraut (ed.), *Cambridge Companion to Plato.* Cambridge: Cambridge University Press, 1991, 277–310.

WIGGERSHAUS, ROLF, *The Frankfurt School: Its History, Theories and Political Significance.* Cambridge: Polity Press, 1994.

WIGGINS, DAVID, 'Truth, Invention and the Meaning of Life', *Proceedings of the British Academy* 62 (1976), 331–78.

WILES, MAURICE F., *The Making of Christian Doctrine.* Cambridge: Cambridge University Press, 1967.

——, *Archetypal Heresy: Arianism through the Centuries.* Oxford: Clarendon Press, 1996.

WILKEN, ROBERT, 'Diversity and Unity in Early Christianity', *The Second Century* 1 (1981), 101–10.

WILLIAMS, M. B., 'Falsifiable Predictions of Evolutionary Theory', *Philosophy of Science* 40 (1973), 518–37.

WILLIAMS, ROWAN, 'Trinity and Revelation', *Modern Theology* 2 (1986), 197–212.

——, 'Newman's *Arians* and the Question of Method in Doctrinal History', in Ian Ker and Alan G. Hill (eds), *Newman after a Hundred Years.* Oxford: Clarendon Press, 1990, 263–85.

——, 'Between Politics and Metaphysics: Reflections in the Wake of Gillian Rose', *Modern Theology* 11 (1995), 3–22.

——, *Arius: Heresy and Tradition,* 2nd edn. London: SCM Press, 2001.

WILSON, EDWARD O., *Consilience: The Unity of Knowledge.* New York: Knopf, 1998.

WITTEKIND, FOLKART, *Geschichtliche Offenbarung und die Wahrheit des Glaubens: Der Zusammenhang von Offenbarungstheologie, Geschichtsphilosophie und Ethik bei Albrecht Ritschl, Julius Kaftan und Karl Barth (1909–1916).* Tübingen: Mohr Siebeck, 2000.

WOLF, ERNST, 'Die Rechtfertigungslehre als Mitte und Grenze reformatorischer Theologie', *Evangelische Theologie* 9 (1949), 298–308.

WORRALL, B. G., 'R. J. Campbell and his New Theology', *Theology* 81 (1978), 342–8.

WRIGHT, N. T., *The New Testament and the People of God.* Minneapolis, MN: Fortress, 1992.

WRZECIONKO, PAUL, *Die philosophischen Wurzeln der Theologie Albrecht Ritschls. Ein Beitrag zum Problem des Verhältnisses von Theologie und Philosophie im 19. Jahrhundert.* Berlin: De Gruyter, 1964.

WULF, FRIEDRICH, 'Christliches Denken: Eine Einführung in das theologisch-religiose Werk von Erich Przywara (1889–1972)', in Paul Imhof (ed.), *Gottes Nähe: religiöse Erfahrung in Mystik und*

Offenbarung: Festschrift zum 65. Geburtstag von Josef Sudbrack. Würzburg: Echter, 1990, 353–66.

WYKSTRA, STEPHEN J., 'Religious Beliefs, Metaphysical Beliefs and Historiography of Science', *Osiris* 16 (2001), 29–46.

YEO, RICHARD R., 'William Whewell's Philosophy of Knowledge and its Reception', in Menachem Fisch and Simon Schaffer (eds), *William Whewell: A Composite Portrait*. Oxford: Clarendon Press, 1991, 175–99.

——, *Defining Science: William Whewell, Natural knowledge, and Public Debate in Early Victorian Britain*. Cambridge: Cambridge University Press, 1993.

YOUNG, ROBERT M., 'Malthus and the Evolutionists: The Common Context of Biological and Social Theory', *Past and Present* 43 (1969), 109–45.

——, 'Darwin's Metaphor: Does Nature Select?' *Monist* 55 (1971), 442–503.

——, 'Darwin's Metaphor and the Philosophy of Science', *Science as Culture* 16 (1993), 375–403.

ZIMMERMANN, WOLFGANG, *Rekatholisierung, Konfessionalisierung und Ratsregiment: der Prozess des politischen und religiösen Wandels in der österreichischen Stadt Konstanz, 1548–1637*. Sigmaringen: Thorbecke, 1994.

Index